DANCE, SEX, AND GENDER

DANCE, SEX and *GENDER*

SIGNS OF IDENTITY,
DOMINANCE, DEFIANCE, AND DESIRE

JUDITH LYNNE HANNA

THE UNIVERSITY OF CHICAGO PRESS
CHICAGO AND LONDON

The University of Chicago Press, Chicago 60637
The University of Chicago Press, Ltd., London

Library of Congress Cataloging in Publication Data

Hanna, Judith Lynne.
  Dance, sex, and gender.

  Bibliography: p.
  Includes index.
  1. Sexuality in dance.   2. Dancing—Social aspects.
  3. Dancing—Anthropological aspects.   4. Dancing—Cross-
cultural studies.   I. Title.
GV1595.H33   1987   793.3'2   87-23784
ISBN 0-226-31551-7 (paper)

To

my father, David Selmont,
husband-colleague, William,
sons, Shawn and Aaron,
and all those who tell us about gender.

Contents

Illustrations

Illustrations follow page 116.

Overture

Sexuality and dance share the same instrument—the human body. Using the signature key of sexuality, essential for human survival and desirable for pleasure, dance resonates universal behavioral needs (Montagu 1981) and particular concerns. With the medium as part of the message, dance evokes, reinforces, and clarifies desires and fantasies, some of which would otherwise be incoherent. Holding up a mirror, dance says to us: Look at yourself or at how you might be. The image we see may be pleasing, awkward, or even terrifying.

Dance is an eye-catching, riveting way for humans to identify themselves and maintain or erase their boundaries. Feelings and ideas about sexuality and sex roles (also referred to as gender) take shape in dance. These visual models of which dancer (male or female) performs what, when, where, how, why, either alone, or with or to another dancer reflect and also challenge society's expectations for each sex's specific activities, whether dominance patterns or mating strategies. Dance, usually more like poetry (with its multiple, symbolic, and elusive meanings) than prose, has qualities that psychologists report arouse viewers and influence their attitudes and opinions. When moving images created by dancers violate expected male and female roles and their conventional expressions, the novel signs onstage charge the atmosphere and stimulate performers and observers to confront the possibility of altered life-styles. Dances are social acts that contribute to the continual emergence of culture.

Anchored in evolution and constrained by biology, the social life of men and women is culturally sex-typed and patterned. Everyday movement nearly everywhere conveys the historically male-dominated culture in the same way that language does with its terms of address and pronouns of power. From the quotidian and special occasion, dance takes the lived agenda of needs, habits, and other actions and tranforms the material into spotlighted kinetic illusions and realities. Thus dance, which requires the body for its realization, often attracts attention to the dancer as self, but more often it calls attention to one of the two types of human bodies—male or female.

Do men and women produce dance and dance differently because of anatomy and physiology? What is the role of culture and cognition? Conclusions emerge from the convergence of what we know. I draw upon the human record for illustrations. What appears beyond our culture at first blush to be archaic and exotic turns out to be no less bizarre than what appears in twentieth-century Western choreography on stages and television screens as well as what occurs backstage and offstage (outside the theater). Moreover, the Western dance culture draws upon the human record of dance as a resource for its creativity.

Within a global, historical, and cross-cultural perspective of sex- and gender-related dance performance, I focus primarily on images and their production in Western theatrical "high-culture" dance of the twentieth century, a period during which dominance hierarchies have been challenged significantly. I look at what takes place offstage, backstage, and onstage. The availability of evidence from personal observation, dance reviews in the *New York Times* since the late nineteenth century, dancer and audience reports, scholarly literature, and films and videos determined my focus.

Societies generally designate occupations according to sex. In the United States, men, especially Anglo-Saxons, have dominated the prestigious and well-paid occupations. Because the esteemed worlds of work have discriminated against the so-called weaker sexes, women and homosexual men have disproportionately pursued the more tolerant, poorly paid, low-prestige dance career.

Over the years, from the epitomized dancing of seventeenth-century French male royalty to the nadir of the "inferior" female predominantly dancing onstage, theatrical dance has become a vehicle of liberation from low, dependent status. Yet a recurring message of the images is male domination and protection of women through partnering in ballet: a strong man supporting and manipulating the woman on her pedestal of pointe. And male producers and choreographers continue to make decisions in the background. Seeking escape from male control, rebellious women in the twentieth century have rendered asunder old patterns of women as handmaidens or illusionary embodiments of men as they create new forms of dance ("modern dance"), manage their own companies, and move barefoot with their own power. (Subsequently, unisex and sex role reversal have appeared in dance.)

Seeing women begin to shatter canons of the past, other groups have taken heed. Homosexual men have created onstage new visions of themselves and their interpersonal relationship. Rudolf Nureyev, with outstanding technical and dramatic prowess, international recognition, and stature that accrues to a person with a six-digit income, heartened heterosexual and homosexual male devotees of professional dance in their effort to improve its status for men. Big bucks and megastars in the United States can make almost anything respectable—even dance as a male occupation. And the tales and images of dance portray changing economic and sex role options for men and women as various choreographies and performances present traditional and contemporary controversies.

This book is intended for scholars, students, and nonspecialist readers in many fields: dance, women's studies, gay studies, American studies, performance, nonverbal communication, the anthropology, sociology, psychology, and semiotics of sex roles and occupations, and sexology. Because I have written this book with a broad audience in mind, individuals may find certain sections familiar and even elementary. I beg their patience; the sense of the familiar, I hope, will offer the specialized reader a comfortable map before moving into foreign areas.

Many books have been published on female and male dancers. Yet at a time when attention is being given to women's achievements as well as obstacles which have hindered these accomplishments from being more plentiful and prominent, no book explicitly examines sexuality, the "battle of the sexes," and the cultural construction of gender options as they are played out in the production and visual imagery of dance. (This is true even though there are studies of images of the sexes in art, photography, and advertising.) Nor do dance biographies, autobiographies, and picture books confront the changing content and context of the feminist and gay liberation movements as they manifest themselves in dance, pushing aside the gatekeepers of social mobility and acceptability. Some books indicate the existence of subtle differences in male and female speech and conversational style that mirror the relative power positions of the sexes. More than ten thousand studies bearing on some aspect of sex have appeared during this century. We also find research on everyday interactions and nonverbal communication (touch, eye contact, and facial expression) that supports the idea of females showing more affiliative and less dominating behavior than males. However, images of gender similarities and differences in dance—the fastest growing performing art—remain to be investigated.

The reason for this neglect may be sexual prudery and sensitivity in some dance circles, because dance has had to fight for pride of place among the arts and in the esteem of the American public. Now that dance has achieved recognition, we step into an unclaimed territory in an attempt to expose and understand what is often out-of-awareness. In dance, messages of power, dominance, defiance, and equality usually can be sent without accountability. The same unaccountability may provide a low-risk route to change. What has been historically constructed can be politically reconstructed. Although seeing is learning and believing, believing is also seeing what we know. Resolution of such a paradox may lie with the potency and sponsorship of the image.

This study, ambitious in scope, is only a beginning; it shows that dance images and their production should be taken seriously and questioned. Renowned dancer Dame Margot Fonteyn might demur: "I don't think that audiences should know too much about what goes on backstage. . . . If you want to preserve the magic, you don't show them how to do the trick" (Rosenwald 1982).

I am aware of the pitfalls and incompleteness inherent in a "global" effort. This work covers such breadth that it is vulnerable to criticism by specialists upon whose domain I have dared to tread. I hope that the inevitable weaknesses do not detract from my main argument about the meaningful relationship of dance to society. I believe an attempt at synthesis is worthwhile. Not only does it tell us what is generally known but, of greatest importance, it raises questions that should stimulate further inquiry.

Chapter 1 sets the stage with a conceptualization of the conflating relationship of sex, gender, and dance and the potential of dance to convey sexual imagery that confirms or challenges attitudes about being a man or woman. Some concepts, introduced because of their explanatory force, are briefly defined because they have different meanings within and between disciplines; their full impact will be felt in later chapters. Chapter 2 describes the odyssey toward this book, its guiding theory, sources of evidence, and the dance critic's role as sage or shaman in "replaying" a performance. This study, not on the impact of dance images but of the perception of them, necessarily moves beyond the boundaries of a single discipline because none has adequately examined the questions at hand.

Chapters 3, 4, and 5 examine erotic and sex role themes in our global dance heritage. Although Western theater dance in the twentieth century has unique dimensions, it shares some affinities and structural patterns with the ritual and social dance evolvements of other cultures and times. This sharing has occurred through various influences that affect independent innovation. Many dance themes and styles from around the world, especially since the Age of Exploration, have been creatively incorporated into the United States's cultural heritage and have entered the repertoires of theatrical dance. Around the world we find aphrodisiac dance, both licit and illicit, whose intent ranges from promoting mate selection and procreation to soliciting for prostitution. Dance is embedded in divine sanction for sex and erotic fantasy, in sex role typecasting in rites of passage, in gender metaphors of movement, and in sexual instruction through the dance. This expressive form is also a means of modulating sex role performance to keep authority figures within bounds. Thus dance parodies and appeases the powerful and powerless in different realms of life and even suggests the reversal of roles. In addition, dance may be a form of sexual sublimation.

Chapter 6 examines male and female patterns of dominance in twentieth-century Western theater "high-culture" art dance in the context of the French, Industrial, and post-Industrial revolutions and the changes they wrought. As in many non-Western cultures, the prestige path in the dance profession for each sex has its own specific history of reputability and disreputability, its own form of bondage and liberation. Seeing feminist women gain a foothold in attacking dominant-culture dictates, homosexual men create new visions of themselves and their interpersonal relations. Unequal distribution among the sexes of production and performance roles provokes reaction.

Chapter 7 explores the awareness of sexuality in Western dance images, sexual signs in everyday life and their theatrical dance transformations, as well as biological constraints on movement. Chapter 8 points to the wide repertory of sexual themes played out onstage. There are markers of masculinity and femininity, portrayals of the life cycle, dances that shock, and choreographies that raise questions. Chapter 9 focuses on new dances for women; these pieces examine changes in roles of stature, equality, guiltless sex, and role reversal. Chapter 10 examines various manifestations of male assertion on the dance stage. Some of these dances ignore or denigrate women, and for the first time some kinetic images publicly delve into gay relationships. In Chapter 11, I summarize and reflect upon some of the issues surrounding sex, gender, and dance and suggest directions for further exploration.

My thematic approach may give the mistaken impression that the issues addressed in one chapter or section are not relevant in others. The reader should bear in mind that many of the categories of dance, rather than being mutually exclusive, overlap and interweave. Similarly, some dance photographs illustrate more than one theme, such as male dominance and shocking sexuality. Both words and still images, however vividly descriptive, rapturous, or interesting in their own right, cannot but hint at the compelling dynamic of actual live dancing with its multisensory, pulsating, and often sensual and electrifying qualities.

Acknowledgments

This book has come to fruition with the help of many people. One grows intellectually through challenges from colleagues and students. I am grateful to them for their curiosity, questioning, and insights. My debts are numerous, and it is a pleasure to acknowledge at least some of them.

The encouragement I received for pursuing this project from anthropologists George Spindler, Ashley Montagu, Lucy Cohen, and Thomas Johnston, semiotician Thomas Sebeok, philosopher/dance aesthetician Gerald Meyer, architect Guido Francescato, psychologist Martha Davis, and political scientist William John Hanna kept me going in spite of financial constraints.

Anthropologist Robert Levine directed me to relevant theory in psychology, communications specialist George Gerbner to research on gender images, psychologist Larry Gross and writer Barry Laine to literature on homosexuality, physical education researcher Joan Hult to work on comparative physical abilities of men and women, and performance studies specialist Kate Davy to critical thinking in feminist studies.

Invitations to give guest lectures, present papers at conferences, and contribute articles to edited volumes helped me work through various problems. My appreciation goes to Judith M. Scalin, Department of Dance, Loyola Marymount University; Martha and Gerald Meyers and Charles and Stephanie Reinhart, American Dance Festival distinguished humanists/choreographers lecture series; Paul Garvin and

Linda Swiniuch, Semiotic Program/Theatre and Dance, State University of New York, Buffalo; Kate Davy, Department of Performance Studies, New York University; Tricia Henry and Nancy Smith, Department of Dance, Florida State University; American Anthropological Association; Social Theory, Politics, and the Arts Conference; Conference on Religious Art: Images of the Divine; David Whitehead, University of Toronto Conference on Dance of India; Simon P. X. Battestini, Georgetown University Round Table on Languages and Linguistics; Conference on Researching Dance through Film and Video, Smithsonian Institution and Congress on Research in Dance; Advertising and Consumer Psychology Conference on Nonverbal Communication; Mircea Eliade, Victor Turner, and Paul Bernabeo, *Encyclopedia of Religion*; Guida West and Rhoda Lois Blumberg, *Women in Protest*; Michael Hill, *Images of Women in the Arts*; and Tony Whitehead, *Gender Constructs and Social Issues*.

My appreciation for resources goes to Joan and Barry Stahl, Enoch Pratt Free Library; the University of Maryland Library; Genevieve Oswald and Monica Moseley, Dance Collection, the New York Public Library at Lincoln Center; National Endowment for the Arts Library; John F. Kennedy Library for the Performing Arts, Library of Congress; Wendy Japhet, WNET/Thirteen; Television Information Office Library, New York City; Don Moore, Dance USA; and the Montgomery County Public Library.

Thanks go to all those who gave me photographs and permissions to illustrate dance themes. Specific acknowledgments are adjacent to the plates.

I benefited greatly from the thoughtful reading of preliminary drafts and parts of the manuscript by anthropology-trained coordinators of dance programs Jean Cunningham, University of British Columbia, and Susan Cashion, Stanford University; Lynnette Overby, coeditor, *Dance: Current Selected Research*; anthropologists Anya Peterson Royce, Indiana University, Karen Sacks, University of California, Los Angeles, and Ashley Montagu, Princeton University. Other individuals who read specific chapters are gratefully acknowledged in the respective chapter notes.

Of course, this study would not have been possible if it were not for the choreographers and dancers who shared their views through dancing and commenting, as well as all those people who make performances possible. I thank them for enriching our lives.

I

SPOTLIGHT

1

Sex, Learning, and Dance Images

What is the relationship between dance, sex, and gender? The interplay
encompasses dance production—how dances come into being and how
they get to the stage (whatever its form), and once there, how the dance
images project the activities of each sex. What are the patterns of
male-female dominance in dance and the possibilities for their promotion and change?

Why focus on sex or gender? A physical endowment noticeable at
birth, sex evolves physically, and socioculturally in terms of gender,
through one's lifetime as a way of knowing about oneself and others.
Survival of the human species depends upon heterosexual relations,
history gives significance to sexuality, and individuals universally
characterize persons by sexual attributes. Moreover, sexual differentiation has served as a basis of dominance and subordination, inclusion
and exclusion.

Why focus on dance? This answer is less well known and requires a
longer discussion. Whether a ritual, social event, or theater art, dance
has important yet little-recognized potential to move and persuade us
about what it is to be male or female. This potential is unrecognized in
part because the heritage of the Puritans and the Industrial Revolution
diverted attention from it: the instrument of dance, the body, had to be
harnessed or denied in service of morality and economic productivity.
However, as I point out in *To Dance Is Human* (1987d), dance may be
an adaptive pattern.

One of the mechanisms of adaptation to an environment is natural selection (the process of reproductive success), and dance often displays a person's sexual appeal, provides stimulating fantasy or foreplay, and communicates information as a prelude to encounters that lead to mating.

For example, in societies where choosing a mate is influenced by the skill exhibited in a dance that incorporates qualities that predict success in life, natural selection favors individuals with dance prowess. Among the Igede of Nigeria, "an outstanding dance performance can win a man a wife (Nicholls 1984, 70). Where social advantage of wealth and rank do not coincide with physical superiority, women may marry wealthy men while taking physically attractive ones as lovers. About his Acholi people in Uganda, Okot p'Bitek says that women discriminate among men on the basis of the vigor and endurance of their dance performance: "A man's manliness is seen in the arena/You cannot hide anything,/All parts of the body/Are clearly seen in the arena,/Health and liveliness/Are shown in the arena!" (1966, 33). Noted African scholar Ali Mazrui sums up the situation: "The dancer, the warrior, the lover, become indistinguishable where the heritage of imagery draws no distinction between valor and virility" (1973, 20). War dance behavior confers a selective advantage if it physically and emotionally prepares a childless warrior for battle success.

In contemporary society social dancing is often part of courtship. Theatrical dance, too, may lead to liaisons between dancers and spectators. More frequently, dancing stimulates sexual fantasy acted out beyond the dance performer–audience exchange.

Of greater importance, perhaps, dance appears to be the result of processes that have been selected for in human evolution: exploratory behavior, a sense of rhythm, symbolic capability, and the ability of the brain to make fine distinctions. Innovations and variations in dance arise, each subject to selective pressures governing its survival and spread (Darwin 1965; Alland 1976).

Nonhuman animals' drive to reproduce stimulates the dramatic and colorful ritualized movement displays that are referred to as "mating dances." Similarly, the impulse for dance among humans may be reproductive, *but* it is mediated by culture. Dance may also be something more than sexual. As humans evolved, the programmed action sequences characteristic of other animals tended to be replaced by actions in which cultural learning and individual choice played a greater role. Consequently, dance may comprise all human emotions and thoughts in some transformation. Through dance training and practice an individual marshals power to discipline the instinctive and culturally patterned everyday movements of the body. As a result, the dancer gains control over the body and freedom to use it in a particular way. Achievement in such complicated dance genres as ballet or Kathakali testifies to self-control, dominance, and ascendance, comparable to the human conflict with nature found in Spanish bullfighting. Consistent with the Enlightenment ideal that the arts be instruments in controlling nature, dancers shape the rhythms of life and make the difficult look simple in testament to human competency and potential.[1]

Another means of human adaptation to the environment is communication, the process of an individual or group intentionally sending a message to someone who infers a shared meaning and responds. As part of a human cultural communication system, dance may purposefully convey information or provide an open channel. Shared knowledge about the form, experience in its use, and information sufficiently lucid to be perceived through surrounding distractions or impediments are conditions for effectiveness. The dancer (encoder) makes ideas and feelings known to another (decoder) by means of a code held in common.

Kinetic patterns evince visualizations of social relations and sexual behavior. Even when a dancer intends only to explicate movement forms, the dancer's body is said to disappear into the movement; even when the shape of the body is obscured by costume, signs and symbols of sexuality may be read into the dance and erotic or lustful feeling aroused. Critic Alan M. Kriegsman (1979) remarked that the sex appeal of ballet and modern dancers, their long slender legs, seductive torsos, bulging crotches, swooning dips, ecstatic leg splits, and so on, may win over those for whom ballet holds no other fascination. John Rockwell, also an arts critic, believes that "sex clearly functions as a motor-force for the arts. . . . a dancer automatically projects a sexual aura" (1976, 1). Rockwell sees Isadora Duncan as a paradigm of the new eroticism in American dance. Martha Graham's "tortured probings of the psyche," the mixed erotic yearning with a strong residue of guilt, is yet another examplar. In what postmodern dancer Lucinda Childs considers pure abstraction, Rockwell finds erotic connotations.

Onstage, dance conveys a host of sexual and gender motifs. Theme and variations range from the sublime to the ridiculous. Dance shows the Christian church–upheld superiority of the virgin and the danger of the siren. Not only are there displays of femininity (the romantic sentiment of imposed limitations) and masculinity (often male chauvinism), but at the same time images embody feminist thought, a critique of male supremacy. We see the tension between the sexes enacted. Weaving prevailing attitudes toward gender before our eyes, dance also challenges us with alternative life-styles: unisexuality, homosexuality, asexuality. Insecurity about one's own sexual identity may galvanize derogatory parody through a monstrously exaggerated dance of another's sense of self. Dancers cut images in space of vain narcissism as well as of selfless loving. Choreographer Alwin Nikolais speaks of "masturbatory tendencies in motion" in which "the parasitic attachment to the dance act overpowers the intended expression, leaving in its stead the communication of the parasitic and/or narcissistic act rather than the art idea" (1967, 322).

I illustrate later how dance can be explicit or ambiguous in its conjoining of mind and body to sexual imagery. How we respond to a sexual stimulus depends on our attitudes, beliefs (sometimes referred to as a cognitive map, schematic, or frame of reference), and experience. Subject to old clichés, fetters of past assumptions, and viewers' cognitive maps, dance may also go beyond the known or acceptable and permit futuristic explorations and otherwise dangerous uncloseting. Distanced from the everyday, the performance is an arena in which we can safely challenge the status quo. After all, dance is illusion and pretend, close yet far.

Theater, from proscenium stage to street space or village compound, is "a mode of discovery," said philosopher Bruce Wilshire, "that explores the threads of what is implicit and buried in the world, and pulls them into a compressed and acknowledgeable pattern before us in its 'world.' Theatre discovers meaning, and its peculiar detachment reveals our involvement. . . . The whole point of art [including dance] is to put us in touch with things that are too far or too close for us to see in our ordinary offstage life" (1982, xiv).

Be a Man, Be a Woman: Nature and Nurture

In humans, *sex* refers to biological distinctions of anatomy, hormones, and erotic behavior. Most notable of the anatomic markers are the genitals and reproductive function. Female genitals are inside the body, whereas male genitals are external to it. With the onset of puberty, girls develop the secondary sex characteristics of breasts; upper torso broadening occurs for boys. Both sexes develop body hair in the genital area and armpit. Facial hair and increased body size become prominent for males. Females' hips become broader. The sexes experience hormonal dissimilarities. Men produce more testosterone. The female hormones estrogen and progesterone affect menstruation, gestation, and lactation functions. During the menstrual cycle it is common for a woman's body to swell due to increased fluid retention and for her breasts to be sore. Pregnancy involves changes that alter her sense of balance: increased weight, enlarged, tender breasts, tiredness, and sometimes nausea and back pain. Differences in male and female body size and composition affect physiological processes and have implications for differences in motor potential, which I discuss in chapter 7.

Biological sex differences are not necessarily universal, nor do they obtain between any male/female pair chosen at random. Members of each sex may have some characteristics of the opposite one (Lambert 1978). For example, female athletes and dancers often diverge from the typical female in having more testosterone, muscle, and angularity, narrower hips, and no menstrual cycle.

Whereas sex refers to biological phenomena, *sex role* or *gender* denotes their cultural, psychological, and social correlates: the rules, expectations, and behavior appropriate to being male or female within a particular society. One of the first and key social roles in a child's repertory, sex role, is ascribed, that is, one need do nothing to be assigned it. Its public and private expressions are "scripted."

Cultures add to nature's distinctions and systematically attempt to teach one set of behavior to females and another (usually opposite) set to males. Societies have specific ways—including dance—of sending messages of sexual identity, and showing us ways to discriminate ourselves as male or female. Thus in the United States visual markers are pink for female and blue for male babies. Later follow skirts and curls for girls and pants, ties, and short hair for boys. The clothing industry broadcasts gender by a full code of design details: round collar for a girl; pointed, never scalloped, edges on a boy. For appliqués, trains and soldiers for boys, no flowers or butterflies. And the bottom line is, "Never Put Fruit on a Boy's Garment" (Hoffman 1984). Sometimes there are rites of passage such as initiation, schools, or debutante balls. Signs of sex become embellished. Anthropologist Ray Birdwhistell calls the nonverbal behavior that accentuates gender differences "tertiary sexual characteristics (1970, 42). Note, however, that male and female cultural, as well as biological, ranges overlap.

People have several identities (Weigert, Teitge, and Teitge 1986, 68). Perhaps as an extension of our animal nature to reproduce the species, sex and gender tend to be the foremost way humans categorize themselves and one another. *Sexual identity* depends on biological criteria of genetic, anatomical, and physiological characteristics. Dichotomized into male and female types of persons, *gender identity* includes the internalization of a sex role typical of the society in which one lives (Taylor et al. 1978). During the second year of life, gender identity begins to form. By three years old, children know how to classify themselves and others. Self-recognition develops into self-concept, while youngsters' rapidly growing bodies send them, as well as others, messages. Adolescence is especially telling. Belief in the absolute nature of men's sexual drive stems from evidence of involuntary erection and nocturnal emission, and the encouragement of men's greater voluntary sexual expression; there are no obvious parallels for women. *Sexual identity* refers to sexual interaction: heterosexual, homosexual (gay lesbian), or bisexual.

Identity evolves through realizing others' perceptions of the self as well as by contrasting and comparing others with oneself in real or make-believe life. Recall Wilshire's comment on the reflexivity of theater performance in showing us to ourselves and presenting alternatives.

There have been several influential theories of gender identification (see Pleck 1981). Sigmund Freud broke through the conventions of the Victorian age by elucidating the role of sexuality in human development. His psychosexual theory states that the penis becomes the center of the libido or sexual energy and erotic pleasure for the male. The clitoris is the female counterpart of the penis, yet for Freud the penis is the valued organ for both sexes; boys are subject to castration anxiety, girls, to penis envy. Furthermore, domineering mothers are blamed for a son's homosexuality and poor mother-daughter relations for a daughter's lesbianism. However, learning theory and women's studies have challenged these views.

Lawrence Kohlberg (1966), a cognitive learning theorist influenced by the Swiss psychologist Jean Piaget, argued that sexuality, a significant domain of interaction between biological givens and cultural values, is in large measure patterned by thought. Through *same-sex gender models*, boys and girls perceive the behavior appropriate for their sex and strive to be self-consistent.

Sexual identity and role are not fixed, and relationships are *environmentally conditioned* and changeable over the life cycle. G. Mitchell explained: "The commonsense notion that the sex of the individual is determined at conception is . . . only a half-truth at best. Sexual differentiation, whether structural or behavioral . . . is a *process*. We begin life primarily as females. Something (Y chromosome, testosterone) must be added for the differentiation of a male. In the absence of a Y chromosome the embryo will develop into a female. The crucial *genetic* determinant is the Y chromosome, the crucial *hormonal* determinant is androgen. . . . Moreover, the interaction between hormones and experience continues after the animals have learned various roles. Androgens, for example, undoubtedly affect neural circuits that are involved in experience as well as those more directly involved in sex differences" (1981, 13). Peggy Sanday (1981) documented how scripted gender behavior, especially through religious charters and symbols, changes in societies as they respond to social stresses and competition for scarce resources. (Chap. 5 explicates this pattern in India.)

Learning conditions can even account for differences in sexual responsiveness to erotic visual stimuli. For example, Alfred Kinsey, in the late 1940s and 1950s, found that fewer women than men reported being aroused by erotic images. He attributed this finding to inferred differences in the central nervous system. But sociologist John H. Gagnon demurred: "Most women in the 1940s seldom saw such materials . . . largely prepared for men (that is, they did not connect with women's sexual scripts, though romantic movies did), and finally . . . women had learned to talk about these materials in a negative manner" (1979, 241). However, since the late 1960s, greater flexibility in women's roles and more openness in sexual behavior have led to fewer differences between men and women.

The concept of *androgyny*, the presence of feminine and masculine dispositions in the same individual, has begun to supplant older either/or notions of bipolar opposites. (*Andro* means male; *gyne*, female). Sandra Bem's (1974) concept of psychological androgyny states that persons whose sense of self incorporates both typically feminine and masculine characteristics have behavioral flexibility and adaptability; advantages accrue to both sexes in the separation of gender from sex. Emancipation from inflexible sex role demands could free men to enjoy the emotional rewards conventionally found women's domain and free women to enter men's competitive public arenas.

Margaret Mead was a pioneer in looking at the way traits are assigned to gender in societies around the world. In her words, "If those temperamental attitudes which we have traditionally regarded as feminine—such as passivity, responsiveness, and a willingness to cherish children—can so easily be set up as the masculine pattern in one tribe, and in another, be outlawed for the majority of women as for the majority of men, we no longer have any basis for regarding aspects of such behavior as sex linked" (1935, 279–80). She found that among the New Guinea Arapesh, neither sex shows much aggression or assertiveness. Michelle Rosaldo and Louise Lamphere extended the argument: "The same sort of variability attaches to almost every kind of behavior one can think of: there are societies in which men trade or garden, and those in which women do; societies where women are queens and those in which they must always defer to a man; in parts of New Guinea, men are (like Victorian women) at once prudish and flirtatious, fearful of sex yet preoccupied with love magic and cosmetics that will lead the maidens—who take the initiative in courtship—to be interested in them" (1974, 18).

Notwithstanding the new knowledge and the changes that have occurred in the United States, sexism persists, and sex role stereotyping oppresses both sexes. Table 1.1 summarizes the stereotypic sex-contingent characteristics—notions of masculinity and femininity growing out of the realities of sex and gender. Among many ethnic and social-class groups, masculinity is more demanding than femininity. If a boy does not display sufficient masculinity, he is thought likely to become homosexual or hypermasculine, even a misogynist, hating women for not making him man enough (Fein, in Sargent 1977, 188). Effeminacy in boys is a source of derision. It is more acceptable for girls to be masculine; they are accepted as tomboys and later admired for "having balls." Stereotypes developed in an earlier time, when technology and society were less advanced than today, make contemporary discrimination against women, who now constitute a large percentage of the labor force, seem legitimate. When women violate these outmoded concepts, they often experience stress, a shaky self-concept, and hostility from men and other women. The sexes continue to be brought up viewing each other antagonistically on the assumption that the male is always superior to the female.

What are the strategies for combating sexism? The mechanisms are similar to those that support it (Sargent 1977). Promoting a feminist political agenda and electing its spokespersons is one route. Another is consciousness-raising through didacticism and subliminal seduction. The arts are often part of this tactic of eroding rigid sex roles.

Danced Sexual Imagery: Modeling

How does dance convey concepts of sex and gender? Modeling theory provides an explanation. According to Albert Bandura (1972), following Kohlberg's social learning theory, an individual tends to reproduce attitudes, acts, and emotions exhibited by an observed model (live or symbolic film or television). A model may be cognitively registered and

TABLE 1.1   SEX-RELATED TRAITS IN AMERICA

Female	Male
emotionally expressive	emotionally sparse
reactive	rational, problem solving, instrumental
dependent, passive	independent, active
cooperative	competitive, ambitious
self-abnegating	self-aggrandizing
hearth, home, school, church	market place, bureaucracy, military fields, mines
nurturer	supporter
sex and intimacy linked	sex apart from close relationship
sex is done to, sex object (kitten)	sex is done by, sex subject or possessor
women compete with each other for male approval	men compete with each other for male approval
soft, weak	hard, strong
pet, doll, sparrow	person
wife	husband
mother	father
prostitute, monetarily motivated sex	worker, naturally driven sex
stress on beautiful, marketable body	body as source of pleasure and strength
circumspect and reserved	direct and relaxed
use of polite language	use of profanity
childlike	grown-up
virgin and pure/siren	naturally sexual and worldly
responds to others	dominates others
moral	pragmatic
object	subject

used or remain in subconscious memory until a relevant situation activates it.

A key premise of this theory of vicarious learning is that first the model must attract attention. The observer's sensory capacity, arousal level, and past experiences affect receptivity. Second, retention of what is seen depends upon the viewer's ability to remember and rehearse through symbolic coding in images, words, or actual behavior. Third, there is evidence of learning through motor reproduction of the model, and fourth, learning must make a difference to the learner. More than simply imitation, modeling includes an individual acting in a way that the model would be inclined to behave under similar circumstances, even though the observer had never witnessed the model's behavior in such circumstances. That is, modeling influences can lead to generative and innovative behavior.

There is evidence that images do influence attitudes and behavior. Through images, manufacturers and service providers sell their own notions of smell, taste, and touch to consumers. Psychologists report that exposure to even a few minutes of sexually *violent* pornography can lead to antisocial attitudes and behavior (Donnerstein and Linz 1984). The arts, too, offer models.

As one of the arts that offers models of gender attitudes and behavior, dancing realistically or symbolically presents courtship, climax, male chauvinism, feminist thought, interpersonal exchanges, group interaction, casual relations, and stable associations. Choreographies derive from and contribute to evolving culture. In much the same way as nonhuman animal ritualized displays and human religious ritual, dance frames messages and thereby bestows power upon them. The optical array of dance messages of sexuality and gender may lead to reinforcing ongoing models, acquiring new responses, weakening or strengthening inhibitions over fully elaborated patterns in a person's repertoire, and facilitating performance of previously learned behavior that was unencumbered by restraints.

Note that the dancing of sexuality and gender may be detached from professional dancers, who do not always embrace the roles they perform. Their bodies are at once the instrument of dance, tool of the choreographer, object of perception, and subject who perceives. Gender involves private experience and public display, both everyday and theatrical, which may not conflate.[2]

Prisoners of our sex roles, we sometimes suppress dreams or visions of alternatives. Since from childhood we fight to establish our identities, even imaginarily crossing stereotypic gender roles may scrape deep nerves and evoke anxiety for the insecure. Lincoln Kirstein, scholar and founder of the New York City Ballet, has said, "Ballet dancing is always a paradigm of potential, a frame that presents facts of the extreme possible" (1973, 303). Sex role expectations inhibit dance less than many other social actions—after all, as noted earlier, dance onstage is only art, recreation, entertainment, or a job for the performer.

What makes dance a potentially potent form of gender modeling? There are at least six factors.

CAPTIVATING

Because the instrument of dance and of sexuality is one—the human body—dancing motion attracts attention. Human survival depends upon alertness to moving objects and reproduction. Peoples' intimate experience with their bodies influence their responses to dance. The body is the first form of power with which all persons can identify. Ontogenetically they discover and master their bodies in time, space, and effort patterns. Through sight and movement they enter relationships. The lived-in body symbolically sustains people's power as they groom and adorn themselves, exercise, watch what they eat, and otherwise try to control their bodies. Humans have an instinctual sexual drive constrained by society and culture. Yet the imagination is free, and dance, an activity that depends on flaunting the body, focuses awareness on the body and its associations. Dance, both expressive and communicative, can mediate between sexual stimulus and response. A dance performance embodies the dancer—a human sexual being—choreographic design, and dancer and audience perceptions influenced by their knowledge of the past and present history of the body, sex, gender, and dance in society.

Theorists in gender studies *separate* sex and *gender*. Using the concept of sex in discussions of discrimination reinforces the idea that foremost and always the female or male represents a romantic possibility. In contemporary Western society the separation of sex and gender becomes significant when we attempt to make political and economic opportunity relevant to qualifications for positions instead of physical markers with which an individual is born.

However, because a gender role for most people is sexual reproduction, a perceived body in dance, especially when performers appear nude, in anatomically revealing dress, or in stereotypic male or female costume, conflates biological thought and behavior (arousal and sexual identity), gender, and the historical relationship of dance and sex. Of course, people express gender signs in situations unrelated to sexual activity, but in adolescent and adult interaction the manifestation that refers to everyday stereotypes and violations of them is most dramatic.

LANGUAGELIKE

Dance is potentially potent because it is languagelike. We recognize the power of verbal language in teaching and persuading. As I elaborate in *To Dance Is Human*, dance is a nonverbal language—a form of communication that requires the same underlying cortical faculty for conceptualization, creativity, and memory as verbal language (1987d). Both forms have vocabulary (steps and gestures in dance), grammar (rules for putting the vocabulary together), and semantics (meaning). Dance, however, assembles these elements in a manner that more often resembles poetry rather than prose. Choreographer Martha Graham (1985) believes that dance is "like poetic lyricism, sometimes like the rawness of dramatic poetry, it's like the terror or it can be a terrible revelation of meaning." In critic Clive Barnes's view (1967), "There is a poetic opacity of dance, a lack of definition in statement, an insistence upon the audience interpreting rather than merely watching. In this, dance does share something with poetry itself—the poet throws a phrase into the air to fall like a seed into our imagination. The dance does much the same thing." Of course in dance, motor/visual-kinesthetic channels of communication predominate rather than vocal/auditory channels as in spoken poetry or prose. Whereas language exists in a temporal dimension, dance involves the temporal as well as the three dimensions in space. Both verbal and dance forms of communication have various devices for encoding meaning, and expressions may have multiple meanings.

I have discovered that at least six symbolic devices may be utilized for conveying meaning in dance. They are listed below, but are illustrated more fully in the following chapters. Each way of forming messages may be part of a group's shared legacy or the choreographer's idiosyncratic expression (Hanna 1979b, 1987d; Sebeok 1987). (1) A *concretization* is movement that produces the outward aspect of something. Courtship dances, for example, imitate or replicate potential lovers' advance and retreat tactics. (2) The *icon* represents most properties of a divinity, and viewers respond to it as if it were what it represents. A case discussed in chapter 3 concerns a Haitian possessed by Ghede, god of love and death, who manifests his presence through dancing and is treated with genuine awe and gender-appropriate behavior as if he were the god. (3) A *stylization* encompasses gestures or movements that are the result of convention. For example, a male ballet dancer points to the heart as a sign of love and gazes directly at a woman, who shows her interest with a stereotypic indirect and shy glance. (4) A *metonym* is a motional conceptualization of one thing representing another of which it is a part or with which it is associated in the same frame of experience. A romatic duet to indicate a more encompassing relationship such as a marriage between two individuals is an illustration. (5) A *metaphor* expresses one thought, experience, or phenomenon in place of another that it resembles, suggesting an analogy between the two: for example, a fairy-tale love story between animals denoting the relationship between human lovers. (6) An *actualization* is a portrayal by the dancer of roles that blur the boundary between "real" and "theatrical" life. Dancers can express their own sexual preferences through dance and be treated accordingly by an observer, especially in theatrical settings where a rigid boundary does not exist between performer and spectator.

The devices for encapsulating meaning in dance seem to operate within one or more of eight spheres: the dance event, as when people go to the ballet to be seen socially or to find sexual partners, dance viewing being incidental; the total human body in action, as in girl or boy watching; the whole pattern of the performance, which may emphasize form, style, feeling, or drama; the sequence of unfolding movement, including who does what to whom in dramatic episodes; specific movements and how they are performed, for example, a male dancer parodying a woman on pointe; the intermeshing of movements with other communication modes such as speech or costume; the emotional turn-on through projected sensuality or raw animality; and dance as a vehicle for another medium, for example, serving as a backdrop for a performer's poetry recitation.

Just as speakers use a language, dancers can embed symbols within one another, use opposites and inversions, situational qualifiers, synonyms, and neutralization. A symbol may have a patent meaning, while its latent meaning may be contained in a constellation of symbols that reveal themselves as the dance unfolds.

Besides being a sign of sexuality and gender, dance may be an instrument of sexuality, a stimulant and direct enactment. In this case dance develops erotic love or lust as the sense of sight mediates the sense of touch.

OPEN-ENDED

Dance is replete with meaning for the audience to discover or create. "Dancing is just discovery, discovery, discovery—what it all means," said Graham (1985; in agreement with Wilshire, mentioned earlier). A way of seeing is also a way of not seeing. Critic Walter Terry noted an evolution in American dance that has required choreographers and dancers to go below the surface attraction of the human body in movement and probe the meanings of movement. "It follows that audiences are going to have to look beyond the outer layers of dance action if they are to savor, to the fullest, the inherent richness of dance itself" (1982, 82).

From years of dance viewing Terry concluded that "meaning is present in every movement from the flutter of an eyelid to a space-splitting leap." In order to see and savor all that is present in a performance, the viewer must look for the choreographer's meanings, respond to the dancers' interpretations, and bring his or her own personal experiences or reactions to bear upon what happens onstage. Terry found apt the French expression *assister*, "to go to the theatre to attend a performance," "to assist" (1982, 165).

Actively participating in the creation of meaning, a viewer may gain power by seizing and pinning down the performer as an object in his or her own world, according to Jean-Paul Sartre (1956, pt. 3; Inoue 1980). He believed that the look or regard of the other also dogs persons in their social lives.

Jill Johnston, radical, innovative critic, wrote of mutual exchange in theatrical performance. "When the actor [read dancer] and spectator embrace in the ritual copulation of theatre, nobody is satisfied unless there is mutual ejaculation." Since this "catharsis" is rare and "in fact impossible in any total sense, the antagonism between actor and spectator is an acute unresolved tension. Who's going to get whom? It becomes a sadomasochistic dilemma. . . . The actor, the hero, is the sadist screwing the passive spectator. Yet the actor sacrifices himself in the fiery outstretched arms of a greedy audience which desperately wants what it has for centuries denied itself—the right to act itself. The actor is that part of the organism (audience) projected outside itself to unfold the misery of its own self-alienation. . . . We are all actors and spectators simultaneously upon the stage of the world" (1971, 188–89).

MULTISENSORY

The potency of dance as a resource for promoting gender continuity and change lies in its going beyond language in involving all the senses and seducing us through a multisensory impact. Education specialists have found that experiential learning changes opinions and attitudes. Dance gives us the feeling of kinesthetic activity or empathy; the sight of performers, and sometimes the audience, moving in time and space with effort; the touch of body to performing area, to the performer's own body, or to another's body; the sound of physical movement, the impact of the feet or other body supports on the stage, heavy breathing in high-energy presentations; and the smell of physical exertion and perhaps food and drink on participants' breath.

Sometimes the realism of dance camouflages an appropriation of a dreamlike symbolic language. The dance transforms complex inner experiences, desires, and feelings, and it coaxes people into acceptance, tranquillity, or arousal. Qualities such as surprise, innovation, and ambiguity, which psychologists have found to evoke multisensory arousal (Berlyne 1971) are often part of dance. It can lead to some degree of altered state of consciousness wherein the individual clearly feels a lesser or greater intensity and shift in mental state.

PERSUASIVE

A performance may have the composite of variables that psychologists have documented are likely to change attitudes and opinions (Karlins and Abelson 1970). For example, strong appeals are superior to mild ones when communicated by highly credible sources, and pleasant forms of distraction can increase the effectiveness of persuasive appeals. Critic Marcia Siegel said that we hardly notice how much dance trades in popular traditional stereotypes of the virile man and the feminine woman and "how this reinforces sexism because it's so attractive and entertaining" (1977, 106). Repetition helps ward off the diminuition of a persuasive communication over time. Some efforts in dance to force a new vision upon us fail if the imagery is not compelling enough to pull us away from accustomed ways of seeing the world (see Yinger 1982, 31).

The power of dance to move and persuade is well recognized in Western theater theory and history (Carlson 1984). Aristotle, whose *Poetics* is a central reference point, recognized the potential of the arts (Greek theater included dance) to arouse, and feared they could subvert state and religion. In the Middle Ages the Christian church used the arts to instruct and delight. Many governments have harnessed the arts in service of the state. George Bernard Shaw believed that the aim of the arts should be didactic—telling truths society would rather not hear. Conceiving the goal of theater to be educative, Bertolt Brecht argued that it could intervene in history by explaining that the world can be other than it is and by altering spectators' consciousness. Somewhat in agreement, Antonin Artaud viewed theater as an instrument of revolution that can reorder human existence. In a similar vein, Sartre considered dramatic creation a process of commitment to personal rights or free choice to define oneself and one's existence in the face of the world's absurdity. Herbert Blau stated that theater should be a forum pitted against the outrages humanity commits upon itself.

One may ask, Is not the contemporary Western theater dance audience atypical of opinion leaders who shape attitudes about sex roles? The ticket-purchasing dance audience does share some characteristics of opinion leaders, especially those who control the worlds of print and moving images. The performing arts audience is, for the most part, middle class, white, well educated, with higher-status jobs and incomes than the general public. Some spectators are opinion leaders. The culture-consuming public as a whole differs from the general public in having a higher female-to-male ratio; this is particularly true of the dance audience (DiMaggio, Useem, and Brown 1978; Wyszomirski and Balfe 1985).

Dance performance is immediate, emotionally charging the performer and audience in sporadic or continuous interchange if both are receptive. However, dancing often generates electricity and reflection about the performance that linger long afterward. As a consequence, images of dancing surge forth in our thoughts to comment upon other aspects of life. We draw upon dance as metaphor in our language. In replaying the affecting dance experience from stage to page, metaphors gain power as they clarify and enliven nondance human activity. In *The Performer-Audience Connection: Emotion to Metaphor in Dance and Society* (1983b), I give myriad illustrations of the metaphoric use of dance in vernacular language and literature to suggest the impact of a performance, especially with sexual imagery, on the public at large.

For example, over the years many proverbs have acknowledged dance as a courtship behavior that may or may not include a serious pursuit of a marriage partner. Now we use the phrase "boy meets girl" when members of the same sex approach each other, or elderly divorced or widowed come together. Thus the metaphor of the "Legal Mating Dance" is an apt description of the fall ritual of platoons of corporate lawyers visiting prestigious law schools to woo top students. In the hiring halls, connections are made in a stylized manner comparable to the decorum of many social dance occasions (*Newsweek* 1980, 111).

It is said, "Dancing is the child of Music and of Love." And, "In dance the hand hath liberty to touch." Saying "My dancing days are done" refers to feelings of remorse or resignation about settling down or getting old. The adage "An old man dancing is a child in mind" describes an elderly person's rousing youthful attitude and behavior.

The dangers of heterosexual dancing were well known: "When you go to dance, take heed whom you take by the hand," it was said. Sixteenth-century moralist John Northbrooke (*Against Dicing*, 1577), remarked, "Through dancing many maidens have been unmaidened, whereby I may say it is the storehouse and nursery of bastardy." Dangers for men appear in the sayings "Twas surely the devil that taught women to dance," and "Refrain from dancing which was the means that lost John Baptist's head."

In the Renaissance, one gloss for *dance* was copulation. There was a ribald association between dancing and copulation in such songs as the "Irish Jigg": "Then nothing but Dancing our Fancy could please./ We lay on the Grass and danc'd at our ease;/I don'd with my Breeches and off with my Whigg,/And we fell a Dancing the Irish Jigg." The bawdy metaphor follows in the tradition of Aristophanes (Henke 1979, 63–64).

ACCESSIBLE

The power of dance to convey sexual imagery is also related to its popularity and accessibility. In the United States during the first quarter of the twentieth century, with dance companies touring the country, there was talk of being on the threshold or even within the portal of a second renaissance. During the 1960s there was another boom. And in the 1970s dance came into full blossom coincident with the adoption of government subsidies for cultural organizations and the dissolution of the puritanist denial of bodily pleasure. American culture's preening hedonism, terror of aging, adulation of youth, and fixation on slimness paved the way for increased dance performance and appreciation. Onstage performers are young, strong, slim, and sometimes defiant of everyday limitations. About twenty-five years ago there were 6 professional dance companies in the United States, the majority of them based in New York City. Now there are more than 120 professional companies and nearly 700 amateur groups reaching out for audiences. The Indianapolis Ballet Theatre educates its public by performing at shopping malls, festivals, fairs, parades, schools, and churches. Dance participation has expanded as has the number of writers, musicians, and artists it has enamored. Dance concerts; television programs, Broadway shows, and films about dancers; and news publications, articles, and books are a bazaar that has captured the American imagination. Complementing this bounty are dance agents, professional associations, connoisseurs, critics, researchers, memorabilia collectors, therapists, studios, university programs, libraries, and curators. And the dance explosion in the United States reverberates elsewhere in the world.

Even sports enthusiasts give dance its due. Critic Anna Kisselgoff (1982d), with obvious elation, wrote, "We know that dance has really made it when Peter Pocklington, owner of the Canadian hockey team, the Edmonton Oilers, calls his . . . center player, Wayne Gretzky, 'the Nureyev of sport, the superstar's superstar.' " An entire article on news of ballet has even appeared on the front page of a major newspaper's sports section (Kornheiser 1984). A decade earlier Nureyev had been called the Joe Namath of dance.

Televised dance won applause in 1937. "The ballet has a bright future in television!" "It is winning a prominent place on the telecast programs" (*New York Times* 1937). No longer the province solely of elite ticket-buying theatergoers and critic-reading audiences, today a melange of dance can reach nearly the entire nation through television. There are special programs and series such as "Dance in America" and "Live from the White House," and performances are broadcast from major theater centers. In addition, old movies and live shows with dancing are broadcast. Televised performances are now seen in parts of the country that cannot accommodate live productions because of sparse population, antidance attitudes, or cultural traditions favoring narrow dance genre (categories of dance characterized by particular styles). Having been a New York City dance-omane who only watched live performances about twice a week, I had no choice when I moved to Dallas but to watch dance on television if I wanted to see a range of genres and excellent performance.

Whereas in 1948 there were about fifteen commercial stations, which were received in 200,000 American homes with television sets, by 1970 there were thousands of stations and 100 million sets. In 1977, 98 percent of homes owned one or more sets. Cable television, video recorders, and video cassettes are increasingly available. Visual imagery is especially important in a generation for which 7.2 hours of television watching per day is average.[3] Current expansion of numbers of television stations, especially MTV, is accompanied by the dance visualization of rock and pop music, eliminating visual slack and creating movement where there is none (Levy 1983). Offbeat dance programs are now available through cable.

Drawing upon the Syndicated Data Service which uses the Nielsen Television Index, researchers at Public Broadcasting System reported that their nationwide dance audience from September 1984 to May 1985 was about 3.5 percent of television households, or 2.93 million households. (Note that an average dance program has approximately three million viewing households, but more than one person may be watching a dance program in the home.) The past eight years have seen similar ratings. Dance viewing has increased from the previous decade and appears to be growing. The programs vary in numbers of viewers. For example, *The Nutcracker* is a certain "sellout," whereas it is difficult to determine which other programs will attract a large audience (Dale Rhodes, pers. com. 1984; Sue Bomzer, pers. com. 1985). The commercial networks have their own ratings.

Television as the media of information for most people appears to validate dance and to promote live performances. The television appearances of ten dance companies in "Dance in America," between 1976 and 1978, led to increases in attendance at live performances, according to a telephone survey with company administrators and managers. Four companies saw immediate effects on box-office receipts after their shows aired. Some companies added new cities and larger theaters to their tours and received increased financial patronage and contributions. The box-office take improved when reruns of the shows were aired near performance dates. All of the companies' directors expressed the desire to participate in other dance/TV projects, except for Paul Taylor, who at the time considered dance a form he wished to present live (Research and Programming Services 1978).

Dance came to television in 1931 with a performance by Maria Gambarelli. In the inaugural years, dance was used as spectacle and diversion. Collapsing life-size three-dimensional dancers to a small flat surface distorted depth, scale, and spatial proportion. There were blurred images, electronically decapitated dancers, and incomplete choreographic patterns. During the 1940s and 1950s, variety shows continued to present dance; however, choreographers began to work with the electronic staff to integrate dance with all aspects of the show and its production. The TV camera was soon freed from its stationary position (Barrett 1968; Penney 1981).

Eventually there evolved dance series in which the producer, director, and crew realized the concept of the choreographer. Phyllis Annette Penney avers: "The dance telecasts of the 1970's consciously aimed to make the viewing audience look at dance through the all-seeing eye of the camera, not merely through human eyes. A review of the content of the comprehensive descriptive [1970s] chronology constructed for . . . [my] study reveals a definite attempt, however subtle, by the networks to portray the worthiness of dance to be a vital part of the social fabric of American life" (1981, 94; Coe 1985). Cable TV's Arts and Entertainment Network, Hearst/ABC-RCTV, airs dance programs and productions filmed abroad.

The growth and popularity of dance in the 1980s, as well as awareness of its sexual and gender signification, are reflected in expensive
advertisements placed in major newspapers, news magazines, and other
widely distributed periodicals, for a remarkable range of products and
services. Sometimes the images speak for themselves. At other times it
is unclear if the image of a beautiful ballerina is a sex object,
idealization of femininity, artist, or worker. A written text may pin
down one of many possible interpretations. The economic world knows
well that images affect how we select our banks, business supplies, home
furnishings, clothing, grooming goods, and leisure commodities, services, and activities, as well as how we react to our environment. Approximately a two-year casual reading netted a survey of these images.[4]

While such advertising images illustrate the accessibility and esteem
of dance, they also tend to emphasize the conservative traditions of
classical ballet, a repository of cultural history in which women are sex
objects or workers directed by men.

There is yet another reason for the growth of the dance audience.
Although the human figure was prominent in the history of Western
visual art, during the mid-twentieth century attention centered on
abstraction and anonymity. If humans appeared at all, they were
disembodied and rootless. Therefore, I submit, dance may have met the
need for the aesthetic presence of the whole human body, and
especially the female body, which has occupied a central place in the
Western cultural imagination (Suleiman 1985).

In sum, the body language of dance may carry a more immediate
wallop than verbal communication in commenting on sexuality and in
modeling gender because of its motion-attracting attention, languagelike qualities, replete multilayered meanings, multisensory assault,
composite of variables that change attitudes and opinions, and accessibility and humanity.

The sexuality of dance and its potential to excite has long been
recognized. Dancing can lead to altered states of consciousness (with
changed physiological patterns in brain wave frequency, adrenalin, and
blood sugar) and hence to altered social action (Hanna 1987d, 1988).
Dance spectators may have vicarious, empathic experiences. The
Greeks linked dance, bacchanals, and political unrest; Plato feared the
subversive impact of the arts—mimesis aroused the feeling being
imitated. The Bible alludes to the corrupting dance of Salome; clerics
speak of abuses of dance, which was an accepted liturgical art form
(Davies 1984); and totalitarian governments demand dance in the

service of the state. Even the denial of sexuality through, for example, costume, which hides sexual identity, may paradoxically make the spectator contemplate the essence of that which is absent. Dance can be understood as a medium through which choreographers/directors/producers interpret, legitimate, reproduce, and challenge gender and associated patterns of cooperation and conflict that order their social world (see Ortner and Whitehead 1981).

2

Odyssey toward Understanding

The pathways and mazes that lead one to explore such subjects as the relationship of dance to sex and gender often have long histories. Multiple stimuli in one's environment may eventually coalesce and lead to action.

A catalytic event for me ocurred in 1980 when Gerald Meyers, Queens College and Graduate Center of the City University of New York philosophy professor and American Dance Festival Town Hall director and master of ceremonies, invited my participation in a public forum consisting of conversations between humanists and noted choreographers. Since I am an anthropologist, Meyers asked me to address the topic "Dance and Cultural Perspectives," specifically, the influence of non-Western culture on American modern dance.

I was paired with Erick Hawkins, a man who created his own modern dance style when he broke away from the innovative "matriarch" of modern dance, Martha Graham, his former mentor, dance partner, and wife. Not only did he develop a movement technique different from hers, in harmony with nature and the body as opposed to her contractive, tense gesture and locomotion, but Hawkins looked to American Indian and oriental cultures for role models of "respectable" men in dance. Because Western culture after Louis XIV generally associated professional male dancing with effeminacy and homosexuality, Hawkins felt that a cross-cultural perspective was more supportive of men charting new directions in American dance.

In preparation for our conversation, I reread some old classics on

American modern dance that I had perused nearly three decades earlier. I also looked at more recent books such as *Where She Danced* (Kendall 1979), which portrays key figures in the development of American modern dance during the twentieth century, a period that witnessed a great change in women's traditional social, cultural, economic, and political roles. During my preparation I also read Barry Laine's "Diaghilev: The Imprint of a Gay Impresssario on 20th Century Art" (1980).

What hit me was how prominently the dance field spoke to sexual preference, role, and behavior as well as to economic opportunity. As I recalled what I had seen onstage in four decades of dance viewing— from male support of female, woman on her own, unisex pattern, to role reversal as in woman flips man or man dances on pointe in tutu— the images seemed to mirror, refract, or telescope into the future, changing gender patterns in society.

Several experiences had earlier sensitized me to gender distinctions. I grew up in a family where the expectations for me were different from those for my brother, who would be the doctor. By contrast, I should not show too much intelligence or I would not get married, and if I had to have a career, teaching was acceptable because the hours and holidays permitted a mother to be with her children. Mine taught piano at home. My father, a musician who played in the orchestras of the Ballet Russe de Monte Carlo, the St. Louis Civic Opera Company, Broadway shows, and Hollywood films, said that female dancers often were "not treated nicely" and discouraged me from aspiring to a dance career, which I had considered. Years later I learned that public theater dance performance had a long history of objectifying women's bodies in association with the demimonde and even prostitution. In the 1950s I read Ashley Montagu's *The Natural Superiority of Women* (1974). Yet traveling alone in Mexico, Europe, and the United States alerts a woman to gender constraints that her male counterparts rarely experience. Sitting in one son's classroom, I listened to the teacher read sexist fairy tales. "They are only stories," she said when I suggested she comment on the old-fashioned gender stereotypes in the tales. Karen Rowe (1979) shows that these entertainments perpetuate a cultural status quo. They situate women in the home, subordinate them to a male prince or father figure, and give them no alternative but to marry. Passivity, dependence, and self-sacrifice are celebrated as the heroine's cardinal virtues.

A sharp reminder that attitudes toward sexuality vary in time, place, and person came after spending thirteen months in Africa, surveying the ethnographic and travelers's literature, and then writing a manuscript on African dance. A white male American reviewer accused me of "racism" and insensitivity for reporting some Africans' actions that he considered improper: "Why, for example, does the illustration of social sanction applied against those who do not join in a dance have to be one in which dancers show their buttocks to the offenders and dance backwards at them singing about the baboon's red bottom? Why does the intellectually impressive framework for Chapter 10 produce such a relatively large percentage of bald description of sweat and phallus, coitus and sexual suggestion? How would we survey our own dancing?" Yet, when I drew upon the same African material at a public lecture on African dance, a Ghanaian came up to me afterward and chastised me for my indirection and circumlocution in discussing sex and dance—a relationship that is direct and acceptable in his culture! Was the American reviewer of my study ethnocentric? To his question of how we would survey our own dance, this book provides an answer.

Over the course of the last decade some of my friends have made their private homosexual lives public, and some have become the butt of others' own sexual insecurities. The recent spate of publications on sex, the women's and gay liberation movements, and changing notions of manhood attests to our insatiable hunger to understand ourselves as sexual beings. In the fall of 1986, Barry Laine was curator for an exploration of erotic expression in dance, called Sex and Dance, a two-week, four-part festival at Dance Theater Workshop and P.S. 122 in New York City. The festival surveyed ritual and fantasy, audience arousal, and sexual identity on and off stage, with performances of classical ballet, classical Indian dance, burlesque, tap dancing, modern, postmodern, Broadway show dancing, and multimedia presentations. A seminar of critics, dancers, and writers active in the field concluded the festival. Elsewhere in the United States, some local communities associate dance with illicit sex, viewed as the devil's doing, and ban dancing. The U.S. Post Office even held up for review the flyer of the Sex and Dance festival because of the title. The post office said sex is commercial and contested its association with the nonprofit educational mission of the Dance Theater Workshop, in part supported by state and federal money.

These stimuli and my earlier work on ethnicity, social mobility, and dance came together for me in what Margaret Mead, pioneer of studies on gender and cultural learning, called my "analogical mind."

This study of sexuality and gender patterns in the production of dance and its images extends my earlier work on dance and society, beginning with an invitation to join Ewe dancers in Nima, Accra, Ghana. As I danced, I received the women's gentle correction for copying the males' energetic movements rather than the females' more subdued style. During field research on Nigeria's Ubakala dance-plays, I learned that women asserted themselves through the medium of dance in much the same way as a special interest group lobbies in Washington, D.C. Furthermore, when the biological and social roles of men and women are most diverse—men as the warrior life-takers and women as the married childbearing life-givers—their dance movements differed most markedly in the use of time, space and effort (this is discussed further in chap. 4 and Hanna 1987d).

Both of my earlier books on dance touch upon sex and gender. *To Dance Is Human* develops a case for dance as nonverbal communication and describes the cognitive dimension of this physical activity. *The Performer-Audience Connection* balances the scale by addressing the dancer's intention and the audience's reception of emotion. When I interviewed performers and spectators, and also surveyed the latter, at eight Smithsonian Institution concerts for different dance forms from the United States and Asia (including modern and postmodern Western theater art and folk and classical arts), unsolicited notions of sexuality and sex roles once again come to the fore. For example, in the Kathakali performance of *The Sacrifice of King Daksha*, a young professional woman economist noted that "most vivid is the clear depiction of the relative status of the two sexes. This permeates the entire performance. The female is always submissive and even an attempt at anger is subdued."

Historian Carl N. Degler (1982) sums it up: "Sexuality is to women as color or race is to blacks: a source of difference from the dominant group, therefore a source of possible oppression. . . . Men wrote history to meet their needs and concerns as men. They did not exclude or ignore women because they were misogynists or malicious; they did so because what women did, felt, or thought was not important to them when they looked to the past for guidance, understanding, and identity." It is the identity, guidance, and understanding that I examine in the production and images of dance. As a woman, I have a female bias. However, as an anthropologist, I try to take the perspectives of those with other gender self-identifications, expectations, and actions.

Anthropologists, stimulated by Mead's work, whatever its shortcomings,[1] have studied the transmission of culture, learning, and nonverbal communication. They draw attention to the means and forms through which values and related behavior are intentionally and unintentionally generated and taught within a group, conveyed from one generation to another, and modified in response to changing environments.[2] Anthropologists are concerned with the controversies of nature versus culture and cultural continuity and change.

The Social Construction of Reality

Shared by members of a community as social beings, *culture* is a system of ideas about the nature of the world and the expected behavior of people in it. Ideas are encoded in public symbols, literary texts, art, drama, religious practice, and dance. These symbols, through which people represent themselves to themselves and to each other, are accessible to observation and inquiry.

Both the reality (actual fact) and illusion (pretend aspect) of performance on stage are socially constructed through individuals producing, choreographing, dancing the dance, and watching it (see Berger and Luckmann 1966). Performers may surrender themselves to spectators' gazes or assert themselves before the gazes and thus manipulate the gazers who partake of fantasy worlds often denied them in real life. For example, the poor may indulge in the luxurious life of rich nobility portrayed in some ballets; the present viewers may be transported to the nostalgic past. Active physical beings create images that are read and felt by performers and audience members. Their social beings play a role in the consciousness and reflexivity of these images. Reports of dance are also social constructions of knowledge, as I explain further on in this chapter.

I accept a key assumption of symbolic interaction; namely, that human social relations require conscious symbolic behavior that is a product of body language. People's perceptions of participants in the dancer-audience exchange are therefore significant data in this embryonic study primarily of discovery and presentation rather than of hypothesis testing. What may matter is not what happened but what people think happened, so that outstanding acts and images outweigh representative distributions.

Dance is merely one node in a performance web within the Kenneth Burke/Erving Goffman dramaturgical model of social interaction whereby the individual presents a version of the reality of a situation by choosing the setting, posture, gesture, and so on to manage a impression. Therefore I consider dance in relation to society. Theatrical and other stages have conventions and rebellions against them, some predictability, certain prescribed roles, and repercussions.

Within the vast literature that must be the foundation for this odyssey, in addition to the works discussed thus far, mention should be made of research on an aspect of the performance web: sexuality and nonverbal gender patterns that draw our attention to both blatant and subtle ways of molding opinion. Western culture has an exaggerated esteem for language and its prerogative for describing reality. Yet as is language, images are a reality-defining discourse (Miles 1985).

In *Body Politics: Power, Sex, and Nonverbal Communication*, Nancy M. Henley summarized the everyday American social interaction that is the raw material from which choreographers-dancers construct a way of knowing through kinetic discourse.[3] In daily life the male tends to be more elevated, in front, to the right rather than the left, to use more space, to touch physically more, and to display less emotion. This behavior is consistent with pancultural findings in a thirty nation study of sex stereotypes: the male is stronger and more active and is "characterized by higher needs for dominance, autonomy, aggression, exhibition, achievement, and endurance, and the female stereotype reveals higher needs for abasement, deference, succorance, nurturance, affiliation, and heterosexuality" (Williams and Best 1982, 245).

Erving Goffman (1979, 35) and Jean Umiker-Sebeok (1981) explained how our notions of gender are coded in the metaphor of visual images in advertising, a male-dominated field. The Marlboro man proclaims that any man can have macho stature with a cigarette in his mouth. We see the woman's personal success story: Dr. Maidenform is displayed looking down compassionately at her bedridden patient. Nearly nude in a Maidenform bra, the professional woman is forced into the image of a sex object. For all the talk, the new woman is merely in updated gear; underneath she is sexually available, maybe just pretending to be a doctor. One does not see such images of male physicians, who are bastions of respectability according to polls of occupational prestige. Rena Bartos (1982) analyzed the changing women's market and appraised ways to reach it through advertising.

Art historians Margaret R. Miles (1985), Marina Warner (1985), and Edwin Mullins (1985) illustrate how people may gain insight and understanding through images in sacred and profane domains. Images were critical to conveying information prior to the printing press and have been since the supreme reign of television. Documenting how the visual arts became "a game in which women are the pieces, and men the players," Mullins says, "Nothing in art has been more persistent than an anxiety to establish what it is that defines a good woman and what it is that defines a bad." Moreover, "much art comes to look like magnificent camouflage behind which the dominant sex hides horrible doubts about his fitness to dominate" (Mullins 1985, 9, 17, and 224).

George Gerbner and his colleagues at the Annenberg School of Communication at the University of Pennsylvania have been discovering evidence of subliminal video conditioning of how we perceive ourselves and others. Summarizing an extensive body of nondance studies on role socialization in the 1950s, Bradley Greenberg (1982) concluded that television supplements, reenforces, and complements other stereotypical information on social roles, but it is also capable of teaching counterstereotypes (see Busby 1975).

Michelene Wandor's *Understudies: Theatre and Sexual Politics* (1981) gives strong precedent for examining the production and performance of images. She describes the male-dominant division of labor in the theater and women's and gays' challenge to it through the representation of sexuality in London's alternate theater during the 1970s.

Sexuality and its political implications (see Weeks 1985; Vance 1984) operate through metaphors and other devices and spheres of encoding meaning. These modes condense anxieties, desires, and aspirations about pleasure and danger, and they mobilize attitudes, energies, and actions. Symbolized sexuality and gender give and take value and meaning in relation to actual men and women. A constant exchange occurs between images and reality (Warner 1985).

We shall see that similar to visual arts, advertising, and nondance theater, images in dance evoke plural significations and mixed moralities among dance creators and dance viewers. Ambiguity creates sexual static. Camouflage is possible, as when hostility of one sex toward the other is dressed up as love. Males primarily have been the choreographers who project fantasies and longings as they conjure women into existence or exorcise them into oblivion. Or they make strong threatening women managable for men. Yet dances with imagery of, for example, Judith or Salome convey the power of women to undo, contaminate, or overpower men. Women viewers sometimes identify with idealized female images, such as the Virgin Mary, as an escape from childbearing biology (Miles 1985, 90). Rebellious women, and empathic men, challenge established traditions by choreographing women in many-faceted roles of stature, independence, and dominance. Unintentionally these new images spawn reactions toward the persisting conflicting notions of woman as life giver, nurturer, sex object, and castrator.

Sources of Evidence

This book combines many social constructions of knowledge: my observations through active participation in the life of people I have studied; firsthand and secondhand reports of dancers, choreographers, directors, producers, and audience members (including critics); the work of other scholars, primarily in anthropology and history; and visual records.

THROUGH TIME ACROSS CULTURES

Beginning with the study of non-Western exotic societies, anthropology, with its theories and methods, can illuminate the dance of a small village in Nigeria or the dance of the United States (see Hanna references). The time frame may be limited or extended, as dance changes. Concerned with culture, anthropologists seek kinds of meanings, indigenous views, and analyst observations.

Anthropological *semiotics* directs our attention to the movement or "text," the choreographer or "writer," "composer," dancer or "maker," audience members or "readers," and the performance-event context, including production, history, ecology, and economics, all of which contribute to the meaning. *Holism,* or the interconnection of social phenomena, is a hallmark. So, too, is *ethnography*, which developed as a reaction to speculative, "armchair" history. A researcher engaged in participant observation, living among a group (usually for at least a year, which encompasses responses to seasonal changes), asking questions, and observing in much the same way as a child learns its culture. Many anthropologists take a *comparative perspective*. From a broad overview of case studies arise hypotheses of greater generality, formulations that transcend the circumstances of any given case, and interpretative insights. A comparative perspective, often a mind stretcher, prejudice dissolver, and taste widener, allows us to discover structural patterns and affinities among peoples distant in time and space. Moreover, "going" to far away places allows people to understand their own cultures better.

Since my parents sent me to ballet class when I was eight years old, I have been a participant-observer of dance. I had a case of *pes planus,* flat feet, and the doctor said dancing would make them strong. My mother became the piano accompanist for Lala Bauman, in St. Louis, Missouri, whose dance studio attracted professionals and me. As an adult I continued to study dance in the United States, Mexico, Africa, Europe, the Caribbean, and the Orient. My dance viewing was most intense and varied when I moved to the New York metropolitan area.

Anthropologists often do historical research or draw upon historians' work. History is a chronicle and explanation of events (Adshead and Layson 1983). Historians use primary sources, materials that come into existence during the period being studied, such as a choreographer's working score, actual costumes, and eyewitness accounts. These materials are often found in archives and attic trunks. Secondary sources are materials that use hindsight to trace developments in the dance over a chosen span of time. These include dance encyclopedias and biographies.

Because sex and gender options lie within an anthropological and a historical context, I have tried to place the issues of dance production/management and images in this perspective, expecially considering values and economic opportunities related to gender.

Moreover, people often look to other cultures, past and present, to enhance their palette of experience. This is especially the case in Western culture where innovation prevails as an aesthetic canon. Much thought and many dances from around the world, in some transformation, have become part of the United States cultural heritage and have entered the repertoire of theatrical dance. Indeed, the "high arts" have always taken from the people for their own creative products. "Exotica" entered European classical ballet during the Age of Exploration. We find the Middle Eastern harem dance in classical ballet, Chinese dancing in *The Nutcracker*, Indian goddesses of the Upanishads in *La Bayadère*, and Ghede, Haitian lord of eroticism and death, in the more recently choreographed *Banda* (performed by the Dance Theatre of Harlem). The 1855 ballet *Abdallah*, choreographed by Auguste Bournonville in Denmark, was set in Bassara (now Basra, Iraq) under the reign of marauding Turks. The ballet dealt with the Muslim religion, sheikhs, soldiers, and harem dancing girls (considered too sexy for the nineteenth century). America's Ballet West reconstructed the ballet in 1984.

The ancient classical traditions of the huge geographical area and large population of India have also influenced ballet. Mohan Khokar (1984, 221–23) points to the efforts made at a time when the art of dance in India was in a precarious condition. As early as October 1830, a ballet having an Indian background, *Le Dieu et la Bayadère*, was choreographed by Filippo Taglioni and performed in Paris. In 1877 another ballet about dancing girls belonging to Hindu temples, *La Bayadère*, by Marius Petipa, was premiered at the Maryinsky Theatre in St. Petersburg and remains a popular piece today. Such famous ballerinas as Marie Taglioni and Anna Pavlova have danced the pivotal role. *Lalla Rookh* (*The Rose of Lahore*), choreographed by Jules Perrot, was first produced in London in 1846. Later in 1858, Lucien Petipa produced a ballet version of Kalidasa's play *Shakuntala. The Talisman*, first performed in 1899, included characters Akbar, king of Delhi, Damayanti, his daughter, Moureddin, maharaja of Lahore, and Amaravati, goddess of heavenly spirits. *Scheherazade*, premiered in 1910, with choreography by Michel Fokine, has also remained in the repertoires of companies in the Soviet Union, Europe, and the United States. In 1912, Vaslav Nijinsky, with Tamara Karsavina, danced in Fokine's *Le Dieu Bleu*, a ballet about the god Krishna. Pavlova, about whom more will be said later, drew upon Indian culture to create new dances. Eliot Feld's *Echo*, premiered in 1986, draws upon Indian temple dancing.

In the modern dance field, Isadora Duncan turned to classical Greece. Ruth St. Denis's obsession with the Orient manifested itself in serious stage treatment of Eastern styles. She was fascinated by Hindu gods who dance and by the dancing girls. St. Denis's 1906 *Radha*, of carnal ecstasy, which she performed in bare feet, legs, and midriff, either shocked or entranced the public. Graham, too, explored the Orient and borrowed from Japanese Nō and Kabuki. Inter alia, she was an Aztec heroine, a Moorish dancing girl, and a lithesome Hindu maiden. Zen influenced Erick Hawkins. T'ai chi ch'uan inspired Deborah Hay (Wheeler 1984).

Outsiders may, of course, see another culture's customs out of context or misinterpret what they see (Kealiinohomoku 1981). Notwithstanding Western assertions to the contrary, Hawaiian dance is supposed to be sexy and fun. Through travel and performance tours to different parts of the world, reading, seeing photographs, watching television or motion pictures, and attending museums, choreographers/dancers learn about other peoples's dances. In addition, foreign groups come to American theaters. Les Ballets Africains from Guinea evoked, in 1959, rules prohibiting bare bosoms in New York City. The mayor later revoked the rule to permit the company to dance in traditional costume. Today bare breasts of any dancer are commonly accepted on stages in major cities.

The depth of choreographic assimilation varies. Scant regard may be given to what is meaningful to the dancer of a particular culture. Diffusion is an easy concept to propose and difficult to substantiate.

Western dancers also leave their mark on non-Western cultures. For example, Anna Pavlova toured Latin America and the Far East in 1917 and the early 1920s. She encouraged respect for women's public dance performance in, for example, Japan and India, and sparked dance renaissances (Money 1982). American modern and jazz dance have had a strong impact throughout the world.

THE DANCE CRITIC AS SAGE AND SHAMAN

In exotic cultures anthropologists seek out key informants—the knowledgeable sage or shaman. Thus Marcel Griaule (1965) sought out one of the best-informed members of the Dogon society in Mali, since there was no written history of its myths, and published an account of the wise man's story. In a similar way, I draw upon the critics' stories for the material on sexuality and gender in dance in America, the bulk of this book. Often considered the cognoscenti in Western societies, dance critics can be viewed as sages or shamans. Moreover, they are creators of historical records.

As social agents of a culture, the critics fulfill a role assigned to clergymen, parents, peers, and others who convey knowledge. Usually self-selected and hired by newspapers and periodicals, critics represent the dance and the public to each other. Respected critics mediate between the performers/managers and the audience. They may disseminate news, improve our knowledge of performance, and capture a slice of ongoing history. Their criticism of the present becomes tomorrow's history, for it is often the only record of a performance. Therefore, much like an archaeologist uses a shard of pottery or other artifact, I turn to documents of dance perception from the "self-appointed historian," as Marcia Siegel (1979) puts it. Reading the critics can be a form of interviewing and historical content analysis.

John Manfredi says that critics' "popularity of influence rests mainly on the extent to which they say what is in accord with the collective consciousness" (1982, 87). They are the mouthpiece and agent of the establishment in the attempt "to relate the work of the artist to the inner ethos of the society and what he sees as its truths" (p. 15). In this respect a film or video recording is no substitute.

Among those making new dances, Murray Spalding (1983) stresses the importance of critics to an artist's work: "We had to depend on our own standards and esthetics. Rarely did reviews appear in the newspapers. It seemed to us that the growth of our art and its audience hinged on reviews. Now we often get vital pre-performance coverage." At the panel entitled The Impact of the Critic, which I organized for the Conference on Social Theory, Politics, and the Arts, choreographer/artistic director Maida Withers said that the artist often appreciated the perspective of a person who is "distant from the creation and from this vantage can provide some illumination to the creator of the work as a cultural phenomenon. . . . When I first started making work, quite frankly, I didn't know what I was making, and I looked for help in terms of trying to understand what my work was as it was viewed and experienced by other people. . . . an artist can get insight. . . . To imagine a critic sitting in the theatre to watch something that I've worked on for four months and to catch in that one evening's performance those movement images and be able to translate them into language and then into an experience for a reader is extremely complex. . . . That's why I'm interested mostly in reading critical work that is fairly extensive" (Hanna 1985b, 146).

Choreographer, artistic director, and former dancer, Russian-born George Balanchine was less sanguine about the aesthetic value of the critic, but believed a favorable review was essential for financial success. "It was very hard for us here in the beginning. Then we were called American Ballet not City Ballet. No one knew who we were, and we need [sic] people to come, buy tickets to survive. There was a writer for *Daily Mirror* who came every night. He had a friend who was a dancer, but not in the company, and every day he wrote awful things in the paper. And, because he wrote column, not review, public read and believed more. So, every morning people read *Mirror*, see ballet was bad, and not come buy ticket to see [for themselves]. We didn't know what to do, but we figured out. We stopped giving him tickets, he wouldn't buy his own, so he didn't come anymore. There were no more columns, people started coming to see and buying tickets. It was a blessing because we needed to survive" (quoted in Livingston 1983, 48).

Critics contribute so much to the record and meaning of dance. Marcia Siegel underscores the challenge of one role: "The fact that dance has no institutionalized history imposes extra responsibilities on its critics. We are its reporters and sometimes its interpreters, but we are also its memory, its conscience. By that I don't mean that critics have the best memories, or possess any unusual moral qualities. I mean that they are professional observers, and that what they tell us is our only systematic account of an ongoing history" (1977, xiv). The trained critic is expected to conduct historical research and write with well-honed vision so that the reader can visualize the report in relation to the art of theater dancing and, according to esteemed critic Edwin Denby (1967, 233), to tell the public what is interesting and original (see English 1979; Hanna 1985b).

A dance critic since 1949, Clive Barnes points out the unique position of this communicative endeavor. "The number of dance critics in the English-speaking world who make a decent living wage, commensurate to say such professional peers as drama critics, doctors, lawyers or principal dancers, is pitifully small. No, you don't enter into dance criticism for the money. Why then? Perhaps it is the challenge—the desire to interpret the nonverbal in verbal terms, to communicate in words the joy of the dance, to analyze the ineluctible" (1978, 33). The critic in this sense is much like the shaman or psychiatrist who is able to see what is actually going on, lay bare some aspect that might otherwise be unnoticed, and improve our knowledge.

How do critics, commonly trained in journalism or English, gain the ability through verbal glosses to direct others' eyes to what is to be seen and to gain insight? They undergo an experiential initiation. Barnes went to performance "after performance. Of every type of dance . . . I could beg, borrow or steal my way into. . . . I also later—after I started to write actually—took classes, and I watched ballet class a great deal" (p. 44). There are other kinds of apprenticeships. A dance student or professional may become a critic. Alan M. Kriegsman, Pulitzer prizewinner for his dance criticism at the *Washington Post*, began in the sciences at the Massachusetts Institute of Technology and then switched to music. Unable to obtain a position as a music critic, he took what was available—dance. Then he read about dance and applied his former training. There are also more formal apprenticeships. Marcia Siegel studied at the Laban Institute (school of dance movement analysis), and Sally Banes earned a Ph.D. in performance studies after an undergraduate degree in literature.

The critic differs from the social scientist, who aims for objectivity, linking observations to theory and discovering underlying principles. One school of criticism takes a subjective advocacy approach based on clearly expressed opinion. Another school takes a stance that is closer to natural history observation and anthropological methods of translating between two cultures. Critics from this school attempt to describe accurately what occurred. They and social scientists would presumably admit that their biases affect their observations. About exponents of either style of criticism Barnes says, "Critics are not Moses coming down from the mountains, they are not even the person who gave Moses the message in the first place, they are fallible human beings offering their throught about an adventure of the soul and spirit. Opinionated, yes. Free of prejudice, no. All we can ask is that their opinions are informed and their prejudices open" (1978, 46).

A third school of criticism attempts to recapture in a transformation the experience of a viewer for the reader who was not at the dance concert. In a letter to the choreographer/dancer Murray Louis, published in *Dance Magazine*, Katherine Block (1976) wrote: "If you read what I wrote about your '73 concert, you may say, 'Oh, God, what's she talking about? She really missed the point!' Yet it was a tremendous aesthetic, emotional, kinesthetic experience for me and I tried to express that experience. Which leads to what I think is the most that can be hoped for in criticism for the general public—give them some of what went on. Really, no way can you avoid the essential subjectivity of that and the best you can do is let the readers know where your (the critic's) prejudices lie. Also give some context—through history or comparison or whatever. Let's face it, writing, verbal arts in general, are not in sync, not appropriate companions to a kinesthetic multidimensional, spatial experience like dance." Historian and critic Suzanne Shelton, writing in the same magazine, emphasizes that "criticism depends primarily on the honest and informed perception of the moment" (1981, 158; see also English 1979; Engel 1976).

Important to a scholar's use of critics' reports is the fact that a critic's response to a performance is "the creation of another work which articulates the first" (Ross 1982, 299). This does not discount the discrepancy between the lived multisensory experience and the paucity of words to describe it. Isadora Duncan is well known for saying, "If I could *tell* you what I mean, there would be no point in dancing." Martha Graham has often remarked, "the body says what words cannot." Nonetheless, through the critic's creation of a surrogate performance, a replay translation, readers become a surrogate audience. Readers who have not seen the performance construct what would have been their own experiences had they been at the dance itself. Audience members who have seen the dance may recognize responses they themselves had, gain new insights, or react with disbelief.

Participants in the performer-audience connection are not always in accord. Critics may use their columns to debate other critics whom they perceive to have misperceived. Critics can also see and write about different aspects in a dance they all like (Siegel 1977, xvi).

Spectators and dancers are known to take exception with the critics. An audience member made this point: "Dance, like any visual art form, is not expected to be entirely directed to nor clearly understood by, the audience. . . . With due respect to Mr. Kriegsman's great knowledge of dance, I feel he overstepped his bounds as a reviewer by criticizing Ms. Wimmer for ambiguities which I feel made the performance even more interesting" (Hyatt 1982). Dancer Igor Youskevitch remarked, "I think the best critic I ever had was my wife [Anna Scarpova]. She was in Ballet

Russe with me, but of course she saw my performances with Ballet Theatre as well, and if I did something wrong or she didn't like it, she would tell me about it most definitely. The critics were helpful, but not always specific enough or constructive enough that you could follow their suggestions . . . and also, I did not always agree. Sometimes critics may not understand what the dancer is trying to do. This happened to me . . . with Helen of Troy. While I was with Ballet Theatre, I danced the role of Paris. Because it's a light, tongue-in-cheek kind of ballet, I decided that I was going to be a dumb football player with big muscles, not quite sure what's going on. . . . Then we danced it in some provincial city, and one of the critics said, 'Mr. Youskevitch didn't look like Paris. He looked like a football player.' Well, that's exactly what I wanted to portray, so he paid me a compliment without knowing it" (quoted in Newman 1982, 56–57).

The power of critics can be enormous. What is said or unsaid may influence and shape dancing. Critics contribute to audience development, which is essential to advance sales—the remedy for theater-goers who might be deterred from attending a concert by inclement weather. A background piece or review is promotion (or anti-motion) and advertisement. Thus critics, arbiters of public taste, often determine the existence and nature of future performer-audience exchanges. Ethnographers have less effect upon dance performances and audiences, although exceptions have occurred. For example, the dances of third world peoples often aroused colonial moralists and missionaries to attempt to eradicate those whose meanings they assumed contrary to colonial norms and beliefs.

Because New York City is the dance capital of the world and the big-money metropolis where performers come for the stamp of approval that provides performance opportunities, the New York City critics of major publications are especially powerful.[4] These high priests of criticism are often opinion leaders for critics elsewhere who draw upon program notes and promotional press packets that describe performers' intentions, techniques, metaphor, and positive New York City reception. Consequently the imprimatur of New York City writers echoes through other newspapers and magazines nationwide. New York critics have a long history of distinction. In 1907 the *New York Times* ran a newspaper caption that said, "Mlle. Genée Admits Fear of Critics." The famous dancer talked about her plans for her debut. "It seemed quite evident that the world's premiere danseuse . . . had been very much frightened by reports of the severity of American Critics" (Dec. 22, 1907, p. III-1). For these reasons, I draw mostly upon New York critics.

AT A REMOVE: TRANSLATIONS OF DANCE

My approach in this book is (in the tradition of Erving Goffman) to analyze images. However, besides looking directly at dances, I look indirectly, at a remove from actual performance images, by examining the critics' reports of them. I identify sexuality and sex role in criticism by such words as *androgynous, erotic, gender, heterosexual, homosexual, sensual, sexual, sexy, suggestive*: by descriptions of sexual themes and gender relationships; and by discussion of male/female contrasts and similarities in the use of time, space, effort, body, costume, and music.

Of course, many reviews do not talk about these issues. The history of a dance, its theme, the ways different choreographers present the same subject, the production circumstance, the use of movement, music, the way the choreographer or dancer captures and interprets aspects of music, costume, or sets, the quality of performance, the evolution of a performer's growth and development, the comparison of dancers performing the same or similar roles, the reconstruction or restaging of a piece—these are all possible themes. At times choreographers or dancers do not focus on sex or gender, and critics do not perceive or choose to write about these inherent dimensions of dance. Moreover, not all concerts are reviewed. Some reviews are written but not printed, or they are printed only in one of a paper's editions. Some reviews are cut by editors. One consequence is that innovative dances or movements may not be credited to the first innovator.

Denby explained one way a review takes shape: "A critic has to risk hypotheses . . . to distinguish in the complex total effect of a performance, the relationships between dance . . . and story effect, between expressive individualized . . . and neutral structural rhythm, dance impetus or pantomime shock, dance illusion or . . . fun, sex appeal or impersonation, gesture which relates to the whole architectural space of the stage and has an effect like singing, or gesture which relates to the dancer's own body and so has the effect of a spoken tone. And there are of course many possible relationships of the dancing to the structure or momentum of the music. . . . What he actually does is to work . . . from the dance image that after the event is over strikes him as a peculiarly fascinating one" (1936, 412–13). Consequently, I have tried to examine several reviews of the same performance.

Of the numerous dance performances in the twentieth century, I focus primarily on those reviewed in a major newspaper (*New York Times* is the most significant), periodical, or book collection of reviews.

These dances are likely to have a greater impact than others because, even if the dances actually are not seen by large audiences, people learn about them through the reviews, a written replay transformation that validates the ephemeral. New York City, the undisputed commercial and creative center of the arts and an "unrivaled" magnet for professional performers, has an unsurpassed density of dance activity, range of dance genres, and extraordinary quality of performance. The city is an incomparable showcase that receives maximum recognition by the national and world media (Bennetts 1983; Hanna 1987d).

Newsweek declared, "No other medium remotely rivals the nearly absolute power of *The New York Times* over the fate of . . . the cultural world. What did the *Times* say? For every artist . . . that can be the most important question of a lifetime" (Nov. 22, 1982, p. 125; see Hanna 1985b on mitigating factors). Since 1927, the *New York Times* has employed full-time dance critics. Carl Van Vechten, assistant music critic for the paper, reviewed dance prior to World War I, and H. T. Parker covered music, drama, and dance at the *Boston Evening Transcript* between 1905 and 1935. However, John Martin was the first critic to write solely about dance and for the *Times* (Holmes 1982); he held this job from 1927 to 1962. The author of six books, Martin taught for four years at UCLA after retiring from the *Times*.

The *New York Times* has been publishing articles about dance since the newspaper's inception in 1851. Most of the paper's early material on dance was concerned with its denunciation and defense. In 1874 an article appeared called "Dancing from the Times of the Greeks to the Days of the Polka." This long scholarly article befits an encyclopedia. An 1892 article called "Man and Beast Love the Dance" reads, "Dancing is of course an art, notwithstanding that the Reformation in Northern Europe frowned it out of decent company, and in modern days Catholicism helps to discredit it" (June 19, 1892, p. 4). Dance coverage has increased since that time.

Dance Magazine and the *Village Voice* are other prominent periodicals that cover dance. Collections of criticism include those by Denby, Martin, Croce, Siegel, and Jowitt. Perceptions of dancers, choreographers, and producers appear in interviews reported in these publications and in such books as Barbara Newman's *Striking a Balance* (1982). (I have delved into the extensive files of television program reviews, begun in 1965, located in the Television Information Office in New York City.)

I consider dance performances that reach a more narrow audience, such as burlesque and drag. These also influence American life and therefore theater arts. Social, folk, and popular dances, too, are grist for choreographic mills. Discussion of these genre appears in newspapers, periodicals, and books. The recent break dance genre, for example, has been incorporated into Michael Smuin's 1984 ballet *To the Beatles.* One can discern the electric boogie, waves, and glides in the opening "Help" section.

ENTRUSTED KINETIC IMAGES

Besides observing dance, interviewing participants, and examining the critics' reported perceptions, I have viewed or re-viewed many twentieth-century dances in which sexuality or gender created unusual publicity: gender/dominance discriminators in the elements of dance space (especially interpersonal touch and support, the closing of space), time, energy, posture, gesture, locomotion, theme, style, costume, and music. These celebrated landmark cases, some of which have been recently revived, broke barriers for what is permissible onstage. Also, for those years prior to the recording of moving images, I examined, for stereotypic gender images, still photographs of dance at the National Archives and at the Dance Collection, the New York Public Library at Lincoln Center.

Whereas in the past, dance performances lasted mostly in memory, critics' reports, and language metaphor, now dance has a more permanent and accurate visible past on film and videotape, another form of replay and translation. As mentioned in chapter 1, filmed or videotaped dance is only an approximation of the live performance with its excitement of the possibility of the unexpected. The two-dimensionality of recordings distorts the three-dimensionality and detail, expanse, and angle of dance. Some dances are restaged specifically for the media play of electronic imagery, because front-on shooting without variation can be boring and can reduce the dancers to tiny stick figures on television. Close-ins may provide greater visibility than from the theater seat yet lose the broader context. Because of recent technological advances and collaboration of choreographers or other dance experts with camera people, television dance is a close facsimile of the carnality of live dance, and for some people, television is the only form of dance they can see.

Whatever the objective reality of a film or videotape as historical record, however, what contributes to sex role modeling is the viewer's perceptions of the images. Written reviews of film and television dances are replays that may influence perceptions of those who saw them and those who did not.

So What?

This book takes the gender gap issue and places it within the context of an unexplored realm of expressive culture. Often this realm provides insights into the foundations of everyday life that might not otherwise be readily discernible. Dance events frame images for our scrutiny. Because dance may reflect what is and suggest what might be, it is useful to analyze how gender patterns in everyday life are present, broken, or parodied in dance.

We know that much culturally patterned nonverbal communication is out-of-awareness. Similarly, in dance production and performance there is "hidden" meaning, with messages tacit or hinted at. Studies of nonverbal communication have generally concentrated on what occurs in verbal face-to-face interaction. The use of touch and space gets less attention than the face and paralanguage. Important in dance, they are only two of the many means of bodily communication. What the anthropologist/semiotician tries to do is to examine what is done, what is said, and to place these actions and views within the context of the broader culture, society, history, and environment, guided by a theory of nonverbal communication, and to offer further insights.

Drawing upon and extending my earlier research and writing in the anthropology of dance, education, nonverbal communication, and political symbolism, this book contributes to the growing corpus of studies that attempt to understand how we come to know what we know. The work should expand our knowledge of an art's relationship to sexuality, gender, and society.

II

A WORLDWIDE EROTIC AND
SEX-ROLE DANCE HERITAGE

3

Sexuality

A "comparative" perspective helps us gain a sense of the uniqueness of our own dance customs and gender modeling as well as realize the similarity of human movement in a host of societies.[1] Furthermore, as mentioned in the last chapter, dance developments do not arise out of thin air. The past and contemporary worldwide situations often prefigure the future. Our changing dance traditions have drawn upon cultural patterns from the far reaches of the globe and through time for inspiration in theme, style, structure, and movement effort qualities. Folk, social, ritual, and other "staged" dances provide grist for the theatrical mill to transform for its own purposes.

Although I present illustrations of sexuality, gender, and dance from different times and places, these illustrations may be specific to a particular group, historical time, geographical setting, and/or situation. Consequently, we cannot generalize these examples to an entire people or continent. Qualifications are necessary. They include types of dance, the segregation or mixing of the sexes, private or public events, a solo performer or a couple in physical contact, and communal or professional performance. Broadly focusing on dance, sexual, and gender images from diverse societies brings seminal issues into clear relief. Taking a slice of human experience out of its embedded context, however, may distort cultural coherence. The following pages present a gender-focused glimpse of the spectrum of dance and often omit the rich contextual antecedents and consequences, the dynamics of continuity and change, as well as non-gender-explicit dances. Whether the dance meets a society's ideals, is considered normal social activity, or is viewed as exceptional behavior of persons who operate on the fringes between societal acceptability and rejection may be discussed in the sources themselves.

By relying upon English-language literature, I am missing perspectives offered in other languages. Also, the dances of one geographical area or historical period may be discussed in this book under several different categories. Japanese transvestite dance, for example, has a melange of functions and meanings.

There are many definitions of dance, but for reasons of cross-cultural comparisons (Hanna 1987d), dance can be usefully conceptualized as human behavior that is purposeful, from the dancer's perspective (usually shared by the society to which he or she belongs), is intentionally rhythmical, and has culturally patterned sequences of nonverbal body movements other than ordinary motor activities, the motion having inherent and aesthetic value. Dance exists in three dimensions of space, one of time, and another in the realm of imagination.

Dance reverberates past and present experience. Linking inchoate feelings and thoughts to the dance enables the mind to grasp these sentiments and ideas. As explained in the first chapter, the human experience of corporeal life makes the dancing body an important communicative vehicle to convey, reinforce, and challenge.

The inherent sexuality of dance may be a reason why dance is a nearly universal activity and why gender is coterminous with sexuality in dance. Sexual intercourse is seen to be life generating, an action with miraculous power and a magical sense of pleasure and relief. Courtship and foreplay arouse and anticipate. Signs of sexuality evoke these erotic images and sentiments. They also serve as symbolic references to other domains of power.

Within a global perspective, sex and dance are associated in multiple ways that are not always mutually exclusive. The associations can be seen to cluster on the basis of purpose, function, and gender imagery. A broad category is aphrodisiac dancing, which conveys the gender role of sexual object or partner. Such dancing may be licit, pre- or extramarital, in a respectable or disreputable vein, or illicit. The purposes include entertainment and conviviality, sexual arousal being explicit or implicit. In some cases, dancing is designed first to display sexual appeal for mate selection and then to stimulate mating.

Different kinds of aphrodisiac dancing include the following:

1. Dance in settings with courtship opportunities and at wedding parties (where courtship often occurs)—whether women and men

dance together or apart, for the opposite sex or for their own sex—encourages culturally licit *procreation*. A group's own members may dance, or it may hire professional dancers of high or low status.

2. Dancing may be for the purpose of alluring a *pre-* or *extramarital* affair, including prostitution. Whether for reputable, demimonde, or disreputable liaisons, dancing tends to be a display of the sexual self, a celebration of sexuality, and often a means to an end.

3. Another kind of aphrodisiac dancing is *sacred*. Dance may intertwine with sexuality to convey messages of spiritual love that finds its analogy in the bliss of sexual congress.

4. In some societies, religious ritual with sexually seductive dancing to cope with the supernatural and natural forces is assumed to be *efficacious*.

5. Dancing belongs to the repertoire of resources for *sex role scripting*, which educates young and old alike about what it means to be a man or woman.

6. Another relationship of dance and sex is *modulation* or controlling the excessive enactment of one sex role to the detriment of the opposite. Communities may be alerted to a possible chink in the armor of the status quo, even to rebellion, through parody and rites of reversal in which women dance men's usual roles.

7. Rather than being a precursor to sexual intimacy, dance may be physical and psychological sexual *sublimation*. Orgasmic gratification may come from actual or empathic dance involvement. Dance often has the excitement, release, and exhaustion characteristic of sexual climax.

The state of the literature on dance is uneven; only recently have scholars begun to study the field, and the historical depth of dance traditions varies. Thus I have been able to discuss more fully than others some dance and sex associations. Consequently, in chapter 5 the categories of sacred dance, erotic fantasy, and sex role socialization are combined in a discussion of Indian ancient traditions that continue transformed into the contemporary era.

Aphrodisiac Dancing toward Culturally Licit Procreation

WEDDING DANCES

Dances celebrate marriages in many parts of the world within the guiding tenets of religion and attitudes toward gender. The Talmud, ancient rabbinic writings that constitute religious authority for traditional Judiasm, describes dancing as the principal function of the angels and commands dancing at weddings for brides, grooms, and their guests. Procreation is God's will; weddings, a step toward its fulfillment; and dancing, a thanksgiving symbolizing fruitfulness. Even in exile (A.D. 130) Jews could dance, because out of the wedding might be born the messiah who would restore the people to the land and rebuild the temple. The Jews danced to praise their God in sublime adoration and to express joy for his beneficence. In a sort of corporeal merging with the infinite God, the God-given mind and body is returned to God through dance (Ingber 1985–86).

By contrast, in Islam (with its various branches and their subdivisions, which have distinct doctrinal interpretations and practices), dancing, for the most part, is viewed as enhancing worldly pleasure and lacking a role in religious spiritual enlightenment. Moreover, "Pleasure in the Islamic legal system is defined as an enemy of order" (Sabbah 1984, 4).

Heterosexual dancing has been banned in an attempt to eradicate goddess worship and isolate a female's sexuality for one man. "Women," says Fatna H. Sabbah, "are ordinarily perceived, conceived, and defined as exclusively sexual objects" (1984, 16). In Sura 4:34, the Koran states that "men stand superior to women in that God hath preferred the one over the other. . . . Those whose perverseness ye fear, admonish them and remove them into bed-chambers and beat them; but if they submit to you then do not seek a way against them."[2] Yet the Muslim jurists, the *ulama* or learned specialists in the religion and traditions of Islam, were concerned with the free married woman's right to sexual pleasure and her own progeny.[3]

A strict code of modesty for women prevailed due to men's belief that women possess animalistic sexual appetites. Seen as "a voracious crack" that "sends out its rays like radar in search of the phallus" (Sabbah 1984, 26–27), women were protected from their own lust through segregation, seclusion, and concealment. Besides, men see femaleness as challenging the social hierarchy.

Consequently, women can dance among themselves and in public in certain situations. Associated with sexuality and fertility, Middle Eastern dancing by women, with its multiple local variations, generally falls within the genre that the West calls belly, oriental, or Arabic dancing. Somewhat like sympathetic magic, dancers, through mimetic dance (a concretization device of encoding meaning) enact wished-for results in their lives—for example, copulation leading to the creation of a human. The dance is also a metaphor for the perpetuation of a man's lineage.

Thus the dance may be an integral part of the important Muslim wedding celebration, which lasts from three to seven days, at great financial expense. The stakes of marriage are high for women whose sphere of influence is the home and whose options for earning a living outside it are limited. A failed marriage can be a disaster.

In a Libyan oasis community, John P. Mason (1975) observed a seven-day wedding rite that highlighted ambivalence, contradiction, and accommodation between the sexes, by portraying act and symbol through dance. During the rite, the women sing and dance in honor of the bride. While the young men impatiently await their three evenings of continuous singing and dancing, they mock the slow, erotic dance women perform for themselves. "One of the men wraps a long cloth or towel around his waist and commences this dance, to the slow undulating beat of a drum, accentuating his hip movement in the fashion of the female dancer. The cloth is then passed to another man (no women are present) who is obliged to follow suit. To refuse is embarrassing, though a refusal can be made if to do otherwise compromises one's position in the eyes of any of his kinsmen who might be present (e.g., his older brother or mother's brother)" (p. 654).

The women, too, dance like men. Mason suggests that this role reversal (discussed further in chap. 4) by members of each sex in their separate ceremonies denotes humor and goodwill, and points to the mutual dependency of the sexes as well as to a certain amount of tension between them.

The highlight of the ceremony begins with the men's dancing observed by women peering through a shrouded window or doorway. To the accompaniment of songs of love and sex, the men thrust their pelvises foward in rapid, repeated motions while their arms extend outward from the sides of the body and then come closer as the palms resoundingly clap. Mason's informants said the dancing simulated the sex act. The women's shrill piercing *zaghrit* or ululation signifies their approval when the men reach a fervent climax in the dance.

Then the groom's younger brother leads the women's veiled representative to the men, by the white baton she carries; she is usually the groom's younger, virgin sister, cousin, or neighbor. "Once the female dancer enters the room, the men recommence their song and dance. She stands completely still for several minutes. . . . Then she begins her dance, which is a rapidly repeated, highly abbreviated twist of the hips from side-to-side. Simultaneously she shuffles on her heels very slowly up and down the line of dancing and singing males. Her baton is held continuously between both hands high above her head, moving horizontally to the rhythm of her shuffle. . . . To bring her dance to a close, she spins completely around in a brisk turn as the baton cuts the still air with a white streak . . . the dancer's signal that she wishes one of the men to sing to her. The male singer, who has meanwhile discovered the identity of the dancer, takes on the appearance of uncontrollable emotion. . . . he must place one hand on the side of his head while he leans his elbow on the next man's shoulder, as if in need of physical support. [Lois Ibsen al Faruqi says this is a directing of the sound of the voice in an attempt to hear oneself better.][4] His free hand is placed over his eyes, to shield his overwhelming emotion about the female to whom he will sing. With a warbling moan, he begins by singing one line, stopping abruptly, and placing his hand back over his eyes. He continues in this manner, stopping and starting several times, describing in intimate, poetic detail the female body. Many of the details fit the young female dancer in front of him. It is then that she may feel insulted to the point of anger by the singer's abusive lyrics, striking him over the head with her baton. Following the song, she returns to the bridal party in the next room. The men pause, then start their song and dance once again, hoping to lure the girl—or a new dancer—back. She usually returns two or three times during the evening, each occasion eliciting the shrill cry of her secluded companions in the adjacent room and the frenzied thrusting pelvic movements of the male dancer" (Mason 1975, 655–56).

Within the framework of local assumptions, the female emissary's role is ambivalent. The white baton represents "the virginity of the dancing girl as well as the protection afforded her (and the bride, too) by her male kinsmen. . . . She is supposed to be anonymous and thus symbolic of women generally" (Mason 1975, 656). (The baton is unnecessary when the women dance for themselves in the bride's home on another occasion.) Serenaded by poetic Arabic lyrics about her magnificent sexual beauty, within customary bounds in the amount of personal reference, and shown the men's unquenchable sexual thirst through their undying dance rhythm, the dancer is both praised and insulted. She may censure the men and with sanctions demonstrate that boundaries exist. Withdrawal and silence in response to an improprietous male singer are the women's strongest ritual weapons for they negate the social interaction between the sexes. In the rite the female world temporarily controls that of the intransigent male. However, when the women's bridal party tolerates verbal taunting about the supposed female sexual appetite, they reinforce the male stereotype of the sexually uncontrollable woman. The wedding dance clearly represents female virtue and male honor in the confluence of symbol and act, and it "affirms the sharp line of demarcation between men and women and the avowed inferiority of the latter" (p. 659).

PROFESSIONAL DANCING

Sometimes women outside a family entertain at Muslim marriages. In this case a female dancer usually regarded as immoral becomes licit. Because the Muslim world cordons off respectable women, women who perform before men outside their own families are seen as violating Islamic laws regarding the secluded, dependent place of women and are assumed to be advertising themselves for sale. Wendy Buonaventura points out that former slaves, poor women who never married, or women whose marriages have failed may turn to the skill they grew up with, "the art which remains under Islam almost the sole means of self-expression open to the female sex: they become dancers. They join a troupe and begin the life of public performers and it is ironic that the entertainers whom we see at weddings may only be there because their own marriages have failed" (1983, 65). She continues, "Alone of all Moslem women, dancers intrude upon a male environment. They are doubly disturbing to men in that they are engaged in an art which draws attention to their sexuality" (p. 97). Recall that the Muslim religion recognizes female sexuality as such a powerful force that its potential disruptiveness must be controlled.

"Free" women may be called to dance in Morocco. Vanessa Maher reports: "Although great importance is attached to virginity and to female submission, two values which are served by the early marriage (age 10–14) of girls, women may enjoy considerable autonomy and even sexual freedom between marriages. Some may temporarily join the ranks of the *huryin* (free women), who prefer the life of the courtesan to the yoke of marriage and subordination to men. . . . The most important and self-conscious category are the *shikhat* or dancers to whom being a free woman is a profession. They live alone or in groups, having in common the characteristic that they have left or been repudiated by their kin, and have thus forfeited lineage and male tutelage. They are popularly defined as 'women who do not want men to tell them what to do.'

"Such women are called to sing and dance at weddings and other feasts (one contacting the others). They perform in the room where only men are gathered, and their behavior, in its detailed reversal of proper behavior for women, seems to have a ritual value. They smoke, drink heavily, joke, talk boldly, and fondle male guests in a way that would be taboo for women in other contexts. However, that they are taking upon themselves the burden of ritual license is suggested by the fact that at weddings of people too poor to employ professional dancers, it is the young unmarried village women (the boldest ones) who go in to dance to the men. Their matronly sisters cry 'Shame!' but receive them equably when they come back. The mother of the bride may herself engage in licentious dancing. On such occasions, the values inherent in the 'normal' restrained relationship between the sexes are made explicit" (Maher 1978, 111).

MARRIED WOMEN'S DANCING

Throughout the Middle East, celebration of the sanctioned uniting of man and woman, the fulfillment of a primary gender role, occurs in decorous female dancing inside the private female section of the house, with its enclosed space, drawn curtains, and closed doors. Respectable women in Morocco dance only for one another—with their daughters to pass the time between cooking lunch and dinner, for their friends when they visit, and at weddings, circumcisions, and name-day festivals. Little girls begin cultivating their stomach muscles as soon as they can stand. Women may, however, dance publicly for the *hadra*, a special transcendent state of soul. In the presence of men, a woman may partake in the Hamadsha curing ceremony, become entranced, and be readily forgiven her immodesty (Crapanzano and Kramer 1969).

Among the Saudi, females, including the prepubescent, married or unmarried, assemble for a dance during the afternoon in a concealed setting (Deaver 1978). The performer is usually married. Viewed as explicitly sexual, the dance displays the perceived inherent, uncontrollable trait. With demur, downcast eyes and flat-footed steps, the dancer's movements begin and radiate from the pelvis in 360-degree rotations that spiral up the trunk. The upper torso shimmies, hips thrust.

Displaying sexual prowess, entertaining, and showing status, the dancer's message is, "I am young, I am beautiful, and I am sexually appealing. Therefore, I can keep my husband, I am secure." The display of wealth, gold jewelry, and rich dressing, signs of the husband's affection, reinforces the message.

DOWRY DANCING

History tells us of dancing as a licit but not necessarily preferred means of earning money for a required marriage dowry (Buonaventura 1983, 67–69). In classical Greece a woman from a poor family performed in the marketplace for money to acquire resources in order to get married. Similarly, Ouled Nail young women, of the Djebel Nail plateau region of the Algerian Sahara, at the age of puberty leave home accompanied by an older woman who acts as a housekeeper. They travel from one oasis to another, dancing in cafes and consorting with migrant tribesmen until, after several years of dancing, for which they have been trained since infancy, and prostitution, they accumulate sufficient wealth to return home with a handsome dowry.

COURTSHIP DANCING

Where marriages are not arranged, wedding celebrations in some societies are arenas for danced courtship practices. A Catholic priest, Fr. Jehan Tabourot, writing in 1588 under the pseudonym Thoinot Arbeau, discerned the social function of mixing the sexes in dancing: "To make manifest whether lovers are in good health and sound in all their limbs, after which it is permitted to them to kiss their mistresses, whereby they may perceive if either has an unpleasant breath" (Arbeau 1968, 18). Van der Leeuw (1963, 20–21) speaks of dance "in the game of love. Dance and love are indissolubly bound. . . . The dance unchains the natural drives, but it also enchains them. Ultimately, it makes possible the game of exploding and controlled passion. Our fathers understood how one danced 'the bride to bed.' "

In Yugoslavia, especially in Lika and Dubrovnik, young nubile women are judged for their strength, endurance, and health in dance performance (Nancy Ruyter, pers. com. 1984). Dance as a medium to display a woman's beauty and sexual attractiveness and as an arena for arranging liaisons is common. Women also judge men in dance, as p'Bitek described for the Acholi in chapter 1.

"Sexuality, its pursuit and control," is the main theme of the rhymes associated with many tunes played at highly charged dance events that are the scene of courtship activity in rural Newfoundland. This is one of the most widely known rhymes: "Chase me Charlie I got Barley/Up the leg of me drawers/If you don't believe me, come and see me/Up the leg of my drawers." The young unmarried men and women instigate the dance events where men display themselves competitively in rivalry for women (Quigley 1982, 16).

Among the Muslim Hausa of Zazzau, Nigeria, feasts associated with marriage, naming the title-taking ceremonies, weekly markets, harvest festivals, and moonlit nights are occasions for dancing. Dancing suggests sexual availability. Young unmarried girls perform publicly before young men, who compete in courtship to arrange premarital love affairs. Small girls, scarcely five to six years of age, imitate the sexually suggestive dance movements of the older girls, but respectable married women do not dance in public. *Karuwai*, courtesans, may be observed dancing in public at festivals, public *bori* (spirit possession) ceremonies, the semipublic courtyard of harlots' compounds, and performances of dance troupes in urban hotels and beer gardens. Young men engage in a form of foot-boxing dance, recreational dances, including ones in which they criticize wrongdoers, warrior dances, and cooperative work dances. These dances, however, are not geared toward arranging love trysts (Ames 1982).

The way of the Wodaabe nomads of Niger is for men in makeup and special dress to exaggerate their features during all-male dances to attract women, who judge them on their charm and beauty (Beckwith 1983). Several weeks after the Worso festivity when a lineage gathers to celebrate births and marriages, two lineages unite for seven days of dancing and seeking permanent or other attachments beyond their circle of cousins. Prior to the *yaake* dance, young men become preoccupied with preening themselves, shaving a hairline to dramatize the forehead, applying pale yellow powder to lighten skin and black kohl on the eyelids and lips to heighten the whiteness of eyes and teeth, drawing a white line to elongate the nose, and adorning themselves in hand-embroidered tunics. Marriageable women stand outside the dance circle, inviting courtship. When a man's wink is met by a woman's gaze, romance is born. "Eyes roll; teeth flash; lips purse, part and tremble; cheeks, inflating like toy balloons, collapse in short puffs of breath as if extinguishing a candle. Elders dash up and down the line, challenging, mocking, and criticizing in an effort to incite the contestants to ever greater contortions. A dancer knows he's receiving favorable attention when an older woman dashes toward him yelling 'yeee hoo' and gently butts him in the torso" (p. 508).

In the afternoon and evening performances of the Wodaabe *geerewol* dance, men compete in an exhausting marathon. They dress uniformly in tight knee-length wrappers, with strings of white beads crisscrossing bare chests, ostrich feathers rising from shell bands atop their heads, and red ocher makeup on their faces. Dancers who endure replace their ostrich feathers with horsetail plumes, as the haunting chants and frenzied jumping and stamping dance steps resume at an even wilder pace. Three unmarried women, selected for their loveliness, judge who are the most beautiful and reap the admiration and ardor of women.

Young male *habodha* dancers of Sudan's Nuba Tira tribe recited their exploits in raiding and mimed their skillful actions, pugnacity, and endurance. "In this dance, male pride and sexual stimuli are inextricably mixed. For by means of these self-praises the young men try to attract the attention of girls, who standing in the centre of the ring formed by young men, will pick out one or the other, and throw themselves against the partners they have chosen (Nadel 1947, 248).

The New Guinea Maring's massed dancing of visitors at the *kaiko* special entertainment not only communicate information about cooperation in later aggressive engagement, but it also permits women to discriminate among the warriors—for their endurance, vigor, and health (Rappaport 1971).

Dance as Pre- and Extramarital Entertainment, Art, and Artifice

DANCE SIGN OF SEXUALITY TO REFERENT

Some societies condone heterosexual aphrodisiac dancing that leads to copulation for pleasure apart from procreation. Terrence Loomis suggests that the imagery of cosmic lovemaking and separation, and the births or creation that flows from it, are crucial metaphors implicit in Cook Islander dancing. "In social dancing sign often leads to referent at the end of the evening" (Loomis 1981, 5). *Ori*, the word for "wander" and "dance," is synonymous with the word for adultery among the inhabitants of Mangaia, a southern Cook Island in central Polynesia (Marshall, 1979, 146, 124–25).

Males and females, trained from puberty in sexual techniques, take pride in their sexual prowess. The ideal male lover has stamina for pelvic thrusting motions, the woman for hip rotations and swings. Stylized lovemaking movements are aesthetically pleasing. Their meanings, symbolic of mythic, romantic, and mundane male virility and female seductiveness, characterize the dance which varies in style and sexual explicitness among the Islands.

Not surprisingly, the nakedness and sexual explicitness of Polynesian dancing was abhorrent to the Christian missionaries. Nevertheless, this cultural expression, though modified in form, has survived their onslaught. Cook Islanders in Auckland, New Zealand, now engage in social and theatrical dancing for themselves and for Europeans; for the latter, the style and atmosphere are more subdued. The metaphors of the social dancing songs translate as joining together, moving about, crushing together as in bananas to make pudding. Women move their hips from side to side, lifting them with each step, while men, in a semicrouched position on the balls of their feet, move their thighs in and out to the music. The man, smiling, looks at his partner's hips; she, aware of his attention, gazes coyly into space.

In the Cook Island *tuki* dance, or challenge, "the woman turns sideways to the man and accentuates her hip movements. The man crouches lower, keeping his thighs moving rhythmically, and moves as close as he can to the woman with arms extended on either side of her. The woman allures and entices; the man thrusts and tries to 'capture' the woman. But the woman also crushes with her hips, bumping his genitals if he gets close enough. The man teases by dancing around just out of reach, or below her dangerous hips. It is in this episode that the categories 'real man' and 'real woman' are epitomized. The woman should remain composed and confident, but supremely evocative before the advances of the man. And the male should get as close and low as possible without losing the dance rhythm or being bowled over by the woman's hips. So there is a complementary opposition of maleness and femaleness, invitation and defense, thrust and counter-thrust, immanent submission with detachment which is emergent both in the ecstasy of the dance and love-making" (Loomis 1981, 16–17).

WOMAN AS OBJECT

Examples of aphrodisiac dancing abound throughout the world. Women (and sometimes young males) dance to entertain men whose prurient interests often override concerns of artistic merit. The dancer's message is sexual service for one or more of the senses. Male-dominant cultures tend to regard women as intended for the voluptuous pleasure of men, as something to look at, a tool to use. The dancing may be for aesthetic appreciation, conviviality, prelude to sexual intimacy, or even a substitute for it. Middle Eastern, Indian, and Chinese treatises on love recognize dance as one of the amorous arts a woman should cultivate to please her lover. For the most part, the dances, complemented by music, poetic song, and mime, depict erotic episodes.

Dancing to entertain men is found in the institutions of the Chinese *chi-nu*, Japanese geisha, Indian *devadasi* and *nautch*, Arabic *guina*, Korean *kisaeng*, Persian *motreb*, Turkish *cengi*, Egyptian *ghawazee*, Greek *hertaere*, and Moroccan *shikhat*. Java had dancer-prostitutes, and Romans turned to women from Cadiz or Syria to kindle loose desire (Henriques 1962, 420, *passim*). Among the Hausa of Nigeria, *bori* dancing and prostitution merged. Unmarried women of childbearing age who were possessed by spirits lived in compounds filled with music and dancing at night (p. 392).

A venal relationship commonly obtains between dancers and spectators, even with the outright slavery of dancing women. A dance performance by itself or coupled with carnality may be purchased for money or other valuable consideration such as jewels, clothing, or accommodations. Salome's dance is legend. The young woman received John the Baptist's head in reward. (Either she obeyed her revengeful mother in requesting this, or she expressed her anger about John not reciprocating her sexual interest in him.)

Some dancer-courtesans wielded considerable power over members of the ruling elite. Dancer-courtesan-prostitute relationships in different times and places could be licit or illicit, for the pleasure of the elite exclusively, or for rich and poor alike. When governments have banned institutions that offer venal dance/carnal relations, they usually go underground.

TRANSVESTITES

In response to the prohibition of women dancing in public, especially in the Middle East and the Orient, young boys (*batcha* in Persia, *gawwal* in Arab countries) have taken women's place in dance and bed (Wood and Shay 1976). Older males dressed as women also practiced their arts of allurement, including dance and music. The boys catered to venal pederasty, enticing sexual partners through terpsichorean performance (Henriques 1962). The Turkish capital in 1805 had about six hundred boys (*kocek* or *cojuk*) in the taverns (Popescu-Judetz 1982). By 1837, so much trouble had occurred because audience members fought over the merits of particular youths that they were outlawed. The Turks considered the dance profession degrading, so most of the boys were Greek, Armenian, or Jewish. "Today, dancing boys can still be seen in the villages of Turkey, Morocco, and other Middle Eastern countries. They continue to parody what was and still is an essentially female style of dance" (Buonaventura 1983, 51). The famous belly dancers of Tangier and Marrakech tea houses and tourist restaurants are boys; itinerant female dancing whores are seen at markets and festivals (Crapanzano and Kramer 1969).

Vern Bullough (1976, 234) avers that historically in the Chinese and Islamic worlds, males who impersonated females in dramatic productions were tolerated because the arrangement allowed men to keep their women to themselves. Although the *khawal* transvestite dancers in Egypt emulated the female *ghawazee* by dancing with castanet self-accompaniment, painting their hands with henna, braiding their hair, plucking facial hair, and affecting the manners of women, the men distinguished themselves from natural females by a costume that was part male and female.

Among the Gebusi people of the Strickland-Bosavai area of New Guinea, Bruce Knauft found that male dancers impersonating women transform male heterosexual desires and the tense divisiveness about their fulfillment into homosexual acts. Gebusi unrestrained sexual desire is antithetical to the nonreciprocal marriage patterns that restrict sexual access to women and create disgruntlement among unmarried men. A potent mechanism of bonding among the male hosts and visitors from adjacent settlements at an all-night ritual dance and songfest "enacts the overcoming of anger through postive affect, and collective camaraderie" (1985a, 245). The transcendence of anger is concretely and unequivocally enacted.

One to five men, usually from the visiting settlement, dance sedately in simple hopping/bending steps syncopated to the beat of their drum. They embody and make manifest the characteristics of the spirit world—the most positive of the Gebusi's own ideals of beauty, health, friendship, and good company. The dancer's costume and body paint signify the red bird of paradise, central in the panoply of spirit images. This bird is "the preeminent natural form of spirit women . . . young, beautiful, and sexually voracious" (Knauft 1985a, 262). Women's singing accompanies the male dancing. About ten minutes long, the songs are usually about a young man and woman, often in the form of birds, who are separated and wish to be together.

"The persona of the beautiful but melancholy dancer arouses a strong and distinct sense of pathos among the audience" (Knauft 1985b, 323). Men interpret the women's songs as scenes of sexual loneliness, innuendo, and seduction. "Hosts and visitors joke hilariously, fantasizing how they will bring to fruition the sexual scenario evoked by the beautiful dancer and women's seductive songs. . . . The transformation of heterosexual into homosexual desire is reflected in the strong transvestite images that Gebusi men project onto the male dancer, and is evident also in their mutual joking. Men often make loud, bantering proclamations that their heterosexual arousal is so great that it cannot wait for an available female, but demands immediate sexual release, that is, with other men" (p. 325). Sexual fantasy transforms from reality and heterosexuality to homosexuality, as pairs of unrelated males slip out into the brush for a brief tryst. "In this context, the persona of the beautiful and seductive male dancer . . . is not only an overt symbol of alluring female sexuality, but also a veiled symbol of transvestism and secret homosexuality" (Knauft 1985a, 264).

Although transvestite dancing had erotic implications and homosexuality was extant, Alan Heyman offers another perspective in light of the rural Korean *nam-sadahng-pae* bands that perform shaman exorcist rituals and other ceremonies: "Flower boys" who wear women's skirts and flowery headbands or hats have a specific role in the dancing. They "step" on the ground and press evil spirits into the earth. "The spectacle of boys dancing in girls' dress is by no means indigenous to Korea alone. Bali had this tradition for a long time; the *suwa-suwa* dancing boys on the island of Jolo in the Philippines could be cited as another example; the young boys in the Kathakali of India, with their yellow-painted faces and false breasts, are still another. Instances can also be noted in ancient Greece, China, and Japan. In Asian aesthetics the principle of transvestism is to give the dance a higher moral quality by making it sexless. Asians delight in artistic interchanges, and if you suggest to an Asian that women dancing as women and men dancing as men would be better, he is amazed. Obviously, you have missed the point and are trying to thrust eroticism where it is not" (1966, 32).

ROYAL PERFORMANCE

Frequently the rich distinguish themselves from the lower classes by stylizing and embellishing male-female erotic relations and by highly respecting artistic talents who present female sexual charm. In kingdoms and their equivalent, dancing girls tended to be lower class, slaves, or prisoners of war. But some were fortunate enough to improve their status. They performed in Rome, for shahs of Persia, sultans of Turkey, various central Asian khans, North Indian rajahs, rulers of the Arab countries, and Chinese kings (Penzer 1952). In some places there were also ragged street entertainers who danced alone or in organized companies for the poor.

Turkey. The harem system (*caoutchouc*) appeared in Turkey in the fifteenth century in tandem with despotism, polygamy, and the development of the empire. Dancing was part of women's training in general coquetry. Erotic dance reigned in the opulent surroundings of a sultan's harem. At the Topkapi harem, concubines danced for the sultan and for each other. Norman Penzer (1952) suggests that many of the women may have been lovers. When the dance was part of religious ceremony, women themselves barred men from seeing it. In the harem the dance became an art performed by women largely for their own sex in seclusion, only this time the seclusion was enforced by men (Buonaventura 1983, 58). Female dancers from outside the harem were brought in to entertain the men and harem women, who learned some new dances or techniques from these strangers. The 1890 revolt against the extant government dealt a deathblow to the harem system.

Bali. In Bali, village girls were recruited to be court dancers. Some became royal concubines and wives. The *legong*, in which young women participated dressed in expensive, elegant costumes, was a dramatic ceremonial court dance that displayed the wealth and magic force of the court (Bandem 1983, 116).

China. Robert Hans Van Gulik (1961) tells us about dance and sexuality in China from about 1500 B.C. to A.D. 1644. In the early Chou period (ca. 1100–77 B.C.), rural communities organized spring fertility festivals, where young men and women danced together. Liaisons formed and became regularized as marriage if the girl became pregnant (p. 21). Upper-class women had a less free sex life. Later in the dynasty, the king's centralized power declined while feudal lords gained ascendancy. At this time princes and high officials maintained not only harems but also their own troupes of *nu-yueh,* trained dancing girls and female musicians who entertained at official banquets and private drinking bouts. These women, mostly slave girls and prisoners of war, were subject to be sold or offered as presents. This class became the forerunner of the *kuan-chi,* "official prostitute," who attained important positions in subsequent Chinese social life (pp. 27–38).

The Chinese did not regard prostitutes with contempt; rather they considered the visitation of prostitutes a legitimate pastime for men. During the Han dynasty (206 B.C.–A.D. 220), the public brothel catered to the "scholar-official class" and to the prosperous merchant class, which could not afford to keep dancing girls or perhaps considered such possession an infringement upon ruling-class privilege. Women and girls were recruited for brothels as a result of economic changes that broke up middle-class and peasant families and left abandoned women seeking employment. The public houses were for drinking, eating, and dance and song performances; men could also stay the night. Furthermore, middle-class men might also purchase concubines from brothels.

By the time of the T'ang dynasty (A.D. 618–907), the dancing courtesan had become a social institution. Men who participated in the elegant life of the capital or province kept wives and concubines. Only the latter left the home to accompany the men and enliven their parties with song, dance, drinking, and conversation. Social relations of officials, literati, artists, and merchants were conducted in restaurants, temples, brothels, or outdoor scenic spots.

Cities took pride in their courtesans, whose ultimate aim was to find a husband; the unlucky aged courtesan earned her living by teaching younger women the arts of dance and music (Van Gulik 1961, 180–81). Because men who could afford to cultivate relations with courtesans belonged to the upper-middle class or elite, and hence had several women at home to whom they were obliged to give complete sexual satisfaction, carnal desire was not the full motivation for the nearly daily association with courtesans. Indeed, men may have found their association as escape from carnal love. Skilled in eroticism, courtesans were even more appreciated for their artistic skills. Moreover, the women also knew much about the public world, which they might share with a favored suitor.

Brothel keepers belonged to trade associations and paid taxes to the government in exchange for the same official protection as other commercial enterprises. Thus a girl who broke her contract could be prosecuted by the authorities, but she could denounce an unjust owner.

A distinction was made between the courtesans and the low-class harlots and brothels owned by the government. The inmates of the latter were often female criminals condemned to prostitution, females whose close relatives had been condemned to slavery, and female prisoners of war. In contrast with the courtesans, these women were prohibited from marrying outside their caste. The courtesan's bondage was based not on legal decision but on a private commercial transaction. The Chinese viewed the lowest class of prostitutes with contempt not because of the work they did but because they were criminals or related to them.

During the Sung period (A.D. 903–1279), foot binding became a fashion and small feet indispensable for beautiful women. A woman's feet became the center of her sex appeal. Foot binding led to the obsolescence of the Chinese art of dancing. After the Sung period, courtesans were praised for their music making. However, the Chinese art of dancing had been imported to Korea and Japan and continued to flourish there (Van Gulik 1961, 232).

Korea. In Korea, according to Byong Won Lee (1979), different categories of professional entertainers corresponded to historical eras. During the Koryo dynasty (918–1392), some dancers became concubines of kings, who gave them noble titles and high rank. However, when Confucianism was adopted, women lost such avenues of social mobility. Separated from men, women entertainers were required to obey; they were considered slave property, and were obliged to perform and serve at banquets. Some even were required to engage in prostitution. Women entertainers were the only females permitted education. In the Yi dynasty (1392–1910), the first-grade entertainer of *kisaeng* monopolized court classical music and dance. Members of the second grade were of dubious respectability because of suspected prostitution, while members of the third grade engaged in outright prostitution. After 1910 when Japan annexed Korea, the status distinctions disappeared. However, the dancers continued to be recruited from poor families of the *ch'onmin* caste, and their profession became commercialized. When Korea gained its independence, the female dancers were called performers or researchers.

Europe. As we have seen, not only has a class or several classes of women to satisfy the men's sensual appetite been permissible and lawful in some cultures, but such institutions have been respectfully approved. European countries and the United States generally considered professional dance activities to be associated with prostitution and therefore immoral. However, the West has a history of the demimonde, a class of courtesan women on the fringes of respectable society. Supported by wealthy lovers, dancers were often envied and admired by men and women alike. A number of European states supported ballet companies that provided opportunities for female social mobility and self-esteem. The stage was a display case of feminine charms and abilities for prestigious males who competed for dancers' favors. The music halls served the lower social classes. Respectability for artistically talented and socially powerful dancers went hand in glove with the social stigma attached to public female dancing, although superstars such as Fanny Elssler and Marie Taglioni seem to have overcome such handicaps.

Middle Eastern Reverberations. The Middle Eastern/Arabic/oriental "belly dance" (promoters trying to lure patrons to the 1893 World's Fair chose this name) exemplifies a form that changes over time, moves across the seas, and has periods of favor and disfavor (Buonaventura 1983). Varying due to cross-cultural contact and historical situations, the dance blends influences from Morocco to India and combines multiple symbols. The genre, says Glenna Batson (1975), imitates the snake (which is associated with seduction, intelligence, and destruction), horse, camel, and the natural waves of the river and wind. A performer brings to the dance contradictory images: spirited, liberated, haughty, and powerful in contrast with submissive and pained female responses (e.g., crawling and dragging the body) to the whims of the male.

In Egypt the dancing female *ghawazee*, perhaps allied to the Gypsies, were available in cities, and they followed pilgrimages (Henriques 1962). The women married men who assisted their dancing and prostitution.[5] The *ghawazees* settled along the lower Nile and in Cairo. After Napoleon and his army landed in Egypt in 1798, the women consorted with French soldiers. Ruler Muhammad Ali, in the interest of modernizing the country, decided that the notorious belly dance did not enhance the dignity of the newly Westernized nation. Therefore he outlawed the *ghawazee* to three towns. The ban lasted until 1854. Young boys originally from Istanbul took the women's place and were supposedly even more suggestive.

Belly dance had a heyday at the beginning of this century in Cairo when princes and pashas haunted the Mohammed Ali Club to select favorite dancers to support lavishly. Gamal Abdel Nasser banned the naked midriff to restore respectability, and in the 1980s dancers continued to sport transparent body stockings. A strict dance code in 1963 stipulated that the only proper dance costume was one that covered the chest, stomach, and back and had no openings. "The Limits within Which the Oriental Dance Should Be Performed" also forbade dancers to "take positions or make movements that carry sexual implications." In 1966 the Egyptian government decided to ease its restrictions on belly dancing. The dancers would be able to express themselves somewhat more freely, bare their stomachs, and wear skirts slit up the sides (Pace 1966).

Oriental dance influenced several forms of American dance. Not only do we see it in the ballets *Scheherazade, La Bayadère,* and *The Nutcracker,* but the belly dance has attained a popularity for two groups: American professional dancers and dancing matrons interested in exercise and eroticism for their husbands and lovers. The American professionals dance in their own country, and, moreover, they have crossed what used to be fairly rigid cultural barriers to perform in the Middle East itself.

For example, in 1984 Tamara completed a three-month stint at the Orient Club frequented by Syrian military officers and politicians. Even the Syrian minister of defense and his entire family celebrated an anniversary at the club and watched her dance. Syrian television filmed the final performance. Tamara, whose father was a sheep farmer in

Montana and whose mother came from Kansas, followed the options of a married Middle Eastern woman who wishes freedom. She married the son of the Saudi vice minister for religious affairs when she was seventeen, moved to Mecca for three years, and gave up the dancing she had studied as a teenager growing up in a Los Angeles suburb to live the secluded life behind a veil. When Tamara abandoned both her husband and Saudi Arabia, she danced in cities throughout the Middle East, Africa, and Europe (Miller 1984).

In cabaret dancing today, producers everywhere are known to exploit women. Nightclub and restaurant managers use tipping as an excuse to pay low wages. Dancers feed a particular female image that many contemporary women reject—glamour, compliance, plaything, sexual object. Artist and audience may hold different views—the dancer seeing performance as artistic skill and work, the audience, the titilation of an erotic fantasy figure and femme fatale.

India. In Indian history, the sacred and secular overlap, each intruding upon the other. A myth says that the god Brahma, in his effort to maintain the population balance between heaven and earth, created wanton woman to delude men and draw them to her. Too many ascetics from earth threatened to overcrowd heaven, so Brahma also sent the *apsaras*, heavenly seductresses who grace all important social occasions with song and dance in Lord Indra's heavenly court, like the earthly courtesans of the rajas' courts, to distract ascetics and thereby prevent them from being admitted to heaven (Indra 1979, 16). In legend the *asparas*'s lovers include gods and mortals.

The Rig-Veda (ancient hymns considered the revealed word of God), epics, and law books speak of the unmarried woman for sale (Meyer 1971, 264, 268). In the Kama Sutra, a treatise on the science of erotics written about A.D. 200, Vatsyayana devotes the whole text to courtesans, although there is no direct reference to sacred prostitution. He states that dance is a key requirement for a prostitute and also for a married woman who wishes to keep her husband's affections. The law books, however, regard prostitution with disfavor (Manu ix. 259; iv. 209, 211, 219, 220; v. 90). Manu, the first Brahman or priest and known as the Father of Mankind, separated wanton woman from mother.

Manu accepted males engaging in extramarital relations with women if the relations did not impair the men's marital duties and obligations, for it was a sin for a married couple not to procreate. "The wife who forgets her duty goes to hell, the husband who does so is an embryo-slayer" (Manu quoted in Meyer 1971, 218). Akhileshwar Jha claims that today a married man remains sexually faithful to his wife until she has given birth to his children, proof of his sexual power. Fear of decreasing his capacity for impregnating his wife by losing his semen elsewhere inhibits infidelity (1979, 58). Yet, as some popular stories enacted in dance often illustrate, the ideal wife, should always be faithful, bear her husband sons, and be ready to sacrifice mortal life for him.[6]

From the two great epics, the Mahabharata and the Ramayana, we glean information about the relationship between the sexes and the underlying philosophy that pertained in India fifteen hundred or more years ago. In an attempt to derive an account of the life of woman in ancient India from this literature, which is dramatically portrayed in contemporary India, Johann Jakob Meyer (1971) found contradictory utterances.

The epics and the Vedas (ca. 1500–900 B.C.) sing the praises of the courtesan, the embodiment of perfect womanhood. Glorified and held in high esteem, these women are an important part of city life and an indispensable part of any hunting expedition, battle, or diversion in the country. In the epics "it is mentioned times beyond number that the 'city beauties' dance on joyful occasions. . . . The very sight of them brings good luck" (Meyer 1971, 268). When Rama is to be consecrated as the young king, the priest calls for the city to bedeck itself in celebration and things that attract good fortune. Among these are the *ganika*, daughters of pleasure, who appear in prideful place along with the king's wives, ministers, soldiers, Brahmans, and nobles. Royalty's guests are welcomed with such women, beautifully dressed and skilled in dance and song. Ordinary politeness requires that when persons of any distinction visit each other, they must be accompanied by some of these courtesans.

Notwithstanding the praise for courtesans, the epics zealously rail against prostitutes, some of whom were associated with drinking and gambling as well as providing sanctuary for thieves in their abodes. A hierarchy of prestige differentiated temple dancers, city courtesans, and lowly harlots. Some Indian kings encouraged public dancing by women because it promoted consumption of alcoholic drinks, over which the government had a monopoly (Gaston 1982).

In the Buddhist age, Brahmans were forbidden to observe dancing because of its connection to prostitution. Yet in Jatakas (tales of previous births of the Buddha), unmarried women who offered sexual services were respected. Occasionally, they enjoyed a privileged position of noble character and wealth. At the court of Chandragupta, they were subject to strict rules and penalized for breaching them (e.g., a *ganika*, the most honorable of nine classes of prostitutes, who refused her favors to anyone whom the king might choose received a one thousand lashes with a whip or else had to pay a high fine). Each woman paid the government two days' earnings every month (Penzer, 1952, 132).

During India's Muslim period, from the eleventh century onward, when the Turks invaded and plundered as far as the central Punjab, until the sixteenth century, when the Turkish Mughal dynasty subjugated nearly the entire subcontinent, came a new stream of religious and artistic experience. The fact that middle eastern men cordon off respectable women and bar them from dancing in public before other men reflects the status of those who perform (Buonaventura 1983, 30). According to Projesh Banerji (1983, 105–12), controversial journalist and former editor of *Sangeet Natak Akademi*, the Muslim practice of purdah, the seclusion of women, did not affect the fine arts; the sixteenth-century Bengali religious group Vaishnavite Chaitanya spread the cult of ideal love and stimulated the florescence of the arts.

However, religious temple dance, performed prior to the advent of the Islamic rules, partially developed into secular arts of entertainment at the Hindu courts of Rajputana (Jaipur) and the Muslim courts of Delhi, Oudh, Agra, and elsewhere. Through a combination of lax religious sentiment, pecuniary stringency, and disturbed political conditions, the Hindu temple organizations received fewer offerings, and the dancer consequently also received less. She had few options to supplement her resources.

Muslim kings, nawabs, and Hindu rajas who considered themselves rulers by divine right enticed dancers in economic difficulty or used force to requisition their services at court, palace, and durbar. Mughals brought professional dancing girls from Persia who were noted for their footwork. The dancers competed with each other to excel in intricate mathematical rhythmic and movement variations (Penzer 1936, 184).

At the same time that artistry was some dancers' concern, others (called *nautchwalis, naachivalis, khemtawalis, bhagtanyis,* and *bayadères*) "realised that their patrons were more interested in the dancers than in the dance, hence to make adjustments, they began to use dance not as an art but as an artifice" (Banerjee 1983, 144).

Not all umemployed temple dancers were absorbed into the entourages of the wealthy. Some joined the ranks of secular dancer-prostitutes. During the reign of Akbar (1556–1605), many of these women resided at the capital within a separate quarter of the town assigned to them. While Aurangzeb's reign (1659–1707) saw an effort to wipe out prostitution, his successors favored gross sensuality and openly encouraged prostitution at the end of the eighteenth century (Roy 1972, 118).

During the British colonial period, there were contradictory attitudes toward prostitution. On the one hand, the British rulers debased part of the courtesan profession—practiced with widely reputed skillful music and dance performance—into common prostitution. About the demise of the courtesan profession in the Nawabi capital of Lucknow, Veena Talwar Oldenburg says, "If the Nawabi had perceived these cultural women as an asset [sons of the urban elite were sent to the salons of the well-known *tawa'ifs* for lessons in etiquette and appreciation of Urdu poetry], the British Raj saw them as a necessary evil, if not a threat, and sought to make them an inexpensive answer to the sexual needs of single European soldiers by insisting on clinical standards of personal hygiene." The soldiers, and the Indian rural gentry on trips to the capital, were uncultured and thus unappreciative of the sophisticated dance (1984, 137). On the other hand, the British attempted to eliminate prostitution and the dancing assumed to be associated with it. Just before India achieved political sovereignty, dance became a symbol of national identity in the pursuit of cultural independence.

Japan. In the erotic realm, gender differences may be rigid or flexible. Highly sensual, Japanese Kabuki, in which dance plays a key role along with other performing arts, as in Western opera, had deep ties first to female and then to male prostitution. Kabuki's sexuality was significant in the evolution of the form and in the gender and age of its performers. Kabuki was a case of woman's creation being usurped by man, a situation that has occurred elsewhere (see chap. 6 on American modern dance) (Hanna 1983b).

Legend places the origin of Kabuki with Okuni's appearance in the city of Kyoto at the turn of the sixteenth century. An itinerant dancer claiming relationship to the great Shinto Izumo Shrine as a *miko*, or sacred ritual *kagura* dancer, Okuni had wandered through several provinces, where she danced and solicited contributions to repair the oldest and one of the most sacred shrines. When she reached Kyoto, she was enchanted with the lively capital and diverted from her responsibilities to the shrine. Okuni reputedly embellished with suggestive erotic movements and skits the religious dance that celebrates the pleasure of the gods and divine spirits. Not only was Okuni highly popular with the masses, who were weary of fighting and destruction, and sought diversion at the end of an era of one hundred years of incessant and meaningless civil wars between rival fiefs, but she also intrigued the nobility who patronized her. She even appeared before the Tokugawa shogun.

In imitation of the Okuni Kabuki, other women formed companies (*onna*). Their popularity was so widespread that a man, Sadoshima Yosanji, began to teach women recruited from the ranks of prostitutes. Other training schools appeared, and talented dancers competed with each other for the public's favor. What had been a genre performed by women soon had the two sexes playing together, with each sex taking the role of the other.

During the primarily female performances, fights frequently broke out among the hot-blooded samurai or foot soldiers in the audience, especially among the unemployed who had drifted to the cities in search of new masters, work, or merely excitement. The brawls, ignited by rivalries over the dancers, led to sanctions against female players. Less concerned with immorality than with curbing disorder, the shogun's government in 1608 limited the Kabuki to the city outskirts. By 1629 female public performances were forbidden in an attempt to create greater social order and stability. Female dancers, however, continued their Kabuki performances at private parties.

Successors to women's Kabuki were troupes of young men (*wakashu*) that had been performing alongside women's troupes. The suppression of *onna* brought them into prominence. Beautiful faces and voices were important, and performances served as preludes to prostitution. As happened with women's Kabuki, quarrels over favorites broke out among samurai; government intervention then prohibited young boys from the stage in 1653. Thereafter only mature men whose front locks had been shorn were permitted to perform Kabuki onstage, since presumably no one would pay to sleep with them.

Strict laws regarding the appearance of women onstage remained in effect until the last days of the Tokugawa shogunate, when its grip on moral and democratic tendencies loosened. The succeeding Meiji era (1868–1912) brought about the revival of women's performance on-stage. World War II with its theater closings halted the momentum of the performing arts in Japan. However, afterward, Western influences encouraged public performance by women primarily in their own dance concerts. Thomas R. Havens (1983) found that a million or so students of classical Japanese dance were dispersed among more than two hundred schools. Major Kabuki companies, however, continue to employ only male actors, some of whom specialize in female roles.

Another notable genre of Japanese women's dance that delights elite men is geisha dancing. Prior to World War II, 90 percent of Japanese peasants were sharecroppers who could be ruined by a bad harvest. In times of disaster a farmer could sell a pretty daughter to the geisha business. Forced into indentured servitude, such girls, some as young as ten, received room and board, and lessons in classical dancing, singing, and playing musical instruments, as well as costly kimono wardrobes. The services of the geisha are expensive (see Dalby 1983).

Love, Life, Death, and Divinity

Sandawe men and women in Tanzania dance by moonlight in the erotic *phek'umo* rites to promote fertility. Because the cycle of the moon coincides with the cycle of women's menstruation, the Sandawe believe that the moon is the source of women's fertility as well as general fertility. In the Sandawe creation myth, the moon is the original celestial body; she is followed by the sun, who marries her. Identifying with the moon, a supreme being believed to be both beneficial and destructive, the *phek'umo* dance both metaphorically and magically conducts supernatural beneficence.

"The dance is begun by the women, who go round in circles. They carry their arms high in a stance which is said to represent the horns of the moon, and at the same time also the horns of game animals and cattle. The women select their partners from among the opposing row of men by dancing in front of them with suggestive motions. The selected partners then come forward and begin to dance in the same manner as the women do, facing them all the time. The women entice the men away in a southerly direction and as the dance warms up the movements become more and more erotic; some of them turn around and gather up their garments to expose their buttocks to the men. Finally the men embrace the women while emitting hoarse grunts which sound like those of animals on (sic) heat. The men and women lift one another up in turn, embracing tightly and mimicking the act of fertilization; those who are not dancing shout encouragements at them. . . . What the women are in fact doing is to re-enact the role of the moon in the creation myth. At first they dance alone in circles, like the moon which was up in the sky before the appearance of the sun; each woman then entices her sun to the south; they ascend into the sky lifting one another up, and finally, in the erotic culmination of the dance, they marry" (Ten Raa 1969, 38).

In Haiti priests conduct ceremonies to salute and summon a *loa*, a divinity who possesses an individual by displacing the soul, spirit, and psyche of the self. The divinity becomes the animating force of the person's physical body and manifests its presence through particular dance movements. As lord of eroticism and death, Ghede's dance movements remind people of the compulsive drive to life and the inevitability of death. Baron Samedi is Ghede's special emissary, a heavy-drinking ladies' man who expresses himself in foul language and lascivious movements. He wears a tall top hat, long black tailcoat, skirt of cloth or grass, and dark glasses, carries a cane, and smokes. Dual sexuality is expressed in gesture, language, and clothing. Broadly sexual and obscene, he breaks taboos while he confronts humans with their eternal eroticism.

Maya Deren explains: "Life for Ghede is not the exalted creation of primal ardor; it is a destiny. . . . He is lord of that eroticism which, being inevitable, is therefore beyond good and evil and is beyond the elations and despairs of love. Of this is he neither proud nor ashamed; if anything, he is amused by the eternal persistence of the erotic and by man's eternally persistent pretense that it is something else. . . . He may mimic the passionate. Or, again, he may invent variations on the theme of provocation, ranging from suggestive mischief to lascivious aggression. His greatest delight is to discover some one who pretends to piously heroic or refined immunity. He will confront such a one and expose him savagely, imposing upon him the most lascivious gestures and the most extreme obscenities. Thus he introduces men to their own devil, for whoever would consider sex as a sin creates and confronts, in Ghede, his own guilt. Such incidents amuse him, but they represent no real challenge, for he knows that no one can elude him . . . master of both life and death" (1970, 102–3). Ghede, in the form of a possessed dancer, "may alternately remind men that he is their past, their present, and their future, and he is master of their compulsive drive to life and of the inevitability of their death; that he is, in fact their total lord" (p. 104).

Seduction of Forces and Female Shamans

Not only can dance be performed to arouse the passion of a human lover, but it has sexual overtones in relationship to overcoming the forces of nature. In the agricultural Chou society (ca. 111–222 B.C.), the *wu*, female shamans, danced for rain to seduce its spirit during the Yu ceremony. Dancing was the classic way to reach the state of trance in which the shaman could fly to meet a descending spirit and probably unite with it in a cloud. "Cloud and rain love" is a romantic expression for lovemaking found in Chinese literature from antiquity to the present (Chee 1983, 129).

In Korea the female shaman, essentially a ritual specialist for housewives, brings the deities from the supernatural world, manifests their presence, and interprets the gods' will in order to bring good fortune, to heal, or to send off the dead. Laurel Kendall (1985) reports that "like the female entertainer, the *kisaeng*, the shaman engages in public display, singing and dancing. An element of ambiguous sexuality wafts about the *mansin's* performance." (*Mansin*, meaning "ten thousand spirits," is the respectful term of address to a shaman.) Folklore and literature portray these shamans as "lewd women." "The *mansin* play to their female audience, but when the supernatural Official sells 'lucky wine,' the costumed *mansin* roams through the house seeking male customers. The men have been drinking by themselves in a corner of the house as far removed from the *kut* [shaman's most elaborate ritual] as possible. Now they emerge, red-faced, and the bolder of their company dance a few steps on the porch. Men buy the Official's wine and tease the *mansin*, flourishing their bills in front of her face before securing the money in her chestband. An audacious man may try to tweak the *mansin's* breast as he secures his bill.

"The *mansin* is caught at cross purposes. By her coy, flirtatious performance, she encourages the man to spend more money on wine. But as a woman alone, she must defend herself from harassment and protect her reputation." When a man grabbed Yongsu's Mother's breast, she said, "I put out my hand so the drummer would go faster, then brought my arms up quick to start dancing. I knocked that guy against the wall." Asked what she meant by that, she answered, "Oh, that wasn't me, it was the honorable Official who did that" (p. 61). Kendall explains: "To the exemplar of Confucian virtue, the *mansin* offends simply because she dances in public. When an officer from the district police station tried to stop a *kut* in Enduring Pine Village, he threatened to arrest the *mansin* because 'they were dancing to drum music and students were watching.' The moral education of the young was thereby imperiled. An envelope of 'cigarette money' finally silenced this paragon" (p. 62).

Although the *mansin* shares in the ambiguous status of other glamorous but morally dubious female marginals (actress, entertainer, and prostitute), and like them makes a living by public performance in a society where "good women" stay home, she serves the "good women." "She came from their midst, lives like them, and speaks to their anxieties and hopes. . . . only by virtue of divine calling is she a *mansin*, and that is a compulsion fatal to resist." The gods who have claimed her as a shaman leave her one lingering shred of respectability. "Her neighbors assume that she did not want to become a *mansin*. She tells her story to clients, describes how she resisted the call with the last ounce of her strength and succumbed only after considerable suffering and in fear for her very life" (p. 63).

Sexual Sublimation

Dance, we have seen, conveys gender roles concerned with sexuality. Thus dance may promote sexual union and its fruits of pleasure and offspring, a glimpse of the divine, or seduction of the spiritual. The obverse, too, occurs. The Ngoni and the Shakers illustrate dance as a medium that prevents sexual behavior: the cathartic energy or orgasm of dance dampens consumation.

Among the Ngoni of Malawi, the *ingoma* dances were the main village recreation for everyone. Young dancers were "continuously being told to dance strongly, *usina na'mandla*, and their leaping and stamping and singing all combined to make the dancing a strenuous pastime." The older Ngoni men asserted that this dancing made a young man self-restrained; sitting about with no fixed activity tended to make a man sexually uncontrolled (Read 1938, 10).

The United Society of Believers in Christ's Second Appearing, commonly called the Shakers because of their dramatic practice of vigorous dancing to crush sexual desire and dispel sin, believed that the Day of Judgment was imminent. With about six thousand members in nineteen communities at its peak in the United States, the group believed salvation would come through confessing and forsaking fleshly practices. Sexual conduct became a bench mark of an individual's morality and the basis for reward or punishment in the next life. If lust were conquered, other problems would solve themselves.

Louis Kern (1981) says that Ann Lee (1736–1784), founder of this utopian, millenarian society, had experiences that played a central role in shaping Shaker theology and practice. Lee had deep feelings of guilt and shame about her strong sex drive, a sense of impurity concerning the fleshly cohabitation of the sexes, and a purient interest in the sex lives of others. Her turbulent marriage led to eight bitter and harrowing pregnancies. Lee's offspring were stillborn or died in early childhood, with only one living to six years of age. Coition caused her suffering.

During one of her periods of imprisonment (the Shakers were frequently persecuted), she received a revelation of Adam and Eve's first "carnal act," which she interpreted as the source of human depravity. She then promulgated a revulsion of sexuality in the sect.

Lee was concerned with the plight of women in marriage, which she likened to servitude, prostitution, and rape, and included the risks of pregnancy and parturition. At that time, women's bodies were often maimed because of primitive knowledge of bodily functions (Shorter 1982). The Shakers thus saw woman as a victim abused by irresponsible men for their selfish pleasure.

Choosing celibacy, Lee became a universal mother and sublimated her sex drives in a spiritualization. "She called herself, and was considered by her followers, the 'Second Appearing of Christ.' . . . As a female Christ she stood in the place of spiritual mate to the male Christ. She is reputed to have told the Elders on one occasion that Christ 'is my Lord and Lover' (a spiritual lover impregnating her with the lives of regenerated souls)" (Kern 1981, 74). A female image of God did empower women in the Shaker community. Their social organization was based on the equality of the sexes and emphasized group rather than individual pursuits. Marjorie Proctor-Smith (1983) argues that the Shakers anticipated several important feminist concerns in their rejection of marriage, establishment of dual leadership, and experience of a dual incarnation and a Father-Mother godhead.

Notwithstanding Shaker attitudes toward transcending the body through sheer willpower, the first adherents were seized by an involuntary and repressed passion. It led them to run about a meeting room, jump, hop, tremble, whirl, reel in a spontaneous manner, and "wrestle with the Devil" to shake off "the flesh" and doubts, loosen sins and faults, induce humility, and purge the body of lust in order to purify the spirit. Toward repentance they turned away from preoccupation with self-concern to shake off, in febrile performance called "laboring," their bondage to a troubled past. The attempt to escape the body while being riveted to it permitted concentration on new feelings and intent. Individualistic impulsive and ecstatic abandon eventually evolved into ordered, well-rehearsed, drill-like group movement patterns over the two hundred years of the sect's existence. Shaking the hand palm downward discarded the carnal; turning palms upward petitioned eternal life. The square, circle, line or march, and endless change comprised the spatial design. Herein male and female often came in proximity to each other, yet they never touched. The shaking off sin movement sequence parallels the sexual experience of energy buildup to climax and then relaxation. In the dancing, both sexes conveyed images of a process of the pursuit of purity and denial of sexuality.[7]

For the Shakers, who believed in the dualism of spirit versus body, dancing appears to have been a canalization of feeling in the context of men and women living together in celibacy, austerity, humility, and hard manual labor. Dancing afforded an outlet for energies restrained by Shaker regimentation and a sanctioned emotional release from the enforced separation of the sexes. Men and women lived apart except for the worship service, of which dance was a central feature, and during the rare "union" or visiting meetings.

Summary

Thus far in the broad examination of the association of dance with sexuality and gender (which is often linked to religion, politics, and economics), I have presented illustrations of gender, especially of women's roles, in aphrodisiac dancing that encourages what a culture considers appropriate perpetuation of the society. Dancing may be prescribed for weddings; the participants in dancing and the places they perform, both before and after marriage, as well as the role of the nonmarried professional dancer may be specified. Examples of aphrodisiac dancing that encourages pre- and extramarital relations followed. Sacred aphrodisiac dancing and dance as an alternative to sexual intercourse, yet other categories in the repertoire of human behavior, were noted.

In this chapter I have shown how dance conveys gender through focusing on sexuality—whether its assertion or denial. In the next chapter I turn to further ways in which dance expresses sexuality and is an element of a culture's resources for transmitting its sex role norms and values.

4

Sex Role Scripting

Scripts for manhood and womanhood may be created and "read" in various ways. This chapter comments on the social construction and transmission of gender knowledge through initiation dances, movement signs, and religious and secular rituals.

Initiation

All people have special ceremonies to recognize an individual's change of status. Puberty rites attesting to physical maturity may require operations on the body, a change of residence, or a formal school. These rituals and those initiating adults who reach a new status often convey gender expectations and requirements through dance.

In Liberia, known for its secret initiation societies whose instruction makes use of dance, the Vai people's Sande plays an important role in the transformation of females from adolescent to adult. Poro is the male counterpart.

Dancing communicates symbolic gender meaning, punctuates phrases of the acquisition of gender knowledge, instills discipline, develops women's muscles that aid in childbirth, builds up endurance, provides recreation, and reflects the personality and physical talents of the individual. Dance may metaphorically enact status transformation from childhood to adulthood.

Moreover, some people believe dance may actually bring about a transformation and new gender script. For example, in the *chisungu* girls' initiation ceremony of the Bemba of Zambia, each initiate must be "danced" from one group to another. "The women in charge of this ceremony were convinced that they were causing supernatural changes to take place in the girls under their care" (Richards 1956, 125).

Among the Ndembu of Zambia, special high-status cults had specific dances for killers; these performances served as markers of identity and prestige. A man who hunted men or animals encapsulated masculinity in a society jurally dominated by the principle of matrilineal descent. Part of the prayer at the onset of the *wuyang* ritual, "We want a man who can sleep with ten women in one day, a great . . . hunter," points to the associated qualifications of virility (Turner 1957, 29–39, 203, 380). The *mukanda* initiation rite for boys inculcated these values with the dominant symbol, *chikoli*, a strong hard tree, signifying strength, an erect penis, and the masculine virtues of courage and skill. During circumcision rites, males danced near the tree and, on the last day, in the rites of return, each boy, holding an axe, performed the *ku-tomboka* solo war dance signifying aspiration to the high-status cult for killers (pp. 35, 259–60).

Gender roles in marriage concerning reproduction are depicted in dance. Harold Schneider describes the first day of the circumcision rite among the Wanyaturu of Tanzania: "The woman stands with her left foot planted firmly on the ground (her left side being the side on which she is supposed to lie during intercourse) with her left leg flexed, toes of the left foot touching the ground. Her male partner stands between her legs, and while she has her hands on his shoulders or waist, his hands are held out from the body or down near her vagina. In this position, the two twist their hips in unison in imitation of coitus, while others sing suggestive songs making references to vagina, penis, and the act of coitus" (1979, 63–64).

The Venda of South Africa and Zimbabwe hold the coeducational *domba* school to prepare boys and girls for marriage (Stayt 1931). A small snake is believed to live inside every woman and play an active part in building up the fetus in the womb. Consequently, a barren woman is given a girdle of python skin in order, by sympathetic magic, to stimulate fertility. Through the symbolism of the python dance, a central feature of the *domba*, youth, performing in single file, learn of insemination, signs of pregnancy, labor pains, partuition, and the pitfalls and dangers they are likely to encounter in their adult lives. The arduous dance calls for incredible powers of endurance.

Movement Metaphor

Movement metaphors distinguish male from female. Danced gender patterns serve to remind audience members of their respective identities and roles.

Male dominance appears in the guise of masked men performing both male and female characters and dance movements. Among the Ivory Coast's Nafana, power is measured by the differential amount of activity and the quality of movement present between the male and female. The male exhibits greater effort (Williams 1968, 72).

Through the Ida annual dance ritual for palm sago fertility and celebration of survival in the face of physical and mystical dangers, the Umeda of the West Sepik district of New Guinea convey gender status. Alfred Gell (1975) explains that while the sexual division of labor is supposedly complementary, the dance reflects the cultural creativity of men pitted against the natural creativity of women. Female culture must ultimately be opposed and conquered by male culture.

Social life male-female distinctions in Sonquo, a Quechua-speaking community in the highlands of southern Peru, echo in dance. Women work with their hands: they spin, weave, and cook in or near their homes. Men work with their feet: they plough the earth and travel. Viewed as horizontal and identified with the earth, women use the horizontal loom, care for growing things, and sit on the ground at public functions. Considered vertical, men use the upright loom with foot pedals, sit on seats at public functions, and pass through a hierarchy of community offices. These patterns of gender in space—female immobility and male coming and going—are expressed in dance: 'The women bend over their full skirts and twirl around in place, while the men go stamping and leaping around them" (Allen 1984, 2).

Who performs together and who dances what are movement metaphors of gender hierarchy among the Beledugu Bamana of Mali. Performers of one sex may accompany the other's performances, but the sexes may not perform the same material together simultaneously. Exceptions occur in the theater of the *woloso*, who have a low legal position in relation to other casted groups and in relation to the free clans that occupy the highest position in society. The *woloso* may give lip service to the appropriate ideology, but they consciously make efforts on and offstage to overthrow the gender segregation norm. Women, too, with a low jural position violate the norms for age segregation and may dance together (Brink 1982).

Among the egalitarian Ubakala of Nigeria, dance movement patterns show a relation to gender at the time of the participant's greatest sex-role and age differentiation (Hanna 1976). Young people of both sexes have relatively similar dance movements in terms of their use of time, space, energy, and body parts. At the other end of the age continuum, elderly men and women have similar dance patterns. Perhaps age and energy determine these phenomena. However, when the age of both sexes is relatively similar but the biological and social sex role differentiation is greatest, the dance movement patterns diverge most markedly.

There is a strong contrastive movement metaphor: women's movements suggest life-creating and nurturing; men's suggest life-taking warriors. Men cut diagonal lines through spaces. Their directional changes are more angular; body shapes are more varied and complex. Whereas men dance in a circle extrusively, stepping in an out, leaping up and down, and moving on the ball of the foot, the women use the circle intrusively, have a more homogeneous spatial level, and move predominantly on the whole foot. Men's rapid speed and varied spatial use resemble destruction, just as women's slow speed and limited spatial use resemble construction. The warrior's killing thrust is swift; he ventures abroad. The woman's gestation and suckling period of about two-and-three-quarters years somewhat restricts mobility. Ubakala men dance to proclaim their power, strength, wealth, and aggressiveness. The women knowingly use the dance-play to assert and laud their creative powers as mothers, maintainers of the male lineage, and family integrators. They also self-consciously dance for political power. More will be said about this in the section on modulating sex roles.

Dance movement patterns and the particular participants in a dance group mark changes in sex role expectations and behavior. Movement labels and categorizes performers who cross social frontiers in much the same way as does costume. For example, the dance-play of young girls from about eleven to sixteen years of age focuses on a girl's imminent marriage, when she leaves her home and goes to live among her husband's kin. The shimmy movements of the upper torso highlight the girl's developing mammary glands, and the innovative, well-executed choreography proclaims the girl's potential for dealing with the trials and tribulations of married life in a changing society.

The dance-play for the birth of a child takes place immediately after a normal healthy child is born and again after the child has survived one year. The performers, from the compound of the infant's father, are at least fifteen years old and have themselves given birth and achieved the status of womanhood. A woman's status in Ubakala society depends upon living children. Using movements and song texts that clarify the meaning of movement, these women glorify fertility and generously praise childbearing women and midwives. After performing for about three hours at the father's home, they move on—dancing, singing, and playing music along the way—to the compound of the mother's parents, where they perform again, informing all of the blessed event.

Another kind of dance-play focusing on women's sex role is performed after the death of an important aged woman. The deceased must have lived at least to the age of seventy, borne many children, and become independently wealthy through trade in agricultural produce or some craft items. This dance-play eulogizes, propitiates, and shows respect for the deceased on behalf of her kin. The spirit of the deceased is believed to exist in limbo between living and ancestral states until the performance of the "second burial," which assists the deceased in joining the ancestors who are believed to be later reincarnated.

Women contribute to defining sex roles through the concretization device of conveying meaning as in mimetically cradling an infant. They symbolize fertility with the stylization of female movement: undulations and hip shifts and rotations. The counterclockwise circle predominates as women move with flexed knees, the upper torso inclined forward at a forty-five-degree angle, and the pelvis tilted backward (the buttocks upward). Movements are small, fluid, and curvilinear. The tempo of the dance movement is slow and even. The feet, flat on the ground or barely arched, move continually; even when in place they undulate against the earth. Women do not defy or leave the ground but move along its surface.

Men engage in warrior dances retelling heroic battles and proclaiming machismo. Such dances are performed for the actual interment and the later "second burial" (ritual to send the spirit of the deceased to the world of the ancestors) of an aged, prestigious man, one who has accumulated wealth, lived a long life, and made a significant contribution to his community. His sons are the core participants. Gatherings of men's special titled societies that recognize wealth and other achievements are also occasions for men's dances.

The dance-play passes on village history and informs all present of valued male perspectives and goals when men vigorously portray as warriorlike the deeds, exploits, and prowess of a deceased or his ancestors in order to bestow praise and honor upon him and his descendants. Movement amplitude ranges from small to large and dramatic, as dancers lunge, jump, and run in mock attacks and defenses and gesture in flailing spoke and arclike thrusts cutting into space with machetes or sticks or brandishing and changing them from the right hand to the left and back again. They move in a quick and febrile tempo with staccato rhythm; indulgent pauses precede sudden action.

MALE IDEAL OF WOMAN

From Japan's Kabuki comes an example of a man's portrayal of an idealized conceptualization of what it is to be a woman that socializes women. Kabuki's *onnagata* is the actor/dancer in an all-male cast who specializes in female roles. Lithe, slender (in 1982) male ingenue Tamasaburo Bando, enraptures the Japanese public. His beauty carries with it a magical power. *New York Times* Tokyo correspondent Steve Lohr (1982) reports that many men, especially members of Japan's homosexual community who traditionally have been attracted to Kabuki's female impersonators, are devoted fans. Yet the majority of Tamasaburo's enthusiastic fans are young women. "We like men we can take care of," one young woman explained. Swarms of female fans ardently await him at the stage door. The women approve of a man who demonstrates his appreciation of females through portraying idealized images of them.

Passing as an exquisite woman onstage, Tamasaburo has feminine qualities in face, body, and gesture, 118 pounds on a five-foot, eight-and-one-half-inch frame. He lives as a woman in his daily life in order to be considered an accomplished *onnagata*. A mild case of polio as a child and the doctor's suggestion that traditional dance would be useful therapy set Tamasburo on the path toward the Kabuki theater. He ended up specializing in female roles because of his build, talents, others' advice, and his mastery of female movement and expression to become "every inch the *femme fatale*." He thinks women's clothes are much less comfortable than men's, but "when they are slightly uncomfortable, women are more erotic" (Lohr 1982, 16).

Tamasaburo has said that an actor lives for the sole purpose of seducing his audience. The women he portrays, "wonderful things which are beyond our reach," are idealized and romanticized. He elucidated his intention never to marry a woman: "Most men would try to make their ideal woman into their wife. But I have made the ideal woman into my business" (p. 16).

MALE ASSERTION

In Indian Kathakali, an all-male caste also portrays male and female characters. "As an example, the gesture for 'I' or 'me' can be shown in different ways. A female character shows this gesture with circular curving movements accompanied by the bending of the upper body; the effect is of softness. The smoothly flowing movements reflect a feminine quality. When the gesture for 'I' is shown by a male character, a stronger, more masculine quality is evident. . . . If the accompanying mood is one of humility, or love, the left hand in . . . a fist is placed in front of the chest, and the right hand . . . flat open . . . is brought near it. To show the gesture with arrogance, the left hand . . . in a pointing gesture points toward the chest and the entire body is tilted backward" (Namboodiri 1983, 199–200).

Manjusri Chaki-Sircar and Parbati K. Sircar (1982) suggest why the Nayar heroic warriors, under the supervision of the Brahmin caste, created such a powerful and spectacular dance drama and staged it as a public ritual for the entire community: Kathakali was a reaction to foreign aggression and a reaffirmation of the warrior-priest social status. Furthermore, in a society where descent and residence are on the maternal side, masculine pride, perhaps, needed to be affirmed. The dramas enacted tend to present the female as submissive and the male as dominant.

GENDER AND PERSONALITY TYPE

The male and female roles of the Wayang Wong, the principal dance form of Indonesia's Javanese Yogyakarta court, were traditionally danced by men or young boys (Oslin-Windecker 1983, 188). Not only is there a male-female distinction on Java, but there are codified intramale differential dance patterns based on psychology.

As in India whose culture spread to Indonesia, some Javanese recognize dance as a model for morally unambiguous behavior and spiritual growth. The stylized movement of dance underscores the stylized social behavior that is part of everyday life. Dance practice and performance thereby reinforce traditional etiquette. Training in following the rhythm and emotional quality of the musical accompaniment prepares males and females for the ideal social interaction: a person is supposed to flow with the group's rhythm and adapt to it without being noticed or obtrusive.

The Natyasastra, India's classic treatise on dance, specifies that dance enactments of myths and legends would "give guidance to the people of the future in all their actions" (Ghosh 1950, 1:34). The dance training in classical Yogyanese, officially created by Sri Sultan Hamengku Buwana I (reigned 1755–92), also called Joged Mataram or dance of the Mataram Kingdom, went beyond aesthetic pleasure and entertainment. The heroes of Javaneses narrative dance, derived form the Mahabharata and Ramayana, uphold truth, goodness, rectitude, and belief in God. Moral strength is acquired through perseverance, concentration, and self-confidence in dance training.

Male and female dancers are given separate specialized training. The female dance (*putri*) is always in the refined mode (*alus*), characterized by small, restrained, slow, subtle, and softly flowing movement, limbs close to the body, and gaze low, whereas male dance falls into categories of refined *alus* (not weak but like a chivalrous knight) or *gagah*—forceful and emphatic, expansive, aggressive, or abrupt gestures and movement. "For instance, a refined male dancer should not place his fingers higher than chest level except when dancing with a weapon in a combat scene. In contrast, a forceful male dancer should always move his hands above chest level except when dancing with weapons and when executing the dance positions called *tanjak* (basic stance for beginning a dance phrase) and *tancep* (basic stance for ending a dance phase)" (Murgiyanto 1983, 180). "From the beginning, a student may be taught to master only a certain character in the refined or forceful mode, in accordance with individual physical appearance" (p. 179). The concept of *pacak* refers to the matching of a dancer's physique with one of the basic modes and the execution of movement appropriate to the character that coincides with mode.

The Javanese recognize five basic human disposition types, each of which is symbolized by a movement motif and dance style called a *ragam* (Olsin-Windecker 1983, 187–88). Only the refined *ragam* (*ngenceng*) is used for all female dancing. These *ragam* differentiate the possible male types: *impur* (*alus*) expresses truthfulness, calm, refined appearance and feelings, and self-confidence with modesty; *kambeng* (*gagah*) is honest, unexcitable, self-confident, and determined; *kalang kinantang* (*alus* and *gagah*) is somewhat harsh, excitable, arrogant and dynamic; *bapang* (*gagah*) is coarse, conceited, uncontrolled, and rough. Because the Javanese recognize the movement code, even non-narrative dancing implies personality.

Even though all female dance is based on one refined movement pattern, different types of females are recognized through slight emotional variations in energy and direction of gaze. One is humble, shy, and quiet; another is more dynamic, active, emotional, and aggressive. The non-narrative Golek dance illustrates an adolescent girl's new awareness of herself as a woman through lively, rhythmic movements, including "playing with earrings," "adjusting and head ornament," "looking in a mirror," "applying makeup," and "admiring finger rings." These movements are often choreographed into narrative sequences depicting love.

Religiously sanctioned possession dance also underlines the stylized dichotomous everyday as well as other dance movements that split along sex lines. In West Java, Kathy Foley (1985) has observed that females move in curves with a langorous, sleepwalking quality, whereas males always move in lines wth tension, angularity, bouncy jerks, and violence.

The female at a certain stage in her life manifests that godly ideal in both trance and semiritual dances throughout the region. "Female dancers are by their anatomy appropriate vessels for the divine refined. . . . Emptied of their individual ego in trance, they will revert to a godly archetype, hence the special importance of female trancers and by association dancers, in these cultures. An analogy with architecture is evocative: curves are lines that foil demons; houses and temples are thus designd so that partitions necessitate taking a curved path through them. . . . Since the female body is the appropriate vessel for the godly, in trance and theatrical dance the motion is all circles; no demon can enter it" (Foley 1985, 40).

In contrast to past custom, when men performed male and female roles, women in theatrical dance now often portray male characters because their build and movement quality are more likely to capture the essence of the refined male character. Given the view that femaleness is next to godliness, the ideal male is female. In a number of Southeast Asian dramas, Burmese *pwe*, Sundanese *wayang golek*, Malay *ma'yong*, one or more female dancers who have no perceptible relation to the plot dance at the opening. The dances appear to be "movement mantras that evoke the mild 'female' godliness to manifest and mediate the more manly business of wars and demons that soon will follow" (p. 41).

Foley describes a 1982 moonlit-night *sintren* performance in a home courtyard on the north coast of West Java: "The audience is packed into the small space, belly to back. The chorus, pounding bamboo tubes or earthenware implements to be found in any kitchen, sings: Make lively, lively,/Make lively for the performance/So the heavenly goddess (*widadari*) will descent./Make lively, lively, by the clear of the moon." After various ritual acts a girl dances dreamily for about an hour in the refined, langorous, flowing classical dance style. "The spine is upright and relatively stationary, the extremities undulate around the fixed point in space created by the torso. A habitual plié is in evidence, but the knees remain close together and little bouncing occurs. The dancer floats through space, as if air were water and she was buoyed up by it.

"The head, arms, and hands draw the viewer's focus. The elbows remain relatively fixed in space as the lower arms transcribe elegant arcs in the air. At the moment when the lower arms reach their rotational limit, the wrists take up the impulse in the curving of the *ukel*, a gesture typical of dance in the area, in which the fingers open out and down, then gently grasp a point in space, holding it while the wrists explore their rotation around it. The head, as if liberated from the trunk, floats above . . . the chin and the tip of the head inscribe fluid figure eights. The dancer advances through space using a circuitous floor pattern. The total impression is of gentle indirection" (pp. 29–31).

Male trances are the vessels for display in the uncontrolled demonic and animal side of the spirit and human worlds. As Foley watched the *dabus* troupe dance, performers drove awls into their stomachs, ate glass, slashed their legs with knives, ate razor blades (joking they taste like candy), and cooked eggs on a fire they built atop one man's head.

"One of the approximately twenty men performing slices off his tongue and dances across the sage with the [still quivering] organ in his hand. . . . Audience members are invited on stage to view the cut-open stomach of one performer. The *seh* [head of the troupe] utters a mantra, takes some clear water in his mouth, and sprays it over the wounds that result from these acts. The tongue is reconnected, the stomach is unscarred.

"The dance movements are strong and direct rather than circuitous and langorous. The movement is related to the . . . style of . . . the martial arts dance found through the Malay archipelago (troupe members later acknowledged that they had all studied this art before undertaking training in *dabus*)" (p. 32).

With an upright body and strong energy, the weight falls heavily toward the earth. While the arms move from the shoulder, the hands extend as if in readiness to deflect or initiate a blow. The dancers, in a position of the legs rotated out at the hip joint, knees spread wide, step in a jerky, bouncing manner. Abruptness marks transitions from one pose to the next.

Another male dance that contrasts with the female style is the *kuda képang* (literally "horse of woven bamboo"). "Two young men strap around their waists the belts attached to the horses. They tip the horse figures up and down and begin dancing in a prancing step-hop-step. . . .

"They start leaping and turning somersaults. Audience members tell me that they have been entered by the spirits of horses. They eat unhusked rice and gulp, without pause, huge buckets of water. They then proceed to less equine activities. I see them eating light bulbs, lying on thorn sticks with three people standing on top of them, gamboling through fire, rolling torches over their bodies, and swallowing flames" (pp. 33–34).

The simple, repetitive step-hop-step dance inscribes the same circle, the center from which dancers in relatively straight lines move in and out as each feat is performed. Trancers dance unceasingly, keeping an upright torso and unmoving hands clinging to the hobbyhorse, as they constantly bounce up and down even when the orchestra stops at the end of each song.

In the possession dances of both women and men, the spirit controller is a man. The dancers view themselves as empty vessels. When magically charged instrument and recited mantras, the controller calls the spirits and assures that the performers are unharmed. If a *dabus* performer gets hurt, however, the harm is ascribed to the performer's lack of belief in the power of God.

While there are many specific male and female movement metaphors, the concept and manifestation of androgyny can also be found in movement. India's Hindu theology is replete with the concept of the unity of male and female. This pertains in spite of the fact that the society is primarily male-dominant. We will look at an instance of sexual dualism in the Kuchipudi dance in a later section on sex role modulation.

TRANSVESTITE RIDICULE

A people may teach sex roles through ridicule. For example, in Zaire, when the Mbuti perform the *ekokomea* dance ritual, women dress as men and "ridicule that sex quite mercilessly, while men dress as women and are equally merciless. . . . while women ridicule the male organ, exaggerating its size to grotesque proportions, men ridicule that (for them) strange life-giving phenomenon, menstruation" (Turnbull 1981, 215–16). Mbuti see themselves equal in all respects except sexually. Female youth celebrate their puberty in the *elima* dance ritual; male youths have exclusive right to perform the ceremony of *molimo made*, in which the trumpet, the main symbol of the forest as a spiritual entity, is used.

Enforced transvestite dance may be a punishment for unsatisfactory sex role performance. The Bamana (Bambara of Mali) use dance as a manifestation of boys' developing control over their physical selves, a demonstration that they have acquired balance, coordination, and suppleness of movement. Requiring a misbehaved boy to dance therhythms associated with women of another caste is strong chastisement (Brink 1982, 422).

Modulating Sex Roles; Transvestism, Adulation, and Appeasement

Sex role typecasting, we have seen, occurs through dance performance at weddings, through pre- and extramarital entertainment, and through rituals for life, death, and initiations; typecasting is also seen in movement metaphors and is used for idealization and ridicule. Dance also serves to modulate gender role excess or abuse. Dance is a means for one sex to appropriate symbolically the power of the other. Each sex has strengths that the other may fear or perceive to be inadequately exercised. Role reversal and lobbying through dance are coping devices that illustrate complementarily, contradictions, and ambivalent feelings. In transvestite dance, caricatures may poke fun at the image of the opposite sex in an attempt to demonstrate a cultural blueprint and the frequency with which it is disregarded.

RITUALS OF REBELLION AND ROLE REVERSAL

Max Gluckman (1954) called attention to "rituals of rebellion" in which a particular kind of behavioral inversion occurred. Women, usually the subordinate sex, engaged in socially approved inverted and transvestite behavior; they dressed as men, assumed their dominant authority roles, and danced warrior dances, all of which were believed to be for the common good.

This inversion behavior may not only be cathartic—the controlled release of tension in which the powerful allow a contest or reversal against themselves so that they might continue to order the usual state of affairs without challenge. The temporary public sharing in high-status behavior and then its loss emphasizes the holder's superiority, reinforce the maintenance of the system, and create order. But more important, the rituals of rebellion may impose restraints on the occupants of high-status positions. Dramatizations of conflict through role reversal and gender inversion offer a latent system of possible alternatives, that is, a veiled threat and prophylactic portrayal of what might happen if authority exceeds normative bounds and abuses its power. Thus men are put on their mettle to act appropriately so that they too receive women's support.

Among the Gogo of Tanzania, dance metaphorically effects a

supernatural change in a curative and preventative rite through sex role reversal in dance. Men have ritual responsibility for controlling human and animal fertility. However, when they fail, disorder reigns. Then women, assuming the men's ritual roles, become the only active agents in rituals addressed to righting the wrong. Dressed as men, they dance violently with spears. Peter Rigby points out that "a major element in all the rituals is dancing (*kuvina*), and the women are said to 'dance away' (*kuvinira*) the ritual contamination. In fact, the dancing is the primary 'curative' aspect of the ritual, and no other medicines (*miti*) are used" (1972, 240). This is a form of sympathetic magic.

APPRECIATION OF WOMEN

In the Nigerian Yoruba hierarchical, competitive society where men dominate yet heavily depend upon women, dance appears to be a vehicle to honor females, attract their goodwill, and assuage male fears of impotency attributed to women. H.J. and M.T. Drewal, in *Gelede: Art and Female Power among the Yoruba* (1983), examine the communication of women's social and spiritual roles in dance performance with its elaborate proclamations maleness and femaleness through a profusion of visual signs. We learn that "the etymology of the word *Gelede* reveals its central concerns and its ultimate significance. *Ge* means 'to soothe, to placate, to pet or coddle'; *ele* refers to a woman's private parts, those that symbolize women's secrets and their life-giving powers; and *de* connotes 'to soften with care or gentleness.' Together these ideas convey the significance of *Gelede*, a male performance carefully conceived and executed to pay homage to women so that the community may partake of their innate power for its benefit (p. xv). Only men wear and dance the female and male masks, which portray the appropriate roles for each sex, although both men and women belong to the Gelede cult to seek protection and blessings and assuage their fear of death.

The Gelede society masquerade figures appear annually at the start of the new agricultural year to dance in the marketplace and through the streets. Men honor and propitiate the female *orisa* (deities) and their representatives, living and ancestral, for the mothers are the gods of society, and their children its members. All animal life comes from a mother's body. Women are also economically independent of their husbands and may even be wealthier than them.

Mothers have both positive (calm, creative, protective) and negative or witch dimensions (unmitigated evil affecting fertility, childbirth, and the functioning of men's sexual organs). The mothers possess powerful *ase* (vital, mystical power), which resides in the *orisa* and ultimately stems from the Earth Mother. A man can have *ase* most fully when he is spiritually united with an *orisa*. When men symbolically externalize the vital life forces in dance, they may be asserting their virility and freedom in the presence of the powerful mothers; in addition, they may be recognizing and honoring the mothers' powers in order to appease them, thus insuring that the mothers utilize their *ase* for male benefit.

The Yoruba acknowledge with praises of "our mother," "the gods of society," and "the owners of the world" their belief that women, primarily the elderly, possess a kind of extraordinary power equal to or greater than that of the gods and ancestors. Women know the secret life itself and have the power to usher humans into and out of society. Gelede is supposed to entertain the women at the same time that it is a sacrifice to them.

With concretization, stylization, metonym, and metaphor, the dance movements and the constumes define and elaborate the physical attributes and styles of men and women and so epitomize maleness and femaleness. In this manner, they engage in the sex role scripting that has been discussed. Female steps are controlled, as is the great mother who is seen as not becoming visibly angered and exacting revenge covertly. "Their very restraint communicates complete control of awesome qualities unequaled by the most commanding male" (Drewal and Drewal 1983, 75). The movement is slow and takes a direct and narrow path toward the drum in sluggish time. Some Gelede images also satirize and criticize female antisocial behavior such as prostitution and other inappropriate sexual behavior.

In contrast with female masks, male masks move fast and take up more space, jumping here and there with strong hard effort, shifting directions, whirling with outstretched arms, and rushing at the audience. In spontaneous movements the male dancer's body levels change from an erect posture to lunge low to the ground.

Dress, a means of expressing status in everyday life, exaggerates gender in the performance. The female's hips and buttocks are accentuated with a wooden spool, woven fish trap, or stick construction tied around the waist and covered with a wrapper. A wooden breastplate with thrusting breasts is fastened above the bodice. The male figure has an expanded girth and chest created with a massive cylinder of fabric.

Seeking meaning between the relationship of dance structure and style on one hand and other aspects of culture on the other, Stephen A. Wild (1977–78) asks this question about Walbiri aboriginals in northern Australia: Why do men dance in women's style in their rituals but the reverse never occurs? He contends that the men symbolically celebrate the complementarity of sex roles at the same time that they appropriate women's procreative and nurturing role to induct novices into manhood. Men are ritual procreators. They symbolize their circumcision ritual as a mother substitute through dancing in women's style.

Walbiri rituals reenact the events of Dreamtime, a supernatural and timeless sphere that existed in the distant past but also continues in the present. Mens's participation in Dreamtime through ritual performance that reveals knowledge of the Dreamtime ensures Walbiri fertility and well-being. Only men perform mimetic dances that represent the behavior of a specific Dreamtime ancestor and wear the fluff obtained from the underbody of certain birds and efflorescent of a local paint. Women perform nonmimetic dance representing the traveling behavior of ancestors writ large. They jump in place or forward, with arms bent, elbows pointing downward, forearms and hands upward.

VISUAL PLAY OF CONTRADICTIONS AND FEARS

In Bali, Indonesia, and Rangda and Barong drama enacts and reenacts the battle of the sexes and the complementarity of male and female (Belo 1949). Rangda, queen of human witches, controls the spirits who at her bidding perform all sorts of horrors. Rapacious and insatiable, this hairy creature is long fanged and bulging eyed, with elongated fingernails and a long pendulous tongue tipped with fire. Her long gray hair reaches to the ground, and her breasts sag, presumably from the suckling of children. She wields a white sling in which mothers carry their offspring. A widow, she may have embraced the role of witch out of anger and frustration at her infertility. Barong is king of the demons, and animal-like creature who has power over demonic beings and evil spirits who accompany traveling gods. He resembles a young dragon and a lion or tiger with fanged teeth. His serpentine body sports an erect tail decorated with shining mirrors.

On the occasion of Galungan, sometimes called the Balinese New Year (it occurs about every 210 days), many villages put on the Rangda and Barong drama. Males play both of these aggressive and destructive characters. The playing of Rangda by a man who becomes possessed by her spirit is identifying with female power and honoring the positive in women. "Rangda, in her connection with death, destruction and disease, it is but the ugly counterpart of living, procreation, and well-being" (Belo 1949, 49).

In Rangda-Barong, a fearsome witch and foolish dragon combat, and the story ends in complete irresolution—no one ever wins. Neither male nor female dominates. The "powers of evil though forever with us are under control" (p. 19). Male and female villagers, aroused by the excitement and stylized interplay between the combatants, go into trance and, in a somnabulistic state, attack the witch with their krises (wavy-bladed daggers), and sometimes work themselves into a climatic convulsive seizure. Becoming possessed by demons, they stab themselves without bloodshed. After the performance, everyone returns home feeling peaceful.

Both sexes want children, and unmarried women are believed to go to hell. Yet men consider women seductive and distracting; they enervate men, causing a loss of power through tumescence, and create fear of future impotence. Sexual abstinence supposedly aids the accumulation of power. On the positive side, women give ecstasy, bear children, and are the link with reincarnation. Procreation is a major source of envy. These dilemmas are under debate in the kinetic discourse of the dance-drama.

The trance is narcissistic, self-induced, accompanied by copulatory movements, and defiant of dyadic or communal dependence. Through trance men express defiance of their reliance on women for nurturant support, ecstasy, and the link in reincarnation. Men help each other out of the trance. The witch thwarts penetration with magic that forces the slayers to turn away from her passive femininity and flourished baby sling and to thrust the kris against themselves. Because a man's phallic kris is an appendage and symbol of himself, this act appears to recognize self-deprecation and weakness. The individual succumbs to trance as to a sex partner, dominant caste, or supernatural, and to the loss of power.

Mary LeCron Foster offers further interpretation: "Since the kris is clearly the phallic element, the body under attack must be interpreted as female-like. This is underscored by the typical male krissing stance; the body bent backward, kris pressed against breast from above. The demon has been incorporated through prior introjection/enclosure, a reversal of the penetration/introjection sequence in coitus. The body which has already enclosed the male-female-animal demon will not receive the instrument of penetration which unaccompanied by intro-jection could mean only death. Thus, the demon within acts as mediator in thwarting the self-destruction attempt that must inevitably follow the desire to kill the mother. He is more powerful than the man, though he is below, a second reversal. The demon without, the Barong, removes the demon within by assuming a sexual position, standing over the possessed person. This is a third reversal from the coitus model in that posture above extracts rather than introjects. The function here is one of *withdrawal/rejection*, which brings the act into analogical cohesion with childbirth instead of coitus" (1979, 192).

The Balinese cross sex roles in assigning the bad traits of both sexes to Rangda, the good to Barong. Rangda "embodies male aggressiveness, female old age, desexualized intellectuality or infertile wisdom, hatred and destructive greed which is death dealing. He [Barong] embodies female lack of aggression, youthful sexuality of both sexes (uteral back, erect tail), female-animal-childlike playfulness and unthreatening animal appetite which is life giving. His strength is in his tail, not in his head" (Foster, 1979, 188). Barong's masculinity appears in his serpentine body and eye-catching erect tail and his stance above the entranced warrior to restore him to his senses. Feminized traits are a tongueless mouth seemingly representative of a vagina, sensuous and circular movements, a concave spine and playful actions, which Gregory Bateson and Margaret Mead (1942) found characterized the Balinese mother. Though ostensibly female, Rangda displays kinesthetic behavior of the *barris* warrior dancer: wide movements with thighs, knees, and feet turned outward, an erect spine, shouts of "wah," eyes round and staring, and sudden and tense movement. Women's movement, in contrast, is narrower, with feet together, knees bent but not outward, spinal curve, and buttocks protrusion. Rangda's tongue gestures are phallic.

Perhaps the play presents negativity to stress the desirability of and hope for the opposite in the presence of reality. The evil of the spirits is posited as evil in humans, which must be kept within bounds.

Asserting life against a fear of disintegration, the dance style powerfully exaggerates fingers in tension, which distinguishes the living from the dead.[1] Moreover, the dance is in counterpoint to ordinary life, with its constrained behavior and rigid code of hierarchical relations. The dance permits a powerful stimulus of mass emotion in which cautiousness, dignity, and fear are loosened from the usual ethos and momentarily overcome. The dance, however, belongs to neither high nor low caste but to *communitas*, a condition on the periphery of everyday life. Here nature reigns at the expense of culture; the dance is replete with symbols relating to biological processes. Hostile feelings are projected and people are spoofed through upsetting their regular erect, seated, recumbent position in space. In the dance there are arched, climatic movements—women bending forward and downward, men jerking backward. Climax and emotion are permitted to degree not found in ordinary life.

Note that the Hindu-Balinese religion, once viewed menstruating women as impure and so excluded them from public performance. Young men or boys performed female characters in Balinese classical dance dramas. Little girls danced the *sano hyang* ritual trance dances and performed in sacred processionals. Gambuh, the oldest of *bebali* or classical dance dramas, came to Bali from the courts of East Java in the eleventh century. At this time female characters were added to the drama and were performed by males until as late as 1922. The Dutch rule in 1906 ended ritual suttee and the harems of Balinese courts and launched other forces of change, including Western education for women. Modernization and Western colonialization led to the transformation of many expressive dance forms for tourists. For example, I Mario, in 1950 created *oleg* for mature adolescents.

FEMALE IMAGES OF THE DIVINE

Although male dominance is the general cultural pattern in India, male and female are complementary in Hindu thought, and each sex has specific power. For example, a man's mother may gain familial power in the domestic realm. A comparative study of sex stereotyping found that Hinduism was associated with a favorable cultural image of the stereotypic woman largely because the pantheon of deities has both gods and goddesses (Williams and Best 1982). By contrast, a less positive image of women was found among practitioners of the Protestant and Muslim faiths. Female images of the divine may empower some women both spiritually and socially. Having deities of each sex, or a deity with attributes of both sexes, in an anthropomorphic religion articulates behavioral bounds for male and female. Implicit is the suggested possibilty that excessive male behavior toward females could cause women to challenge the social order of male dominance.

Kuchipudi dance—theater illustrates messages of female power that may modulate the exercise of male power. This dance form began with Brahman male dancers and actors, who at some time taught the art to the guilds of male teachers, who instructed women. Today, however, women are responsible for its survival and performance.

Chamudeswari Shadbam, one of the episodic dances I observed Indrani perform at the Smithsonian (Hanna 1983b) tells the tale of the unconquerable Goddess Durga and the evil buffalo-headed demon Mahishasura. Durga is a universal spirit, a deity with male and female qualities. She represents female energy on earth and the potential to destroy evil and bring justice. Mother of all living things and creator par excellence, Durga also possesses the characteristics of power and victory. She is savior of the gods and killer of demons. The majestic

Durga, an important divinity in the sacred Indian tradition, rules the heavens with Lord Siva. They are a loving couple devoted to divine children. Hindus believe Durga and Siva dwell on the high peaks of the Himalayas and in humble temples. Capable of taking any form, they are timeless creators, rulers, and destroyers of the world. Their cosmic dance dissolves and re-creates the world. When these deities are angered, they strike the offender. When they are pleased, they bring joy.

The evil demon Mahishasura received boons from Lord Siva as reward for his devotion and asceticism. However, the demon later created havoc on earth and went on to terrify all the gods unable to withstand him. The demon declared himself god and destroyed good holy people. Siva rose in anger, and Durga appeared to save the gods.

Indrani danced the impersonations of Goddess Durga, Lord Siva, and Mahishasura. She set the mood with an expressional abstract dance and a Sanskrit hymn of praise to Goddess Durga. Then in the role of narrator, the dancer depicted the demon's conquest of the universe and the defiance of the gods. Indrani impersonated his boastful proclamation of supremacy and danced his challenge. She presented the anger and dismay of the gods who appealed to Lord Siva for assistance. Subsequently she danced Siva's reply. From the divine, radiant splendor of all the gods, the dancer portrayed the creation of Goddess Durga. After becoming Goddess Durga and displaying her divine weapons bestowed by all the gods, Indrani swiftly assumed the role of the monstrous demon. In the battle dance she alternated the roles of the two combatants, dancing to accented drumming. The dramatic sequences climaxed Durga's supreme victory.

SITTING ON A MAN

The Ubakala women of Nigeria induce moderation of men's power through the dance practice referred to as "sitting on a man" (Hanna 1987d). Only men participate in the formal, traditional political and ritual decision-making bodies of the culture. However, Ubakala women are not merely subordinate domestic creatures of exchange and family alliances. They also provide men with mates, privileges in a new group (husbands gain special support from a wife's family), and labor. Ubakala recognize that female fertility and energies complement male virility and strength in human and economic production. Furthermore, women have prestige and power apart from that of their husbands; achieving wealth through marketing agricultural produce and other goods, developing persuasive verbal eloquence, and bearing many offspring are indicators of a woman's success. With these assets, women past menopause may even attend men's political meetings if they choose. Women have their own groups and leaders who are considered powerful among both women and men.

Because women marry outside the village group into which they were born, their kin organization cuts across the goes beyond any one level of political structure. The organization, which is potentially powerful in rallying numerous groupings behind any single member, uses the dance-play as a boycott. The aggrieved gather at the compound of an offender and dance and sing to detail the problem. Movement presents a dynamic image emphasizing the argument as well as releasing and generating physical and psychological energy and tension. The accompanying song, with its potent ridicule and satire, serves as a vehicle for specific social criticism.

The famous 1929 "women's war" in which the dance-play communication went unheeded illustrates the potential of this expressive form. Repercussions of the war were widespread both locally and across continents. Contemporary politicians and leaders—again, male—frequently refer to this notorious episode of feminine protest. They remember how the women moved the mighty British to alter their colonial administration of eastern Nigeria. Generally aware of the potential for public disturbance in the dance-play, the British colonial government of Nigeria required licenses and permission from the British district commissioner in some areas to hold performances.

The first phase (Turner 1974) of the social drama that resulted in the women's war began with a *breach* of understanding between women and the British colonial government. After the British government introduced taxation of men in 1928, women incorrectly believed that they too would be taxed. The women considered taxation as an infringement upon their competitive economic patterns. Since women had not become representatives of the colonial government as Nigerian men had, the women saw no benefits from taxation. Indeed, their economic and political grievances coalesced. They strongly disliked the abusive and extortionist practices of many British-appointed Nigerian male warrant chiefs who violated traditional practices protective of women, for example, obtaining wives by paying full bride wealth.

The spark that ignited the conflagration occurred when a young assistant British district officer decided on his own authority to obtain information on the number of men, women, children, and livestock in order to make the cencus registers more complete and accurate. A warrant chief employed a schoolteacher to take charge of the census.

The man inquired about the possessions of a local woman, Nwanye-ruwa, who became incensed. She then reported the incident to her village women's meeting.

A mounting *crisis,* the second phase of the social drama, rallied women from near and far to discuss what had happened. They initiated the third stage, the potentially *redressive* process of "sitting on a man," which usually works to resolve conflict. The irate women trooped to the mission that employed the chief's messenger to demonstrate against him. They camped in front of his compound and kept him from sleeping and carrying out his usual tasks. Improvising to meet the situation, the women danced and sang all night, eating, drinking palm wine, and singing that Nwanyeruwa had been told to count her goats, sheep, and people.

The next day, with the problem still unresolved, the social drama reached the *schism* phase. When the women excitedly went to the chief's compound to demand his resignation, he escaped. The British officer then met with twenty-five thousand women in the market to assure them they were not to be taxed. Skeptical of government assurances—the British had deceived the Nigerians before—the women went on a rampage. They forced warrant chiefs to surrender their caps, symbols of authority. Some proceeded to attack and loot the European trading stores and Barclays Bank and to break into the prison and release the prisoners. The riots spread, involving about ten thousand women in two provinces. Destruction was directed primarily toward the warrant chiefs and building representing this detested authority. A car accident and heated passions triggered the most extreme violence. At some point the police opened fire and thirty-two women were killed and thirty-one wounded. In 1930–31, following reports of two commissions of inquiry and an anthropological study, the British reorganized their colonial government. The women succeeded in destroying the warrant chief system with its male abuse of women. The cost would have been less had the male audience been more attentive initially.

Thus the contemporary women's dance-play performance serves as a metaphor for their power. Because men have a range of vehicles to express their identity and will, the dance is of less importance to them than to the women and youth.

Dance has played a role in European politics as well. In the French ballet *La Déliverance de Renaud,* Louis XIII's performance as a demigod was a metaphorical message of the triumph of his orderly, exalted monarchy over anarchy (Kirstein 1970, 62). Female political leaders also used dance to assert themselves. Catherine di Medici of

France commissioned a lavish production of *Ballet des Polonais* in 1573 to impress the Polish ambassadors arriving to negotiate a royal marriage. The goal of the 1581 *Ballet Comique de la Reine* was to send a message that the queen's treasury was full.

Summary

In this chapter I have illustrated how people learn through dance what it means to be male or female. Distinct roles for the sexes and male superiority, dominance, and greater range of opportunity for men are pervasive messages. By depicting gender roles at different stages of the life cycle through movement metaphor, criteria for who dances, and idealization or ridicule, men often tell women how they should behave. Men may direct women, even when women are considered vessels for possession by the divine. The female is usually more passive, gentle, the male more aggressive, bold, and energetic. Generally the stereotypes described in chapter 1 are upheld. In stratified societies, social class may also be demarcated in dimensions of the gender-related dance performance. The contest and complementarity of the sexes, the power of women, and even aspects of androgyny are played out in performance. Men may pay homage to women even as they attempt to appropriate their powers. Yet through dance women may set limits on male assertiveness, especially in egalitarian societies.[2]

Before completing the historical and cross-cultural contextual dicussion and moving on to sex and gender in twentieth-century Western theatrical "high-art" dance, we give further consideration to India's classical dance. Special attention is given to Indian classical dance because of its antiquity, complexity, broad geographical impact, rich literature in English, and strong influence on Western ballet and modern dance.

5

India's Dance Kaleidoscope: Divine Sexuality, Sex Roles, Erotic Fantasy, Profanity, and Emancipation

This chapter gives further attention to Indian dance because its bounteous past extends into the contemporary era and its influence has spread beyond the Indian subcontinent. To a great extent, the importance of dance to India lies in its embedding in the Hindu faith, predominant in India and held by a large portion of the world's population. India, the second most populous nation in the world, has a dance heritage that ramifies through Southeast Asia, where local groups have adapted Indian cultural forms to their own needs and aesthetic, and through communities worldwide. This includes the United States, where Indian dancers have performed and immigrants have settled. American choreographers have also drawn inspiration from Hindu dance expressions. (There are also non-Hindu dances, such as Kathak, which is Mughal and Muslim, and some forms use dances of different religions.)

Indian dance includes aphrodisiac performance, pre- and extramarital entertainment, art and artifice, erotic fantasy, sex role typecasting, and transformations in response to the clash of cultures through war, imperialism, and technological change. Sex, gender, divinity, and dance conflate. In Indian culture, the gender role of woman is to serve

Some material in this chapter was presented in "Feminist Perspectives on Classical Indian Dance," a paper given at the conference Dance of India, held at the University of Toronto. Chapters 3, 4, and 5 benefited from the conference discussion and from comments on drafts of my paper by Serena Nanda, Joan Erdman, Medha Yodh, Ann-Marie Gaston, Carol Martin, and Manjusri Chaki-Sircar.

man and God, including sexually. Males are, however, considered to be females—submissive before God. There is also a third institutional gender role manifest in the dance.

Sacred and Secular Merge

The sacred and secular, ritual and play, spiritual and sexual do not everywhere have the dichotomous character so common in postindustrial societies, especially Christian ones. Whereas Christianity separates the sacred and sexual (even though it uses the sexual metaphor "the passion of God's love"), a common strand of Hinduism merges divinity and eroticism in felicitous union. "The consistent fabric of Indian life was never rent by the Western dichotomy of religious belief and worldly practice" (Banerji 1983, 101). Hinduism is also more tolerant and embracing of contradictions and variations in human behavior. Rather than considering carnal love a phenomenon to be "overcome" as in many Christian denominations, Hinduism accepts sexual congress as a phase of the soul's migration that is analogous to mystery, potential danger, heaven, and ecstasy. Dance, often a devotional obligation, conveys such a vision of life. And in so doing, it creates attitudes about the conduct of social life for each sex as it honors the deities.

In response to Christian Westerners' misconceptions about Indian dance, Banerji writes, "Since the celebration of the sexual has been the matrix of traditional religion in India, all Indian art in consequence is basically erotic in nature. Indian dance, classical or popular folk, is much more so." Moreover, "the major gods, along with the lesser gods and goddesses, their attendants and celestial nymphs (*apsaras*) propagated the Art of Dance with its main feature and ingredient viz. Sex" (1983, 41).

Hinduism is similar to Christianity in comprising a medley of hundreds of belief systems that share commonalities. Hinduism has a pantheon of deities. The supreme all-powerful God is sometimes manifested in a trio of anthropomorphic divinities: Brahma, Vishnu, who appears in one incarnation as Lord Krishna of amorous nature, and Siva, Lord of the Dance, who created the universe and balances the eternal cycles of destruction and regeneration (Gaston 1982). His rhythms are those of the world. With pleasure he exuberantly dances out the creation of the world. But just as a human dancer tires, so Siva periodically relapses into inactivity (Banerji 1983, 14). Siva's violent, frenzied *tandava* (virile, manly) dance causes chaos and represents the destruction of the world. For his creative dance, his consort Parvati's dance of *lasya* (tender, womanly) is imperative.

Hindus conceive of dance as metonymical, a part of the whole of life. Gregory Bateson tells us, "Consider Shiva, the Nataraj figure, the Dancing Shiva. This is a paradigm, imposed upon the entire world of experience, in which it is assumed that everything that happens, ranging from earthquakes to gossip, to murder, to joy, to love, to laughter, and all the rest, is an incredible zig-zag of what might seem otherwise to be unclassifiable and disordered experience, but is, in fact, all framed within the Shivaite concept as *The Dance*" (1977, 14).

Dance has power as a metaphor for the significant god's dancing, which makes human dance, by extension, esteemable. Indeed, divine origin is ascribed to Indian dancing. Although both male and female royalty may have been well versed in dancing in early India, the Natyasastra classical dance treatise is said to be the work of a male sage, Bharata Muni (sometime between 100 B.C. and A.D. 200). Receiving instruction from the gods, he handed it down through his sons (Chosh 1950). This treatise is often called a fifth Veda (an ancient sacred text of Hinduism. It specified that dance enactments of myths and legends would "give guidance to the people of the future in all their actions" (I:34). During the epic and classical periods (440 B.C. to A.D. 600), the elitist religion of the Upanishads was democratized and made available to the common people through two great epics, the Ramayana and Mahabharata. Portions of these blends of ancient legends, ballads, and esoteric teaching are enacted in dance.

Centuries later, in the 1930s, Uday Shankar saw the instructional value of dance and attempted to spread "through the world the knowledge that there is a native Indian culture, with all the social and political concomitants of such a culture clearly in mind" (Martin 1933; see Erdman 1987). Shankar became torchbearer of a dance revival movement in India.

Given the preeminence of the dancing god and the danced enactments of the lives of deities, some of whom also dance, it is not surprising that believers have historically paid greater attention to dance than do those people whose cosmologies do not so prominently feature this form of expressive culture. Another reason for the importance of dance is the essential role of the visual in India, prior to the era of motion pictures and television. Worshipers make gods and icons. Through image making, shape is given to what cannot be readily seen. This is the concept of *murti*, in which the deity is embodied in the human body which is therefore also divine (Waghorne and Cutler 1985). Hindu worship is an awakening of the senses and a directing of them to the divine, an exercise of beauty as specified by canonical texts. The worshiper and the deity see each other. "The contact between devotee and deity is exchanged through the eyes." (Eck 1981, 5). Seeing is a form of touching and knowing. Moreover, the bhakti religious movement originating in the medieval period (sixth to tenth century A.D.), in contrast with the earlier Vedic or orthodox religion, permitted salvation to anyone, including the poor, women, and lower castes, by means of devotion. Dances based on the epics and Puranic themes were an expression of devotion. Bhakti religious egalitarianism, however, was separate from political ideology.

Ancient tales of Krishna, cowherd incarnation of Vishnu, who is full of pathos and love and represents emotion over intellectuality (Vaishnavism), and Siva, who represents the supremacy of the intellect (Sivaism), are popular today. "The love episodes of Shiva and Parvati or the amorous dalliance of Krishna and Radha [his consort] and the *gopis* [milkmaids who leave their husbands, family, and respectability for the pleasure of Krishna], the erotic dances of the *apsaras*, and their endeavours to seduce the sages, are all sanctified by the Hindus, and no iota of sensual vulgarity or indecency is attached to the doings of the heavenly creatures. Sex is regarded as divine, with complete negation of human lust" (Banerji 1983, 22).

As oral and written religious texts come into being, vary in their fluidity, and transform over time, so do the dances that enliven the texts. "For example, from the tenth to the twelfth century the function of Krishna changes, from his having been born solely to kill a tyrant and rid the world of demons to having been born to impose impassioned adoration of God as the most valid way to achieve salvation. . . . the facts as given in the *Bhagavata Purana* are . . . [not] disputed; rather . . . their emphasis and viewpoint . . . are changed. Radha, the Gopi, comes to the fore and Rukmini, his wife, is relegated to the background. . . . Krishna's chief function is now, with Radha's help, to declare passion as the symbol of the final union with God" (Martland 1984, 259).

In Hindu theology, there are many ways of worship and paths to reach the ultimate goals for humans: salvation, bliss, knowledge, and pleasure. An erotic/aesthetic tension exists. Within the cult of Siva, the yogi is one who has renounced ordinary human duties and concerns in saintly training to unify the body and the soul. Dancing is one of the media for attaining this objective.

An alternative and more popular philosophy has been Bhoga, release through sensual enjoyment "in variations of coital postures, which excite . . . reference towards the fire, which rages on lips that blossom like flowers and eyes which look gently up to the splendour of the deity in the beautiful warm human face" (Banerji 1983, 67). The sensual religious practice of the Vedic era became widespread through the doctrine of the Tantras, which entered both the later Hindu and Buddhist traditions.

"The conception of Bhoga naturally ushered sex in dance, sculpture, painting and literature, but there was always the divine touch in it" (Banerji 1983, 68). Banerji thinks that scholars of the Tantric texts provided justification for practices so prevalent that they considered it useless to fight them (pp. 79 80).

The Tantric cults raise enjoyment to its highest power and use it as a spiritual rocket-fuel to enlightenment. Following the path of devotion (bhakti), surrender in love is an appealing form of worship, a symbol of divine communion, and a microcosm of the macrocosm of divine creation that reveals the hidden truth of the universe. The sensual female helpmate plays the part of Sakti, the female life force (god's energy), while the male assumes the role of Siva. Some Tantras declare that Supreme Knowledge, *prajna*, resides in the female genital organ. A man and woman attain spiritual illumination momentarily when they glimpse a sense of the desired absolute union with divinity in the physical, erotic self-oblivion of becoming one in carnal love. Sexual union is thus the symbol of the soul's intense longing for God. Distortions of Tantrism are that a man has unlimited scope for indulging in sex and other forms of licentious behavior. However, doctrinal strictures call for strict moral discipline and self- and sense control.

Note that in the Bhagavata philosophy, humans in quest of the universal and infinite are in the role of women, the brides of God. The Lord alone is male. This view explains the acceptance, in religious practice, of males dressing and dancing as women.

Mrinalini Sarabhai, a classical Indian dancer writes: "There is in Hindu thought, an essential similarity between the saint and the lover . . . the *ananda* or bliss of the Supreme Brahma cannot be measured by the physical and mental rapturous involvement of lovers; yet the utter surrender of the two merged into one and the complete though momentary peace is an infinitesimal glimpse of that absolute union with God." And further, "The dancer expresses in her interpretation the most intimate secrets of love, dancing with symbolic duality, the lowest and highest forms of passionate love through the labyrinth of each state of erotic love towards the final transformation" (1976, n.p.)

A student of Indian dance in Vancouver, British Columbia, Jean Cunningham, reflects: "I cannot help thinking that the longevity of the classical dance has been due to the mythology which can be interpreted by each according to his or her perceptions and by dance which is both erotic yet sanctioned, and transformed by each (again) according to his or her perceptions" (pers. com. 1983).

COURTESANS

As discussed in chapter 3, courtesans have had their times of respectability in Indian history. In chapter 24 of the Natyasastra, Bharata enumerates a number of feminine erotic styles; chapter 25 deals mainly with courtesans who are not excluded from the benefits of religion. They usually worship Kama, God of Love, most handsome of the deities, who enjoys perpetual youth. "He has a sugar cane for his bow, humming bees for his love strings and he wounds by flower shafts. The parrot, his charger, is the Indian love bird" (Banerji 1983, 88).

AESTHETIC GOAL

For dance, and the other arts, Hinduism encourages the artist to strive to suggest, reveal, or re-create the infinite, divine self. Artistic creation, conceived as the supreme means of realizing the Universal Being, is a sacrifice, a dedicated offering of the best one has to the best one seeks. The dancer expresses feeling moods or *bhavas*, situations and acts that evoke *rasa*, a specific response in the spectator. Through the inner force of creative intuition, the dancer tries to evoke in the spectator emotional states of consciousness—feelings of love, anger, laughter, disgust, sorrow, fear, amazement, valor, and peace—that lie dormant in each individual.

Faubion Bowers explains the *rasa* of love: "*Bhavas* may be either enduring or transitory, a cause or effect, or even an ensuant or excitant. . . . *bhavas* can be the causal one between a husband and wife or between two strangers. The *bhava* of effect will be that of undying devotion, if it is permanent, or longing, despondence or doubt, if it is transitory. The ensuants can be sidelong glances or coquettish smiles, and the excitants, moonlight, a beach, or a soft zephyrous breeze. When all these minute *bhavas* are properly portrayed, the *rasa* is an overpowering aesthetic delectation which according to the Hindus only true art can arouse" (1956, 31).

Dancing symbolic of love (*sringara*), a key sentiment implying the intimacy and secrets of desire and cause of all creation, conveys the amorous mood through posture, gait, gestures, glances, adornment, perfume, and accompanying song. Natyasastra describes it as an offering and demonstration of love to God, a cleansing of sin, a path of salvation, a partaking of the cosmic control of the world, and an expression of God within. Adoration of God is embodied in the dancer's expression of erotic desires for union with the divine.

In classical dance, males and females have different dance styles, the virile *tandava* and gentle *lasya* (for the development of the erotic sentiment) respectively, as Siva and his consort Parvati. Manjusri Chaki-Sircar (pers. com. 1983) points out that masculine and feminine dance do not necessarily convey only sexuality. *Lasya* may express maternal or sisterly affection and devotion. Moreover, both styles are cultivated by dancers of each sex; that is, if a male or female dancer chooses to portray the warrior goddess Durga riding on a lion, he or she would use *tandava*. The same Durga may also be depicted through *lasya* to express maternal love for the devotees or wifely devotion to Lord Siva.

Female as well as male dancers commonly dance sexuality in the *lasya* style. In Bharata Natyam and Odissi dance forms (both developed from the *dovadasi* temple tradition), female sexuality predominates, whereas in Kathakali, male sexuality is more vibrant. Kathak shows both male and female styles. However, in Manipuri Vaisnavite dancing, one finds a transcendence of eroticism. Only very young boys (six to seven years), young girls, and women are allowed to perform Krishna's role in order to remove any possible physical connotation of divine love. The Meitei society of Manipur, however, forced to accept Vaisnavite Hinduism in 1735, retains some of its pre-Hindu traditions. The Meitei did not accept the Brahmanical pattern of the polarity of sexes (or repression of women). Men and women participate in different spheres on an equal basis and with ample opportunity for premarital romance (Chaki-Sircar, pers. com. 1983). For them, the dance is both entertainment and an offering to the ancestors.

DEVADASIS

Male Brahmans, members of the priestly caste, initially "choreographed" (received from the gods) the dance that male professionals, non-Brahmans who come from hereditary families of teachers and musicians (Nattuvanaras or gurus) and were versed in Sanskrit and

Sastras, taught to *devadasis*. These women, called servants or slaves of God, vestal virgins, temple maidens, *maharis* in Orissi state, and even prostitutes, were dedicated to temples and pressed into service to dance for the deities inside the temple as well as outside for festivals involving the larger community.[1] The *devadasi* prototype is the heavenly nymph (*apsara*) who dances for the gods. Voluptuous, beautiful *apsaras* inspire love in paradise as well as upon earth. Gods, Gandharvas (renowned male musicians, bards, and singers who accompany the *apsaras*), and mortals are their lovers. Temples housing the gods became pivotal in all aspects of Hindu life because of the belief that no place is fit for human habitation without earth, water, and a deity. There are home altars everywhere. Kings usually built the temples and supported their various rituals and services, which included dancing. The dancers and their families lived near the temple. In the Odissi tradition, the *devadasis* through example taught the dance heritage to their natural or adopted daughters.

Probably established between the ninth and eleventh centuries, the *devadasi* institution exhibits unique features as well as common patterns in the various regions of the Indian continent with its Hindu diversity. Generally the women had high-ritual status and lived in the public eye. Because the temple dance, known as *sadir attam* (in Tamil), *sadir nac*, or *nautch*, was a votive offering, rigid rules governed the dancer's training (usually beginning at age five to seven) and method of performance. She learned, scholar Kapila Vatsyayan has said, to seek the perfect pose that conveys a sense of timelessness (Jeanes Antze 1979, 8). At the same time, women's dance movement, in all its demanding exactitude, emphasized the beauty of the body and the erotic appeal of dance for an "other"—god, husband, lover.

Several circumstances prompted parents to give their daughters to a temple. Parents might need to fulfill a vow, have no male issue (a *devadasi* could inherit), or be too poor to afford a daughter's dowry. A woman could offer herself out of devotion, for the prosperity of her family, out of weariness of her husband or her widowhood. She could sell herself or be enticed. Extraordinary freedom was allowed these women at a time when wives and daughters lived in a kind of purdah.

The *devadasis* were "dedicated" to a god in ceremonies in which they became his brides and servants and were given to particular temples. They received a *tali* (necklace), the marriage insignia of the South Indian woman. Because the relation between human and deity is analogous to the relation between lover and beloved, the professional temple dancer's requirement of individual service to the deity was incompatible with human marriage and motherhood. (In this sense the Hindu ethos is similar to the Christian view of separating the wife/mother from the public woman. In contrast to the *devadasis*, Catholic nuns who marry Jesus deny their sexuality.) The initiation into temple dance service was a marriage with a god, and, therefore, it exempted a woman from the uncomfortable state of widowhood. Besides gaining freedom from the constraints of human marriage and widowhood, the "dedicated" also learned to read and write, an opportunity not allowed other women. Furthermore, some dancers acquired wealth through gifts of admirers, owned land, and made large donations to temples.

In Tamil, the cost of temple dedication might be met by a man who hoped to receive a woman's favors. Her dedicated status made it a social privilege to maintain her. Such support was a symbol of success among a man's peers. Moreover, it enabled him to approximate and imitate the Lord of the Temple in human terms (Srinivasan 1976, n.p.).

The honor of helping with temple duties, such as cleaning devotional vessels and decorating shrines, belonged to the *devadasis*. More significantly, following the heavenly nymph prototype, they worshiped, propitiated, and entertained the seeing deities (embodied in images) with dancing. Daily rituals of Hindu temple worship have their textual base in ritual manuals and Puranas (legends) and dramatic content in devotional literature and oral traditions. Offerings of prayer, incense, light, and food pay homage to the deity. In Tamilnadu, the *puspananjali*, *devadasi* song and dance, concluded the offering of light. (Kersenboom-Story 1983–84). Festival ritual involves a grand procession of the deity(s) outside the temple, accompanied by *devadasi* song and dance. At night a dance-drama (*kaman-kutta*) is performed. "One *devadasi* appears dressed up as *Kama* (Cupid), while the other *devadasis* are his female victims, suffering the pangs of love intoxication inflicted by Kaman's arrows" (p. 23).

Rosemary Jeanes Antze (1982) interviewed three of India's last Odissi dancers who were dedicated to temple service. Hari Priya calls the devotion (bhakti) of the dancer an anchor without which the mind would be disturbed or unsteady. The devotion permits a modest young woman to overcome her shyness in order to reach the sense of union with the Lord. "We have to generate a feeling inside ourselves that we are sparks of him, and after death we will go back to him" (p. 57). Sasi described the power and energy she received from the deity Lord Jagannatha as a "current," comparable to an electric charge: "When we stand before him, some sort of current is produced in our body. When we are decorated, vermillion is put on our forehead and that vermillion dazzles with a strong glow. If any man will look at us with evil intention (i.e., with desire) he will burn up and be destroyed. God has given us that power." And Chanda explained, "When we go to the god our bodies glow" (p. 73).

Sasi said a *devadasi* must have a sense of *tapas,* which refers to warmth, heat, fire, light, meditation, and service. She believes that dancers broke with tradition long ago by taking human husbands or lovers.

Devadasis performed not only before temple shrines and during the ceremonial procession of a deity; they also danced at private parties and at the royal courts, especially for marriages. The temple dancers were regarded as auspicious and believed to possess power to ward off the effects of inauspicious omens.

GOTIPUAS: BOYS AS GIRLS

In Orissa, the custom of small boys performing dressed as girls coexisted with the female temple dancer tradition since the fifteenth century (Kothari 1968). The cardinal tenet of the Sakhi-bhava cult is that the Lord alone is male and all devotees are *gopis* (milkmaids). God could be approached only through ecstatic devotion. Since Krishna was male, the most effective way of showing devotion was as a female, similar to the *gopis* who dance their love for Krishna. The *gotipuas,* as the boys were called, also *akhad pilas* because they apprenticed in the centers of physical culture (*akhadas*), danced outside the temple during religious festivals and other social gatherings. On the occasion of Chandan Jatra, when the Lord is taken on a ceremonial boat ride for twenty-one days, a *gotipua* performs on the boat before the deity. For their services the boys receive some offering and the patronage of religious and wealthy people.

The former governor of Rajahmundry introduced the custom of temple dances (traditional classical Odissi style) performed by boys dressed as girls and not by women as was the custom. The boys trained in physical culture with acrobatic feats, beginning at age seven. In adolescence, when the boys lost their delicate appearance, they became teachers.

After Ramachandra's rule in the fifteenth century, the next three hundred years in Orissa witnessed a succession of ruling groups. In the last century the Sakhi Nach, a voluptuous dance of *devadasis,* and later the cinema, corrupted the art of the *gotipuas*, and increasing vulgarity manifested itself.

HIJRAS: MEN AS WOMEN

It was common in some parts of India for men and natural eunuchs to voluntarily dedicate themselves to temple service and dancing as women. Of the *jogati muttus*, who devote their lives to the service of the goddess Renuka in northwest Karnataka, only the men learn the art of dancing, and some learn to play instruments. As *jogati* the men switch to women's dress—the sari, bodice, and bangles. When B. R. Patil (1977) asked the men their reasons for becoming *jogati*, they took refuge in the name Renuka. There were, to be sure, material benefits. As religious mendicants, not as beggars, they collected alms.

According to Serena Nanda (1984), who has conducted extensive research in India, *hijra* refers to eunuchs, hermaphrodites, and impotent men, especially to those whose genitals lack a normal male appearance in infancy or childhood. Men who identify themselves as "in-between" or as women, whose dress, demeanor, and legal and social status they espouse, comprise an institutionalized third gender role, neither male nor female but with elements of both, that includes men with a variety of gender incongruities. The *hijra* form a community with its own rituals and "family" houses.

Indian mythology provides ample illustrations among deities and humans of androgenes, impersonations of the opposite sex, and sex change (O'Flaherty 1980). Thus the Hindu tradition provides models for the *hijra*, although they occupy a marginal status in India. Primarily North Indian cultural groups, such as Gujeratis, Panjabis, Sindhis, and Marwaris, believe the *hijra* have powers to bless and to curse. As conduits of Bahuchara Mata's power (she is one of many versions of the other goddess figure), *hijra* receive respect and awe in Indian societies.

By asking *hijra* to dance and sing or allowing them to do so when a baby is born, the public shows respect for their powers. Singing and dancing hold the highest status in the *hijra* community. Its members perform at weddings, births, festivals, male stag parties, and college openings. They often dance to film music, improvise, and spoof grooms at their weddings. Dancing is not only a means of earning a livelihood, but some performers personally enjoy the arts. The *hijra* act in sexually suggestive ways that would be considered inappropriate for ordinary women in their roles as daughters, wives, and others. *Hijra* outrageously burlesque female behavior by dancing in public, using coarse and abusive speech and gestures, smoking hookah, and lifting their skirts to expose mutilated genitals when their authenticity is challenged.

Hijras who are not talented in music and dance earn their living through owning or working in bathhouses and as prostitutes. Because sexual activity is considered offensive to Bahuchara Mata, those *hijra* who practice prostitution are often not permitted to live in "respectable" family houses. Sexual relations also run counter to the *hijra* community interest in maintaining its tenuous hold on respectability. However, as the economic status of *hijra* has declined since independence when raja and nawobs, important patrons of ritual dance performances, lost their offices, prostitution has become a "necessary evil" for some. The *hijra* community has always attracted men with an interest in active homosexual relations; it has also attracted men who merely seek the economic options of the *hijra*.

From New Delhi, William Claiborne (1984) reported on the crisis of the eunuchs, who were often inducted into their elite vocation by ritual castration and once pampered and indulged as the traditional guardians of princely harems: "Now scorned as deformed parasites of society, India's estimated 50,000 eunuchs [this figure may include other types of *hijra*] are at a crossroads of survival in their shadowy half-world of superstition and extortion."

Gulzar, apparently given to a group of eunuchs by his parents when they discovered he was sexless, said the cult that worships Bahuchara, an incarnation of the goddess Durga, now rarely gets such babies. Tipped off by a network of spying household servants, bands of eunuchs appear uninvited at weddings and births to dance and bless brides, grooms, and progeny in exchange for payment. "We have to dance to survive. What else can we do?" Gita asked. He said most of the forty or fifty eunuchs in his neighborhood behind Turkman Gate in teeming Old Delhi earn about $100 per month; the police claim the figure may be up to $4,000 for some groups that tour the countryside (Claiborne 1984).

In 1986 *hijra* held a conference in Bhopal, the first time since 1916. They met to publicize their plight—existing on crumbs thrown to them by others (Bumiller 1986, C1).

A. P. Sinha (1967) describes the eunuchs of Lucknow, homosexuals who seek to live in communities where they will be considered normal. Their self-identity, dress, and other behavior are female. The men are born with normal genitals and may or may not be castrated. *Hijra* is a developed stage. A new entrant to the community is called *janka* and is initiated in a ritual symbolic of a mother breastfeeding her new bornchild. Becoming a "mother-master" *hijra* requires removal of the genitals.

Sex Role Encoding

In general, religious ideas explain and justify human thoughts and actions and are a paramount force in shaping relations between the sexes (Hoch-Smith and Spring 1978). Because a significant part of the Indian population was illiterate, the arts became an entrenched dramatic medium used to communicate the Hindu philosophy of good, evil, social hierarchy, and inequality in the human and divine worlds. The lives of anthropomorphic deities appear as enlarged, intensified, or distorted reflections of human ideas, feelings, and behavior. Hinduism uses human analogies to explain the divine, and in turn, the god's actions provide sanctified models for human behavior or fantasies and vicarious thrills. Manisha Roy points out that "the Vedic and epic gods, like the Greek and Roman deities, are a lecherous bunch constantly seducing the wives of sages and mortals. The sages and monks, surprisingly enough, are also depicted indulging in active sexual pleasure even though living as hermits" (1972, 117–18). Tales of the deities' scandalous behavior project human ideals, foibles, and failures to meet social norms.

Although India may have originally been matriarchal, patriarchy and male dominance came to prevail in early history. Males apparently were primarily responsible for creating the ancient Vedas and later scriptural texts, major epics, and legends that dancers kinetically visualize. Moreover, male temple priests and court rulers supported the dance, and male professional teachers and musicians usually taught it to women. Thus males have been the key architects of dance productions and images.

In the Vedic texts the image of woman is that of an "insignificant receptacle for the unilaterally effective male fluid." She is a "thing to be possessed" (O'Flaherty 1980, 29, 30). Later texts and philosophies perpetuate such views or give the female a more important role. Hindus generally agree that a woman should be and give the appearance of being subordinate to the men closest to her. Manu, male codifier of ancient law, specified that in childhood woman must be subject to her father, in youth to her husband, and when her lord is dead, to her sons. A woman must never be independent.

Nonetheless, Hinduism recognizes an ideal harmonious union of male and female energies within oneself, *purusa*, the primal human being identified as male spirit, and *prakriti*, or *sakti*, identified as female matter. Indians say, "Without Shakti [goddess and female energy], Siva is nothing." Siva is worshiped in Indian temples in the *linga* form: the male vertical stone shaft and the female circular horizontal base called a *yoni* or *pitha*. It is seen as "both Siva and Sakti, male and female, divine spirit and divine matter, transcendent and immanent, aloof and active" (Eck 1982, 17).

Hinduism also takes notice of the instability of power relations among goddesses as well as gods, and of goddesses' power. Even though there are many heroines in the various danced stories, including powerful and wise goddesses (for example, Kali and Saraswati), eight heroines (*nayika*) appear in the Natyasastra treatise. Here the plight of woman is depicted as a life of longing, hesitation, sorrow, loneliness, anxiety, fear, parting, yearning, pleading, forgiveness, faithfulness, despondency, envy, self-disparagement, depression, derangement, madness, shame, grief, and being rebuked, insulted, and mocked by one's family, and deceived by one's lover. These many manifestations of love afford dramatic dance themes (Sarabhai 1965).

When a goddess is dominant, she is dangerous. Making her subservient to her husband tames her power. Thus there tends to be an inequality of power structures between male and female deities. The female requires male control to channel her natural force. For example, variants of legends tell the story of Siva and his counterpart, the goddess Kali, competing in dance contests that Siva wins. He performed many dances that Kali was able to imitate perfectly. Out of frustration, Siva exploited her sense of modesty and raised his right foot to the level of his crown and danced in that pose. Kali could have emulated the pose, but feminine modesty led her to withdraw from the contest. Kali lost not because she was an inferior dancer, but because she was a woman; her subservience is affirmed in this role (O'Flaherty 1980, 142; Khokar 1984, 17–18). As testimony to their faith and respect for Siva's dancing, worshipers built a majestic temple of Nataraja at Chidambaram. One of the shrines houses Siva's image in the attitude in which he defeated Kali. Dancer Mamata Niyogi-Nakra, at the age of ten, asked her male guru if goddesses could not win over gods; he said no (pers. com. 1985).

Popular themes danced by *devadasis, gotipuas, hijras,* and many other groups are about Lord Krishna, described as eternal lover dancing in the heart of everyone (Sarabhai 1965, 5). A. Coomaraswamy (1971) in the *Dance of Shiva* refers to the allegories of Radha (loveliest of the milkmaids) and Krishna in which their illicit love becomes a spiritual freedom, a type of salvation, and a surrender of all that the strict Indian social conventional world values. Radha and Krishna represent the female and male who yearn for each other.

Men, concerned with their sexual drive and perpetuation of their lineages, have imparted dances about male-female actions (dancers of either sex may perform male and female roles). Through the dance theme, style, and gesture, dancers, mostly female, send messages to men and women about the enjoyment and divinity of sex, the acceptance of men's lustful/divinelike/symbolically one-with-the-universe wanderings outside of marriage, and women's faithfulness, giving, and forgiving. Women also send messages to other women to serve their husbands and bear children in spite of the pain and risk of death and agony from high infant mortality (Shorter 1982). Ann-Marie Gaston (pers. com. 1985) pointed out that in Indian dance the main purveyors of gender messages include costume and makeup; the female dancer is often bedecked as a bride.

Erotic Fantasy

More than providing sanction for gender-related behavior, dance offers opportunities for fantasy. Historically it was customary for men and women to be rigidly segregated until marriage. Married women are restricted to carnal acts with their husbands. Because sexuality was socially repressed, love often was sublimated or channeled through poetic appreciation or the divinizing of the opposite sex (Yati 1979, 15). The love-life stories of anthropomorphic gods, as portrayed in dance, may evoke erotic fantasy, provide avenues for repressed and suppressed energies, and allow women temporary escape from human toil (and, a feminist perspective might add, from male dominance) through identification with the prestige and freedom of the *apsara* or *devadasi* (and today with motion picture stars). Women may imagine themselves as *gopis* (milkmaids) who sport with the deity in wild carnal love (Singer 1972, 235). Men also relate to Krishna as *gopis*.

A specific case of married women's erotic fantasy occurs in Orissa where *habisha* rites are associated with the Jagannatha temple of Puri (Freeman 1980). The *habisha* is a vowed observance by menopausal upper-class women who wish to prevent the death of a husband who provides both security and status. As older women they are not supposed to be sexually active, but they reenact the legend of Krishna in dance, song, and games. Perhaps their identification with the milkmaids recalls their youth and fertility at the same time that they vicariously become Krishna's lovers.

Profanity and Further Exploitation of Women

Traditionally it was socially sanctioned for Brahman male temple servants or other men of higher castes than the *devadasis*, who fulfilled their marital obligations, to have sexual license with temple dancers. *Devadasis* were the crucible through which auspiciousness and identity with the Lord could be attained in addition to prestige among one's peers.[2] To the king of Orissa, believed to be the incarnation of Vishnu, belonged the privilege and duty of deflowering the dancers (Marglin 1980).

Over the past few centuries, as a result of the Muslim political rule that weakened the Hindu kings supporting the temple dancers and later the British imperial hold that destroyed other patrons, the temples in Orissa and South India became vehicles of the sexual exploitation of women. The dancer's fixed salary for religious duties became small or nonexistent and alternative economic opportunities were limited.[3] Some women were kept as concubines by new well-to-do patrons. Although a North Indian Muslim ruler, Aurangzeb, in the seventeenth century, regarded dancing as improper for women of good virtue and attacked the *devadasi* institution, other Muslim rulers supported dancers who were housed in the women's quarters or outside the palace. Stories of kidnapping girls for the temple and of priests deriving a key source of income from the temple dancers' prostitution made the news. Furthermore, caste behavior violations and pollution may have occurred.

Male British rulers and Indian social reformers in tandem waged an "anti-naucth" campaign at the turn of the century to prohibit temple dancing and the "dedication" of girls to the temples. As late as 1912–13, girls were being purchased for two thousand rupees each. Not only had the imperial rule economically diminished the dancers' patrons, but the Hindu interlaced sacred/secular philosophy wherein sexual ecstasy is a path of spirituality was an anathema to the British, who were ensconced in the Christian denial of the flesh which they viewed as the root of all evil.

Chaki-Sircar (1983) points out that Indian nationalists such as Mahatma Gandhi campaigned against the institution of *devadasis* because it had become corrupted under priestly order. About 1909 or

1920, campaign efforts in Mysore helped abolish the practice of dedicating women to a temple. Madras in 1927, Travancore in 1930, and Bombay in 1934 took action. In 1947, Madras State's Act 31 went so far as to formally forbid temple dancing (L'Armand and L'Armand 1983).

Renaissance

Although the colonial era did not lead to widespread Christian conversions, it did have a dampening effect on open expression of Hindu sexuality. Chaitanya Nitya Yati said, "After the advent of Christianity, Indians as a whole became oversensitive about erotic references, and the general tendency in present-day India is mostly to keep away from erotic expression in art and literature" (1979, 21).

Yet, as human history testifies, when dance is suppressed, it rises phoenixlike to live again in some form of re-creation. The ethereal beauty of the Russian prima ballerina Anna Pavlova's 1929 performances in India helped rekindle enthusiasm for Hindu dance. She astonished India not only because of her artistic distinction, but because she performed dances based on Indian themes. In the 1920s, Indian art inspired her to create the ballet *Ajanta Frescoes*. Uday Shankar choreographed *Radha and Krishna* and *Hindu Wedding* for Pavlova. The music of these works used Indian forms (ragas, raginis, and talas), composed by Comalata Bannerjee-Dutt. Moreover, Pavlova posed the simple question to Indians: "Where is your dance?" (Bowers 1953, 9; see Gopal 1956, 102ff.).

Teaching *devadasi* (Bharata Natyam) and other classical dance to non-*devadasi* girls began in the 1930s. Intellectual leaders in urban areas who were at the forefront of Indian nationalism began to reevaluate Indian cultural traditions and brought about a renaissance of Indian classical dancing (Chaki-Sircar 1972). The national integrationist policy of postindependence India "promoted the concept that classical arts helped unite India culturally," while "fears of unruly and fissiparous regionalism were met by giving particular regional forms of classical arts national recognition" (Erdman 1983, 262).

Chaki-Sircar emphasizes that the renaissance not only gave dance a regenerated environment in which to be cultivated, but it also gave women of the high castes, who were previously barred from the art, the opportunity to become dancers. Expertise in dance is at this time a much-prized attribute for a girl of the privileged classes who is seeking a husband. Girls from influential and wealthy families study dance as many middle-class girls in the West study ballet. However, few married women are permitted to pursue public performance, that is, to undertake a dance career. The high school and, in diluted form, the cinema, stage, and private gatherings have also embraced dance performance. Clifford Jones reports that "there is still a fairly widespread feeling that 'reformed' traditional art as practiced in polite urban society by nonprofessionals, and 'acceptable to Europeans,' is superior to traditional art as performed by traditional artists" (1982, 5).

The life history of K. Venkatalakshamma, the last surviving representative of the Mysore court tradition of Bharata Natyam, exemplifies the ambiguous status of dance and its fluctuations of respectability and disreputability. Jeanes Antze (1985) collected the great dancer's story. Venkatalakshamma began classical dancing when it still retained its former high status in the traditional contexts of temple and palace. Later she experienced the demise of the traditional religious and political structures that supported the dancers and the consequent fall in the prestige of the dance. Unmarried women were identified as prostitutes, and her own community regarded her as a social liability. Therefore she stopped dancing for about ten years. To be accepted and to arrange suitable marriages for her son and later for her granddaughter, she went to elaborate financial efforts. These included paying a tax to the community elders and providing a feast for the whole village. Ultimately she gained status through her excellence in dance and became one of the living treasures of India's cultural heritage. In the 1960s she received many honors, notably the State Academy National Sangeet Natak award. The 1965 founding of the faculty of dance at the University of Mysore led to Venkatalakshamma's appointment as the first reader in dance, a post she held for nine years. After retiring, the university gave her an honorary doctorate of literature.

Not unexpectedly, following the ancient tradition, the primary gurus or teachers of the dance renaissance have been male. Now, however, economics, traditionally important in the teacher-student relationship, has overshadowed the also critical bond of devotion. Some gurus are no longer instructor and "parent" for many hours of the day. Instead they give group lessons to anyone who can afford to pay for the classes, regardless of birth or caste. Many of the known gurus travel beyond their home areas to key cities to teach special courses, and they even go abroad.

During Jeanes Anzte's fieldwork in 1980–81, she learned that one of the main Odissi gurus charged 1,000 rupees (at 7 rupees to the dollar) per student for a month of intensive group classes. She was told that 600 rupees for one hour a day class for a month was not uncommon, and gurus had seven to ten students. By contrast, university lecturers earned about 2,000 rupees per month (1982). Gaston, also a student and performer of Indian dance, said that several dancers estimated that it cost 10,000 rupees to learn the dance and another 10,000 to 15,000 to prepare for the debut recital. Over a period of six years a dance student's family may spend 60,000 rupees or more.

Gaston (1983) points out the aesthetic implications of the traditional guru-student relationship that pertains today. Imparting his own vision and music upon a dance, a guru expects respect and credit for a piece he has taught a dancer. Usually accompanying students' performances, he tends to be jealous if a student studies with another teacher or creates her own dances. If a dancer wishes to be creative, it breaks the dependency mold. Then the dancer has to find and teach another musician to accompany her, who may leave her for better economic rewards, and then she must begin again.

Not only is classical dance an expression of Indian identity and esteem for those in the homeland; for those who have immigrated it also reflects the traditional culture in a changing context. During her field study of Indians in Vancouver, British Columbia, Jean Cunningham was practicing the *puja* devotional portion of Bharata Natyam together with Roheema, a classmate in the Nataraj school of classical Indian dance. She asked Roheema what meaning the dance had for her.

"The dance for me is first a discipline, second a special role, and third, it is fun as in play, in that play is an absorbing way of spending time the way you want to spend it. The religious elements of the dance make it very profound. The role, which is the ideal Indian woman, is linked in India to both God and the family, and the reason that the dance is a play is that my everyday life is the total antithesis of the ideal Indian woman," Roheema explained. "The dance allows me to act the pleading, teasing, coquettish movements, and they imply a female subjugation. The subjugation or deference lies at the very root of the Indian family tradition. So although I couldn't be the person in the dance, in reality I can experience it through the dance." Roheema thinks that the eroticism of the dance is what makes it profound, "because it is so elemental. . . . Now when we roll our eyes and look very flirtatious in the dance, there is the same sense of shyness, but also a sense of that same profound nature." Her relationship with her mother, with whom she has disagreements, was affected by the dance. "But when I am dancing I am playing the role of my submissive mother and in this way, I share an experience with her." Roheema plans to choose her own husband rather than accept the choice of her parents as is traditional. She also thinks there are Indian men who are looking for independent young women to marry and even with whom to share domestic chores. The dance allows Roheema a momentary partaking of two contradictory worlds without compromising either (field notes 1984).

Medha Yodh considers Roheema's comment about playing and the play directly related to the Hindu concepts of *lila* (play) and bhakti (devotion) which meld in the classical dance. Yodh thinks a modern young woman in India has a similar need to integrate her present reality with the Indian "ideal" woman. Classical Indian dance may have become a tool to mediate the dichotomy between traditional and modern roles. Gaston (pers. com. 1985) proposes yet another reason for the current resurgent interest in this dance: the perceived need to teach traditional gender patterns in the face of the assault of modernity.

Summary

From a worldwide overview of sexuality, gender, and the dance in chapters 3, 4, and 5, we found numerous motifs: aphrodisiac dancing toward culturally licit procreation; pre- and extra-marital entertainment, art, and artifice; love, life, death, and divinity; seduction of forces and female shamans; sexual sublimation; sex role scripting; modulating and coping with sex role performance; transvestite parody and adulation; and India's dance kaleidoscope of divine sexuality, sex roles, erotic fantasy, profanity, and emancipation. Now we turn to twentieth-century American theatrical dance, where we find some similarities and differences.

1. Louis XIV as "Sun King" in *Ballet Royal de la Nuit* (Bibliotheque National, Paris). Courtesy of Dance Collection, The New York Public Library at Lincoln Center, Astor, Lenox and Tilden Foundations

2. Vaslav Nijinsky in *L'Après-midi d'un Faune*. Courtesy of Dance Collection, The New York Public Library at Lincoln Center, Astor, Lenox and Tilden Foundations

3. George Balanchine and Tamara Geva in *Enigma*.
Courtesy of Ballet Society, Inc.

4. George Balanchine rehearsing five "girls." Courtesy of Dance Collection, The New York Public Library at Lincoln Center, Astor, Lenox and Tilden Foundations

5. Margot Fonteyn and Michael Somes rehearsing. Courtesy of National Archives

6. Nora Kaye and Igor Youskevitch. Courtesy of National Archives.

7. Melissa Hayden (pagan) and Francisco Moncion (Christian) in *The Duel*, by William Dollar, New York City Ballet. Courtesy of National Archives

8. Marie Taglioni in *La Bayadère* (English lithograph). Courtesy of Dance Collection, The New York Public Library at Lincoln Center, Astor, Lenox and Tilden Foundations

9. Caroline Lassiat in *Paquita*, 1846. Reproduced from Parmenia Migel Extrom, *Great Ballet Prints of the Romantic Era*, by courtesy of the author

10. *Les Biches* by Bronislava Nijinska, 1924. Courtesy of Dance Collection, The New York Public Library at Lincoln Center, Astor, Lenox and Tilden Foundations

11. Maud Allan in *Vision of Salome*, 1916. Courtesy of Dance Collection, The New York Public Library at Lincoln Center, Astor, Lenox and Tilden Foundations

12. *Prodigal Son* by George Balanchine, American Ballet Theater production (Robert La Fosse and Cynthia Gregory). Photograph by Martha Swope. Courtesy of Barry Laine, *Stagebill*

13. Sally Rand. Courtesy of National Archives

14. *Bugaku* by George Balanchine, New York City Ballet (Jorge Donn and Suzanne Farrell). Photograph by Costas

15. *Mutations* by Glen Tetley and Hans van Manen, Netherlands Dance Theater (Anja Licher and Gerard Lemaitre). Photograph by Anthony Crickmay. Courtesy of Netherlands Dance Theater

MODERN DANCE PIONEERS

17. Isadora Duncan dancing in a Greek theater, Athens. Courtesy of Dance Collection, The New York Public Library at Lincoln Center, Astor, Lenox and Tilden Foundations

16. Loie Fuller (playing with light). Courtesy of Dance Collection, The New York Public Library at Lincoln Center, Astor, Lenox and Tilden Foundations

18. Ruth St. Denis, 1913. Courtesy of Dance Collection, The New York Public Library at Lincoln Center, Astor, Lenox and Tilden Foundations

WOMEN OF STRENGTH

19. Martha Graham in *Cave of the Heart*. Courtesy of Dance Collection, The New York Public Library at Lincoln Center, Astor, Lenox and Tilden Foundations

20. Martha Graham in *Letter to the World*. Photograph by Barbara Morgan. Courtesy of National Archives

21. Martha Graham in *Frontier*. Photograph by Barbara Morgan. Courtesy of National Archives

22. Ted Shawn in *Kinetic Molpai*. Courtesy of Dance Collection, The New York Public Library at Lincoln Center, Astor, Lenox and Tilden Foundations

MALE REBELLION

23. Martha Graham with artistic progeny in *Death and Entrances*: Erick Hawkins as the Dark Lover and Merce Cunningham as the Poetic Lover. Photograph by Barbara Morgan. Courtesy of Dance Collection, The New York Public Library at Lincoln Center, Astor, Lenox and Tilden Foundations

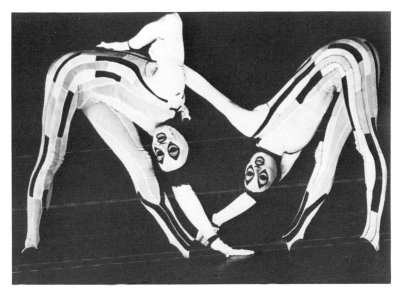

24. *Gallery*, Nikolais Dance Theater. Photograph by Jack Vartoogian. Courtesy of Nikolais/Louis Foundation for Dance

25. *Grotto*, Nikolais Dance Theater. Photograph by Oleaga. Courtesy of Nikolais/Louis Foundation for Dance

26. Bill T. Jones and Amy Pivar
in *Shared Distance*. Photograph
by Lois Greenfield. Courtesy of
Bill T. Jones and Arnie Zane

27. Senta Driver's *Missing Persons*
(Alan Danielson and Susan Hadley).
Photograph © 1987 by Johan Elbers.
Courtesy of Harry

28. *The Cage* by Jerome Robbins, New York City Ballet (female predator
Nora Kaye attacking Nicolas Magallanes). Courtesy of Dance Collection,
The New York Public Library at Lincoln Center, Astor, Lenox and Tilden
Foundations

29. Rudolf Nureyev in *Le Corsaire*. Photograph by Louis Peres. Courtesy of Dance Collection, The New York Public Library at Lincoln Center, Astor, Lenox and Tilden Foundations

30. *Dionysos Suite* by Maurice Béjart, Ballet of the Twentieth Century.
Photograph by William Dupont. Courtesy of ICM Artists Ltd

31. *Swan Lake* (prince and princess, Alexis Lermontov and Tamara Boum-
diyeva). Photograph by John L. Murphy. Courtesy of Sheldon Soffer Management

32. *Swan Lake* (Odette with her swans). Photograph by John L. Murphy.
Courtesy of Sheldon Soffer Management

33. *Relativity of Icarus* by Gerald Arpino, Joffrey Ballet (Russell Sultzback and Ted Nelson). Photograph by Herbert Migdoll

34. Bill T. Jones and Arnie Zane (choreographers/dancers). Photograph by
Robert Mapplethorpe. Courtesy of Bill T. Jones and Arnie Zane

35. Bill T. Jones and Arnie Zane challenge racist, sexist, and sexual assumptions in *Rotary Action*. Photograph by Lois Greenfield. Courtesy of Bill T. Jones and Arnie Zane

36. *Pli Selon Pli* by Maurice Béjart, Ballet of the Twentieth Century. Photograph by Costas

37. *Dionysos Suite* by Maurice Béjart, Ballet of the Twentieth Century (Tony Fabre and Philippe Lizon). Photograph by William Dupont. Courtesy of ICM Artists Ltd.

38. Jacques d'Amboise teaching National Dance Institute Class in
San Francisco, 1986. Photograph by Kim Stolper. Courtesy of National
Dance Institute

39. Kathakali male performers. Courtesy of Performing Arts Department,
The Asia Society

40. Indrani: Female dances male
and female roles in Kuchipudi.
Courtesy of Performing Arts
Department, The Asia Society

41. Eighteenth-century Turkish boy
dancing as female. Courtesy of Centre
for Dance Studies

42. Tamasaburo: male as female in Kabuki *Koyohime* (*The Cape of the Temple Bell*). Photograph © 1984 by Linda Vartoogian

43. Ubakala women. Photograph by William John Hanna

44. Ubakala men. Photograph by William John Hanna

III

WESTERN THEATER DANCE

6

Patterns of Dominance: Men, Women, and Homosexuality

Turning to American theater dance, I examine the dance occupation, its patterns of personnel recruitment and internal stratification, and the historical influence of social, political, and economic factors. These dance production and contextual factors help account for the social construction of knowledge through dance images of sexuality and gender that are described in the following chapters.

Dance today prompts an inevitable question question: Why do women and gay men predominate in Western theater ("high-culture") dance?[1] And why are men disproportionately the well-recognized choreographers and managers, and women the dancers (workers), notwithstanding a more balanced picture in the dance genres that developed after ballet? Although dance is an art form, it interweaves the

This chapter is a revision of papers presented at the Conference on Social Theory, Politics, and the Arts, University of Maryland, 1984, and the Annual Meeting of the American Anthropological Association, 1985. After my 1984 presentation, a male colleague said he was disturbed that it was not clear where I stood; I sounded like a feminist who did not deliver. However, my intent is to present facts, issues, and perspectives of participants involved in a process, not to advocate. Parts of this chapter appeared in *The Drama Review*, 1987, at the invitation of Richard Schechner, editor. I appreciate the helpful comments of Judith Scalin, Joan Zimmerman, Elizabeth Zimmer, Abbie Relkin, Anni Coplan, Daniel O'Connor, Tommi Short, Paula Levine, Jean Cunningham, Judith H. Balfe, Susan Cashion, Nancy Ruyter, Carol Martin, William John Hanna, Richard Schechner, and Ann Daly on various drafts. My gratitude goes to Barry Laine who shared his views and to Judith Schwarz who went through the Lesbian Herstory Archives for data on dancers.

ramifications of dancers, choreographers, and producers as individuals and as members of gender, ethnic, and/or economic groups also in a milieu of the cultural history of the women's and gay liberation movements and reactions to them.

History attests to the liability of being female or recognizably gay in the United States. Prestigious careers have been closed to the "weaker sexes" as they have been to waves of slaves and immigrants. Not only does work determine status and the use of time, but work reflects physical, psychological, social, and symbolic power.

How do nondominant groups cope with entry barriers to prestigious careers? In biological and social evolution, groups seek niches to which they adapt. They create new niches or fill those vacated or permitted by socially mobile groups. Notable examples of ethnic adaptation include hiding minority identity through assimilation (Thernstrom 1980). In the United States, the Jews found an occupational niche in the garment industry, as well as in film and entertainment fields not dominated by and exclusive to WASPs. Kept out of mainstream economic positions, the Chinese opened laundries and restaurants. Barred by discrimination from most of Los Angeles's economic activity, the Japanese moved into segments that whites did not want or had failed to exploit. On land considered too arid for farming, the Japanese grew and marketed various foods and flowers.

Women and gays, groups stigmatized in the United States in the sense of being subject to prejudice and discrimination, have sought escape from social and economic constraints. (Of course, some homosexuals easily hide their sexual preferences.) One option among many was to go into dance, a metonym and metaphor of existence, for life is movement. Since the French Revolution, dance has been a low-status occupation not sequestered by the dominant male group. Margaret Mead pointed out that "in every known society, the male's need for achievement can be recognized. Men may cook, or weave, or dress dolls or hunt hummingbirds, but if such activities are appropriate occupations of men, then the whole society, men and women alike, votes them as important. When the same occupations are performed by women, they are regarded as less important" (1949, 125). This chapter examines dance as a reflection of occupational opportunity and self-expression for males and females who have common as well as different goals and recruitment pathways to dance.

The reasons individuals go into dance vary (see Halpern 1981; Angioli 1982; Kirkland 1986). Economic opportunities are important. However, some people simply seek the pure joy of movement. Narcissism, desire to control audience reactions (seduce the audience), and exhibitionism are other motivating factors. Exhibitionism may be an attempt to confirm one's adequacy and self-worth through attracting positive audience acclaim. Dance may be partly an effort to enhance self-esteem related to a faulty body image, a need for others' approval, or proof of independence from one's family. Dance may also be a continuing reenactment of an approach-avoidance relationship with a parental figure. Although audience appreciation may temporarily enhance self-esteem, it may be counteracted if the individual has grown up or lives in an environment in which a stigma is attached to dancing.

Dance shares with other arts a gender-related prestige hierarchy. Like theater and symphony, dance is to some degree occupationally differentiated and sex segregated, separating the performers, choreographers/ composers, and directors/managers—the nondancing positions being more powerful and male-dominant. Women have less mobility across these career segments than men. They are rarely trained in other disciplines or in team sports that aid managerial skills. Whereas marriage or teaching are postperformance options for women, and most university dance departments are chaired by women (from modern dance), teaching, choreography, and management of larger-income enterprises have been career developments for men. For example, at thirty-seven, principal dancer Peter Martins retired, at the summit of his performing career with the New York City Ballet, to codirect the company and create dances. Ballet dancers are stratified into superstar, principal, soloist, and corps member. Sometimes there is also a male straight/gay distinction, the former considered more prestigious. Historically female dancers, and other female performing artists, have been perceived as immoral and peripheral to the main economy (Simpson and Simpson 1983). Dance performance offers seasonal rather than full-time employment and accepts people with alternative life-styles who deal with their differences, including homosexuality, through the artistic medium.

The dance world is unique among the performing arts in at least two respects. First, female challenges to male dominance have led to new genres and styles, as I explain later. Second, a person's career as a performer is short-lived because the instrument, the human body, ages and can no longer meet the physically strenuous demands; consequently, dancers retire in their thirty's and forty's, usually without pensions or retirement plans. The dancer also risks the ever-present hazards of physical injury (Hanna 1988).

Classical or dual economic theories (Linder 1983) alone are inadequate to explain the predominance of women and gay men in dance, with men disproportionately found in managerial roles. Classical economic theories postulate that workers earn the value of their products and that pay disparities between men and women reflect quality differences. Women are assumed to anticipate discontinuous employment and select occupations accordingly. The dual economy approach locates the source of earning differential between the sexes in the structure of society that is partitioned into distinct sectors, each with its own rules. To some extent, the typically low pay of predominantly female occupations may reflect their unequal location in the periphery sector.

Cultural history, including attitudes toward the body, emotion, and gender, must also be considered if one is to understand the patterns of male and female in dance. Today the American majority is beginning to view women in the dance profession as respectable and men who choose this career to be not deviant.

In the following overview of an art occupation, I sketch the reasons for various attitudes toward dance as a career in the United States, suggest how a nonprestigious domain of human behavior is used as a mechanism to cope with limited opportunity, and note how an occupation changes over time in a dialectic of the "battle of the sexes," with male dominance a persistent motif. Cutting a broad swath through western European and United States history, source of much theater dance heritage, I must simplify what is complex. And certainly there are exceptions to the trend. Although American and European cultures are unique, they share some developments. Parts of Europe experienced the feminization of culture (Douglas 1977) heralded by female American modern dancers who performed abroad (e.g., Loie Fuller and Isadora Duncan). Their counterparts in Europe founded and directed dance companies in Germany (e.g., Mary Wigman and Pina Bausch), Sweden (e.g., Birgit Cullberg), and England (e.g., Marie Rambert and Ninette de Valois). Today Europe and America also share each other's choreographers, dancers, and repertoires.

Gender and the Evaluation of Dance

Why did not prestigious male groups monopolize Western theater dance after the French Revolution? After all, throughout history renowned men have danced; societies have deemed dancing a natural male purusit and accorded such performance great esteem. Louis XIII danced and took on women's parts, in one piece playing the innkeeper's wife (Kisselgoff 1986).

Louis XIV of France (1643–1715), dancing in his roles as milkmaiden, king, or god Apollo, was glorified as the "Sun King," the epithet coming from a role he danced at age fifteen. The nobility acclaimed male peer dancing.

When Louis XIV ceased his dance performances, and his emulators among the twelve princes of the royal council also abdicated as centers of their respective dance universes, courtly social dance developed into a professional theatrical genre. The Judeo-Christian heritage that excluded women from active roles in public religious ritual carried over to secular theater (Brierley 1979). Because well-bred women did not appear on the public stage, men danced women's roles in travesty. Furthermore, because their dress was not so physically confining, men could be more virtuosic and thus gain respect for their individual dancing.

The French and Industrial revolutions (in the eighteenth and nineteenth centuries) dealt serious blows to the prestige of dance, sending it from the epitome of royal male performance to the nadir of "inferior" female performance. Among the sociopolitical elite, activities of the body became associated with moral laxity and impediments to economic productivity. Drawing upon the age-old biblical and Greek views of the potency of dance to express performers' emotions and to arouse spectators' feelings, the leaders of these revolutions negatively assayed male dancing as a distraction from their goals (Kern 1975). With its multisensory stimulation, coupled with cognition, the dancing body calls attention to sexuality and arouses emotions.

Other arts, too, have been considered outlets for emotion. Yet they do not use the body so directly and so primarily in their products. Bodily efforts are transformed and made "respectably" intellectual through brush, pen, violin, or verbal sound.

Because the cognitive dimensions of dance were generally unrecognized (Hanna 1987d, 1983a, 1983b), the kind of emotion linked to it contributed to perceptions of it. Although the Bible discusses two forms of dance—prayerful dance to God as a demonstration that no part of the individual is unaffected by the love of God, and Salome's immoral dance—popular unrestrained sexually arousing dances for men and women attracted church attention. Clerical distress about this kind of dancing led to its periodic proscription. Furthermore, Christianity has had a love-hate relationship with the body, the instrument of dance.

Christ was flesh, God's creation. Yet the flesh was denied. Western European culture for about two thousand years was based on the pervasive notion that the human is essentially a soul imprisoned for mysterious reasons in a body (Fallon and Wolbers 1982; see Davies 1984). Rejection of the body also reflects the inability to come to terms with the passing of time and death.

Already implicated in sin and deemed the enemy of spiritual life, the body became the foe of economic productivity (Kern 1975). Because the emergent French bourgeoisie attributed the collapse of the French monarchy in part to moral laxity, they transformed the body from an instrument of pleasure into one of production. In this way the middle class could protect its power. Self-control meant control of the body and, further, control of people who were primarily of the body. Similar attitudes developed with the rise of Protestantism and the machine age in England. Consequently, the dance profession received low financial remuneration and career interest from dominant-culture males.

Descartes's mind/body split survived capitalism, in which the foundation of work, not management, is "the selling of one's body to another for the purpose of making profit (surplus value)." The capitalist, on the other hand, exerted mental effort to increase profits (Goodman 1979, 116). The dance world reflects this pattern.

As the importance of dance declined, traditional ties between dancers and noble patrons disintegrated. Moreover, as men abnegated the dance profession—they had danced both male and female roles— women gained more performance opportunities.

However, female dancers on the public stage were thought to be part of the demimonde or echelons of prostitution.[2] "Ballet girl" had a pejorative connotation until the mid-twentieth century, and in some places it still does. Young female dancers were a source of sexual titilation and even gratification. Abonnés, regular opera subscribers, were their protectors. The ballet "leg show" enticed wealthy men who relished the sight and fell in love with the beautiful dancers, enduring their punishments of neglect and begging their rewards of intimacy. Becoming mistress to a wealthy man usually meant success and the option of leaving the stage. Some less fortunate dancers in the "parade" left the theater to become teachers or common prostitutes.

Today's respectable is often yesterday's outrageous or repugnant, as illustrated in the case of Indian classical dance. Until the mid-twentieth century, female performers generally came from the lower classes. For an attractive girl, dancing was an avenue of social mobility, an alternative to factory sweat shops, agriculture, or domestic work.

Certainly talented women who achieved acclaim and the attention, dalliance, and commitment of wealthy admirers were envied. Respectable wives envied the dancers' freedom from the burden and hazards of childbearing and from being "sexually cowed and emotionally brutalized" by husbands (Shorter 1982, 16). But respected, in the sense of the dominant culture's view of the proper female role, dancers were not. Ballerinas were branded by the stigma of working-class origins and sexual impropriety. The Paris Opéra backstage was the privileged venue of sexual assignation. Only a few superstars could overcome this handicap. Western dancers reported to share favors with well-to-do men include Albertine Coquillard, Pauline Duvernay, Fanny Elssler, Pauline Guichard, Cleo de Merode, Pauline Montessu, Lola Montez, Adeline Plunkett, Elisa Scheffer, and Clara Webster (Migel 1972).

In the mid-eighteenth century, when Marie Camargo shortened her skirt and removed her heels, gaining new physical freedom for active, proficient dancing, she, along with her peers La Barberina and Marie Sallé (reputed to be a lesbian) (Migel 1972, 25–29), entered what had been the male preserve of dance. Yet when Sallé danced to George Frideric Handel's *Alcina*, she was hissed because of her innovative yet "unbecoming" man's costume (Murphy 1985).

The eclipse of male supremacy in dancing onstage began in the 1830s when Marie Taglioni established a foothold for women, employing the toe dance as an essential element of ballet. Ushering in the Romantic Age (1831–47), a theater of dreams, Taglioni elevated herself on pointe, a prowess that became reserved for women. While the tight-fitting toe shoe, hardened by sturdy fabric and glue, restricts natural movement and perpetuates the ethos of female frailty and dependence upon male authority (even if played by a female), it also permits the dancer a range of movements, positions, and height impossible in other footwear. In a sense, the toe shoe raised women above the herd and out of the house. Engravings prior to 1820 provide evidence of the beginning of women's special technical innovation and virtuosity—a new fleet, subtle style with exotic, ethereal quality and precarious balance. Taglioni epitomized the fantasized ethereal centerpiece of the Romantic era in *La Sylphide*, choreographed for her by her father, Filippo Taglioni, in 1832. She expressed and embodied "the longing for the ideal . . . a skimming the earth, belonging less to it than to the night and sky" (Dunning 1984a).

Ballet celebrated the female dancer as its aesthetic quintessence. Ascendance of the female by 1840 created a revulsion against male dancers, and the audience discovered the charm of danseuse *en travesti*.

(On the courtly stages of Denmark and Russia, however, the male retained recognition even if overshadowed by the ballerina.) Female hussars danced in *Paquita*. In 1870 the prettiest girl in the Paris Opéra danced hero Franz in *Coppélia* (Guest 1966). Donning male clothing did not, as assumed in cross-dressing (see chap. 10), mean assuming the powers and prerogatives that go with male identity. Lynn Garafola (1985–86) suggests that the development of the danseuse *en travesti* eliminated the danseur, the remaining in-house obstacle to sexual license in the social class and bordello politics that governed theater corridors.

As I discuss in succeeding chapters, women's romantic ballet roles generally did not depict independent women but untouchable, elusive sylphs or earthy, sexual peasants, though not chattels for male enjoyment. There were also erotic, macabre *willis*, vengeful ghosts of betrayed women who died unwed; they condemned faithless men to dance to death. Perhaps the role of sylph symbolized the idealization of the female as "lady"—compensation for middle-class women's loss of a key economic role in the family with the onset of the Industrial Revolution.

Beautiful nineteenth-century ballerinas with uncanny skills of speed, technique, and elevation dominated onstage, while their stage partners bowed and scraped in the background. Most of the important male dancers of this period were married to female dancers in the traditional pattern of a theatrical family (e.g., Jules Perrot to Carlotta Grisi; Arthur Saint-Leon to Fanny Cerrito, and Salvatore Vigano to Maria Medina). Yet after the French Revolution, men who became professional dancers in Europe and the United States were increasingly assumed to be homosexual. Sometimes marriage was a cover. Ballet was tagged the "pansies' ball game" (Barnes 1974). In Russia, where dancers were recruited as children to audition for government-supported training out of economic necessity, heterosexuality may have been more common.

Although women came into the limelight and appeared to reign supreme, ballet continued under men's three-hundred-year dominance. We often speak of the woman behind the successful man. On the ballet stage, males were literally behind the females, not merely in partnering roles, analogues of patronage by the stronger of the weaker sex. Offstage, men retained control as ballet masters, choreographers, directors, and producers, and theater directors. They determined the work rules and chain of command: who held which rank and danced which role, how often, and with whom. Men aided Marie Camargo, who achieved equality with the premier danseur when she made her debut at the Paris Opéra in 1726. Marie Taglioni's father taught and managed her to create a legend.

Male dominance in ballet began with Louis XIV; Pierre Beauchamps was his dancer, choreographer, and recorder. Later, Jean-Georges Noverre argued for *ballet d'action* in which movement conveys dramatic action. In 1760 he laid the cornerstone of contemporary theatrical dance in *Lettres sur la danse et les ballets*. Then came such figures as Enrico Cecchetti and August Bournonville, the former noted for his method of ballet training, the latter for his choreography. Michel Fokine broke tradition by choreographing more equally featured movements for men and women during the Nijinsky era and eliminating the artificial conventions and acrobatics in ballet in favor of expressive movement. Impressario Sergei Diaghilev revived ballet as collaborative art.

Data on contemporary male dominance in dance comes from Don Moore, executive director of Dance USA, a service organization of the major ballet, modern, and ethnic dance companies in the United States (with the exception of the New York City Ballet). Member companies must meet minimum criteria—a $750,000 annual budget, full-time artistic director, twenty-two performances a year, and eighteen paid dancers for ballet companies; a $100,000 budget, paid artistic director and dancers, and regular performances for other companies. In 1984, out of seventy-five companies, approximately three-quarters had male managers. By 1986, out of sixty companies, 57 percent had male managers (34:26). However, the largest ballet companies, New York City Ballet, American Ballet Theatre, San Francisco Ballet, and the Boston Ballet, have male managers. A glance through the lists of companies in the United States and abroad in *Dance Magazine Annual* over the years nets a more male-dominant pattern.

In spite of ballet companies founded by women (for example, Ballet Rambert by Dame Marie Rambert, England's Royal Ballet by Ninette de Valois, American Ballet Theatre by Lucia Chase (and Richard Pleasant), Chicago Ballet by Ruth Page, Pennsylvania Ballet by Barbara Weisberger, and Boston Ballet by E. Virginia Williams), and the recognition of choreographers and directors Natalia Makarova, Twyla Tharp, Lynne Taylor-Corbett, and Martine van Hamel, male dominance persists to this day. The heritage of George Balanchine (creator of more than 150 ballets during his fifty years in the United States) and the activity of Jerome Robbins, Peter Martins, Robert Joffrey, Rudolf Nureyev, Mikhail Baryshnikov, Arthur Mitchell, and others is strong. Indeed, many companies founded by women were taken over by men (for example, Anthony Dowell at the Royal Ballet and Baryshnikov at American Ballet Theatre).

As wife to husband, so the dancer has been to choreographer: "Wives, submit yourselves unto your husbands as unto the Lord. For the husband is the head of the wife, even as Christ is the head of the Church" (Ephesians 6:22–23). Ballerina Gelsey Kirkland, formerly a Balanchine dancer at New York City Ballet and then a star at American Ballet Theatre, writes in her autobiography, *Dancing on My Grave* (1986, 40), that Balanchine was jealous of his female dancers dating. He wanted their sole devotion. Anthony Tudor said he, as all other choreographers, expected his dancers to treat him like God (Hunt 1987, 36).

Contemporary ballet choreographers and directors—"almost always male—mold ballet's young women to the ideal of femininity that equates beauty and grace with excessive thinness," an aesthetic that is punitive and misogynist (Gordon 1983, 173, also 155). Pert-breasted, narrow-hipped women evoke the male fantasy of deflowering the virgin. Relentless pursuit of the unnatural "ideal" female body arrests puberty, imbalances hormones, contributes to hypothermia and low blood pressure, and often leads to psychosomatic disorders of starvation, vomiting, and use of laxatives that are related to injury. Balanchine receives much credit for the female "anorexic look." Kirkland recalls his demand for starvation: "He halted class and approached me for a kind of physical inspection. With his knuckles, he thumped on my sternum and down by rib cage clucking his tongue and remarking, 'Must see the bones.'. . . He did not merely say, 'Eat less.' He said repeatedly, 'Eat nothing'" (1986, 56).

Male choreographers and managers treat dancers like children, school them in obedience and deference, call women "girls" (and men "boys"). Richard LeBlond, sociologist and president of San Francisco Ballet, was shocked at first to see "an enforced infantilism" in some ballet schools (*Update Dance USA* 1983, 2).

In her journal, Toni Bentley, another Balanchine dancer, reflected, "It's a pity he needs 100 individuals as his tools rather than paint brushes. What would have happened if Van Gogh's brushes one day had refused to be manipulated because they wanted better living conditions?" (1982, 89). Women dancers are a garden of beautiful flowers, and man is the gardener. For Balanchine, they were angels through which he shaped icons for the laity (Kirstein 1984). "Like the pope represents Christ, I represent terpsichore" (quoted in Saal 1983, 89). Kirkland confirmed: Balanchine "assembled steps that were supposed to have been predetermined by God and humbly described himself as an instrument of divine will. His word was holy" (1986, 50).

Alan M. Kriegsman (1983) observed: "There was a conspicuous irony in his admiration of America and its ways—he adored democracy, insisted on a 'no-star' system of rank and publicity in his company, and ruled it in as absolute and totalitarian a fashion as those of the czars and commissars. He looked upon the company as his children, and they submitted to his hegemony over their lives, for the most part, willingly and unquestioningly. He was also capable of being petty, even cruel, on occasion, and he could be ruthlessly demanding in pursuit of perfection: the number of dancers reduced to tears in class or rehearsal was legion." Former Soviet citizen and dancer Ivan Valery Panov, who had lived in a political system with tight control over nearly every aspect of an individual's life, said of a New York City Ballet visit to the USSR, "I felt a certain dehumanization of company talents in the brilliant but easily forgettable scenes. The expression of the choreographer's genius reduced dancers to marvelously precise moving parts of his schematic machine. I could actually feel their subordination to his will—which is why I saw Balanchine and only Balanchine, even in his most gifted ballerinas (1978, 340).

Even when a woman contributes to ballet choreography (a male bailiwick), she is not likely to receive due recognition. Bronislava Nijinska made an important career as a classical ballet choreographer, with about fifty ballets to her credit. (Marie Sallé and Birgit Cullberg also had choreographic careers of some importance.) When poet-critic Edwin Denby saw Nijinska's masterpiece *Les Noces* (*The Wedding*) performed in 1936 (first produced in 1923 by the Diaghilev company), he said it was one of the finest things one could see anywhere. John Martin (1937) called it "a work of undeniable genius in an even more radically reformed style of movement." About fifty years later, Kriegsman, asked how so highly esteemed a masterpiece could have escaped the attention of the contemporary ballet public, which by and large had heard of Nijinska only as the sister of Vaslav Nijinsky. Kriegsman proffers that *Les Noces* has evaded its due fame, not merely because of the cost and difficulty of producing the work, but because "it was [her lot] to be both a woman in a man's profession . . . and the sister of the most prodigiously adulated virtuoso in ballet history."[3]

The deprecation and relegation of dance to the nonessential, the vulgar, and the primitive created an obstacle for the growth of dance in the United States until the mid-twentieth century. Furthermore, at the end of the American Revolution, dance style echoing European courtly demeanor was an anathema to other than the rich.

Less than half a century ago, the downgraded ballet began gaining a more respectable status in America, partly due to a decrease of puritanism and an increase in exposure to Diaghilev's superb dancers and choreographers. Dance was given a boost toward respectability when high society and great family fortunes, followed by foundation resources, supported American ballet companies. The establishment of the National Endowment for the Arts Dance Program in 1965 provided further legitimization of dance.

Prior to these developments, many literary and artistic individuals had fixated on the dancers (the good-time girls or prostitutes) of the "decadent" music halls of the 1890s, which continued in some transformation up through the topless and bottomless discos of the later twentieth century. Vaudeville was the setting for the incipient ballet in America and the development of what was called modern dance (a new form of theater art in rebellion against ballet), both of which flourished by the 1960s (Kendall 1979). Pioneers of modern dance drew themes and strategies from the popular theater of their times rather than from the tradition of ballet.

The advent of modern dance in the 1920s, pioneered by educated middle-class women of strong character (such as Ruth St. Denis and Martha Graham, both of whose parents trained in medicine), and the creation of university dance programs (Margaret H'Doubler's at the University of Wisconsin in 1926 was the first), helped make a dance career respectable, at least for women. A dance career for men continued to be questionable.

For example, choreographer Brian Macdonald said his family wanted him to be a lawyer, and his refusal was paramount to disinheritance: "The day I joined the National Ballet of Canada in 1951, my father changed his will. He died without ever changing it back" (quoted in Stoop 1984, 62). Of the younger generation, choreographer/dancer Douglas Dunn, trained in art history at Princeton University, said his parents, both doctors, were not happy with his career choice. A 1980 "pulse reading" on attitudes toward dance came from Ronald Reagan's campaign headquarters: the politicians, concerned with reactions of the Moral Majority, seemed embarrassed that, as the *Washington Post* (June 25, 1980) put it, "While his dad does the White House waltz, Ronald P. Reagan, 22, is jete-ing for the Joffrey II Dancers." Only in movies did men have big careers in dance, and their genre was not ballet or modern but jazz, tap, social, and popular.

Dance for Women's Liberation: Indict, Dismantle, Create

Turn-of-the-century modern dance was in part a rebellion against male domination in both dance and society. Role strain characterized the Victorian era, a period of rapid change. While men were expected to be sexually aggressive, the middle class was at the same time expected to be self-denying so as to serve the needs of the bureaucratized industrial society of managers, professionals, and entrepreneurs. Charles Rosenberg speaks of the expository metaphor of the mercantilist body, an image of "a closed energy system, one which could be either weakened through the discharge of energy or strengthened through its prudent husbanding" (1973, 243). The work imperative demanded that men bottle up emotion, repress sex, and regulate population. There were also conflicting streams of religious thought about sexuality. Whereas some theologians embraced sexual passion as redemptive and innocent ecstasy (the body was redeemed by accepting its desires) (Gardella 1985), other theologians adhered to a degeneracy theory (too much sex made people sick) (Money 1985).

Women's bodies were viewed as thoroughly saturated with sexuality and governed by sex-linked irrationality (Foucault 1978, 6). Slotted as they were, daring women in the nineteenth and twentieth centuries who were cut off from male prerogatives took advantage of the behavior attributed to their gender: they acted emotionally through the physical medium of dance, drawing upon what researchers have recently documented to be their superior sensitivity to nonverbal communication as well as their "emotionality" (Henley 1977; Hall 1979a). Men generally manifested emotion indirectly through other more "intellectual" arts.

Women's critique of the nineteenth-century system that excluded them from key economic and political roles and relegated them to the home and the realm of morals took a variety of forms. Women created new fields such as modern dance, social work, kindergarten teaching, and librarianship rather than compete in male professions. Affirmation and female control of the body was one thrust of the women's critique. In the birthing and further development of modern dance, women looked to themselves for inspiration as they formed female-dominated dance companies similar to the small businesses that ethnic groups owned, controlled, and found to be vital instruments of upward mobility. About her 1937 *Trend*, a signature work that depicted a society being destroyed by its false values, early modern dance trailblazer Hanya Holm reflected in 1984: "The subject matter would still be good today. . . . only women danced it. There were no men then. . . . women at that time had to be as strong as a man would be (quoted in Dunning 1984b).

Emphatically beyond traditional domestic life to which women had been relegated, theater dance epitomizes a public world. From a cross-cultural perspective, women appear oppressed or lacking in value and status to the extent that they are relegated to the domestic world: "Women gain power and a sense of value when they are able to transcend domestic limits, either by entering the men's world or by creating a society" (Rosaldo and Lamphere 1974, 41).

Through modern dance and its affirmation of the female body, women chose to be agent rather than object. Constrained economically as well as physically by male-imposed dress styles that distorted the body and hampered natural movement, by restricted education, and by health practices that prevented, them from breathing fresh air and eating a sensible diet, some innovative women displayed their strength and their displeasure with traditional roles by breaking the rules of the rigidly codified traditional ballet. They extended the boundaries of dance with revolutionary movement vocabularies, grammars, composition techniques, themes, and costumes. Women offered new dance systems and images alongside the *danse d'école* developed by men. Showing their new choreography onstage invited audience admiration, empathy, and contact, perhaps relieving some women's male-imposed feelings of social and physical insignificance.

The dance medium also permitted women to control and sublimate their sexuality, which had been dominated by men. To get ahead in an uncharted avant-garde, some women needed a nunlike dedication; other middle- and upper-class respectable women in dance had love affairs in and out of marriage to show their new sense of social/sexual equality.

Asserting themselves as individuals against traditional female destiny, ground-breaking American modern dancers through onstage dress helped to de-corset wasp-waisted females. Tight lacing oppressed the body and enforced sexual taboos, whereas unlacing signified sexual release. While the corset worn in ballet helped pull up the body and enabled the woman's male partner to get a good grip when lifting her, it also prevented from feeling her flesh (Kunzle 1982, 84). What women wore closely mirrored their changing role in American society. The rigid female silhouette of earlier years collapsed with the quest for changes in feminine education, health, and professional opportunity. Intrigued with the interplay of body, intellect, and spirit, female dancers investigated and experimented. Braless, corsetless, and bare-foot, most modern dancers' free style of dress symbolized physical freedom and a renewed, diversified self image.[4] As the twentieth century progressed, taboos on what parts of the body could be shown slowly disappeared. With the advent of tights and new dance movement, spectators saw the body—crotches, asses, thighs, and breasts—from every possible angle.

Modern dancers' aggressiveness paralleled women's late nineteenth- and twentieth-century questioning of patriarchy, which included change in conventions surrounding choice of a spouse, rise of marital equality and mutual decision making, campaigns for women's suffrage and higher education, and middle-class women's entry into the labor market during and after World War II. Modern dancers extended women's fight to gain control over their own bodies (Degler 1980; Douglas 1977).

Initially women's achievement, modern dance bore their style-setting stamps. Females were choreographers, dancers, company founders, and managers. They established schools. Harbingers of innovation include Loie Fuller, Isadora Duncan, and Ruth St. Denis; later, Martha Graham, Doris Humprhey, Agnes de Mille (combining modern and Broadway styles in the ballet idiom); and more recently, Yvonne Rainer, Trisha Brown, Twyla Tharp, Laura Dean, Senta Driver, Johanna Boyce, and Lucinda Childs. Critic Anna Kisselgoff (1985) notes, "A premise about movement became a basis for a dance technique in each case and, by extension, became a metaphor for an esthetic—for what each dancer wished to say through her dancing." Modern dance stood for freedom for personal expression through one's own movement idiom.

Duncan (1938, 49, 56, 69, *passim*) believed ballet projected a socially pernicious image of women: virginal, disembodied *sylphide*, frail, sexually passive. She denounced the recruitment of dancers from the slums as exploitation of the rich by the poor and a perversion of artistic values in favor of the prurient. Considering movement to be an antidote to the rigidities of modern life, Duncan, with messianic zeal, founded schools for children.

St. Denis, mother of the most flourishing lineage of modern dance, began her career in the flurry of vaudeville. There she had performed her rapid-fire stunts about eleven times a day on a stage adjacent to the presentation of midgets and two-headed calves in jars. She turned to exotica, for non-Western cultures offered visual beauty and spiritual messages, in contrast to Western industrial life. The critique of traditional women's options through new forms of dance was thus in some ways indirect and symbolic; ballet choreographers had also drawn upon exotic cultures, but to make their art innovative.[5] In a 1932 address to the students of Barnard College, St. Denis said, "Today is woman's hour. It is woman's chance to offset what men may be doing in the realm of politics and war. It is woman's place to foster and develop the cultural forces of civilization." She lauded the plans for a new World's Fair that would include the placing of "the dance upon a level of dignity and power" (*New York Times*, June 4, 1932).

Graham's movement vocabulary redefined the art of dance: stunning, sharp, and percussive patterns of torso contraction and release (movements corresponding to life's breathing, sexual tension, agony and ecstasy), twisting and spiraling spinal movements (ballet focused on limbs, with the torso held as a single unit), parallel and inwardly rotated positions of the legs (ballet uses a turnout), flexed feet (ballet feet are pointed), an Egyptian-inspired walk in which feet move in one direction while the upper body twists open against that base, pelvic isolation, and falls to the floor. Graham thematically presented earthy and socially relevant Sturm und Drang dynamics dealing with dominance, unbridled passion versus duty, attraction and repulsion, and submerged guilt and open eroticism to counter ballet's ethereal fantasies. She began teaching in 1925. Former Graham dancer Ernestine Stodelle (1984), in an uncritical apologia for her mentor, believes that dancers who flocked to Graham (active as a dancer and choreographer over nearly six decades—the longest creative period of any choreographer) came to identify with an ideal and a person greater than themselves who symbolized the creative act.

A younger writer and dancer, Eleanor Luger, puts into words what has been a resoundingly female theme: "What I have been interested in from a woman's point of view, what I have experienced in my own dancing, is trying to tie up movement with one's own image as a woman" (Luger and Laine 1978, 66). Movements carry the inner feelings and cultural overlays of sexuality and sex role identities. As I elaborate in chapter 9, much choreography by females centered on heroic women who took fate into their own hands, if only, says critic Jochen Schmidt, "with an axe, like Lizzie Borden in Agnes de Mille's *Fall River Legend*, who murdered her parents in order to free herself from their rules and strictures" (1983, 18). Graham portrayed settler women of America's pioneer history in *Frontier* and *Appalachian Spring*. She also dealt with the great lovers and haters of Greek tragedy.

Contributing to the foundation for the popular androgyny of the 1980s, exemplified by singer Michael Jackson, some women such as Anna Halprin and Meredith Monk fulfilled their gender movement impulses and went on to express in performance the male and female possibilities within us all. That is, either or both sexes do the same movements in abnegation of stereotyped gender actions. Monk also has experimented with makeup and costuming to obscure sex identity; for example, she sometimes wears a mustache. Senta Driver's choreography extends women's early use of "male" weight and power by reversing dancers' traditional gender roles: her women lift and carry men.

Participants in postmodern dance (Banes 1980), a rebellion against modern dance that both women and men have been developing since the 1960s, have tended to deemphasize sexuality and gender-specific movement, which audience members may, nonetheless, still perceive. Growing in tandem with an increasing acceptance of recreational sex and unisex dress and behavior, a postmodern dance gained much of its inspiration from Merce Cunningham, who had been a Graham discovery, protégé, and company member. As part of the movement to give men more substantive roles onstage, discussed later, Cunningham did away with the need for dance to follow a musical structure, story, psychological pattern, or even the demands and rules of traditional theater. "His experiments with chance procedures and his attempts to defocus the conventional proscenium stage have resulted in dances which affirm the trained body's ability to move in any direction at any time across any space at speed and intensity" (Anderson 1970). Cunningham did, however, retain the Graham curved back and free spine and upper torso as well as the turned-out, extended legs of classical ballet.

Barry Laine noted a gender bias in the New Wave 1981, 1982, and 1983 Brooklyn Academy of Music series of interdisciplinary, collaborative presentations, an avant-garde sequel to post modern minimalism. "Of eleven programs of produced choreography . . . only one featured male choreographers (Bill T. Jones and Arnie Zane). . . . Can we conclude that . . . [new] dance is still dominated by female creativity?" (1983b, 64).

Female dancers have thus challenged the typical male supremicist and female submissive scripts. Women, and some men, now call for men to pay attention to their own bodies and sensuality so that they may discover physical desires apart from a socialized desire to dominate. Joseph Pleck (1979) argues that the relative privilege and false consciousness of it that men get from sexism may allow them to reconcile their subordination in the larger political economy. Keeping women as an underclass reduces the stress of competition and preserves a level to which man cannot fall. Because male powerlessness or refusal to compete becomes imbued with the imagery of homosexuality, male domination of females in dance may prop up the level of social prestige to which men cannot fall.

Gay and Men's Liberation

Having addressed the part of the question about female participation in dance, I now turn to why male homosexuals are disproportionately attracted to dance. On the fringe of society and receptive to the unconventional, the art world offers gay men an opportunity to express an aesthetic sensibility that is emotional and erotic, an insulation from a rejecting society, an avenue of courtship, and an arena in which to deal with homosexual concerns. It has been argued that "the male homosexual has found the means to *pass* by identifying himself as artistic/romantic rather than simply gay. So the social rejection on the basis of sexuality is refocused by the justification of art."[6] Especially important for the perpetuation of dance as a magnet for gays was nondancer Sergei Diaghilev, himself gay, founder and director of the Ballets Russes, and renowed in the twentieth-century art world for over two decades. Gay dancers basked in the aura of the respect showered upon Diaghilev. Seeds for homosexual themes onstage were sown when he introduced his lover Vaslav Nijinsky to the West in 1909.

Barry Laine, a gay American writer and amateur dancer, has said that homosexual males who pursue a dance career do not have as much to lose as other males (pers. com. 1980). Because gays have already broken the compact of mainstream sexual behavior, their occupational deviancy is less threatening to them. Although some Americans consider homosexuality immoral or sick behavior, the arts professions, marginal themselves, historically have been tolerant of all kinds of marginality, including homosexual orientation.

In *Alienated Affections: Being Gay in America*, English professor Seymour Kleinberg writes about the homosexual sensibility of elegance, sensitivity, and ironic distance between the self and the world and "aesthetic discrimination of the finest sort"—whose mythic impact has been felt in the elite culture of the arts (1980, 38, *passim*). Writer Stanley Crouch remarks that elitist members of scorned minority groups, "rather than accept inferior definitions of themselves or develop a stoic dream of equality . . . they draw up their own maps to the land of the aristocrats and define themselves as a chosen people suffering at the hands of insecure and sadistic barbarians. This probably accounts for the obsession so many homosexuals have with taste, art, style, and minute detail—in lieu of procreation, it allows association with the ageless greatness of human history" (1982, 13).[7]

Kleinberg (1980) calls male homosexual sensibility feminine and erotic. Male dancers share more with females and are expected to be more emotionally expressive than mainstream American men, who are allowed to show emotion physically only in such well-defined situations as celebrating athletic success, when they break taboos against men touching by patting each other on the buttocks and hugging. Gay men identify with the effeminate yearnings, feelings, and romantic idealization of the ballet, which is not marked by sexual preference so much as by sexual grace for both sexes.

Moreover, in presenting an image of interaction between men and women that is rarely consummated, ballet presents an illusion experienced by some gay men as parallel to their relationships with women and the difficulties some gays have in establishing long-term relationships with each other. Dance themes may permit homosexuals to play roles demanded by society that they cannot fulfill in real life.

Asked about whether there is such a thing as gay sensibility, choreographer Christopher Beck replied, "It goes beyond homoerotic themes. . . . I'm striving to balance out 'male' and 'female,' 'form' and 'feeling.' This is a very important aspect of the gay aesthetic" (quoted in Laine 1980a, 30).

Dance companies usually have a self-containment that insulates a male against the plight of being homosexual in a heterosexual society that assaults their ego and validity; this plight conjoins with that of the low-paid artist in a materialist culture. In the world of ballet, male homosexuals can compensate for self-questioning, and even self-loathing, and can sustain a sense of personal and social strength through identification with a powerful ballet master, choreographer, or director as well as an accepting group. Besides, gay men as men can still feel themselves to be superior to women in Western culture. Gay male dancers attain perfection and power through the rigorous, esoteric demands of ballet training with its ritualistic language, dress, and studio-stage routines. But this concentration brings with it the danger of ridicule from males engaged in athletics, business, or war. Through dance, gay men set themselves apart from the outside world to which they assign imperfection and from which they feel rejected. At the same time, positive heterosexual audience reaction to "superhuman" physical and artistic achievements onstage indicates acceptance and enhances a performer's self-esteem.

Kenneth Plummer (1975, 180) suggested that although homosexuality was a stigmatized and feared identity, some individuals declared their homosexuality because they were unable to withstand the pressure of leading a double life. It is possible that some men who entered dance may have chosen this way to "come out." Access to supportive others neutralizes or strengthens homosexual sensitivity (p. 136). Another possibility is that the public openness facilitated meeting sexual partners—dancing may be an audition for lovers. By the same token, the hours of intense sensuality and physicality in dance can substitute for sexual consummation.

Because the dance profession offers a more physically and psychically integrated presence than the typical nine-to-five world of work, dance provides opportunities to explore the range of unconventional options without the consequences of real-life sanctions. During times of men's somber dress, ballet has had the attraction of colorful costume, glamour, and makeup.

Men in America aggressively compete in sports, business, and love. Not only does dance combine this masculine expression with unabashed athletic feats, but it also allows graceful communicativeness or romantic interdependence. The act of men dancing together may create a sense of belonging and a return to basic human relations unimpeded by industrialism's distortion of the natural rhythms of social life. Laine (1979) said that gay or bisexual men often find their way into the arts because they sense (consciously or not) that the arts make it easier for them to explore their homosexuality.

Members of the Mangrove all-male workshop (which includes straights and gays) explore their physical parameters in contact improvisation, a dance form that arises from spontaneous interaction rather than from a predetermined pattern. They play with the physical laws of mass, gravity, momentum, and inertia. Eventually they lose the self-consciousness that accompanies close physical contact with another person's knees, chest, pelvis, soles of the feet, neck, and armpits. Improvisors take risks in the "on-goingness." One dancer said, "We struggle to share our vulnerabilities as well as our strengths." Another remarked, "The impact of several men dancing in a group can be overwhelming: our size, our smell, our presence, not to mention the social/sexual dynamics which arise." Emile Durkheim pointed out, "It is only by expressing their feelings, by translating them into signs, by symbolizing them externally, that the individual consciousnesses, which are, by nature, closed to each other, can feel that they are communicating and in unison." (1964, 336).

Certainly money and its power were not the attractions for men who followed a dance profession, because dancers are paid very little. Most could not easily support a wife and family on their earnings, a requirement to be a "real man" in America. Because women could marry and be supported by their husbands, they could indulge in the arts, which most Americans considered a luxury rather than a necessity.

What about lesbians in dance? They were probably always present, as in other fields, but were not visible. The literature on this subject is scant. Perhaps gay men were more visible because male homosexuality was against the law and harshly punished in some Western countries; thus men became politically active to confront the discrimination.[8] Male homosexuality was a capital crime at the time of Henry VIII. The English law that Americans inherited in the colonial era led to male homosexuals being hanged, castrated, jailed, and lobotomized (Oaks 1980). However, although a 1656 New Haven law prescribed the death penalty for male homosexuality, lesbianism was not generally a crime (Katz 1976). Puritan men may have thought only males were capable of experiencing and acting on sexual attraction to their own sex. Furthermore, lesbianism is often sexually arousing to heterosexual males.

According to Vern Bullough, one reason lesbianism was not prosecuted was that the "male establishment was convinced that most women knew nothing at all about the subject, and to pass a law against lesbianism would make women feel guilty about their own gregariousness. The male establishment was willing to tolerate lesbianism, convinced of their own superiority" (1976, 582). These men dismissed what women could do together on the grounds that it did not amount to much. "Only when it threatened their status or position in society did they move against it" (p. 446). Men may have denied lesbianism because "to see women as sexually independent is bound to challenge notions of male dominance and seeing women as mothers touches on the deeply-rooted ambiguities about women as life-giver or castrator" (Wandor 1981, 78).

Without court cases against them, lesbians had no compelling reason for a public campaign on the matter. Their interests were closely associated with the oppression of all women, and they did not want the added burden of society's hostility to their sexual preference (Wandor 1981; Katz 1976; Vance 1984; Weeks 1985). Women are vulnerable financially and socially. After a woman has trained herself to her

potential in dance, given the difficult, time-consuming work demanded, she may not want to take on publicly, in addition to the
identity of a dancer, the even less acceptable identity of lesbian. Loie
Fuller, choreographer-dancer Wendy Perron (1980) argues, would have
been more generally seen as a founder of American modern dance if she
had not been so obviously a lesbian. Fuller predated Duncan in her love
of natural movement and in her belief that individuals can find their
own approach to dance. In 1900 it was Fuller who presented Duncan
to Viennese society. However, Duncan was reluctant to be associated
with Fuller's dozen or so beautiful girls who grouped about her, stroking
her hands and kissing her.

Over the past two hundred years society has been slow to accept men
as professional dancers. (The show business dance of Broadway musi-
cals and Hollywood films, which permitted conventional male images
and incomes, was exempt from the sissified and effete image.) Critic
Walter Terry said, "Equal rights for male dancers in America has not
been really realized even as the 20th century draws to its close" (Terry
1978, 28; see Bland and Percival 1984).

Men's reemergence in dance, the abatement of audience preference
for female dancers, and homosexual expression onstage gained impetus
when Diaghilev introduced Vaslav Nijinsky, forerunner of the
twentieth-century American male dancer, to the West. The Diaghilev
era (1909–29) lauded the virtuosity and passion of the Russian male
dancers and of Adolph Bolm and George Rosai. Nijinsky created a
sensation with his unsurpassable standards of excellence, phenomenal
technical pyrotechnics (as in his enormous leap through a window in *Le
Spectre de la Rose*), mesmerizing stage presence, and sensuous virility.
His provocative androgynous mystique appealed to both women and
men. Perhaps the first ballet that totally belonged to its male lead, *Le
Spectre de la Rose* was, Marcia Siegel notes, "an extension of both the
effete prince and the sensuous but not quite real character part" (1977,
104). The ballet is a vision conjured up by a girl who has just been to
a ball; the male character is perhaps "a virgin's ideal man in 1911," a
nonthreatening, nondemanding partner who defers to her and allows
her to assert herself without losing her femininity.

Another of Diaghilev's ballet stars who promoted the role of the male
dancer was Serge Lifar. He embodied the physical beauty and nobility
of the romantic hero and excelled as a dancer. "In addition to successes
in the classical repertory, Lifar created roles in such precedent-
shattering works as Balanchine's *Apollon Musagète* and *The Prodigal*

Son . . . true heroes at last, not just gilded playthings come to life"
(Siegel 1977, 105).

Recall that before Nijinsky's time, the proximity of dance to social,
economic, and political power (as in the era of Louis XIV), had sharply
declined with the French and Industrial revolutions. Men were less
attracted to professional theater dance, and women in the profession
outnumbered men. Then, with the invention of the toe shoe in the
nineteenth-century, the role of the male dancer was reduced still
further to that of a simple porteur, sometimes a handsome cavalier foil,
lugging the ballerina around while making her look charmingly
featherweight (the women were not as thin nor as well-trained as they
are today!). But the impetus for dance to become a respectable
profession for men did not go far after Nijinsky and Lifar.

While numerically women dominated ballet onstage but not off
during the first half of the twentieth century, they dominated the "first
phase" of modern dance both onstage and off, as choreographers and
company managers. With the exception of Ted Shawn and Charles
Weidman, few men were in modern dance during its early years.
Shawn, the self-styled "papa" of American modern dance, eventually
married Ruth St. Denis; they cochoreographed many works and
cofounded the Denishawn School. Later, Shawn, a bisexual, founded
his own all male company. Charles Weidman, a 1920s student of Doris
Humphrey's at the Denishawn School, formed a company with her in
1928.

Women's dominance in modern dance catalyzed a reaction from
men. Shawn said male dancers were necessary if dancing was to have
any weight or depth at all. For him dance without men was like a
symphony played only by piccolos and violins. Reflecting a prevalent
male chauvinism as well as his turbulent personal relationship with St.
Denis, Shawn wanted to restore male dancing to the dignity he believed
it possessed in ancient Greece. Breaking away from St. Denis, he
selected proven athletes and established the Ted Shawn and His Men
Dancers company in 1933 to present the male dancer as "jock." He
proselytized dance through athletics (his dances include fencing,
dribbling a ball, and shooting baskets) and championed "virile" dancing. *Kinetic Molpai* was one of his most famous works. The 1936
Olympia piece on sports was also a success. Terry (1976), who meets the
issue of Shawn's homosexuality with candor, finds irony in the effort
and time Shawn's Men Dancers spent trying to prove that they were not
what Shawn and many members of the company were. Barton

Mumaw, a principal Shawn dancer and his lover, said that their relationship could not be divulged because knowledge of it would have destroyed Shawn's campaign to establish a respected role for men in serious dance. Mumaw was even forbidden to use Shawn's first name in public. Shawn was fortunate to have the cooperation of those who were in a position to reveal his secret and wreck his enterprise (Sherman and Mumaw 1986).

Shawn developed a training system for the American male body that was based upon experience with his own six-foot, 175-pound frame. This heroic, athletic "he-man" stance seems to have been a defensive reaction to society's negative attitude toward male dancers. Later, José Limón created dances for an all-male cast. But he tended to choreograph for the particular qualities of men as a contrast or complement to those of women.

One of the most famous Denishawn students was Martha Graham, whose own dances until the late 1930s were for women. Then, in 1938, Erick Hawkins, a Harvard University student captivated by dance, became a member of Graham's company and in 1948 her husband for a short time after nine years of their living together. Graham's choreographic use of strong effort, resistance, sheer physical strength, gymnastics, and simple, direct angular patterns, as well as her portrayal of key male characters from Hebrew and Greek mythology and American history, appealed to American men, even though the central role was always danced by a woman.

Like St. Denis, Graham spawned a male reaction. Graham's artistic progeny determined the profile of the male-dominated "second phase" of modern dance. Hawkins went on to become one of America's prominent dancers and choreographers. He saw that ballet favored the· female and that modern dance glorified women. Disturbed about his own identity as a male dancer in America, he went on a pilgrimage of insight, spending an entire summer driving through New Mexico and Arizona where he watched American Indian ceremonials. "I had to see and feel whether a grown man could dance without being a fool" (quoted in Kisselgoff 1980, 43). He looked to non-American cultures in the world for male role models in dance. (Indeed, as exemplified by St. Denis and Hawkins, America's modern dance strength stems in large measure from its cross-pollination of different peoples' aesthetics.) Moreover, Hawkins developed a movement idiom influenced by Buddhism that emphasized harmony with nature and human constitution in contrast to the ballet and Graham styles.

Key male dancer-choreographers besides Hawkins also began with but then broke away from Graham, for example, Paul Taylor, John Butler, and Merce Cunningham. Other notable male choreographers, too, were protégés of women. Alwin Nikolais studied with Hanya Holm; José Limón with Doris Humphrey; and Daniel Nagrin with Helen Tamiris. In 1961 John Martin commented on how times had changed in the modern dance: the bulk of the season was male. However, he thought only one choreographer, Alvin Ailey, had come up with anything "that invites a second seeing," namely *Hermit Songs*.

Choreographers of the 1950s and 1960s, such as Nikolais and subsequent postmodern dancer-choreographers, eschewed male and female polarized stereotypes in favor of unisex movements and androgynous dancers. About sexuality and gender, Nikolais explained, "I've always abhorred the idea of male and female as opposed, as if we were all walking around in heat. Modern society forces you to be a sexual object rather than a person" (quoted in Dunning 1985).

Dance was an open field for some groups to enter and develop, although women and men of respectability did not dance onstage. But dance has been a vehicle to transform stigma to stardom; a deviant figure on the knife's edge of creativity could become a charismatic attraction.

Big Bucks and the Challenge

Since the 1960s and the resounding dance boom following World War II, male superstars such as Soviet defectors Nureyev and Baryshnikov have earned "big money" and the respect it brings. Six-digit incomes encouraged heterosexual men to enter dance and claim an honorable status. Sexual identity, dance, and economic opportunity jostled comfortably together.

Nureyev's 1961 defection from the Kirov Ballet marked the full re-ascendance of the male dancer begun by Diaghilev's stars. In 1987 the thirty-sixth Capezio Dance Award recognized Nureyev for revolutionizing the male role in contemporary ballet. He made the male adagio as exciting as the ballerina's, and, melding animal agility with human finesse, his dancing was bigger and more sexual than other men's. Protean Nureyev, a leading example of a danseur's bravura, resembled some athletes—dashing, flamboyant, temperamental, arrogant—but not heterosexual. He reached an audience in the tens of millions through a phenomenal schedule of appearances on five continents during more than twenty years and through television and films.

Asserting male dominance in areas once securely reserved for women, Nureyev stole the spotlight from "ballet is woman," as Balanchine, Russian émigré with a predilection for ballerinas, put it. "Born into an age of resurgent male dance, Nureyev," wrote Arlene Croce, "has become the usurper, encroaching on the ballerina's territory with extensions of the Prince's role. . . . Nureyev's career may be understood in part as an attempt to gain and hold center stage without a repertory that places him there" (1982, 165). In the Russian tradition of changing the classics through the sensibilities of successive choreographers, Nureyev modified the nineteenth-century fixation on the ballerina at the expense of the male dancer and expanded male roles. In his first reworking of Marius Petipa's *Don Quixote* in 1966, he retained the story of the love between the barber Basilio and the young girl Kitri but changed the choreography to give the male role more emphasis. He also created original works such as *Tancredi, Romeo and Juliet,* and *Manfred.* The latter, based on Byron's 1817 poem of the same title, highlights the Byronic male outsider hero who is not bound by society's mores and expectations (Steinbrink 1983). Nureyev has said that men are better at everything. "You don't kneel to women. You mistrust them" (quoted in the *Washington Post,* July 25, 1983, p. 3).

Maurice Béjart, choreographer of the Ballet of the Twentieth Century, also pioneered an antidote to the female preeminence onstage in classical ballet. Preferring the male image, and finding inspiration in folk dance where men dance much and strong, Béjart gave pride of place to males onstage through solos, duets, and all-male ensembles.

This reemergence of men in dance was only part of the story. The 1960s search for human contact and feeling fueled the dance explosion. People had more leisure time, First Lady Jacqueline Kennedy promoted the arts and French culture, and respectable families permitted their daughters to become ballerinas. As noted in chapter 1, the widespread interest in dance was further spurred by the "Dance in America" television series and the National Endowment for the Arts Dance Touring Program (twenty years ago dance was limited almost exclusively to New York). Dancers were plastered on the covers of weekly news magazines and portrayed in newspaper and periodical avertisements for a variety of services and products, and Broadway plays and movies about dancers were produced. Baryshnikov defected from the Kirov in 1974 to become a star not only of the ballet stage and artistic director of American Ballet Theatre, but a star of films and television. Modern dance gained increasing recognition as it further ensconced itself in the halls of academe. Yet, Croce observed, "Nothing galvanizes the general public like the advent of a male star in ballet (in Steinberg 1980, 123).

The dance boom extended Shawn's effort to promote dance as a sport (Acocella 1985). "Dancing—A Man's Game," a 1958 Omnibus television program narrated by motion picture dancer and choreographer Gene Kelly, placed dancers among the world-class athletes of the day. In well-publicized lecture-practicums for youth who think "the ballet might be effeminate," Edward Villella, formerly a fine danseur with the New York City Ballet, quickly appealed to America's success syndrome by comparing his salary to that of baseball pitcher Tom Seaver (quoted in Gardella 1979, 83). In 1969 *Life* magazine ran a story about Villella, "Is This Man the Country's Best Athlete?" Two years later, *Sports Illustrated* featured him in the profile "Encounter with an Athlete" and cited his $100,000 yearly income (Kram 1971). Recently several books about men in dance have portrayed them as gods, heros, and craftsmen. In 1980 in New York City there was even a concert performance of six companies and eleven male soloists called A Celebration of Men in Dance. Thelma Hill Dance Awards went to twenty men, and an annual tribute to men (mainly black men) in dance has continued.

Jacques d'Amboise, hailed by *Life* magazine in June 1963 as America's first great male ballet dancer, also challenged the dance domain as belonging to women and male homosexuals. A former principal with the New York City Ballet, d'Amboise and his son, who also joined the company, defied the traditional image of who's who in dance and let boys know that dancing is as physically exciting, manly, demanding, and dangerous as any sports activity (Gelb 1981). D'Amboise dreamt of having dance become part of the everyday life of all Americans. He began by teaching free classes at New York City's Dalton School, Collegiate, the Town School, and Public School 191.

A longtime crusader, d'Amboise pursued his determination to reverse entrenched prejudice against men in dance and created in 1976 the nonprofit National Dance Institute to "demystify the world of dance" (Solway 1983, 20). By 1983, assisted by seven professional dancers and four musicians, he was bringing dance to twelve hundred children in public, private, and parochial schools in New York, New Jersey, and Evanston, Illinois. Whereas the School of American Ballet, the official school of the New York City Ballet, had eighty-six boys out of the three hundred young students in 1969, nearly half the students were boys a decade later. In 1985, d'Amboise made the history of the War of 1812 come alive with a production of *Andrew Jackson and the Battle of New Orleans*. It had a cast of more than twelve hundred students and included appearances by the New York City Dancing Police and Boston SWAT Team (Rimer 1985). In 1986 d'Amboise made his annual spectacular at the Felt Forum of Madison Square Garden especially grand by recruiting Chinese children from Peking to participate.

Nonetheless, in spite of efforts to establish the respectability of a male dance career, problems remain. Ballet student, teacher, and anthropologist Daniel O'Connor (pers. com. 1982) observed that in New York City, dance capital of the world, male dancers still feel threathened to find their occupational choice considered deviant by mainstream America. Moreover, he found within the male sphere of ballet, as in other career domains, a homophobia in which straights were perceived to be of higher status. Thus, there are several approaches to the problem in addition to the d'Amboise strategy of upgrading the status of male dancers and destigmatizing the profession. O'Connor noted the following: A male dancer (straight or gay) might handle the issue with nondancers by first acknowledging the stereotypical image and then establishing himself as an exception. He does this by revealing, for example, that he has a girlfriend, that he finds gays disgusting, or that his love of ballet makes him "put up" with gay men. Other men deal with the perception of the suspect male dancer by offering information that would lead an outsider to believe the stereotype of the male dancer is unfounded. A number of dancers said that there are very few gays in ballet today, in contrast to just a few years ago. Another strategy of managing impressions outside the dance world includes dressing like a successful businessman or gentlemanly scholar and communicating machismo through body language. Of course, some men may act in ways that confirm the stereotype of the homosexual male dancer.

In spite of the efforts made to make male dancing an acceptable profession, attitudes are slow to change. During the 1980s when the major TV networks explored the life and art of prominent male dancers Nureyev, d'Amboise, and Martins, a critic remarked that the interviewers proffered a "gee-whiz" attitude that "male dancers were some odd yet awe-inspiring breed from outer space." Critic John Gruen (1980) was further struck by the delegation of a female reporter to conduct the interviews "as though having a male-to-male confrontation on the subject of dance would seem ever so slightly embarrassing." It is unusual when a man puts on a leotard even though, as Laine (1981) points out, "social change has brought about a new receptivity to demonstrative emotion by men on stage." The public glimpses of Gene Kelly and Fred Astaire showed them dancing in men's day and evening clothes. Perhaps "Dancer," a 1985 television series that approaches the male dancer in light of ballet history, may help change attitudes.

Conclusion

Male liberation in dance has its glitches. Yet, "When a woman dances, nobody cares. . . . All women can dance. But when a man dances, now that's something," a high school dance teacher told Wendy Perron and Stephanie Woodard (1976, 59; see also Gordon 1983, 34–37), themselves dancer-choreographers. In an insightful article, they point out that men in dance become a special kind of minority. "Dancers and critics alike are proud of the ever-increasing number of men in dance because their presence has legitimized it. No art is recognized as an art until men do it, from cooking to medicine to dance. And then it becomes dignified, arduous, skilled." Echoes of Margaret Mead!

Perron and Woodard compiled data on nineteen hundred students and company members of six major New York City modern dance and ballet companies with affiliated schools, recipients of 316 grants given by the National Endowment for the Arts (1974–75) and the New York State Council on the Arts (1971–74). They concluded that women were good enough but not man enough for the goodies: "Male dancers are getting hired, and male choreographers are getting grants way out of proportion to their numbers. The men require less performing skill and experience" (p. 59). Whereas the male-to-female ratio of dance students was 32 percent male versus 68 percent female and of dance company members 45 percent male to 55 percent female, scholarship students were 38 percent male to 62 percent female, grant recipients of $15,000 to $70,000 were 73 percent male to 27 percent female, and grant recipients of $70,000 or more were 100 percent male.

Not only has modern dance become a male province, but the situation has gone as far as a male dancer Satoru Shimazaki, in 1982, restaging and performing pioneer Duncan's two Scriabin works, *Mother* (1929) and *Revolutionary* (1922) (Dunning 1982a). (After the tragic death of her two children, Duncan created *Mother*, a poignant dirge for every mother who has lost a child.)

The experience of women in dance is not unique. Gaye Tuchman and Nina Fortin found that when the novel, which had been the province of female writers, became associated with high culture (as writing professionalized and publishing centralized), men increasingly wrote novels and successfully edged women out of their own turf. "As more people move into any field of literature [and I would add dance], the gain by men is almost always greater than that by women" (1984, 86). Mary Shelley, for example, invented science fiction in 1816 with *Frankenstein*. When men viewed her invention as viable literature, they took it over (Keller 1980). Moreover, dance companies as an idealized form of American capitalism—businesses run by self-employed individuals—were overcome by the emergence of national corporations run by men (Robertson 1985). In many arts organizations, "corporatization" has occurred in management and on the boards of directors.

Women are concerned about their status in dance, a field they have numerically dominated as workers and in which they have made progress as dancers, choreographers, and managers (as well as critics and scholars). In December 1981, an all-day conference in New York City called Networking for Women in the Performing Arts was sold out. This parley to aid women had twenty-four panel workshops on different aspects of the arts, each led by women who have achieved recognition in their fields. How do they feel about losing preeminence in a field, albeit a comparatively nonprestigious one, to men? How will they respond when men's "big bucks" make a dance career acceptable for male dancers and push women back into the stereotypic secondary place in the various sectors of the profession? It is noteworthy that as more "respectable" and "masculine" men are moving into dance, more women are moving into sports and business.

In sum, the ambivalence about dance dating from biblical times lingers. Still dance is terrain to shatter canons of the past with audacious danced transformations of feeling and thought. Who performs what and how in dance tells us many things. The body is a subject and purveyor of messages about opportunities and expectations. Dancing is about itself (technique and aesthetics), its creators, and their society's nondance life. The story of theatrical dance in America in the twentieth century is a tale of changing economic and sexual options for men and women, as well as of changing developments in dance and attitudes toward dancing. Over time we see a transformation from reputable to disreputable and back, and we see recurring male dominance. Although the dance world has a degree of insulation that fosters creativity and challenges the status quo, it also contains, expresses, and fuels the prejudices of the larger society about sex roles and career choices.

With this overview of dance as an occupation and its context for producing dance images that tell us what it is to be male and female, we now turn to chapters on the images themselves. The focus will be on sexuality, spotlighted performances, and changes in choreography by and about women and men.

7

The Sense and Symbol of Sexuality
and Gender in Dance Images

This chapter discusses critics' and dancers' awareness of images of
sexuality and gender in American theatrical dance. Because choreographers and dancers take from the everyday, and performance viewers
are influenced by it, a summary of offstage quotidian gender-related
movement markers follows. I have commented on some of the
biological and culturally patterned differences between men and
women in earlier chapters. Here I consider how these affect what each
sex is able to do in the physical activity of dance. Finally, the danced
transformations of signs of sexuality are explored.

Awareness of Sexuality

Western philosophers and aestheticians have reflected religious, moral,
and industrial/technological biases in denying or downplaying the
body's sensuous presence and erotic heritage in theater art dance.
Perhaps out of concern for the respectability of dance, tastefulness
demanded no talk about sexuality—what critic Jill Johnston called "the
bullshit of Western body sickness" (1971, 207). As we have seen,
contrary to some cultures, such as those in India where sexuality is part
of divinity, the Western tradition generally denies the flesh or sets it
apart from the spirit.

In earlier chapters I noted the ambivalent relation of sex and dance.
The Greeks feared that bacchanalian dancing would release unbridled

150

passions. Rabbinic decree at the time the Temple stood in Jerusalem commanded brides and grooms and their guests to dance at weddings. The Bible speaks of David dancing in praise of the Lord. But there is also the salacious dance of Salome. From "meat market" to dream emporium, dancing has served as sexual arousal for licit or illicit liaisons and purposes. Sometimes dancing has even been a sublimation of sexual behavior.

But sex in theater art dance? Yes, say critics Kriegsman and Rockwell. Nineteenth-century critic, poet, novelist, and journalist Théophile Gautier, in his 1837 piece on renowned ballerina Fanny Elssler, concedes that dancing is "nothing more than the art of displaying beautiful shapes. . . . Dancing . . . only expresses the passions, love, desire with all its attendant coquetry; the male who attacks and the female who feebly defends herself" (1983, 433–34). About five decades ago, dance critic John Martin of the *New York Times* noted decorously: "Any theory of dance that attempts to make use of the body as an instrument of pure design is doomed to failure, for the body is of all possible instruments the least removable from the associations of experience" (1936, 92). Lincoln Kirstein, historian and director of the New York City Ballet, admits, "Ballet, since it involves bodies in close contact, possesses erotic dimensions that have long been presupposed" (1973, 129). He calls the three-hundred-year-old art of ballet "a perfect metaphor for erotic sport" (1970, 98). *New Yorker* critic Arlene Croce claims that "derogatoriness, obscenity of every description, is one of the two great driving forces behind the ballet" (1982, 333).

Graham Jackson, another critic, refers to "the highly physical, often erotic nature of the art which brings out defensiveness in many critics. Ballet is all about bodies, bodies in motion, about line and curve and bulge, about arms and legs and backsides, as much as it is about princes and swans. There's no escaping it, although many hotly insist that to talk of ballet as physical and erotic is to demean the art. What shows through their indignation are signs of the age-old dilemma of integration: is sexuality something one keeps carefully apart from the other activities one engages in like eating, bathing, thinking, dancing, or even appreciating dance; or should it be integrated naturally into the fabric of human experience?" (1978, 40).

The classical ballet aesthetic is usually about the romantic attraction of man and woman. Men dance together in rivalry for the some woman or in athletic-type competitions, as in Jerome Robbins's *Dances at a Gathering* or Gerald Arpino's *Kettentanz*. The socially defined gender roles have been "straight." In *Dance Is a Contact Sport*, Joseph H.

Mazo (1974) claims that ballet is about the penis-vagina variety of sex. Marcia Siegel describes George Balanchine's choreographic career, in one sense, as elevating "the pastime of girl watching to a classic art" through the "process of continual refinement and elaboration of ballet's feminine ideal" (1972, 17). Croce puts it this way: "With a Diana Adams crooking her beautiful length of leg in its female arch of complicity, with an Allegra Kent stretching her spine in kittenlike contortions, Balanchine was able to draw miracles of erotic suggestion from the sparse structures of serial music. . . . After one of the first performances of *Agon*, a well-known New York writer said joyfully, 'If they knew what was going on here, the police would close it down'" (1977, 419). Siegel compares the new and the old: "When the ballerina languidly unfolds her leg into a high extension or stretches her torso into an arabesque, she's calling attention to a shapely ankle, an arched instep, the long straight bones, and the round hip and ribcage. You can't mistake it if you're alive yourself. Nor can you be unaware of the sexuality of modern ballet's strong, sleek, handsome men showing you things, buttocks, bulging baskets. The nineteenth-century ballet functioned quite openly as a showcase where dandies picked out their mistresses and little chorus girls found lifelong protectors. Perhaps inevitably, the featuring of men in ballet has created a new theatrical meat market. . . . so much dance these days is primarily a homosexual pitch" (1977, 109–10).

Ballet, moving from its origins of royal respectability to a position of disreputability and then reemerging with a dignified aura, appears in the mid-twentieth century, along with modern and postmodern dance, to assert sensuality within a mechanized and bureaucratized impersonal society. Choreographers have responded to technology without abandoning the meshing of mind and body, ideas and feelings. The choreography of a solo or a work for groups of dancers reflects possibilities in space for the individual, duos, and groups, in offstage public and private.

Contemporary ballet is at once antitechnology in its physical recoiling from the enslaving machine and protechnology in its emulation of the machine's precision, economy, and speed. Ballet experienced an increasing development of technique as more was learned about the body and sports medicine: *fouettés* (a series of rapid turns on one leg, as the foot rises *en pointe*, while the other makes circles at hip level) became flashier and more numerous, elevation and extension higher, speed greater, bodies sleeker and as angular as the skyscraper, and movements sharper. However, as Mazo points out, the dancer who performs with the technical prowess of a highly refined instrument and also projects human emotion (constrained animal sexuality) in ballet becomes the star and creates the peak excitement that thrills audiences. "Only when skill is illuminated by animal power does the stage begin to glow. . . . the animal power is high-octane emotion—life, trying to burst through the performer's body. That emotion, that life force, is indivisible from the sex drive. It takes us very close to the ultimate, orgiastic release that is the closest we can get to the instincts of our own private animals" (1974, 159).

In *Untitled Lecture*, a dance performance, (1968), dancer Steve Paxton explored a certain energy common to sex and ballet: "I speculate that some of the qualities which have made ballet, in spite of its practitioners, the second oldest professional physical tradition, is an early infusion of physiologically basic modes of energy use which I find similar to the ecstasy of stretching such as is experienced during certain types of orgasms . . . a positive and energized stretch. . . . Everybody knows what Graham's 'contraction and release' syndrome is all about. A sex physiologist could probably make a critical contribution to dance literature with some scientific analogies . . . although the motives are different, the pervasive 'stretch' in ballet is similar to the orgastic stretch, not only in position but in the energy employed to get there and stay there" (quoted in Johnston 1971, 198–99).

The 1960s gave impetus to acceptance of the body and its sensitivities. Deborah Jowitt observes, "The vanguard of dance . . . very quickly reflects how we as people feel about our bodies. The choreographers of the '60s complained about the puffed-out ribcages and rigid spines of trained dancers, even as the flower children fled from what they saw as inflated and rigid military and social conventions" (1981, 75). Moreover, the so-called sexual revolution was a broadening of viewpoints about sex that widened the group of people with whom one can licitly experience love and intimacy (Perper 1985). Liberation movements began to free men and women from the fetters of strictly defined sex roles.

Siegel offers a less sanguine view of the impact of the 1960s: "I think the dregs of the sexual revolution may have imposed another burden on the arts. New York is full of would-be swingers and the entertainments that cater to their pent-up eroticism; and it's fallen to the arts, especially dance, to project the fantasies we can't act out. There's no use pretending that dance doesn't turn people on; it always has. What's new is the extremity of violence, aggression, and ugliness cast as sexual encounter that audiences will accept. Dance can so easily take abstract forms; we can always think we're applauding the technical skill of the dancers or the intensity of their performance, and not the anomie, the ruthless exploitation, the sexual despair. Perhaps we see that too, and secretly subconsciously thrill to it, even long for it" (1977, xiii).

By the 1980s choreographers such as Michael Clark, with "blond wig, a frilly apron and a large fake penis," work hard to be outrageous in choreographing plain and fancy sex (Shapiro 1986, 85; see Friedman 1986). Critics mostly report the irreverent and attrocious but do not interpret it.

Although the 1960s opened our eyes and mouths and let pens flow and bodies speak about sexuality, the heritage of dance lingers and makes some people nervous. In Western culture there seems to be latent guilt and anxiety about the body as an instrument of pleasure. Recall the views of the body as a bestial adversary of mind and spirit which had to be denied or overcome. We read in a contemporary tract published by a religious firm: "I flatly charge that dancing is the most advanced and most insidious of the maneuvers preliminary to sex betrayal" (quoted in Fallon and Wolbers 1982). Douglas Fallon, 1982 president of the National Dance Association, distinguishes between provocative dance movements based on sex appeal and accepted as foreplay, a prelude to a sexual encounter, on the one hand, and dance that is aesthetic and artistic, on the other. However, there are problems with this distinction. First, provocative dancing, as in disco, may substitute for sexual intercourse, and aesthetic/artistic dance may lead to it as indicated earlier in this book. Second, the association of sexuality and aesthetic, artistic dance only demeans this kind of dance if sexuality is denied its contribution to humanity—the production of an individual and other creations.

In the 1980s the Paul Taylor Dance Company reversed its policy of not talking about sexuality in advertisements and created a hullabaloo. As critic Jennifer Dunning (1982c) put it, in a time when dance companies are beginning to look increasingly like "endangered species . . . A frisson of dismay ran through the dance world . . . when the first advertisement appeared. . . . 'Suddenly you'll understand sex, power, gravity, music, fear, humor and joy better than ever before,' the advertisement promised. ('All that tonight?' one newcomer to Mr. Taylor's dance murmured nervously.)" According to the Taylor company general manager, "Just about everything doubled. Window sales tripled. Over all, we were up 12 percent over last year, selling 84 percent of capacity for the season." The company also got its first hate mail.

Other perspectives on dance play down open awareness and saliency of sexuality in dance. One view is that humans can distinguish themselves from other animals and thereby cloak raw sexuality in the symbolic forms and self-disciplined rule over the flesh realized in the visual kinetic patterns we call dance. Stéphane Mallarmé explained: "The ballerina is not a girl dancing . . . she is not a girl, but rather a metaphor which symbolizes some elemental aspect of earthly form . . . she does not dance but rather, with miraculous lunges and abbreviations, writing with her body, she suggests things which the written word could express only in several paragraphs of dialogue or descriptive prose" (quoted in Maynard 1979). A second view is that spectators may identify with the technical prowess of the dancer, a model of human potential, who surmounts limitations by defying gravity and overcoming the natural constraints of the body through rigorous training and marshaled talent.

A third perspective is that qualities of formal style are the magic and defining characteristics of ballet rather than sexuality. An "aesthetic of immanence" (much like the modern art and music that annihilate or suppress figurative tendencies, mimetic connotations, and transcendent symbolism) arouses, pleases, and fascinates. Form and content are identical. The expression of body sensuality may not necessarily be excluded in the abstractness, although it seems to evoke plateau rather than peak experience, in psychologist A. H. Maslow's terms.

Whether theorists think sexuality is inherent to dance, or whether dancers intend to convey sexuality, the spectator may perceive it. A dramatic example occurred at the January 12, 1981, Smithsonian Institution performance of postmodern dancers Douglas Dunn and Deborah Riley in *Foot Rules* (Hanna 1983b). In response to the question What kinds of feeling do you want to convey? Dunn told me, "My intention is just to do the dance. . . . And the feeling, whatever it is, remains . . . open. So I can do my dance, and I can feel one thing, and the audience can see it and feel another. . . . It gives everybody a lot of room."

Spectators offered opposite views on whether or not dancers conveyed feeling in the dance performed before the first intermission and how they felt in response to what happened on stage. Forty-six percent say *no emotion*. An observer felt angry by the lack of feeling perceived in the dancers: "They are more concerned with movement than emotion." There were descriptions of the movement style as mechanical, stilted, robotlike, computerized, and processing a tense, bound quality. "An intellectual non-emotional quality was projected," remarked a viewer. Another said the dance has "the feeling of New York art, especially the costumes, and made me feel like I was watching androids or mechanical mannequins." Some audience members faulted the dancers for their lack of playfulness. "I'd say they take themselves so seriously, play or communicating seems the last thing they think of doing. They've forgotten how to have fun. A sense of play is one of the most important things, along with truth, beauty, etc. in all art, and they need a reminder."

In contrast with spectators who saw absolutely no emotion, forty percent of the respondents at the same concert observed *eroticism*, one of the strong emotions that causes physiological perturbations. A male engineer perceived eroticism in the intertwining and rolling of the couple on the floor, and he said it made him feel "horny." Another person viewed the dancing as "X-rated." A male lawyer saw ecstasy as the dancers were "lying as if spent," and he felt "excited." Remember that nearly half of the audience respondents reported that they saw no emotion! People's perceptions may well be affected by the relationship of dance to sexual markers in everyday life as well as to knowledge of artistic conventions and innovations.

Gender Signs in Everyday Life

Dance, as noted earlier, transforms everyday movement for its material. A multitude of studies have documented gender-related nondance messages of nonverbal movements, many of which are often out of the communicators' awareness.[1] The constant occurrence of sex-associated movements contributes to the information that individuals, often unknowingly, use to classify others whom they observe and to model their own gender behavior. Furthermore, the importance of these presentational cues in daily life lies in their regulation of social interaction.

Male-female stereotypic movements learned early in life operate as implicit beliefs and expectations. Sexual movement markers tend to merge with those of interpersonal and male domination in our society in this way: signifiers of social inequality appear in contrasts in posture, precedence, elevation, movement quality, and touch. In lateral opposition, the right side is associated with strength, justice, moral integrity, and beauty.[2] Asymmetry indicates imbalance in status, whereas symmetry or reciprocal behavior suggests affiliation and equal status. Verticality expresses deference and authority. The upper to top height is high status, carrying over the parent-child relationship; the lower, becoming horizontal in bowing and prostrating, connotes inferior status. Strong movement conveys authority; weak effort suggests the opposite. Higher-status people touch lower-status people more than vice versa. Touch may convey power, dominance, aggression, comfort, intimate love, and sexual arousal.

Thus movement is similar to verbal language. Superiors may say certain things, dominate a conversion, and speak in ways to inferiors that may not be reciprocated: terms of address, pronouns of power. The sexes differ in expression. Women (stereotypically inferior) allegedly chose refined, euphemistic, and hyperbolic expressions more than men, who, less polite, cheerful, and emotional, prefer slang and profanity (Jesperson 1922). It is more of a stigma for men to use women's speech than the reverse. "Switching styles means downward mobility" for men (Thorne and Henley 1975, 12). A nonmasculine manner is beyond the ken, derided, feared, and scorned.

With the use of video cameras and frame analysis, researchers have noted courtship readiness behavior when two people are sexually attracted: increased muscular tension, self-grooming, a more erect posture, and a facing of the other person (Scheflen and Scheflen 1972). Biologist Timothy Perper (1985) found, through more than nine hundred hours of observations and interviews at single bars, train stations, parties, and church socials, these five distinct steps in male-female attraction: approach, look, turn, touch, and synchronized movement.

BIOLOGICAL BIND ON MOVEMENT

Sex-linked patterns have origins in human evolution; we see the ritualized often agonistic displays between and within the sexes, males competing over females and males versus females. Groups of human animals select from an array of options in what Perper referred to as biological semiotics.

The human species is sexually dimorphic; that is, distinctions in body shape and composition, physiology, and functioning exist between male and female. On the average, women have a higher proportion of body fat distributed differently, less dense bones, wider pelvis, slightly shorter legs relative to the length of trunk, and less cardiovascular power than men. Men are generally heavier, taller, and more muscular than women, which gives men superior speed and strength.

Men have greater hand width, chest and head circumference, and thoracic and sitting height. At 20 percent to 30 percent heavier, men have more muscle tissue—lean body mass—than fat compared to women, who have twice as much measurable fat. Because of the female hormone estrogen, females are larger in the breast and have more fat deposits than males in the thighs, buttocks, and hips. Weight in the lower part of the trunk lowers the center of gravity. The hip swinging gait of women is due in part to the structure of the wider female pelvis. For any given length of stride, women must rotate through a greater angle than men.

Body size and composition affect physiology. The male's comparatively larger heart copes with a larger proportion of muscle and tissue, which requires more energy from the circulatory system than the larger proportion of adipose tissue found in the female. A larger heart requires less pumping to supply the same amount of energy. Not only is the female's thorasic capacity smaller, but so are her lungs. Therefore less gaseous exchange takes place. During physical activity, higher pulse and respiratory rates cause extended recovery rate.

Because women sweat less profusely and are able to conserve body fluids more than men, women may do well in endurance activities and compete successfully with men. The natural supply of air keeps women from tiring.

Having said that generally men have certain physical advantages over women, it is essential to state emphatically that women athletes and dancers differ from the average female population. Moreover, assumptions concerning differences in the ethos of the "biology is destiny" saddled upon women are being challenged. Scientists are exploring the extent to which some differences have been created and hence can be modified. Athletic and other physical training for women has differed markedly from such training for men. The games the sexes are encouraged to play surely affect what they are able to do (Lowe 1983). More than thirty years ago Ashley Montagu (1974) debunked the belief in male superiority which he attributed to jealousy of the female reproductive capacity and noted the strength of females to endure all sorts of devitalizing conditions better than men: starvation, exposure, fatigue, shock, illness, and the like.

In reflecting what is, the arts perpetuate notions of male superior strength and speed. The arts also challenge tradition as choreographers present new visual images. The sense of limitations is weakening in the face of knowledge and opportunities. Women's performance in various sports and dance events has improved as sophisticated training and coaching methods have become available. Girls used to fear developing big legs, turning into men, losing sex appeal, and not getting boyfriends. In the 1980s the athletic woman and dancer with a taut, fit, muscular body has become sexy.

STEREOTYPIC GENDER MOVEMENT

Each culture has its own clichés, new images, and counterimages. And within each culture, as the Dunn concert so vividly illustrated, multiple meanings can be read into the same "text" of sexual symbolism (Katchadourian 1979). In American culture sexuality tends to be perceived and expressed as achievement. The dominant, aggressive male conquers the female and outdoes his competitors. The male-female relationship may be used as a means to other achievement such as status or money. Male-female encounters are sometimes a game in which male and female are pitted against each other. Women tend to be commodities on the field men play, whereas men are manipulated for what they can give.

Table 7.1 presents stereotypic male-female patterns of movement that relate to status, power, and attraction.[3] Table 7.2 presents homosexual courtship/cruising patterns (Kleinberg 1980; Webbink 1981).

There is, of course, a repertory of movements and gestures common to both sexes. For example, the hand on the heart is a gesture of sincerety; pointing the finger, a sign of emphasis; upraised hands with palms together, an indication of blessing.

Body movement typecasting is emphasized by artifactual signs—the way the body is adorned and displayed. Males, associated with threatening behavior, defense, and strength, wear clothing that permits easy movement. By contrast, females, supposedly protected by family at home, wear clothing with rounded contours that does not easily enable physical activity—skirts, high heels, easily snagged/torn stockings. And yet, that women's half-nude bodies are, says Elizabeth Dworan (1983), systematically displayed throughout the city in subways, newsstands, and magazine centerfolds does not expand the possibilities for women's power and pleasure because those images are not meant to do so. "In this culture the penis is hegemonic, a symbol of power and pleasure; the vulva is not." Among the population at large there are ambivalent or negative attitudes toward transvestism and homosexuality because they defy the normal categorization of male and female.

Sexual Symbols in Western Theater Dance

Many meanings in movement are so well established in culture that they are part of a choreographer's inheritance. The choreographer seeks signs and symbols people can relate to, as well as sometimes creating original ones. Meaning of gender movement appears in spheres of

TABLE 7.1   STEREOTYPIC NONVERBAL GENDER BEHAVIOR

Male	Female
SPACE	
As the case with dominants in the animal world, males control greater territory, move in others' or common territory. They are accorded greater bodily space.	Females yield space to dominants when approached or passed; "shrinking woman." Women are approached more closely by both sexes.
Movement occurs in office, outside home.	Movement in home, outer office.
Movement is more vertical.	Movement is more horizontal.
Initiate directional changes in group interaction.	React to such changes.
TIME	
Dominant does not wait.	"Women-in-waiting."
Begins actions.	Responds to actions.
CARRIAGE STYLE	
Allowed more movement and relaxed body comportment.	More circumspect and constrained body comportment (clothing—skirts and heels—constrict action and act as armament to place in ladylike position).
Options of firm stride and width in stance and sitting; use of ankle-to-knee cross in sitting.	Narrow stance and sitting with legs together; thighs may cross in sitting, but feet are still close.
Pelvis rolled slightly back in walk on flat shoe.	Walk has pelvis anterior roll and mincing step on high heels.
GAZE	
Direct gaze and look more while speaking/listening.	Submissive watching and averting of gaze.
Prolonged gaze indicates sexual attraction.	Prolonged eye contact with aversion indicates attraction.

TABLE 7.1   (*continued*)

Male	Female
GESTURE	
Larger, more sweeping gestures.	Smaller gestures.
Arm and hand held as solid unit.	Fingers, wrist, and forearm articulate more.
Use less facial expression.	Use more facial expression and smile.
Less likely to return smile when smiled at.	More likely to return smile when smiled at.
TOUCH	
Touch nonfamilial women more often; encompass women, hold shoulder, lock arms.	Touch nonfamilial men less often.
Shake hands with men (ritual bracketing of coming together).	Embrace women.
Touch each other and themselves less.	Touch each other and themselves more (grooming).
QUALITY OF MOVEMENT	
Nonemotional, reserved.	Emotional, expressive.
Body expands in energy when meeting authority.	Body expands and contracts in energy when confronting persons of significance.

conveying meaning in dance: the body, especially its adornment and effort qualities; the unfolding of movement revealing who does what, when, where, why, how, and with or to whom; the movements themselves in terms of their historical origin, dancer's gaze, and spatial distances; or the sphere in which movement intertwines with narrative text.

THE CAGING AND RELEASE OF SEXUALITY

Different patterns of sexuality are seen in the development of social dances originally taken from peasants to nobles' courts, and then in yet another remove transferred to theatrical stages, and time and again through the years transformed in ballets. "Ballet is conservative," says Kirstein. He calls it an extant exemplar of the metaphor of human possibility "mastered by mind and muscle, schooled by history, reincarnated in styles and visions of a hundred generations of repertoires"

TABLE 7.2   HOMOSEXUAL COURTSHIP PATTERNS

Initiatory Contact

Gaze: Prolong eye contact, stare intensely.

Locomotion: Walk past object of interest more than once.

Gesture: Turn head in direction of someone walking past.

Touch: Touch or bump "accidentally" without withdrawal.

Space: Enter places known for sexual encounters.

Confirmatory Response

Gaze: Stare intensely.

Gesture: Escalate strategies of auto petting, heavy breathing, erection, thrusting pelvis forward to stance to display "basket" (genitals) if male.

Negative Response

Withdraw gaze, touch.

Ignore initiatives.

(1970, 71). These include the peripatetic minuet, waltz, polka, and polonaise, and the more recent tango, and jazz or vernacular dance with their urban and rural roots. In these dances, with few exceptions, the man leads the woman. Sometimes there is comparatively little distinction between steps and styles of the ballroom, dance hall or parlor, and the stage.

Elegant demeanor, style, and pace characterize the minuet, an undramatic, slow, graceful dance with forward balancing and bowing, toe pointing, artifice, and reserve. The minuet was vertical, with the performer's torso still, while the head tilted and turned in theatrical understatement. Forearms, wrists, fingers, lower legs, and feet of each sex moved mincingly and decoratively, contrary to the later delegation of this stylistic pattern to females (Wynne 1970; Cohen 1974, 42–51). From the late seventeenth century to the revolutionary eras in France and England, the minuet was a class badge of the elite. The French court tamed for its use what was originally a fast, joyous folk dance from the Poitou region of France. Untutored peasants, indulgently physical, danced with unfettered gusto as their torsos initiated and responded to bold movements of the arms and legs. In contrast, well-bred gentlemen and ladies danced with refinement and the restrained classical values of clarity, balance, and regularity as part of their formalized social exchanges. Manuals explained the rules and intricate steps, which precluded individual expressiveness, and dancing masters spent hours with aristocratic students before they could perform in public. Since dance protocol reflected the performers' social rank, hosts for minuets carefully researched the background of each guest to determine who would open the ball and in what order each guest would step out onto the floor. With highly controlled vitality and disdain for revealing inner feelings, as well as ordered equilibrium and weightlessness, couples moved away and together again and again, usually keeping their focus on each other.

The waltz of the 1800s contrasts with the courtly minuet that preceded the French Revolution (Katz 1973). A mere twenty or thirty years but a whole historical epoch separates these two dance forms as appositely seen at the 1814–15 Congress of Vienna. Crown heads of Europe assembled, in company with their chief ministers and the high society of the Austrian capital, to reestablish an ultraconservative Europe freed from the democratic specter. While the diplomats worked at map-covered tables, the kings danced, but this time to the musical strains of the waltz. This dance, in three-quarter rhythm, accent on the first beat, combined the Landler traditional whirling steps of Austria's German-speaking mountain peasantry and the gliding motion of the more sedate Schleifer dance. The waltz conquered more than the Congress of Vienna. It soon dominated the middle class festivities of a whole continent. The minuet disappeared fast; the polonaise survived longer. There is some irony in the triumph of the ecstatic waltz at so conservative a time; with the basic face-to-face position and physical contact (the man's hand on the woman's torso and hers on his shoulder) of the later ballroom dances, the waltz became an assertion of individual expression such as the minuet had never been. More important, the waltz was a popular art form in the service of a freer, more open, and eventually more democratic society than the congress ever envisaged. During the French Revolution there was talk about putting the arts at the disposal of society in general: the waltz, independent of social hierarchy and the petty tyrannies of the male dancing master, and allowing personal choices of partner and movement, became an assertion of increased freedom in a crumbling conservative social order.

By 1830 the waltz was danced in Boston assembly rooms, in the Manchester Free Trade Hall in England, and in the cafés of the Champs Elysées. Couples held each other at arm's length or closer as they revolved around their own axes, vibrantly spinning among others.

Mothers, of course, were still concerned about the backgrounds of young men willing to dance with their daughters.

The waltz is now viewed as graceful, dignified, and orderly, as in Balanchine's *Waltz Scherzo* or *Vienna Waltzes*. However, when it was first danced it scandalized many people. The clergy feared the lust aroused by partners grasping each other and throwing and twirling each other about. When the whirling dance entered the salon, the dancing teachers tried through formal rules to tame the spontaneity and self-expression of the waltz.

Danced in Poland and all over Europe, the polka originated in Bohemia Czechoslovakia about 1830. The man leads his partner in a boisterous manner. This peasant dance with its hop and skip was in two-four time and usually ended with a fast gallop. It reached the fashionable ballrooms of Prague, Vienna, and Paris in the mid-nineteenth century. For many mid-European ethnic groups in the United States today, the polka is a symbolic and emotional link with the "old country." Polish immigrants who became workers in mining, steel, tanning, and meat packing identified with the polka. The relatively small Polish-American middle class, however, seeks a different image associated with the aristocracy and intelligentsia (Keil 1979). Consequently it prefers the polonaise, a dance that originated about the mid-seventeenth century as a dignified, ceremonial warriors' triumphal march. The polonaise appears in classical ballet, for example, in *Swan Lake*; the polka appears in Jerome Robbins's *Circus Polka*.

Evolving from the *milonga* dance, the tango originated about 1880 in taverns and dance halls of lower-class districts in the slums of Buenos Aires (Jimenez 1964; Taylor 1976). Immigrant experiences of a transient, isolated, and frustrated existence, life of migrants from the pampas, and the gaucho traditions, in addition to men's fears of social, economic, and sexual failure, constitute the lore of the tango. The dance reflects the pimp's repertory of carefully studied postures and gestures. His nearly straight, unmoving upper body and smooth steps mirror patterns in the underworld's duels. Perhaps the pimp's elegant high-heeled shoes caused him to have the slightly forward-tilted spine seen in the tango.

Male-female relations is the central theme of what was a daringly suggestive dance. The man (active, powerful, and dominant) advances, slightly inclined over the woman (passive, docile, and submissive), who never escapes his embrace and overpowering control. Danced by pimps and whores, and then by their johns, the tango was learned in brothels by "respectable" wealthy men who later took the scandalous dance to

Paris, from where it eventually spread to respectable society throughout the world, including Argentina. The hot hip contact initially caused the pope to issue a judgment on the morality of the tango. The vicar-general of Rome condemned it as an "offense against God" in a 1914 letter in *Osservatore Romano*, the Vatican paper. Cardinal Amette, archbishop of Paris, called the tango a sin.

The tango has had its metamorphoses. In 1912 New York City cafés inaugurated afternoon dances called *thé dansants* or "tango teas." For the price of a drink or a relatively small admission fee, single and married women could dance; management hired partners for the women (Erenberg 1981). Popular ballroom dancers Vern and Irene Castle sanitized the tango when they took the hip contact out. Eliot Feld's ballet *A Soldier's Tale* is about the horrors of war—including the pimp and prostitute who prey upon its men, living and dead. The tango herein evokes mixed feelings of arousal and contempt. For the New York City Ballet's 1982 Stravinsky Festival, Balanchine choreographed *Tango*, emphasizing the emotion of love. Hans van Manen created *Five Tangos*, and Luc de Layresse, *Three Easy Tangos*.

Other forms of popular social dance, along with their cultural meanings, have been incorporated in high theater art. D. H. Lawrence had contempt for the Charleston and other couple dances of the twenties because they "were narrowed to 'either bounding toward copulation, or sliding and shaking and wagglin', to elude it" (Elsbree 1968, 4).

During Shakespeare's time dancing was a common way of wooing. His audience was familiar with specific dances and understood and empathized with the metaphorical allusions to sexuality and courtship. In *Much Ado about Nothing*, Beatrice speaks about the "hot and hasty" qualities of the jig and the early stages of courtship. Vigorous dances such as the jig and galliard (a lively, seductive dance in which the couples dance variations around each other) were favored courtship dances. The galliard, performed with four leg thrusts alternating from right to left, culminates in a leap, the *cinquepace*, the most difficult step.

Shakespeare employs dance, part of the folk and court traditions in sixteenth and seventeenth century England, as a dramatic technique and storehouse of imagery in his plays. He allows lovers to "speak" to one another without words through the mute rhetoric of dance. Certainly not everyone who danced was looking for a sexual relationship. Yet it was mostly the young who danced, flirtatiously displaying their charms and skills. Not only did people see dancing, but its impact was reinforced in the theater, in vernacular speech proverbs, and in church commentary.

I have described several social dances and their popular sexual meanings that classical ballet incorporated in some transformation. Ballet also relies on conventionalized understandings of the roles of men and women, which are deeply embedded in courtly roots of romantic attachments. These form the skeleton of dance stories and images. Certainly ballet changes and choreographers add their own symbols from exotic and contemporary cultures as well as from their individual psyches. For example, the loosened hair of Balanchine's women in *Serenade* (1934) symbolizes personal grief.

Mark Franko (pers. com. 1984), specialist in French literature, found that the old ballet treatises clearly worked through the interdiction against unbridled sexuality in dance. Thus ballet incorporated movements of immobility—poses and rests—that specifically signified the virtue of respectability and conveyed a notion of propriety. Movement occurred with an illusion of stasis. Women pulled back against their corsets as they pulled in their stomachs and lifted their rib cages. The erect airborne woman at times signified antisexuality. In court, dancing displayed one's God-given grace; thereby this activity ordered society through the senses of seeing and smelling in a marriage market. Sex role stereotyping was also clear. Arbeau in 1589 noted that men's legs show in their tights and the feet should not be too wide; the "second position" is feminine.

PAS DE DEUX

The outstanding and widely recognized sign of sexuality in ballet is the heterosexual pas de deux and partnering style in which the man supports, manipulates, and often conquers the woman. Love, with its smell and sight of partners at close range, is signified in the concretization of the embrace, and prolonged ecstasy, through the adjustment of weight and sustained balance. Today the pas de deux is often a metaphor for the American ideal of romantic love, a romanticization of romance.

Reflecting its origins in the ideal of courtly love, partnering has at the simplest, the male dancer making his ballerina securely comfortable and giving her added freedom in and out of certain combinations of movements, while he projects a dramatic, elegant body line. He must balance the ballerina in pirouette: he grasps her waist so that she can whirl her body on one foot either on pointe or demipointe and not wobble. There are complicated tricks, too, which require timing and physical strength: one-handed hoists as the man lifts the woman high in the air, the dare-devil fish dive as the woman flies into her partner's lowered grasping arms, or the cantilevered poses in which the woman retains contact with the floor solely with the tip of her toe shoe. The opening section of the classical ballet pas de deux is the adagio, which came into existence during the latter part of the eighteenth century, although men and women have danced together since the mid-seventeenth century.

Kirstein believes that the "grand" adagio is the "emotional climax" of a ballet: "The big *adagio* of the classic Russian repertory may be considered as highly conventionalized love-scenes, in which the climax is not an actual embrace, but the most delicate support or adjustment of weight, which enables the ballerina to accomplish spectacular feats of sustained balance or elevation with the least *apparent* aid of her partner" (1967, 4–5). Johnston points out that the ballet is rampant with representational orgasm. "There are climaxes by the dozen in any one ballet. . . . An ascending accumulation of energy is a favorite device" (1971, 200). Weighted lunges are a metaphor for devouring appetite.

Initially the pas de deux was not universally accepted. *The Black Crook*, an opulent extravanganza opening on September 12, 1866, in New York City introduced a popular ballet troupe. Rev. Charles B. Smythe denounced the dancers' "attitudes [that] were exceedingly indelicate. . . . When a danseuse is assisted by a danseur, the attitudes assumed by both in conjunction suggest to the imagination scenes which one may read, describing the ancient heathen orgies." Moralistic editorials about the dancing fired enthusiasm at the box office, and *The Black Crook* was performed for over forty years by touring companies everywhere (Root 1981, 81).

For renowned danseur Igor Youskevitch the classical pas de deux is an overstatement of a life situation where man, as gallant gentleman, helps woman and voluntarily endures hardship for her comfort. She, through her submissiveness, leads him to virtuosity. The nineteenth-century pas de deux style has a solo for each sex. Youskevitch's relationship with the ballerina, he said, has "a certain feeling between us that I felt should be the same as in any classical *pas de deux* [he was conceptualizing *Theme and Variations*, whose male role Balanchine created for him]. Without very realistic lovemaking, it's still a kind of refined love affair. No matter how abstract, that should go on" (quoted in Newman 1982, 58).

Kirstein continues, "The characteristic stage-gallantry of the male partner in adagio need not necessarily echo the feudal courtesies of European courts. Tenderness, playful solicitation, and a subtle, teasing flattery are the twentieth century equivalents for the devoted, dazzled, chivalric plume-sweeping behavior, of the nineteenth century *danseur noble*" (1967, 5).

Overt sexuality is pressed into highly stylized movements in Romantic ballet male-female encounters. A woman may appear as a dryad, *willi*, or *sylphide*. Exalted to ethereality as she is borne aloft by her partner, she is glorified in ways that might seem to transcend sexuality. Yet there are symbolic yearnings as partners reach out toward each other in erotic foreplay and come together, one partner passing over or through the other's personal space of legs and arms in sexual fulfillment or conquest.

Dance transforms animal ritualized patterns at mating time by using abstract stylization and other devices to encode sexual meaning. The ballet pas de deux may also be a metaphor for male domination and patriarchy. In the duet, a man manipulates, controls, and plays with his female partner besides, perhaps, seeing his own desire played out. Mazo speaks of those "magically desirable, vulnerable but strong, fragile yet enduring" women entrusted with key roles in classical ballet. The woman, a prize to be won, contrasts with the whore and "slack-bellied" housewife (1974, 9).

Partnering roles are often analogues of patronage by the stronger of the weaker sex, referred to as sex kitten, vulnerable child-woman, or siren. The pas de deux draws upon the stereotypic quotidian nonverbal gender behavior noted earlier in the use of space, time, carriage, gaze, gesture, and quality of movement. Postmodern choreographer-dancer Bill T. Jones says partnering "seems offensive because it contributes to the way we perceive the roles of men and women offstage" (quoted in Laine 1985, 23). The woman "looks up" to the man, rises *en pointe* to meet him. Rising *en pointe* in some positions renders the dancer insubstantial. Unable to stand alone, the male supports or assists her. When a man carries a woman draped around his shoulders like a scarf, as Balanchine carried Tamara Geva in 1923 dancing his pas de deux *Enigma*, chauvinistic overtones are unmistakable (plate 3). As an ethereal creature, the woman may, however, surpass the base man.

The pas de deux involves touch, the most basic sensory process and earliest form of communication. As noted above, it can convey a host of contradictory messages—caring as well as power relations of dominance and submission, invasion of privacy, and norms of body accessibility. Sometimes meaning appears in the form of a concretization, as when a couple embraces "realistically" in an erotic duet.

Balanchine's ideas about the significance of the pas de deux have influenced male dancers, to be sure. Desmond Kelly, a preferred partner of Margot Fonteyn and a *danseur noble* of distinction at the Royal Ballet, remembers when Balanchine came to London to set his ballets for the company. Balanchine taught him so much "without saying anything. I mean, he's not the kind of person who sits down and gives you a half-hour's talk about what you should be doing with this interpretation. He can say one word, or get up and grab a girl around the waist—he adores holding girls up, doesn't he?—and says so much by that movement. . . . I couldn't take my eyes off him. He has this completely man-woman thing, and it's not very usual in ballet. I'm not saying that because there are homosexuals—that's apart. It's this love Balanchine has for a woman's body and the things you can do with a woman's body in a *pas de deux* that's so great" (in Newman 1982, 319).

Peter Martins explains why he stayed with Balanchine for so many years. "When I was a little boy, before I even met Balanchine, I always had ideas of what dance should be. . . . Balanchine was the first man for me, and also the only man since, who had this incredibly sophisticated outlook towards what dance was all about. It was never just one thing in his mind. It could be anything. Look at the ballets. They're so much, and yet they're all basically the same, right? They're all a man versus a woman. Whether it's *Agon* or *Diamonds* or *Apollo*, it's always this enormous adoration for women. Well, I've always adored women. Not meaning that I am a runaround, but a woman onstage is beautiful, and I've always thought that she was number one. Everything choreographically speaking, is centered around her" (in Newman 1982, 357).

DISTINCT MALE AND FEMALE MOTIVATION, MEANING, AND CHANGE

Reflecting the quotidian stereotypes described earlier, Youskevitch refers to the essential participation in dance of each sex in a particular male and female way to "keep the basic form of the art from distortion" (1969, 13). He believes the appeal of a particular dancer was based upon the "sincere presentation of individual sex characteristics" (p. 19).

According to Youskevitch, women's range of acceptable mannerisms is greater than men's. "That's ballet." Women's calculated small-step walk, arm gestures, detail, perfect positions, and turn-out reflect "feminine instincts" of display. Their internal motivation is to please the opposite sex. "Women's attractiveness to the opposite sex has always been one of the main goals of her existence and all her actions have been a constant, if sometimes camouflaged, display of her best physical characteristics." Sex appeal was the key that opened the dance world door for women and assured them of "its most privileged position." Youskevitch attributed the woman's onstage supremacy in ballet to the "result of instinctive and spontaneous acceptance by all. She as achieved her position, not by aliveness, cunning, ingenuity or knowledge; but by virtue of her natural feminine beauty and quality of action" (p. 15).

The stimulus for the male to move is the desire to please by showing off his strength and prowess in combat and the hunt, asserted Youskevitch. He equates technique with athleticism. "For a man, the technical or athletic side of dance is a rational challenge. Reason has always been the basis of his innovation. . . . There was always purpose in his dance reflecting his masculine inclinations to lead, to go forward, to achieve. Civilization does not change basic masculine nature; it develops progressive images of the man-hero. A man must keep in his dance the seeds of this heroic nature" (p. 18).

Reflecting gender stereotypes, Youskevitch alleged, "For the female, a dance does not need to have a meaning" (in Newman 1982, 58). Yet, Croce reported Balanchine's "long struggle to get American girls to stop thinking and start *dancing*" (1977, 417). However, from her own experience, ballerina Merrill Ashley said of Balanchine, "He tells stories or uses some analogy, and it's not that simple. He makes you think for yourself" (in Newman 1982, 399).

Youskevitch emphasizes, "For a man dancer, it's very important to justify the action. If you know why you're doing a certain step, or you make up your own story—'I'm doing this step in order to reach the sky' or whatever—the step acquires a better importance and a better expression than if you just perform it without a goal. And I feel it's also a more masculine way of performing, because men in general are more rational and less emotional than women. When I know that I have justified everything I do, I know also the feel of how I should do it" (in Newman 1982, 58).

Both Bruce Marks, who began his career as a modern dancer, became principal of the Metropolitan Opera Ballet, and later joined American Ballet Theatre, and Edward Villella, discussed briefly in chapter 6, identify masculine dancing with weight, a feeling of heaviness. Villella explains, "We have a more substantial base than the woman who is on *pointe*" (1969, 34). Croce, however, accuses Villella of excess ostentation: He has the "air of overdefended masculine dignity that has been so oppressive. . . . He's so concerned with projecting his virility that he seems insincere whenever he isn't dancing" (1975, 403). Marks thinks the quality of weight and the dancer's special relationship to the ground makes male dancing exciting: "Rudolf Nureyev has it tremendously. There's a kind of cat-like clawing of the ground before he goes up into the air; it's as if he grabs the ground with his feet before he goes up. . . . Women can't do it the same way; their bodies lack that kind of weight. The man can go after the ground with aggressiveness. I think my starting out as a modern dancer helped by giving me a feeling for weight and relationship to earth. Yet the Danish school, which has no modern training, is very involved with a kind of down-ness. When the Danes do a demi plié, it's enormous, and it's one of the great assets of their male dancers. They go down, down, down before they take off" (in Newman 1982, 206).

As does Youskevitch, Marks thinks a great male dancer must have "a kind of easy assurance" and "positiveness," a predetermined, planned approach. However, Marks notes changes that have occurred in male dancing. Of the mid-1950s he recalls, "Male technique at that point was very different from female technique and . . . [Antony Tudor] was . . . teaching that difference. For instance, for a man to lift his leg higher than hip level in extension just wasn't done. A man's leg was to be kept at a forty-five degree angle. And men were not to stretch. There was always a mystique about losing your jump if you stretched too much. Tudor didn't like the modern dance bow because it looked like you were stretching—you know, when you drop your whole upper body with your hands touching the floor. He said, 'Why that bow? How does that relate to the audience?'" (in Newman 1982, 206).

Marks points out that there has been an enormous change in dance style: "Men's legs now go up very easily in a stretch. There was no one who could do a split on the wall, like Misha [Baryshnikov] does, when I started studying ballet—no men. None of them wanted to. The first year I danced, I remember Pierre Lacotte came from the Paris Opéra and stretched constantly. I had never *seen* a man so stretched; it was considered taboo. We made fun of French male dancers for that. They were considered effete because they were looking for a kind of line that was forbidden to us as men. And, as a man, you turned in a *coupe* [foot at the ankle] position. To turn with your foot at knee level was like donning women's clothes. I sound like ancient history, but that's what Tudor and Craske and Corvino were teaching. A lot of that is getting lost. People are dancing more and more technically. . . . A whole different emphasis is being given" (in Newman 1982, 223).

Although Balanchine comes from the old world, his neoclassic ballet in the new reflects a contrasting ambience. Croce calls attention to contemporary symbolism in gender roles in the pas de deux. "Balanchine's world is pervaded by a modern consciousness; his women do not always live for love, and their destinies are seldom defined by the men they lean on. Sexual complicity in conflict with individual freedom is a central theme of the Balanchine *pas de deux*, and more often than not it is dramatized from the woman's point of view. The man's role is usually that of fascinated observer and would-be manipulator—the artist who seeks to possess his subject and finds that he may only explore it. . . . When the man sometimes does not 'see' (one thinks of *Orpheus*, or the lone male figure in the Elegy of *Serenade*, or *Don Quixote*, who hallucinates), he continues blindly on his mission, passive in the grip of fate.

"But when the woman is passive and sightless it is because she is without a destiny of her own. She can belong to a man. This is what the Sleepwalker suggests to the Poet in *La Sonnambula*; it is what Kay Mazzo suggests to Peter Martins in *Duo Concertant* and *Stravinsky Violin Concerto*. In both these ballets, Mazzo is blinded by Martins in a gesture both benevolent and authoritarian. . . . Even the Sleepwalker does not surrender to the Poet she tantalizes. And even Allegra Kent, who in the roles Balanchine made for her was so supple she practically invited a man to turn her into a docile toy, was uncapturable. Think of *Episodes*, in which every trap her partner set seems to contain a hidden spring by which she can release herself—or ensnare *him*; or her role in *Ivesiana* (*The Unanswered Question*), in which she is borne like an infanta on the shoulders of four men, lifted, turned in this direction and that, dropped headlong to within inches of the ground, delivered for one burning instant into the arms of a fifth man, who is crawling wretchedly after her, and taken away into the dark whence she came. Like the Sleepwalker, she does not seem to belong to herself, yet she doesn't belong to her manipulators, either—they're a part of her mystery. (In the same ballet, another woman enters blind, groping her way forward; what seems to happen between her and the man she meets is rape.)" (1977, 126).

Nineteenth-century Romantic ballet ushered in the image of the unattainable woman who is a supernatural or enchanted being. Balanchine's ballerina is unattainable "simply because she is a woman."

Balanchine is unique in "going beyond the limits of what women have conventionally expressed onstage. In *Diamonds*, the ballet that follows *Emeralds* and *Rubies* in the three-part program called *Jewels*, Suzanne Farrell dances a long, supported *adagio* the point of which is to let us see how little support she actually needs. There is no suggestion here of a partnership between equals, of matched wits in a power play such as there is in *Rubies*, with Patricia McBride and Edward Villella" (Croce 1977, 127).

For Farrell, Balanchine choreographed continually risky off-center balances "to suggest what no ballerina has suggested before her—that she can sustain herself, that she can go it alone. . . . and it makes *Diamonds* a riveting spectacle about the freest woman alive" (p. 128).

However, Farrell's role in *Bugaku* notably contrasts. "The woman is seen ribaldly as an object . . . though there are moments of satire in the geisha-girl pantomime. . . . Farrell brought out some of the acid below the surface. . . . [Allegra] Kent can bring it all out—complicity carried to the point of mockery—so the piece becomes nearly a feminist statement" (p. 129).

OTHER SYMBOLS

Classical ballet tended to present two contrasting images of woman— the unattainable, idealized, or repressed virginal love or the passionate heartthrob. The ballerina in bridal roles appears in white transparent layers of tulle or viole over satin and dances graceful, lyrical movements. By contrast, red costume often accompanies the dancer's stronger, more explicitly sexual hip-swinging movements and accents the secondary sex characteristics of pelvis, breast, and mouth and earthward movements as male partners push downward.

In the nineteenth century the writer Théophile Gautier distinguished between the two famous contemporary ballerinas. Marie Taglioni's consummate artistry personified Christian ethereality, whereas Fanny Elssler captured the escape from everyday life through the languor of exotic lands, the rhythms of the slaves, and the passions of Spain. The dancer in the United States is a symbolic image of eternal youth and sex appeal. In dance the individual dream life and culture's myth life merge.

Gender-related gestures-movements and meanings in ballet include the dancer pointing to him or herself to indicate "I," and to another to indicate "you"; arms folded across the breast symbolize mother; crossed wrists held low in front of the body signify doom or death; arms raised with clenched fist denote male villainy or anger (Terry 1982, 179). Shorn braids and second position (legs wide apart) symbolize the loss of virginity. Consequently, small *bourrée* steps in Bronsilava Nijinksa's 1923 *Les Noces* suggest braiding, as dancers cross and recross their legs while on toe. The male dancer balancing the female is a phallic pillar of strength. Many sex-related symbols are culturally specific and require background knowledge to understand them. Walter Terry points out, for example, that "when Giselle points to her ring finger, it is apparent that she is telling someone she is engaged to be married. When the Princess-Mother in *Swan Lake* points to her son and then to the ring finger . . . she is telling him the time has come for him to marry" (1982, 179). The eunuchs in *The Prodigal Son* are bald; hair signifies fertility.

Johnston perceived several other symbolic images in ballet. The dancer soaring is a soaring phallus that, once erected, must fall (ejaculate). The ballet "stretch" or leg extension is "an unrelieved exercise in phallic erected exhibitionism." Johnston sees the paradox of the ballet "in its phallic nature masquerading as a pitifully romantic searching etherealized unearthly body" (1971, 199–200). Dance therapist Elaine Siegel says of the open crotch in ballet positions, it "not only allows for the 'line' most pleasing to the balletomane but also reassures the audience that the dancer's physical prowess is not a sexual attack" (1984, 219).

There are various ways to tell a story in dance. The concretization or pantomime is the favored device in *Swan Lake*. Marcia Siegel submits: "There is nothing more jarring to the sensibilities than Margot Fonteyn in the second act semaphoring to Nureyev: 'Him Rothbart. Have heap big power from across water. No shoot um!' We have already extended our imaginations rather far to be able to accept all those girls as a flock of swans" (1972, 44–45). Siegel preferred New York City Ballet's *Swan Lake* in which Allegra Kent used her face and body as one coherent expressive instrument: "No elaborate histionic gesture spoils her portrayal; when she takes leave of Siegfried, for instance, she simply goes to him and gently puts his head down, conveying plot, character, and emotion in one lyric phrase. Allegra Kent is not a ballerina playing a swan, she is the essence of swan. She does not merely stretch her neck or flap her arms. All her dancing has the quality of floating, of unearthliness. . . . When she falls backward into Siegfried's arms, she creates a breathtaking effect of total submission that is beyond dance or acting technique alone" (p. 56).

Toni Lander, principal with the Royal Danish Ballet said, "Because the Prince is a stranger, she [Odette, the entranced princess] has to feel tremendous trust for him just to be able to say [unless somebody loves me or swears he will marry me, I will always be a swan]. . . . a lot of people like to do the *battu* at the end very strongly, bang the foot and do many strong *pirouettes*. But to me it was almost like a shivering— without touching the other foot—almost like having sex, in a way. And I always wanted to avoid noise . . . I wanted to make it like quiet love" (in Newman 1982, 182–83). About Susan Jaffe's Swan, Anna Kisselgoff (1982a) wrote, "What was different was the youthfulness of Miss Jaffe's imagery. Even her Odile was a sex kitten, and the poignancy of her Odette came from a child-woman's vulnerability and helplessness."

Modern dance which has infused ballet, developed its own symbolic vocabulary in large measure based on the work of François Delsarte (1811) and transmitted through his students. His studies of human movement led him to believe that "movements emanating from the hips down were primarily physical; from hips to shoulders, emotional; from shoulders upward, spiritual-mental. The space areas lying outside those designated segments of the body partook of the same qualities. Thus it could be said that hands resting on thighs mirror the physical, the sensual, the sexual; those same hands, pressed to the breast, reflect the emotional; hands raised upward to the head, thought or contemplation; and above the head aspiration" (Terry 1982, 81). Isadora Duncan, Ted Shawn, Martha Graham, Doris Humphrey, and Charles Weidman were among the Delsarte-endoctrinated. Graham's new style of sexuality featured the pelvis, bound (restrained) movement qualities, and torso contractions (muscles squeezed together and back toward the spine) and releases.

Jazz dance, too, has become a part of ballet and modern dance. Jazz combines aspects of earthy African uninhibited sexuality and body fluidity with theatrical, disco movements featuring easy direct enjoyment of provocative pelvic thrusts and swivels. A strand of the jazz idiom requires flaunting movement with rhythmic compulsion to project a state of orgasmic excitement.

Summary

We began this chapter with well-known critics' and dancers' perception of sexuality in dance. Because everyday markers of gender provide the pool of knowledge that participants in the arts bring to their roles as dance maker, performer, and spectator, documented gender movements were identified. So, too, were the physical limitations that set constraints for the realm of the possible in breaking traditional gender markers in dance movement. In exploring how signs and symbols of sex and gender are transformed in offstage and theatrical dance, we noted how dances mirror the cultural life of ambiguity toward sexual expression as well as the patterns of gender and socioeconomic class that reflect male upper-class dominance.

Although quotidian gender postural movement, touch, space, walk, gesture, and asymmetry commonly pertain in ballet dance, the female is vertical much of the time. Verticality is usually associated with male authority. However, the woman is often on pointe or lifted at the man's sufferance. Conventions of what is male and female both linger and change. Now male ballet dancers may lift their legs higher in extensions, stretch more, and turn with the foot at the knee rather than at the ankle, whereas in the past these movements were considered female. Dance movement perhaps changes more than the tenor of male dominance. Males attack and conquer the women in social and dance scenarios. Yet here, too, transformations occur. The European Balanchine, whose dancers are his tools, conveys in America the image of women who are free and undefined by the men they lean on. Many of his ballets are about the male would-be manipulator who does not have a controlling role.

8

Spotlighted Performances: More on Telling Sex Stories

A leitmotif running through the human record is that people explore sexuality and gender roles in dance. The overview in chapters 3–5 identified many themes of the past and in non-Western dance that we also see in dances performed on twentieth-century Western stages. No doubt choreographers have traveled, read, visited museums, or seen films, videos, and performances that have influenced their work. Equally likely, the similarities are affinities, aleatory phenomena, or deep structures of human thought and behavior emanating from the origin of the species and its evolvement in somewhat comparable ecological or socioeconomic contexts. Choreographers' work may reflect personal experience or themes that move them.

We also find that history is witness to recurrent demands for liberation from the bonds of tradition as well as urges for ties to it. In the West, the nineteenth-century Romantic era, reacting against the Age of Reason, reveals fascination with the occult, exotic, supernatural, and mysteries of the mind. Like fairy tales and their degenerate offspring of pornographic and melodramatic pulp romances, dance images give shape to romantic musings and illuminate psychic sexual anxieties and ambiguities. Enchanting fantasies of beautiful ladies, gallant men, and Gothic and exotic situations gloss the lack of woman's independence and point to her eventual submission to man. This general tendency in various stagings of classical and contemporary choreography (with a range of themes and multiple layers of meaning) continues onstage. More recent ballets, however, often deviate markedly from stock stories and traditional images to reflect the social construction of contemporary realities onstage.

After the French Revolution, the arts sought out the poorer classes as theater clients. Democratization meant that the new audience was unimpressed by academic conventions and classical allusions. These spectators demanded "entertainment," which fueled new developments in art, including the bedazzling virtuosity of innovations in ballet; thus attention to technique produced multiple pirouettes. The cataclysm of the Industrial Revolution led to fascination with the human body's comparability to the machine, a complex relationship that exists today and continues to call for yet greater physical feats onstage.

The 1920s and 1960s heralded revolutions of sensitivity in which morals changed. The women's and gay liberation movements gained momentum and pushed through new themes, and the goal of zero population growth and introduction of the birth control pill encouraged sex pleasure.

Choreographers reflect their times. Challenging their predecessors, twentieth-century dance stories, motifs, or abstractions address equality between the sexes, female empowerment, and male intimacy. There is also a reemergence of male emphasis on dominance. A backlash against new female images kinetically portrays her as calculating bitch, clinging vine, and male castrator. This chapter presents examples of persistent gender stereotypes as well as challenges to past views of sexuality. The dances described often fit into more than one category and may be referred to more than once.

Insistent Traditional Masculinity and Femininity

Critic H. T. Parker noted two facts. First, modern dancer Mary Wigman and her female dancers performed at Boston's Symphony Hall. Second, the following month on March 22, 1933, "Mr. Shawn and his attendant youth redressed that balance. Overmuch we in America believe the practice of the arts the vocation and concern of women. Our red-blooded still look a bit askance at the man who gives himself to an art of the stage; most of all if it be the art of the dance. Yet a more masculine company than Mr. Shawn and his ensemble, thirteen strong, were hard to imagine, in body, in movement, in the nature of their dances. It was indeed this insistent masculinity that, now and then, set the spectator craving a lighter touch in lighter exercise" (Holmes 1982, 163). The program included *Los Embozados, Dance of Greeting, The Cutting of the Sugar Cane,* and *Workers' Songs.* The athletic "he-man" stance of early male modern dancers was both a representation of reality—"the modern dancer was heroic," said Daniel Nagrin (quoted in Laine 1981), performing since 1940—and a defensive reaction to society's rejection of dance as an acceptable male career.

However, by 1983, critics were questioning new choreography with traditional sex roles. Jack Anderson, (1983b) called Gray Veredon's *Koan* for the Joyce Trisler Danscompany a "bore." "In Zen teaching a koan is a deliberately paradoxical statement that a Zen master gives a student to ponder to free the student's mind from the limitations of rational thought. However, Mr. Veredon's dance resembled a mating ritual. . . . The men . . . were usually aggressive, while the women . . . were frail and submissive. The choreographer did little to make this somewhat old-fashioned view of sexual differences attractive. . . . *Koan* appeared to go from courtship to marriage to possible divorce without ever revealing much about human affections."

By contrast, Twyla Tharp's blatantly old-fashioned, male-dominant yet erotically electric romantic images given shape in *Nine Sinatra Songs* were better received, because "all is beauty: a mirror ball sparkles overhead, seven women wear a rainbow of gorgeously fluid Oscar de la Renata gowns, the men are in chic tuxes. And that music—a selection of Frank Sinatra's greatest hits. Tharp has found the sweetness and sexiness in Sinatra's songs, and her dance shimmers with love" (Draegin 1984). The apogee of aggressive stereotypic male-female relations occurs in the chronicle of a hot stormy affair with sultry langorous intimacy when the man drops and drags his partner.

Classical ballet has bequested a living legacy of sex and gender images in which heterosexual chivalrous relationships create a romantic illusion that validates, idealizes, and veils male dominance. Illustrative is the neoclassic 1960 Balanchine ballet *Liebeslieder*, an hour's dance without orchestra or story. Instead there are two Brahms song cycles in waltz time and with German text. Using eight dancers Balanchine "makes the process of transformation—from the clichés of a 19th-century courting ritual into a dance poem of unutterable sublimity—central to the ballet," said Kriegsman (1984b). "We see four couples in evening dress, full of courtesy and reserve, dancing in a salon. Nothing happens, and everything happens. By purely choreographic means . . . Balanchine follows the deepening course of Brahm's music into a vortex of romantic feeling. We sense every last nuance of emotion as the couples swirl and swoon—the exaltation and pain, the joy and fragility, the passion and vicissitude and tragic mortality of their loving."

Tobi Tobias spoke with the dancers in a 1984 revival: " 'None of us,'

[Violette] Verdy observes, 'ever abandoned our grace and composure.' Yet just under the surface lay ecstasy and heartbreak, those charged feelings as evanescent as the capricious moods common to dancing in company, and all the more poignant for their being only glimpsed.

"The idealized behavior was, of course, part of a Romantic vision, 'the whole attitude,' [William] Carter says, 'of the way a man thought of a woman in the nineteenth century. We wore white gloves, and I had read stories where, at the time in Vienna, a gentleman would place a handkerchief between his hand and his partner's when he embraced her to dance, so that he wouldn't touch her even with his gloved hand. Spiritually and aesthetically, a woman was untouchable, unobtainable, the dream for which one longed' " (1984a, 40–41). One only has to read Edward Shorter's book on women's bodies and their suffering as a result of gynecological ignorance in both the lay and medical world to appreciate women's enjoyment of this illusion.

In *Bugaku*, Balanchine presents the traditional Western gender pattern in the guise of a Japanese wedding ceremony. The ballet blends certain Western steps and gestures with the Japanese ritual ambience of traditionally distinct gender roles and male dominance, perhaps the most entrenched among contemporary internationally competitive nations.

"The core of *Bugaku* is an erotic duet . . . so stylized that some members of the audience see it initially as just another example of convoluted choreography in Balanchine's experimental style. . . . It has the same earmarks of inverted classicism and the same basic faith that ballet's academic idiom can absorb these aberrational movements and 'classicize' them." The male, however, is "violent, transforming the macho flavor of the choreography into wonderfully weighted lunges—metaphors for a devouring appetite" (Kisselgoff 1984d).

Marcia Siegel speaks about "a core of American truth" found in Agnes de Mille's choreography: "One must conform to traditional sex roles or pay the consequence. . . . She buys the whole American Dream and then wreaks punishment on her characters when it doesn't work out. . . . de Mille's heroines . . . resist the roles that seem ordained for them in life. The ones that finally accept these roles live happily ever after, and the ones that don't get branded as outlaws or lunatics. . . . it's peculiarly American for adolescents to question the stability symbols that other cultures take for granted. . . .

"the de Mille heroines I've seen are adolescent, the kid growing out of tomboyhood in *Rodeo*, the soon-to-be-spinster Lizzie Borden in *Fall River Legend*, the old-maid Southern recluse in *A Rose for Miss Emily*.

They're all posed, or arrested, at that point before they have to take on the responsibilities of adult sexuality. . . .

"Lizzie and Emily carry out what must be for both of them the single most positive act of their lives, by murdering the people they love and hate. This explosion of anger is followed by a retreat into numbed silence—neither one of them lives in the real world again. De Mille revised Lizzie Borden's story by sentencing her to death; in fact, Lizzie's own community permitted her to go free—probably they knew she's exhausted all her resources and would never threaten anyone else.

"The Cowgirl in *Rodeo* . . . sees in a moment of clarity that she can solve all her troubles by being a conventional girl. . . . [She] learns you can catch a fella better with a bow in your hair than a lariat in your fist" (Siegel 1977, 52–53).

Not surprisingly men underscore the need to conform. Valery Panov's first ballet for an American company, *Heart of the Mountain*, is "all done with the high-macho insistence that passes for modernism in present-day Russia. The men swagger around, showing off for the women with a stick-twirling dance. The women droop and sway in a line, their arms twined together." Panov said the work is his tribute to freedom. From Siegel's perspective, "The real tradition-breaker is the recalcitrant bride; she gets bumped off for defying the rules of the tribe. . . . Conformity is the constantly reiterated message of the unison group dances, the men and women of the community hovering around to make sure the prescribed ritual is carried out" (p. 97).

Felia Doubrovska, dancer with the Ballet Russe, described the traditional male-female relationship in her preparation for the 1929 ballet *Prodigal Son*. A shocking ballet for its time, it is about adolescent sexual initiation and the old-fashioned two-sided view of woman as virginal or wanton. "My role was to try to please him, to conquer him— but not the regular way. When a woman does a little coquetry with a man, she smiles, she turns, she does different things to attract him. I tried to do the Siren that way to begin with teasing, flirting. But Diaghilev and Balanchine said, 'No. Something is wrong. . . . And then Balanchine said . . . 'You have to be a snake. . . . You hypnotize him. You don't kill him, but . . . ' Everything was in my eyes and in showing myself. Not one smile. . . . the legs are talking" (in Newman 1982, 7–8).

Playing the boy, Desmond Kelly described what happens when the Siren comes on stage. "By the middle of her solo, you can't help yourself. . . . And then she does that fabulous step with the cloak. That's a climax point for me, because immediately after that he plucks up enough courage to take the cloak off because he wants to see what's underneath. . . . You step away because she hasn't looked at you. . . . But then she does the kicking, takes the cloak off, and does that movement down the leg, and that's the first eye contact. . . . And that's frightening. So you back away . . . she actually takes his hand halfway through and puts it on her breast. . . . After that . . . you actually touch her. . . . You've got to build yourself to the point of touching her crotch, which you—because your daddy's told you—you must never do until you're married—and here I am doing it. And then you get carried away by the *pas de deux*. And the end of it, the boy's lying back and she lies back on you. Then she has a *rond de jambe* with the leg, and there's a movement of the boy's leg coming up. I always think of that marvelous crossing over as the actual penetration, the leg being the penis. So it's really got quite erotic by then" (in Newman 1982, 322).

Derogatoriness and obscenity and the belief in forgiveness and salvation are driving forces behind the ballet which is still being performed (e.g., in 1986 by the New York City Ballet). Croce (1982, 333) thinks young dancers growing up in our permissive society, however, do not understand what the Son is guilty of and why he must suffer, and therefore they miss the point of the ballet.

Three Virgins, Agnes de Mille's satire on virginal vanity, gives direction to audience perception through the title. Edwin Denby described the 1943 performance this way: "The dances slip from old country dance forms into burlesque bumps and bits of Lindy steps (Flying Charleston, Suzie-Q, and Pecking). The meaning of the pantomime is unmistakable" (1936, 144).

Salome is another transformation of the standard wanton woman imaged in dance. Although about ten lines are devoted to the story of Salome in the Gospel of Mark (6:14–27), Salome's elusive legend and its elaboration have been portrayed in all the arts and may be the most often used biblical character on the dance stage (Manor 1978). The Salome story seems to be that Herod, the tetrarch (Rome-appointed ruler) of Galilee, married his brother Philip's wife, Herodias. Jokanaan, John the Baptist, publicly decried the alliance as adulterous and called Herodias a whore. Herod therefore imprisoned him. Salome, perhaps Herod's own daughter, invited to dance at the court in celebration of Herod's birthday, pleased the king who then offered to give her whatever she asked. She requested advice from her mother who said to ask for John's head.

In Oscar Wilde's play *Salome* (1893), the biblical story is transformed from Salome as a good girl obeying her mother's desire for revenge to a lascivious creature with passion for Jokanaan's wild eyes and red lips. Loie Fuller danced the role in 1895. When Maud Allan, dressed in many rows of large pearls, performed her *Dance of Salome* throughout Europe in 1907, she created quite a stir. In response, a British member of Parliament, Noel Pemberton Billing, accused her of being a lesbian and a sadist in an article, "The Cult of the Clitoris," in his paper *The Vigilante*.

A Salome craze raged in Europe at the turn of the nineteenth century before it came to the United States. The fashion of Salome reached its height in Germany in 1904 (Pollard 1908). At the International Dancing Congress held in Berlin in 1908, the following story circulated:

"It seems that Miss Allan's Salome dance has so fired the imagination of London society women that one of the great hostesses of the metropolis . . . issued invitations to twenty or thirty ladies whose names figure in Court and other fashionable lists, to attend a 'Maud Allan' dinner dance, which would be undesecrated by the presence of any man, and at which the guests were bidden to appear in Salome costumes. The idea created intense interest and much enthusiasm among those honored with invitations. Each of the ladies proceeded to outvie her sisters in providing herself with . . . the undress effect of Miss Allan's scanty attire. . . . Dinner was served to an accompaniment of Salome music tinkled by an orchestra hidden discreetly behind the fortification of palms and flowers, and when the coffee and cigarette stage had been reached, some of the most graceful members of the party demonstrated that they had not only succeeded in matching Miss Allan's costume, but had learned some of her most captivating steps in movements. It was the intention of the British delegates to the international terpsichorean conference to tell this story in horror stricken accents as convincing proof that the classical dances make for public immorality" (*New York Times*, Aug. 23, 1908).

Actress Marie Cahill wrote to Pres. Theodore Roosevelt, the presidential and vice-presidential candidates, national and state chairmen of the political parties, and the leader of Tammany Hall requesting that they check the "Salome craze" in the United States. She urged putting the stage under strict state censorship and assailed Salome as a disgraceful, vulgar exhibition. Two years prior she had startled Broadway by protesting to theatrical managers against compelling chorus girls to wear tights and excessively short skirts against their will (*New York Times*, Aug. 24, 1908). Theater managers in New York City were "exceptionally active in guarding against outbreaks of Salomania" (*New York Times*, Aug. 16, 1908).

Salomes in dance continue. They include creations by Alexander Gorsky (1921), Kassian Goleizovsky (1924), Ruth St. Denis (1931), Ruth Sorel (1933), Martha Graham (1944), Serge Lifar (1946), Birgit Cullberg (1964), Joseph Lazzini (1968), Peter Durrel (1970), Maurice Béjart (1970), Lindsey Kemp (with an all-male camp version in 1977), Lester Horton (between 1931 and 1950), Carmen de Lavallade and James Truitte (1973), Flemming Flindt (1978), and new versions by Béjart (1985) and Bill Cratty (1986). Béjart's *Salome* was inspired by a passage from Solomon Volkov's book *Balanchine's Tchaikovsky* in which the author says that Balanchine suspected that Salome in Oscar Wilde's play might represent a young boy. Béjart's Salome is a man, who performs a solo (Taub 1986; see chap. 10 for a further discussion). Cratty's version transported the Salome of biblical times into the roaring twenties. Here Salome is an innocent girl; the vain stepmother is the murdering temptress.

The predatory-female-luring-reluctant-male encounter appears in modern scenic guise. Ballet Théâtre Contemporain's *Violostries* is a duet "produced for maximum excitation. Glaring white light from the sides of the stage slams starkly into the areas of combat, like TV going after a riot. The woman's hideout is a glimmering showerbath of plastic streamers. The couple's tense stalkings and devouring sexual meetings acquire superimportance in such a brilliant arena" (Siegel 1977, 99).

Life Cycle Portrayals

The above discussion of machismo, old-fashioned views of woman as virginal or wanton, pressures to conform, and pain from nonconformity touched upon aspects of the life cycle—adolescent sexual awakening, and adult romance and antagonism. These two themes are prominent in performance repertory and directly relevant to gender role definition.

L'Après-midi d'un Faune fascinates. Vaslav Nijinsky choreographed this ballet and performed the title role in the 1912 premier in Paris. A great favorite of the Parisians, Nijinsky was, nevertheless, "roundly hissed at the end of the piece" because it surpassed "all limits of convention." The press was hostile; *Figaro* and *Le Galois* strongly condemned the ballet for its "morbid mimicry" and disregard for decency and propriety. The ballet lacked virtuosity but projected elemental stillness and force, animal magnetism, sexual awakening, and measured eroticism. A faun, half man and half animal, resting upon a rocky crag frightens nymphs who approach to bathe. In the finale the faun retrieves a nymph's fallen scarf and returns to his perch by thrusting himself upon the garment as in an act of love.

The famous sculptor Auguste Rodin rallied to defend Nijinsky's ballet with a letter printed in *Le Matin*: "No part has ever brought out the Russian dancer's extraordinary qualities like *L'Après-midi d'un Faune*, in which he presents the beauty of antique statuary and shows himself the ideal model which I would be only too glad to reproduce in stone." The uproar caused an immediate rush for seats to see the ballet. Moreover, the controversy caused a storm on Rodin's own head; a national debate erupted over state support for a hotel to house his art (*New York Times*, June 2, 1912, III:4). The *New York Times* editorial reported that it could derive no clear idea of the objectionable features of the performance from the politely worded Marconi despatch. The French called *Faune* "humanital," but the newly coined word was "ugly enough to mean almost anything." The editorial asked, "Is Paris really growing moral?"

Nijinsky danced superbly, had an affair with the famous impresario Diaghilev, eventually married, and suffered from mental illness. "Nijinsky made the relation between the dancer's sexuality and the dancer's art absolute. . . . If the trilogy of *Faune*, *Jeux*, and *Sacre* has any biographical meaning at all, it is a biography of the orgasm: at first self-induced, later consciously manipulated through the piquancy and perversity of intimate relations, and finally a vast and sweated communal seizure, with death and life occurring together in a shattering rhythm. . . . In all this, Nijinsky may not be reflecting on his own sexual progress so much as responding to the pressure of his time. It was an age of revolution, and in his own way he was as much a prophet as Marx or Freud. One may say that the ballets form a parallel to Nijinsky's sexual life (adolescent soloist joins human race, fathers two). In *Sacre*, though, there is also an opening out into the political world (Croce 1982, 277).

Serge Lifar choreographed his version of *The Afternoon of a Faun* in 1935. Jerome Robbins's 1953 version for the New York City Ballet changed the Nijinsky setting from idyllic hillside with a part-animal youth and seven nymphs to a modern-day dance studio in which a narcissistic boy is visited by a girl.

Dance may portray sexual awakening as in *Faune* or what Anna Kisselgoff perceived to be love deepening as in *The Leaves Are Fading*, Antony Tudor's ballet to music by Dvořák. This dance is "plotless, and its central figures do not even appear until midway through the work. Yet it is precisely the amplification of the love theme around them—by other couples—that brings them into relief. The mood, moreover, is of love recollected. A woman in a long chiffon dress . . . walks across the stage at the start and also closes the ballet. In the interim, young people seem to discover new aspects about themselves as well as about one another. There are gestures of girlish friendship, solos and quartets for adolescent male bravado, and progressively, pairings of obvious first love." When Gelsey Kirkland danced this ballet with Kevin McKenzie, she offered "a performance of risk and excitement. . . . she has retained the sharp changes and dynamics, the astonishing plasticity that makes her every swoon in the central *pas de deux* an outpouring of passion. She is both woman wooed and the wooer. When she breaks loose, Mr. McKenzie has actually to run across the stage to catch up with her" (Kisselgoff 1984c).

Eliot Feld's *Harbinger* (1967) portrays woman pulling away from man while man desires to contain her (a traditional theme), other pairings, the extra woman, group massings, and partings. "We see the solitary boy in the beginning . . . repeatedly folding and extending his body; the reminder is fetal. . . . A youth posed on the brink of manhood, alternately reaching out to life and retreating into himself. Six girls come in, and the boy dances around them and in front of them but never with them. They're like his daydreams. One by one they slip away, then come back. When he's got them all docilely following his lead, he abruptly sinks down, and they huddle over him protectively.

"The fast duet (created by Feld and Christine Sarry) is . . . a *tour de force*. . . . Every time she reaches out, he grabs her and reins her in. She makes one last huge dive for freedom and he pulls her out of the air by clasping her around the middle. . . .

"Part three poses a self-absorbed couple against a group of seven other dancers. . . . Feld shows us various possible combinations of people—the men and women pair off, but there's always one extra woman; people walk quietly around, touching hands and parting; at times the whole group packs together in one anonymous, solid clump that includes the now-separated lovers. . . . Feld builds to a restatement of the duet's climax, and on three decelerating chords from the orchestra, all the men snatch all the girls out of the air and the curtain falls" (Siegel 1977, 56).

The life cycle may be conceived as a continual effort on the part of humans to deal with their animality through modulating their sexuality. Kriegsman (1982) described Glen Tetley's far from traditional treatment of *The Firebird* presented by the Royal Danish Ballet in 1982: "In place of the Russian fairy tale of the original ballet, Tetley attempts an allegorical abstraction. The roles of the magic Firebird and the Princess are rolled into one; the Prince becomes the Lover; and the evil

Katschei is the Keeper of the Garden. In addition there's a sextet of stiff-necked Women in Black (the costuming at the start is Victorian in look), and hordes of Young Maidens and sleek young males called Ravens. The general idea is clear enough—the Firebird, as symbol of revolt against sexual prudery and repression, is set free when the Lover vanquishes the Keeper in combat. You can make what you will of the theological or metaphysical implications . . . the ultimate effect is to reduce everything to . . . heroic Libido defeats nasty Prudery. . . . As for Tetley's choreography, it is, as ever, full of writhing torsos, entwining limbs, cascading leaps, swirling formations, all in rather fulsome profusion." In short, Kriesgman considers Tetley the "incontinent apostle of carnality."

Earlier I mentioned that ballet has incorporated aspects of modern dance. In John Butler's abstract synthetic group work *Landscape for Lovers*, Marcia Siegel tells us that "Butler uses erotic gesture, which would be taboo in classical ballet, in the same stylized way that ballet uses its own movement conventions. The girl will rub her buttocks against the boy's thigh, or he will clasp her breasts in the same cool, studied manner as if they were going through the rituals of a classical adagio. . . . Butler [switches] his male protagonist's role from that of *danseur noble*—with erect torso, sweeping arm and hand gestures, solicitous, elegant support of the girl—to modern partner with emotional expressiveness and distorted movements" (1972, 93). Butler appears to be displaying changing courtship patterns over time with the different movement vocabularies.

The life cycle usually includes not only matters of love but the related conflict between freedom and its limitations that brings about anguish. In the 1930s, Antony Tudor extended classical ballet vocabulary into an expressionist mode and presented "adult" themes once deemed unsuitable for dance. In his *Lilac Garden* an "about-to-be abandoned mistress sees her lover standing alone, facing her at a distance. Desperately she rushes at top speed across the stage; she seems to leap straight on his shoulder. He holds her tightly by the waist, she crouches there above his head, tensely arching her neck. He does not look up. . . . the pose also brings up the sudden sense of a private physical intimacy" (Denby 1986, 7).

Similarly in Tudor's 1942 *Pillar of Fire*, a tale of repressed sexuality, "a chaste and frenzied young woman sees a vigorous young man. He looks at her suggestively. She leaps at him through the air in *grand jeté*. He catches her in mid-leap in a split and she hangs against his chest as if her leap continued forever, her legs completely rigid, her body completely still" (p. 7).

Tudor uses movement styles to portray social class attitudes and codes of behavior. *Lilac Garden* "exaggerates the constraint of ballet carriage, the dancers dance rigidly, hastily, with dead arms—as beginners might. But the ballet constraint they show portrays the mental constraint of the characters in the story who rigidly follow an upper-class convention of behavior. Artificial upper-class constraint is the theme and the pathos. . . .

"In *Pillar of Fire* Tudor goes further. He shows two different ballet styles: an improperly strained one that characterizes the anguished heroine, and a smooth, proper style for the nice untroubled neighboring boys and girls. In addition, both kinds of ballet are set against the non-ballet dancing of the exciting low-life crowd—they dance and whirl in a sort of wild rumba style, swivel-hipped, explosive and frenzied; while the calm hero, in contrast to everyone, comes on not as a kind of dancer, but walking across the stage as modestly as a Fuller-brush man" (pp. 8–9).

Béjart's *Pli Selon Pli* portrays the life cycle, fold by fold, from birth to death. Once again, sensuality reigns. A man in whiteface represents the life-giving force and death.

Robert Joffrey's *Remembrances*, based on Wagner's "Wesendonck Lieder" and other music associated with the composer's lost love, evokes unfulfilled love. "The ballet is dark and luxurious, a mood, an atmosphere. Maybe it's meant as a soothing accompaniment for the audience's reveries" (Siegel 1977, 46).

Sometimes misfortune and good luck in love combine in comic ballets. *La Fille Mal Gardée* is a "couth, eighteenth-century precursor of the farmer's daughter joke. Lise, the daughter of the Widow Simone, loves Colin, a country lad, but her mother is determined to marry her off to the feeble-minded heir of a rich farmer. After a series of slapstick mistakes, Lise accidentally gets locked in the hayloft with Colin. Her purity thus compromised, she's now unfit for marriage with anyone else, to the lovers' relief.

"Most of the characters in this ballet are freaky in the extreme: the Widow Simone is traditionally played by a man; Alain, the rich man's son, is a blithering idiot who likes to chase butterflies; the rich man himself is a waddling, red-nosed fool; there's a bunch of silly neighbors and superfluous friends; and even Lise and Colin act about twelve years old, except when they do a serious *pas de deux*" (Siegel 1977, 51).

Banda, choreographed by Geoffrey Holder and premiered in 1982 by Dance Theatre of Harlem, is an exciting Caribbean genre piece on sexuality, life, and death. Dedicated to André Pierre, Haitian painter and Vodoun priest, the work is a theatricalization of a Vodoun funeral rite, for an infant mourned by its mother, in an admixture of Christianity and African religion. In the second half of the ballet, the village folk, three priests, and a lay priest call up Baron Samedi when they are unable to rid the grief-stricken mother of her misery. Exuding erotic qualities, Samedi explicitly offers solace in his *Banda* dance with what Kisselgoff (1982b) calls "Donald Williams's fabulously uninhibited pelvis-popping performance." He "suddenly trots down a ramp—backwards and daintily on the balls of his feet, in top hat and cane with buttocks bare beneath his white tails. . . . he struts, twirls his cane, gyrates in every way that would make a burlesque queen green with envy. One could believe that Karen Brown, totally convincing as the mother was left spent or dead after the mystery figure drew her into the dance."

Thus in Western theater dance, life events of love, marriage, and coping with economic reality and social morality are depicted.

Sexuality and Shock

Several ballets that shocked the sensibility of their audiences by portraying sexuality have been mentioned. *L'Après-midi d'un Faune*, about adolescent sexual awakening that ended with a masturbation gesture, *Salome* and *Prodigal Son* with their stereotypic images of wanton woman, and *Bugaku* with its image of insistent virginity and femininity. *Bugaku* has a centerstage stylized erotic nuptial dance in which the man tightly presses the woman against his torso; with her hands she grasps her feet and opens herself to her fullest split position and holds the position before the audience. Using "some nasty pseudo-Oriental mannerisms," Balanchine "seems to have derived his inspiration for the pas de deux from Japanese pornographic prints" (Croce 1975, 129). Kisselgoff (1984c) describes a 1984 revival of the 1963 piece as the "sexiest show in ballet if not in town. . . . There was a period when the acting on stage was politely described as a Japanese wedding ceremony. Now . . . it emerged as what it has always been beneath the niceties—a mating ritual in borrowed Japanese theatrical trappings."

Nijinsky's *Le Sacre du Printemps* caused a near-riot by the Parisian bourgeois audience at its 1913 premier. The sexuality of a fertility ritual, rendered with a departure from traditional ballet movement in favor of the "undisciplined barbarities" of angular turned-in placements of the limbs and with a departure from customary music in favor of Igor

Stravinsky's demonically dissonant music, stunned and outraged the audience.

Another milestone shocker was the 1967 intense, sexual, psychedelic "trip" ballet *Astarte* that Robert Joffrey choreographed to hard rock music and with search lights splayed on the audience. From out of a seat in the audience, a male dancer reaches the stage where he peels to his shorts and then engages in lovemaking with his partner, while above on a huge billowing high screen a film gives an interpretive duplication of their actions on stage. The filmed images of the dancers are dematerialized, larger, and more variable than life. *Astarte* made *Life* magazine (1969). In this innovative "theater of the senses," one feels gripped by the pounding rock music, imploding films and movement patterns, and envelopment of the performance.

"The duet begins, a slow, controlled wooing in which each partner seems to be answering some internal needs of his own, rather than the demands of the other. Each one seems to be spiraling ever deeper into an accelerating and intensifying inner vortex.

" . . . She is Astarte, the inviolable moon goddess, remote and unyielding. He is the seeker, the moth consumed in flame. His movement is sustained strong, always directed to the object of his desire, but cautious, not too familiar. She moves with percussive emphasis and swooping assertion, never adapting her body to his embraces, but angling herself around him, or extending her arms and legs out of his reach. For much of the dance they occupy separate areas of the stage, but even when they dance together, they have little sense of each other's space. Each one, separately, reaches a climax that is expressed in destructive fury. Each one, in a sense, rapes the other. When they move apart at the end, neither one has been satisfied or changed" (Siegel 1972, 122–23).

Critic Clive Barnes (1983) notes the detachment conveyed: *Asarte* is "the American dream of sex—clean, mystic, and uninvolved; a man finds his ideal, goes to her as to a priestess, they love with cool deliberation, and he passes out into the world, a new man cleansed by a cold shower of passion."

A more recent shocker is Mark Morris's *Lovey*, a dance described as "raunchy, petulant, autoerotic." Set to music by the Violent Femmes, the piece reflects the song themes of the downside of love—sex as destructive obsession and weapon. Each of the four dancers, two women and two men, carries a pink baby doll. The dancers rub these across their bodies, "smashing up their breasts, pushing into the bellies, jabbing into their crotches. The autoerotic gestures are assaultive, and the dancers fuck the audience with their anger as they fuck their bodies with the dollies. . . . Morris saves the piece with humor, and controls the passions by working in very dancerly and formal structures" (Sommer 1985).

Stark naked dancers with dangling penises, bobbing breasts, and visible pubic hair call attention to the lack of customary costuming, even if it has become skin tight and nearly nude. The rock musical *Hair,* which opened at New York's Public Theater in 1967, set a precedent in featuring a nude duet. Les Ballets Africains had already performed bare breasted to much hullabaloo. A decade later nudity occurred at the New York City Metropolitan Opera House during the 1976 three-week engagement of the Royal Danish Ballet. Flemming Flindt, in his pessimistic 1972 *Triumph of Death,* had dancers perform nude to a rock score. The ballet dramatizes the manner in which human existence is threatened by environmental pollution, political tyranny and corruption, and bustling cities contaminated by nuclear fallout. A bacchanalian orgy of degeneration marking the decline and fall of civilization climaxes the work. First commissioned by the Danish Royal Theater and premiered in 1972 in Copenhagen, the ballet caused a sensation because of its gloomy social messages. Nudity, however, caused the sensation in the United States. Critic Hubert Saal found it "pointless." Flindt believes nudity to be relevant to the production: "It's a fact of life that human beings live as much outside their clothes as inside them—a fact that should be established on the stage" (quoted in Mork 1976).

The 1960s-inaugurated sexual freedom reflected in dance imagery does not satisfy everyone. Many critics take Béjart and his Brussels-based Ballet of the Twentieth Century to task for presenting sexuality that goes beyond the limits of present-day conventions into supposedly melodramatic sensationalism. But Béjart also has his supporters, such as Barry Laine: "Physical sensuality, literary and philosophical themes and overt theatricalism are decidedly Béjartian. The choreographer's dictum, 'A beautiful *arabesque* is one well felt,' may not sit well with those who prefer to argue about placement or count *fouettés,* but it expresses an important aspect of Mr. Béjart's performance credo. 'Ballet is part of the theater,' he says. 'I want my dancers to be on the stage like human people . . . who give emotion to the audience'" (1983a). George Jackson says of Béjart: "For those who are undone by beauty, no other choreographer arranges physical moments so seductively. Whether it is the representation of male or female, human or animal or immortal one is watching onstage, in Béjart one looks with the eyes of a lover. Americans who claim to be Apollonians should remember that what is forbidden to puritans is permitted pagans. Pagans may worship at more than one shrine, at Dionysus's as well as that of Apollo. Who but a priest of Dionysus could choreograph the eternal embrace with merely the motion of breathing and a meeting of eyes?" (1983b, 19). Béjart explains his choreography this way: "Making a ballet is like making love, you don't do it alone. . . . When I create a ballet, I try to enter the form of the dancer, I try to enter his personality, his world" (quoted in Anawalt (1987a). For Béjart, "eroticism is the will to deny death; it is the affirmation of life. . . . Despite war, epidemics, devastation, all races, thanks to it, exist, spread out and perpetuate themselves. Eroticism then derives from the sacred" (quoted in Davies 1984, 107).

Sensual and shocking, but not to their usual avant-garde audiences, Eiko and Koma create imagery of "being filled, of spewing seed" in their work *Grain*. "When the audience enters the deep, narrow performance space, Eiko and Koma are sprawled far apart, face down, naked, on a white platform less than a foot high that almost fills the room. . . . Blackout. And in the darkness we hear the dry spattering sound of seeds falling. . . . when the lights come up, we can see that it's rice. . . . Afterward, pondering the slow, beautiful, violent, shocking images we can understand them all as aspects of fecundity, of nourishment. 'Wild rice growing on an unmarked grave . . . ' says the press release; the corpse fertilizes crops that feed ensuing generations—symbolically if not actually.

"Koma is lying on a white mat close to us. Eiko stands at the rear of the platform. Both are now dressed. While he slowly, slowly rolls over, knees in the air, until he is crouching, rump up, face down like an awkward newborn, she weaves her body and arms delicately in the air, twisting and bending. From her hands, sleeves, and from inside her short kimono, rice rattles down onto the platform. At some point, he makes his way to her and pulls her, still waving her arms, onto the lap he makes by squatting.

"Blackouts mark off the work. In a black-and-white film of a video . . . veiled limbs, seen in extreme closeup, tangle gently; a back looks like a ridged desert landscape. Eiko, alone on the white mat, does the same agonizingly slow roll Koma did at the beginning. Crouching, she folds up her body in ways both beautiful and grotesque; one groping leg slides past her ear. She could be a fantastic insect, an unfledged bird, a plant sending out roots and tendrils. Slyly, she picks up one corner of the mat; there's more rice under it. Koma wearing a colored blouse, dances along. Earlier, he hurls himself to the floor, making the platform bang. But now he's quiet—solid, but fluid; his upper body, arms, head ripple and wobble gently as his feet slide him into deep lunges and kneebends.

"The several times they come together, it is to mate. Again he drags her backward to his groin, and they fold up together. He puts a necklace around her neck. In all these encounters, she arches and stretches herself into accommodating positions like an animal in heat. He enters with a little tray of candles and cooked rice. She crawls, and he nuzzles his head into her crotch from behind. While he pulls her back onto him again, she crams the fluffy white rice into her mouth" (Jowitt 1983).

About their strange "cold-blooded" work, the couple say, "When we perform, we like to imagine that each of us is a fresh fish which was just caught and is on the cutting board. The fish intuits that somebody will eat it. Not room to be coquettish. The fish's body is tight, shining blue, eyes wide open. No way to escape" (Kriegsman 1985a). When the 1985 Washington, D.C., production I saw began, only Eiko was onstage. Naked, with her head facing toward the audience and her lower legs lying on a long mat beside a mound of rice, she offered the audience an almost inhuman sculptural image created by a raised back and buttocks.

Beauty and the Body

Mutations (1971), by Glen Tetley and Hans van Manen, makes a "statement about the beauty of the human body in movement, first clothed and then, very briefly naked." "There is no story. A ramp reaches from the back of the theater onto the stage. Down this ramp the dancers enter, the first of them dressed in white-like chic spacemen in an antiseptic parnassus. . . . Tetley's choreography, with its simple unfolding patterns . . . is interspersed with . . . films. . . . A naked man dances a slow celebrationary solo or a couple writhe their gradual way through a love duet.

"The essence of the piece is ritual. A couple in masks and high-soled boots parade on stage; other couples daub themselves with savage red paint. And finally a nude couple . . . perform a ceremoniously entwining duet, while three naked henchmen garb themselves in transparent plastic bags, and an echo-image of the duet is projected upon a screen behind them," writes Clive Barnes (1972). He rapped the Brooklyn Academy of Music management for capitalizing on the "shock" value by advertising, "featuring the nude ballet *Mutations*." Barnes found it "prurient-sounding, tasteless, distressing and vulgar."

"Some ballets," wrote Siegel, "are frankly about how beautiful the dancer's body is. They're made to show off finely modeled planes and surfaces, texture, and weight, just like a gallery for statues—except that, since the audience can't move around to see various angles and perspectives, the dancers change position now and then" (1972, 83).

Eliot Feld's *The Gods Amused* is in this category. "Feld appears not to have troubled himself much over the choreography; in addition to striking heroic poses, these gods disport themselves by running and leaping back and forth, and impersonally admiring each other" (Siegel 1972, 83).

Lar Lubovitch, too, "luxuriates in his dancers' bodies, especially those of the men, who are bare-chested as often as possible. The sensuality of rippling muscles and hard physical work and long, flowing hair is what claims your attention" (Siegel 1972, 126).

The beautiful body magnetizes as choreographers knowingly or not suggest gender behavior for both men and women. One message is greater bodily freedom.

The Nutcracker: Christmas and Unconscious Cruel Sex

Ambiguity in meaning is the hallmark of lasting artistic productions. Influenced by psychoanalysis, Edwin Denby in the 1930s reflected on the masterpiece *The Nutcracker*; created in 1890 and an acknowledged classic of the ballet repertoire, it is a sure money-maker in the 1980s for dance companies large and small. This standard-bearer appears every Christmas season on stages throughout the United States. The ballet comes from a long fairy tale of E. T. A. Hoffman's "The Nutcracker and the King of Mice." Hoffman was apparently a "master of the free association device . . . as familiar to educated persons in 1820 as it is to us, and practiced by them with more sense of humor" (Denby 1936, 102).

The Nutcracker . . . The story begins on Christmas Eve in an upper-class home, the *locus classicus* of ambivalent anxiety. An elderly bachelor with one eye gives a pre-adolescent girl a male nutcracker (the symbols and inversion couldn't be more harrowing). Her young brother tears it away from her by force and breaks it. But she takes it up from the floor and nurses it; she loves it. She dreams that the nutcracker turns almost into a boy. Then she dreams of a deep forest in winter with restless girl-snowflakes and a handsome young man who keeps lifting up a young lady (and who is this lady but the little heroine's own dream image?). And after that she dreams she is watching a lot of dancing

Chinamen and Russians and oddly dressed people—all of them somehow 'Sweets'; and at last the previous young man and the previous young lady turn up again, too. They furnish a brilliant climax, and that leads to a happy dazzle for everything and everybody everywhere at once. . . .

"At the start of the piece, the effect of the pantomime scene—sadistic in content for all its upper-class Christmas party manners—is gloomy and oppressed; the dancers don't really get off the floor. . . . when the dancing begins with leaps and airy lifts in the next snow scene . . . the choreography . . . preserves a coolness and remoteness. . . . The third, last scene, is friendlier, lighter, more open to the audience, more animated, more playful in detail. . . .

"And there is another unconscious satisfaction in the sequence of the dances. For the strictness of bodily control inherent in dance virtuosity, a strictness that grows more exacting as the dance becomes more animated and complex, seems at the end a satisfactory sublimation for the savagely cruel impulses suggested in the disturbing pantomime opening of the piece. And so *The Nutcracker* is really a dream about Christmas, since it succeeds in turning envy and pain into lovely invention and social harmony" (p. 101).

Against Their Wills

Researchers have demonstrated that exposure to pornography that depicts violence against women can lead to antisocial attitudes and behavior. Repeated viewing of violence desensitized men to violence against women. The more films the subjects saw, the less debasing and degrading to women they found them (Donnerstein and Linz 1985).

Rape, sadism, and incest surface in ballet. A *Song for Dead Warriors*, choreographed by Michael Smuin, codirector of the San Francisco Ballet, is a contemporary docudrama morality play. With a cast of thirty-one dancers and spectacular effects—ghostlike sheriffs standing twenty-feet tall and huge photographic blowups of bison—the 1979 stage premier of the sensational indictment of native American oppression caused quite a stir at the time. Smuin found his inspiration in the two-year occupation of Alcatraz by a group of Indian dissidents more than a decade ago; in particular, he focused on the career, both heroic and melancholy, of one of the group leaders, an Indian youth named Richard Oakes.

"In the ballet, Oakes becomes a young brave who dreams of ancestral rites and glory. At a reservation dance, he and his sweetheart are menaced by state troopers, who proceed to rape and murder the girl. Turning to drink, the young Indian is savagely beaten by pool hall thugs; after a further vision of the chiefs who were his forebears, he rouses himself to fight, kill and scalp the sheriff, only to be shot down himself by the troopers.

" . . . the dancing is wedged between . . . an introduction that depicts the native Americans' saga in voice-over narration and a montage of 19th-century photographs by Edward Curtis, along with later shots of urban degradation, and an excerpt from a '60s rally address by Marlon Brando" (Kriegsman 1984a).

Peter Martins's 1984 *Tango* raised an interesting issue: "What may have been an attempt at parody turns uneasily into a portrait of a manipulative, sadistic relationship of a man toward a woman. The final image is less than reassuring—Heather Watts lies limp across Bart Cook's knee and her slick-looking partner raises his arms triumphantly over her. Dracula as dude.

"Is this nastiness what Mr. Martins intended? The audience began to laugh and then, realizing the ambiguity of the situation ceased to do so. Miss Watts, in a fringed burlesque-queen outfit and Mr. Cook, a gigolo in shirt sleeves . . . are first seen in separate spotlights. . . . When they meet in their symbolically fused spotlights, Mr. Cook supports his partner in the sexy, arching, leg-lifting. . . .

"From the start, Miss Watts is the object of manipulation rather than desire. Mr. Cook is there to hoist her legs up and step between them as she finds herself on the floor prior to be yanked into a series of clever convolutions. Each dancer does a mock tango. Miss Watts then falls limp after some jumps on toe, only to slump into a split. She folds up like a package in Mr. Cook's arms before the final lifeless image" (Kisselgoff 1984a).

With a merciless eye for Americana, Paul Taylor confronts duplicity and sexual perversity; society's taboos surface. *American Genesis* is an evening-length biblical-historical-allegorical dance with period dance styles used to evoke period behavior. "The hillbilly Eden and the bouncy cakewalk and minstrel dancing in the final section, The Flood, convey to the audience something of the innocence of Adam and Eve in the Garden and the spirited irresponsibility of Noah's children. In "Before Eden," Taylor sets up an air of seductiveness and sexual intrigue within the contained manners of a minuet. . . .

"Taylor takes some very unusual—you might say liberated—views of sex. . . . Women play male—parts—or the part of angels with male names. Adam and Eve try a *ménage à trois* with a fellow called Jake;

then, after each one is left out in the cold while the other duet, they all decide to go their separate ways. Some early Americans are caught wife-swapping. As often as there's a character who goes naughty-naughty at some sexual innuendo, there's another character who's touting the benefits of Sin. Fun-loving Lilith's Child appears to inherit the earth after the Flood, but stalking off close behind her is Lucifer, who first introduced Adam to her mother and, in the guise of Noah, later banned her from the Ark. . . .

"In West of Eden . . . he presents an orgy of lust, rape, and fratricide, with Cain and Abel being comforted impartially at the end by one Elder while the instigators—two other Elders who've previously been identified with Good and Evil—wash their hands of all responsibility" (Siegel 1977, 224–25).

Taylor's *Big Bertha*, is "funny, macabre, garish, low-keyed, and provocative, all at the same time. It's about an all-American tourist family mesmerized into bestiality by a nickelodeon. . . . the folks next door, Mr. and Mrs. B, come sauntering in with their cute daughter . . . a typical bloodless, 1946-nice family that doesn't have problems.

"Taylor puts a coin in Bertha's hand and as she begins to play, the family dance for each other, shyly at first and with polite nods of appreciation. Suddenly Big Bertha points her baton and Mr. B. goes goggle-eyed and slaps his wife. Then he's his old bland self; you hardly think it happened. But it did happen, and as Bertha pulls them into her power, the whole family turn into fiends. Mr. B. starts fondling his daughter, then drags her off to the bushes. She's shocked at first, but later she likes it. Mrs. B. meanwhile strips to her red undies and stands on a chair wiggling, something she has no doubt considered shameful all her life.

"As the orgy is building up, you remember that at the beginning of the dance you saw some exhausted red-clad figures crawling away, and you realize that Bertha is going to wring out the hapless B's the same way. She does" (p. 213).

William Forsythe's ballet *Say Bye-bye* given its American premier by the Netherlands Dance Theater in 1982, was one of the most important of the season. Without literally depicting physical abuse, the ballet is "aggressive, powerful and downright hysterical, both a pop ballet and a sharp commentary on the society." The entire atmosphere with loud sound, high-energy flinging movement, and stylized lack of emotion among the characters "sports its alienation motif with the spiffiness of a new-wave rock group. Its powerful imagery is nonetheless a condemnation, not a glorification, of the mindless joyless gaiety it depicts."

Onstage "six men, in white shirts and ties (but threatening in their tic of punching one black-leather-gloved hand into another) and six women in black, bounce, dance and neck as if there were no tomorrow. . . . a seventh woman, neurotic in her more conservative black dress . . . attempts to drown out the din. She screams 'Stop,' twitches and retreats to the symbol of American car . . . parked in a corner of [the] three-walled no-exit set. . . . The controlling image, actual and metaphoric, is of going nowhere. Abruptly, the ballet comes to an end" (Kisselgoff 1983b).

Like the scandalous *Le Sacre du Printemps*, in which Stravinsky and Nijinsky recall human primitive nature to a fashionable audience, Forsythe's work upsets some genteel ballet sensibilities when spectators recognize their own society.

Ambiguities and Sexual Options

The Still Point, choreographed by Todd Bolender for the New York City Ballet in 1954, was part of the 1980 Alvin Ailey American Dance Theater repertoire. A young woman, left alone by friends who go off with members of the opposite sex, is assaulted by other men. Then another man quietly wins her over. Whether he is sinister or reassuring is ambiguous.

Le Sacre du Printemps choreographed by Glen Tetley raises disturbing questions about meaning. Marcia Siegel saw it as violent—bodies "thrust in distorted shapes, knot together in agonized copulations, or stiffen in rigor of ecstasy . . . mass, the pounding of the blood" (1977, 178).

Mikhail Baryshnikov's initial long solo could be one of searching, growing, yearning, dying, pleading. After much orgiastic dancing by twelve couples, he looks transfixed at Martine van Hamel standing downstage while the couples bundle on the floor.

As he begins to approach her, a group of men lift him and shove him lengthwise at her. "The men throw him around, unresisting, and I conclude he has died of mysterious causes. He's dragged out. Van Hamel dances the closest thing in the ballet to a love duet, with Clark Tippet. Baryshnikov is carried back on. He's manipulated into several bizarre positions by the men, all of which I take to be phallic. Finally the whole ensemble forms a line down to the footlights, the women on the floor, the men in wavelike . . . hand-falls, through which Baryshnikov somehow makes his way" (Siegel 1977, 178).

He pushes himself out through dancers' legs or between dancers, and is—well "reincarnated"? Onstage by himself, he dances rapidly, brilliantly, and desperately. When the group returns to perform an orgiastic circle dance, he fastens himself into a trapeze-harness which exits him up toward the audience.

"I guess he's supposed to be the Spirit of the Eternal Screw or something, if you consider screwing to be the ultimate legal act of aggression, and if you are male. The women in the ballet are forgettable, passive, except for van Hamel, and her apparent importance to Baryshnikov is never explained. She and Tippet convey something beyond pure biological attachment to each other, but like everyone else their dominant emotion is pain, not joy.

"Or maybe Baryshnikov is some sort of sacrificial figure—he does, after all, dance in the ensemble, partnering Rebecca Wright, before turning into a phallic object. Maybe this ballet is a sort of pessimistic Après-Sacre, a sequel to the original in which a Chosen Maiden comes from the ranks to die in order to renew the procreative urges of the tribe. Or maybe he's a sort of modern-day Christ figure" (Siegel 1977, 178–79).

The Pilobolus Dance Theater's *Untitled* is highly evocative and definitely contemporary. It presents images of the masculinized female and feminized male, intimacy and rivalry between women, competition among men, birth and separation, sexual jealousies, costume and identity, and family relations. We first see two women properly attired and demeanored in Victoria style. They grow into ten-foot-tall giantesses perched on the hidden shoulders of naked men whose legs show beneath their gowns. Two clothed male suitors of "normal" height pass by the women and, at the tip of a gentleman's hat, the women give birth to naked full-grown men who emerge from beneath the women's skirts. Everyone dances in various relationships. There are hints of incest and female predatory behavior as the women spend time capturing the men with their skirts, women rest and rock quietly on men's legs, clothed men with top hats lock in combat, and men's feet point daintily.

In the dancing performed by all men, Pilobolus creates kinetic sculpture of unique patterns of lifting, hanging, balanced cantilevered interlocking bodies as dancers move off each other and also on the floor as most dancers do. Movements such as those in *Ocellus* become sensual experience, "stylized skin" as Barry Laine (1978) puts it. Emotional excitement comes in "watching touch that is direct and proximity that is downright intimate. Thighs grip heads to provide support and groins slide up to asses as arms wrap around chests." The dancers reject a homo/hetero sexual as well as sport/dance or dance/theater dichotomy.

The David Gordon/Pick Up Company dances have many layers of meaning and insinuations of significant love relationships that change irrespective of the performers' sex. Dancers change places as in traditional square dancing. Deborah Jowitt (1982) remarks, "Ingeniously Gordon intercuts material or lets one idea wash over another in such a way that both are transformed."

Conclusion

As in non-Western culture, theater art dance in the United States conveys messages about maleness and femaleness. Being sexual is a key gender role. Whatever the intent of the choreographer, dances perceived as beautiful may make restricted traditional gender roles for women attractive. Dances idealize and validate stereotypic femininity and masculinity through chivalrous relations that mask the realities of male dominance and female drudging responsibilities following romantic play. The dichotomous view of woman as virgin or whore as well as the need to control animality and contest sexual prudery and repression are played out onstage. These themes appear in dances about phases of the life cycle.

Sometimes shocking presentations create compelling images. Shock, shame, and sin are in the eyes of the beholder. Yet because dancing frames visual enactments for our scrutiny, it has subversive potential in times of fluctuating mores. The dance stories and motifs of attracting the man and conquering the woman, of virginal vanity, predatory females, violent males, unrequited love, consummation, woman's patience and submission to man and marriage, cruelty, and perversity are at times diatribes against violating social customs and taboos and the impact of technology on human relations. At other times we see danced imagery influenced by the 1960s worldview that accredited a broadened range of relations with whom it was appropriate to initiate relationships and to share intimacy.

There are firsts, premieres of dances that create a furor or otherwise break conventional bounds. Although there are many artistic "starts," few take root and appear onstage over time. These dances may appear in original choreography, or they may be reset or completely rechoreographed. Sometimes the meanings are as compelling as when the work was initially viewed.

9

New Moves for Women

Now my concern is to discuss ground-breaking choreography that specifically illustrates new notions of women's sexuality and gender; in the next chapter I shall do the same for men. Once again there is some overlap. For example, the image of a woman catching an airborne man can also be seen as a man "flying" through the air and being caught by a woman. The earlier chapters have laid the framework for this discussion: In chapter 6 I sketched out women's revolt against traditional sex roles and male dominance in dance and society. Challenges to these roles occurred in ballet but most forcefully in modern dance. Its vocabularies and themes have blended into ballet during the twentieth century at the same time that major companies continue to present old classics. Chapter 7 presented twentieth-century stereotypic gender behavior and perception and the transformation of the everyday into dance signs of identity, dominance, defiance, and desire. Chapter 8 spotlighted some traditional and innovative presentations of sex roles and sexuality in dance.

Although women in modern dance may initially have heralded new moves for their sex, men are equally effective harbingers of new directions. We gleaned a sense of how Balanchine's American choreography, in contrast with his Russian classical ballet training and managerial style, responded to its time and place with a changed vision of the pas de deux. In some ballets he depicted woman as strong and independent, needing little or no support from a man, and thus his European legacy was transformed.

New guises of women in dance show them as more complex than virgin or whore, taking on roles of stature, as human (rather than supernatural) partners with and physical equals to men, guiltless protagonists rather than pawns of gods and men, antagonists confronting inner fears and thoughts, victims confronting their identity in a social order that resists change, women bonding and exploring romantic encounters with other women, in gender role reversals or blending, as asexual, and as fulfilling multiple roles.

Two Temperaments—One Woman

Not until Anna Pavlova (ca. 1881–1931) does the idea of combining two stereotypic temperaments of woman—chaste or wanton—in one ballerina achieve force. Pavlova was probably the greatest emissary of all forms of dance until the advent of television. She toured the globe for more than twenty years giving approximately four thousand ballet performances. Daughter of a laundress and a peasant, she studied at the Russian Imperial Ballet School and danced at the Maryinsky Theatre and with Diaghilev's company in Paris. Her performances in the United States, India, and Japan inspired women to step out of their private spheres and dance in public (Money 1982).

"Pavlova was both Taglioni and Elssler, virgin and bacchante," says Croce. "The sacred-profane Christian-pagan stereotypes of Western dance were a venerable tradition that had been defined, seemingly for all time. . . . In *La Bayadère*, Eastern dualism seems to have played a part in breaking down the Western either/or stereotype of the ballerina. The role of Nikiya is really more advanced psychologically than the dual role of [*Swan Lake's*] Odette-Odile. . . . Nikiya, the keeper of the flame, is one of those archetypal ballet characters who symbolize the life and art of the dancer" (1982, 283). In the Hindu tradition, the goddess may have several transformations and simultaneously possess opposing principles.

Roles of Stature

Kenneth MacMillan, in a number of his dances, has provided roles of stature for women, a contrast with the ethereal (humanlike nonhuman), wanton, and virginal traditional images. Since the 1960s he has adapted literary or historical material: *The Burrow*, based on the Anne Frank story; *The Invitation*, from two novels that had inspired movies; *Las Hermanas*, from Lorca's play *The House of Bernarda Alba*; and

Romeo and Juliet, Anastasia, Manon, and *Mayerling. Mayerling* has "not only the Mary Vetsera figure but the Countess Larisch, Rudolf's procuress and former lover; Empress Elisabeth, his mother; Princess Stephanie, his wife; and Mitzi Caspar, a prostitute who was his mistress. The ballet traces the events that led to Mayerling in a series of encounters between Rudolf and these women. . . . each duet is a variation or a comment on the theme of venery, which MacMillan places at the heart of poor Rudolf's misery" (Croce 1982, 97–98).

MacMillan, however, is irreverent toward women of stature in the field of dance. In his ballet *Isadora,* he denigrates a modern dance pioneer by ignoring her aesthetic contribution; instead, he portrays her as a foolish lesbian and men's sexual object. MacMillan also satirizes "the fossilized ballet of Duncan's period (the Alhambra, not the Maryinsky) with a vengeance that Duncan herself might well have thought excessive, and he has his merry way with a tribe of vaudeville flamenco dancers, with all social dances from the tango to the Charleston, and with Loie Fuller . . . celebrated by poets and artists of her day, [who] presented abstract spectacles of light on waving silk. . . . But while Fuller's historical importance is ground to ruble, the episode of the Fuller dancer who accosted Isadora is inflated into a full-blown lesbian pas de deux. . . . (Duncan's problem with Nursey, as she relates in *My Life,* was not lesbianism but homicidal mania. And in Duncan's version the whole episode is comically dismissed.)

"The Nursey incident is the first of many in which Isadora is treated by MacMillan as a sex object. . . . There are so many floor-slamming, whizbang adagios, with so many acrobatic crotch-held lifts . . . sex is the ruling metaphor" (Croce 1982, 394–95).

A woman's stature may appear through her symbolic dance style. Balanchine made Merrill Ashley, a "flatly American, romantically unresonant dancer," into a star. "She's the modern liberated woman as ballerina—aggressive, work-proud, mistrustful of glamour, dependent on no one for her effects. Her independence of her partner is not an illusion but a fact, which she demonstrated . . . when Robert Weiss became disabled in the middle of *Ballo della Regina* and she finished the performance without him. . . . Ashley hardly ever looks at her partner; she glances, she smiles, but she never really looks at him" (Croce 1982, 278–79).

The Pennsylvania Ballet took a unique step toward giving women roles of stature when it offered a program called In Celebration of the Woman Choreographer, with works by Isadora Duncan, Doris Humphrey, Loyce Houlton, and Senta Driver. Benjamin Harkarvy, the company's artistic director, originated the idea because of his interest in the women's movement. "And some of my most deeply moving experiences in the dance theatre have been the work of women choreographers. I was absolutely flattened by Bronislava Nijinska's *Les Noces*. I think her career was a phenomenon of our time. You can't really point to the women choreographers of the 19th century or before" (Dunning 1982).

Men and Women Sharing

Danced images suggest more than complex and significant women. In this era of equal rights for women and popularized androgyny, we see kinetic visualizations of men and women in relationships without dominance and subservience. Eliot Feld "uses technique to say something about how the people in the ballet are feeling and how they are related to each other. . . . Boy and girl are more nearly equal here." A folk quality animates the dancing in *Intermezzo, At Midnight, Meadowlark*, and *Harbinger*. With unrestrained vitality and pleasure in dancing for its own sake, the "men and women . . . partners adapt to each other rather than dominate each other." Marcia Siegel claims Feld is important "because he is the first choreographer of this generation to break with the idea that ballet is about another world—a universe peopled with invincibly beautiful beings who are possessed of superhuman powers. Feld's ballet is about this world" (1972, 74–70).

The Joffrey Ballet has taken the path between old-fashioned, woman-centered, male-dependent ballet and a new antifeminism discussed in the next chapter. In company choreographer Gerald Arpino's neoclassic ballets, the men and women often are evenly matched. Physical homogeneity between male and female is increasing.

Guiltless Female Protagonists

Martha Graham bequested future generations a history of dance refocused from a woman's point of view. Born (1894) into a respectable family headed by a physician, she has been concerned with issues of dominance. Almost every one of her dances contains a dagger or a bed, because "'those objects are so close to life. We sleep in a bed from the time we are born,' she explains, gliding serenely over the sexual issue that her dances grapple with so forcefully, 'and while we don't, perhaps, actually *use* one, there are many times when we do wield a dagger in speech, or surreptitiously in our hearts'" (Tobias 1984). Graham's strict

Presbyterian upbringing and California residence during her adolescence created a polarity manifest in the dual forces appearing in her work: unbridled passion versus duty, love attraction and repulsion, submerged guilt and open erotica, sexual inhibition and freedom—themes that others also attempt to work through in their choreography.

Graham's dances speak of the American temperament, especially of "woman's struggle for dominance without guilt." Siegel thinks that Graham's most important statement as a preeminently gifted feminist was to make the women in the stories of Oedipus, Jocasta, and Orestes human protagonists, where previously they had been "the pawns of gods and men. The Joan of Arc story usually comes to us as a tale of woman's martyrdom. Joan herself is less important than her religious fanaticism and her temerity in playing a man's role in the wars that are the business of kings." In Graham's version, *Seraphic Dialogue* (1955), "there are no kings or prime ministers in the dance; no peasants or armies or bishops or judges. Joan, played by one dancer, sees her former selves, played by three other dancers, enact her interior struggles, doubts, and spiritual joy. The only other dancers in the work portray Sts. Michael, Catherine, and Margaret" (1977, 205).

When Graham mocks Jason (*Cave of the Heart*) and Agamemnon (*Clytemnestra*), who strut with elbows spread and clenched fists, bodies bending only from the tops of the legs, "she mocks the arrogance of all kings and the rigidity of kingly succession." Graham's women "shrink back in fear, narrow themselves in repressed fury, wriggle seductively, flatten out, and expand in their rare moments of calm." *Death and Entrances* (1943) also disapprovingly shows "three women trapped by their own indecisiveness and gentility" (Siegel 1977, 200).

Night Journey is a love duet based on the Oedipus legend in which the hero flees his alleged parents in Corinth to escape prophesied incest and patricide and then unknowingly kills his real father and marries his mother, Jocasta. Ultimately he learns of his own sins and consequently blinds himself in bondage to the fate he decreed for his father's murderer. However, Graham has changed the focus from Oedipus to Jocasta as earth mother. "The Aristotelian model of tragedy is symbolically presented, but the twenty-nine minute work has little of Oedipus" (Oswald 1983, 45).

In *Errand into the Maze* (1947), "a huge bone or a branch or yoke spans the man's shoulders, and he must keep his arms wrapped around it, but robbed of his arms and hands he's still a formidable attacker. The woman is alone at the beginning of the dance, and survives alone at the end, having wrestled the man to the ground after a decisive third encounter. Narrow and tentative in her body at first, nervously poking and slithering through space, at the end she swings open her lower body, pelvis and leg, in wide, slow figure eights, as she gazes out of the entrance to the maze . . . a serpentine path made by a tape laid on the floor. Later she pulls the tape up and slings it back and forth between two branches of a tree-like structure, barring herself inside, or keeping the man out. After vanquishing the man, she undoes the tape and frees herself" (Siegel 1977, 203).

Graham shifted the focus of the Greek myth of Theseus and the Minotaur by making the Creature's antagonist a woman. "Gone is the standard tale of a hero who saves his people by seeking out an oppressor in its lair. Now it is an investigation of the hero's—heroine's—mind; her inner state of fear and tension, her positive action in going to confront the thing she fears. . . .

"Above all, what *Errand into the Maze* shows us . . . is a woman who thinks, acts, makes more room for herself to operate in. . . . Graham . . . couldn't entirely shake off society's expectations for her, or the armor of guilt, conflict, repressed violence that society decrees for its female mavericks. Graham's heroines are all nonconformists—artists, doers, women with power beyond their sexuality. And they all suffer for their unorthodoxy" (pp. 203–4).

Siegel believes that "the dignity and power of Graham's women emanate from her sense that women do have an independent existence, as rich psychically and creatively as that of men." She explores that interior existence deeply in *Letter to the World*, a dance about the New England recluse-poet Emily Dickinson (p. 206). When Graham recognizes her occasional need to depend on a man, she feels diminished. "Her two self-satires, *Acrobats of God* and *Every Soul is a Circus*, both show the heroine as a star but a star who turns all silly when a man cracks his whip. Clytemnestra consciously assumes a kittenish attitude when she's luring Agamemnon to his death. For Graham, a traditional feminine stance can be adopted only as a weapon or a sign of weakness. She seldom found a way for men and women to be equals" (pp. 204–5).

Identity as Victim

In the last chapter, the section "Against Their Wills" included examples of violent incidents choreographed by males. Female choreographers, recognizing the anguish women face in life, turn to the classics of Greek tragedy, the Bible, early well-received dances, and contemporary vignettes. In some of their choreography, a key aspect of female identity is that of victim—of love, bodily violation by men, and the battle of the sexes.

Critics refer to Graham's sex and gore, with the Jocastas, Clytemnestras, and Medeas of her psychologically oriented, erotic mythical dramas devouring their own hearts because of male victimization. *Phaedra's Dream* is an explicit homoerotic duet that suggests more than one reason for Hippolytus's rejection of his stepmother's advances in the original myth. In her 1962 version, "Graham graphically detailed Phaedra's lust for Hippolytus amid the sexually explicit sculpture of Isamu Noguchi—to the point that two members of Congress protested the State Dapartment's financing of a European tour by Graham with the work" (New York *Times*, Sept. 10 and 23, 1963, pp. 16 and 28). "Typically, the dramatic action [of the dance] was seen from the point of view of the suicidal queen, who was portrayed as the victim of fate in the personification of a malicious Aphrodite. Graham will go so far as to say that her new version 'is taken from the point of view of Hippolytus,' but she has purposefully left his relationship with another male figure open to interpretation, calling him only The Stranger" (Kisselgoff 1984f). In the unhappy triangle a woman desires a young man who desires her too but is also desired by another man. Jowitt (1984b) finds the dancers howling "I WANT!" with "their bodies all the time as they grab each other, stroke their hands down another's body, hurl themselves in frustrated anguish onto one of the Noguchi structures when the desired partner is unavailable." The talk was that the dance was about a personal incident in Graham's life, similar to her mentors' (St. Denis–Shawn) own life experience (an older woman marries a younger man who takes male lovers).

Graham's 1984 *Rite of Spring* cannily builds suspense into a rite whose outcome the audience knows in advance. "There is no elaborate procedure for the choosing of the maiden to be sacrificed; the selection is as arbitrary as destiny. Three couples perform a brief twining dance— amorous, but controlled; as they leave—the men carrying the women on their backs—the watchful Shaman comes forward without warning and plucks the last woman down. . . . And for just a second, we see members of this tribe caught off guard—not only the terrified, struggling girl, but the young man suddenly bereft of his partner.

"Soon, while the victim . . . stands twitching and shuddering, the Shaman fetches a pile of thick, white rope, loops one end around her feet, and begins to walk in a circle around her; the rope spirals gradually up her body, immobilizing her arms. Is she to die so quickly, we wonder, and how will it be done? But the Shaman releases the rope and it crumples to the floor around her feet. This was a symbolic birth then; there's more in store for her.

"The Shaman, doffing his cloak, reveals himself in spring green. The coupling is rapid, perfunctory, although we wonder for a second if the maiden is to be raped by the whole watching tribe of men. . . . the women pass across the back, spinning, as if making an agitated, but formal comment on their companion's plight. She dances her long solo. Graham has made this so agonizing in its almost constant trembling that when the girl falls and rolls down the stairs, she seems not to have danced herself to death, but to have perished from sheer terror" (Jowitt 1984b, 73).

Pina Bausch's *Rite of Spring*, says Kisselgoff (1984e), turns out to be a "recension rooted in a conventional idea, the battle of the sexes." The dirt-covered floor, natural pedestrian movement, strong formal structures, focus on repetition and cumulative phrases, flow of imagery, controlled energy, cinematic overlap, and chilling atmosphere create the mood of a stoning in a small village. "There is no promise of rebirth. The only one who dared to love becomes the victim, and falls seemingly dead."

In the lustful ballet *Amnon V'Tamar*, choreographer Martine van Hamel returns to "the compressed emotional shorthand that ballet choreographers have rarely used recently. . . . Her terse story comes from the Old Testament. King David's son Amnon rapes his half-sister, Tamar. But David is also depicted as torn by a secret of his own, his love for Jonathan. Miss van Hamel's approach is to raise questions and leave them nicely unresolved. Does Tamar consciously arouse Amnon? The choreography conveys a clever mix of sensuous self-awareness and innocence. Is David's righteousness complicated by the fact that he may have broken a taboo himself? In a duet with his current wife, Bathseba, he is haunted by the figure of Jonathan, visible only to himself and the public" (Kisselgoff 1984b). Amnon is killed for the rape by Tamar's brother Absalom.

Pina Bausch's Wuppertal Dance Theater is one of Germany's most controversial companies and one well received in the United States. She is preoccupied with themes of identity, impediments to communication, persistence of male dominance in spite of efforts to the contrary, and the penalties and pains of attempting to make chinks in the armor of the status quo. Bausch is obsessed with the oppression of women; her men and women are locked in ugly power plays. Critics refer to her theatrical idiom as one that mingles tenderness with savagery, celebration with despair, eroticism or sexual excess, and male-female violence. Roland Langer called her first premiere, *Fritz*, "a ballet about childhood fears. Fritz is a typically German being. A woman danced the title role, a man's role, and the ballet explored the question of who Fritz really is. Bausch also identified herself with Fritz—the character an adrogynous cross between different social and sexual milieus." Bausch's *The Seven Deadly Sins* and *Bluebeard* dealt with themes of angst and the emancipation of women. Her later triumph, *Komm, Tanz Mit Mir* (*Come Dance with Me*), pushed to the foreground tension between the sexes. "Men in black suits with hats pulled deeply over their faces had an aggressive macho look. The women adapted themselves, courted the men, tried to please them. Gradually they began to feel discontented with their situations, and rebelled. Male dominance won out in the end" (Langer 1984, 46).

With gloomy pessimism and a montage technique, Bausch bitterly underlines gender issues. The most powerful impression that Kisselgoff got is "the isolation of human beings from one another, and from their own impulses. In *Bluebeard*, a woman (identifiable as that last young wife) kneels between the legs of a man in an overcoat who is sitting on a chair (Bluebeard). He places one hand on top of her head and pushes her down, lifting his arm high in order to simulate great force. She immediately kneels up again. He pushes her down. These two actions escalate in speed and intensity until they dissipate in a blur. . . . To use a wife-killer and his victim as a metaphor for the impasse reached in the battle of the sexes is to say something less than hopeful about the basis of male-female relations.

"A fascinating aspect of Miss Bausch's theatricality is that her characters look so anonymous and thus, universal. If her Everyman is Bluebeard, then any woman who plays wife to him becomes the victim of spiritual murder. As physical as Miss Bausch's imagery is, and it is violently so at times, it is the emotional hurt that she appears to be symbolizing.

"D. H. Lawrence would have been at home here. Only blood and instinct—that is, the erotic impulse—count. . . .

"Jan Minarik, a bulky performer with an extraordinary capacity for repressed tension, offers a virtuoso performance as the all-round brute. And yet this is a brute with a tinge of sensitivity. The long-suffering dejection that permeates every muscle of Mr. Minarik's face has seemingly no outlet except the sudden bursts of violence and sexual compulsion that seize him throughout the work.

"Beatrice Libonati, as the Judith-wife figure, is a lumpen-wife. She exists to be hurled around, and in this respect, the endurance and stamina, not to speak of the painful intensity of her own performance, are mind-boggling" (Kisselgoff 1984e).

Gender identity may be generated by social relationships. Victimization of females by males is one such relationship; another is same-sex interaction.

Female Bonding and Lesbianism

Les Biches (meaning the little does and colloquially young women or little coquettes), created by Bronislava Nijinska in 1924 for Diaghilev's Ballets Russes, is a daring ballet that has received scant exposure since the 1930s. In 1982 the choreographer's daughter Irina and notator Juliette Kando reconstructed the piece for the Oakland Ballet, and the following year Dance Theatre of Harlem offered audiences a view of this work that explores sexual roles. Nijinska had also explored sexual roles as a dancer. She portrayed Hamlet in a piece she choreographed and with strapped breasts even played the Faun in her brother's famous *L'Après-midi d'un Faune.*

Les Biches uses classical ballet and yet reflects Jazz Age images, with body-shaking movements, hip twists, and hip-insinuating flirtatiousness. Into an airy leisure-class drawing room inhabited by women, three narcissistic, muscular young men enter, turn in the air, strut, and preen as flappers tease and chase them with curiosity. The Hostess, an older woman in beige lace and pearls holding a long cigarette holder, attracts two athletes. One of the men flirts with the page boy, or La Garçonne, the other principal female role, an androgynous figure.

David Vaughan said, "Many commentators have suggested that she is in fact meant to be a boy. Perhaps even Diaghilev was not daring enough to depict male homosexuality on the stage, though some have perceived hints of it in the interchanges of the other two Athletes, and a duet performed by two of the women clearly, though delicately, portrays a lesbian relationship" (1983, 15; see also Kriegsman 1983; Jowitt 1983). At one point two girlfriends pop their heads over the back of the drawing room sofa and then drop out of sight. Somewhat later the men abruptly turn the sofa around and discover them, as composer Frances Poulenc remarked, "lying in a position head to tail." The two shy girls, attracted to each other, briefly dance together and embrace, then flee in shock at the revelation of their furtive sexual involvement.

Certainly, *Les Biches* reflects the easy amorality of the twenties. The images of romantic encounters and odd pairings reflect an aura of exploration. Poulenc wrote: "In *Les Biches*, it's not a question of love, but a pleasure. You don't fall in love for life, you go to bed!" (quoted in Vaughan 1983). Nijinsky's *Jeux* (1913) prefigured Nijinska's *Les Biches* in its treatment of contemporary sexual mores. *Jeux* has a triangular relationship of two women and a man, which in his diary Nijinsky said was really three men making love to each other. Given the brutal treatment of male homosexuals (referred to in chap. 6), it is not surprising that men were discrete.

Ambiguity is what *Les Biches* is about says Kisselgoff (1983b). "The very sexual identity of its characters is purposefully ambiguous, and the best-known symbol of the ballet is the figure of a girl in a blue velvet jacket, white gloves and white tights and toe shoes. The British, who imagined the whole setting to be a houseparty in which partners were swapped along emancipated lines, dubbed this figure a 'page boy.' To the French milieu that saw *Les Biches* and found itself reflected in the ballet, she was an even more familiar character. . . . a novelist . . . Victor Marguerite . . . invented the boy-girl figure of the 'garçonne' and it was his novels that were forbidden fare for adolescent girls in the 1910's. Prior to recreating her usual gentle evocative style in the decor for *Les Biches*, Marie Laurencin had done the stage sets for a play called *What Young Girls Dream About*." Jennifer Dunning (1983), noting that Nijinska may have been the first and perhaps only overtly feminist choreographer in ballet, calls attention to the Hostess with the "big, slow jumps and traditionally male steps in a trio the character dances with two of the men."

Antique Epigraphs, Jerome Robbins's female version of a "fraternal" relationship with, as he put it, "understated hints of close spiritual and physical affinity" (quoted in Kriegsman 1984c), uses Debussy's flute solos "Syrinx" and "Six Epigraphes Antiques," which were inspired by the *Songs of Bilitis*, a sapphic poem by Pierre Louys. Sappho was the sixth century B.C. Greek poet who lived on the island of Lesbos and trained young women in the arts and cultural service to the gods. Controversy exists about whether she was a prostitute or a lesbian. In the ballet for eight women, dancers strike more with sensual intimacy and figural poses suggesting images on a Grecian urn. I noticed two women lifting another. Women form a line, two place their hands on the buttocks of the woman next to them, the others grasp linemates' waists. From a flat-footed, linked-arm pose they break into pirouettes *en pointe*.

"Robbins does not shy away from the image of Sappho and her amorous circle; with tender partnering and gentle support among the women and through interweaving of solo, trio, quartet and full ensemble patterns, he suggests an integral female community. But this suggestion—perhaps acknowledging the true provenance of the literary model—is never made pointedly. The dance is at once affectionately sororal and abstractly formal. For Robbins, ambiguity provides not equivocation but rich possibility" (Laine 1984, 9–10).

More explicit is Johanna Boyce's choreography *Ties that Bind*, based on life history interviews with lesbians performers Jennifer Miller (naturally bearded) and Susan Seizer. The Dance Exchange, in Washington, D.C., on March 19, 1984, featured the dancers' auto-biographical contact improvisation duet about their relationship, its intimacy, and outsiders' curiousity about them.

Role Reversal and Androgyny

In the early days of ballet, men played women's roles onstage. Then women danced their own gender roles themselves and later men's as well. Fanny Elssler, the nineteenth-century superstar, foreshadowed contemporary androgyny. "The most surprising aspect was Elssler's androgynous image when the plot called for male disguise. Gautier [French poet] was so confused that after extolling her breasts as a rarity in the land of *entrechats*, he also likened her to a hermaphrodite!" (Kisselgoff 1984g).

The ballerina in Balanchine's *La Sonnambula* emerges from the black arch of a castle portal, candle in hand, eyes fixed, in a blank, aggrieved state. She floats on toe. She exists eerily with the body of the slain poet in her arms. Here a role reversal occurs—the woman carries the man—but the woman is in an atypical state.

Intentional Divisions/Implict Connections, conceived by Bill T. Jones and choreographed in conjunction with Julie West, is a jolting reminder of yet further change in the generation of the ERA (Equal Rights Amendment). Jones, a large, muscular black man who exudes strength, danced with West, a petite white woman under five feet. Jones throws West over his shoulder, not an unusual act onstage. However, moments later, in a reversal noteworthy for the dramatic contrast in the two dancers' looks, the diminutive woman flips a man at least twice her size and weight!

A similar deliberate incongruity of body size and type appears in the 1981 *Shared Distance* that Jones choreographed. Partner Amy Pivar is as apt to carry and support him as the converse. Loving and combative, in addition to maintaining contact and independence, they struggle for equality and equilibrium. The usual expectations for male and female strength and initiative are confounded as are race relations. Blacks in the past carried whites, not vice versa.

Gender role reversal in movement appears in ballet as well as in modern dance. The Houston Ballet performance of Jiri Kylian's *Symphony in D* to classical music (portions of *Clock Symphony* and Symphony No. 73) by Joseph Haydn is illustrative. In an about-face from classical ballet in which women "fly" through the air into the arms of men who catch them, Kylian has women break the flight of an airborne man. Three extend their arms to catch the prone body of a man as he terminates his leap. I also observed two women lift a man. Later a man joined a woman's dance and displaced her in the women's group of partners lined up in a row. Obviously the ballet is a joke about ballet. It parodies partnering conventions and in so doing reinforces what could be and challenges the status quo.

In Senta Driver's *Resettings* we see the customary—men lifting woman. In addition, however, the women lift the men and wrap them around their bodies; one successful huntress carries her prey offstage. *Missing Persons* also shows that a female can assume formerly all-male roles.

Originated by black males, tap used to be performed by them only, although some white men became tappers (Hanna 1983b). Nowadays, quite a few young white women are displaying techniques learned from the jazz dancers of former generations. Both gender and racial patterns have been reversed. Black men such as Stanley Brown, Charles Cook, Honi Coles, Sandman Sims, Bunny Briggs, and Chuck Green serve as teachers to white female modern and postmodern dancers. Croce reported, "They want not so much to revive a bygone era as to develop tap into a contemporary art form. But at their concerts one tends to hear pre-rock jazz and see the dancing that went with it. . . . Gail Conrad . . . may be the only woman choreographer in the currently expanding tap field whose objective isn't laying down irons like a man" (1982, 125–26).

Senta Driver, mentioned above in regard to role reversal, often in her work reveals androgynous attitudes. Her company's formal name is Harry, which Laine (1982) says "captures her irreverence and non-categorability." Driver's dancers are weight-grounded, working in an antiballetic aesthetic in the tradition of modern dance. Her women are strong; they lift, carry, or drag a partner, male or female, around the dance floor. Driver does not think it is possible to tell if a male or female choreographed a dance. She rejects gender as relevant to using one's mind or body; either sex is capable of intellectual, aesthetic, and physical accomplishments.

In the Douglas Dunn and Dancers performance of *Game Tree* (1981 premiere), "for most of its length the dancers pair off in androgynous couplings; men support women, men men, and women women" (Vaughan 1982). At the Washington concert I saw a woman hold and support a man, women touch and lift each other, two men touch, flip each other, grasp each other's hands as one dips the other, and one jump and be caught by the other.

Men and women in the Netherlands Dance Theater often have equal dancing responsibilities—athletic, spiritual musical, moralistic, or humorous. All dancers may be nude or costumed in streamlined leotards and tights (Siegel 1977, 109).

Other examples of androgyny can be found. For example, "Paul Taylor sends his dancers hurtling through space and into and out of each other's arms with no regard for the conventions of partnering or sexually determined dynamic modulation. In Pilobolus's *Ritualistic Day Two*, there are paradoxical moments when sexual differences become erased as the men and women, all casually topless, engage in mostly comparable activity onstage" (Dunning 1984b).

There is even a dance group called Andronyz. The three-male and two-female troupe has a repertoire of approximately sixty-five numbers, the majority of which present erotic, contemporary theater in jazz dance vocabulary (Alliotts 1982, 67).

Asexual Female Dance

Historically perceived as sex objects, women's denial or downplaying of their sexuality conveys a strong statement of choice and autonomy. Johnston described Yvonne Rainer's *Trio A* as the "doing" of a thing rather than the "performing" of it "toward a removal of seductive involvement with an audience. The performers of *Trio A*, for instance, never confront the audience; the gaze is constantly averted as the head is in motion or deflected from the body if the body happens to be frontally oriented" (1971, 39–40).

As chapters 3–5 amply documents, dance has traditionally offered voyeuristic and erotic pleasures. Roger Copeland (1982) notes the feminist perspective that developed against this age-old backdrop: "Unlike the feminists of Duncan's generation who longed for sexual freedom and viewed puritanical repression as an obstacle to the emancipation of women, many feminists of the '60's and '70's eye the sexual revolution with considerable suspicion, fearful that is hadn't really liberated women, but had simply made them more sexually available . . . no longer free *not* to be sexy." He goes on to suggest that "the austere, cerebral, antivoluptuous quality of the early post-modern dances reflects these concerns of being reduced to the status of sex objects."

Multiple Roles

Twyla Tharp began her choreographic career in the 1960s as a stark, austere minimalist, resentful of physicality. That changed. Her *Rolls* immortalizes women alone. In the 1970s her dancers performed simple lifts without regard to gender. Women lifted women or men. However, *Baker's Dozen* shows that the males are boys while the females are women. *Short Stories* was a negative vision of disturbing, brutal men and women. A mischief-maker who uses balletic legs while the upper bodies speak of an inner rhythmic world of social dancing. Tharp has presented a range of gender options in her dances, including the traditional male dominant-female submissive ones. Tharp has attempted "to shatter convention and reconstitute it in contemporary terms" (Coe 1985, 216; see 205–28). She thinks that "societal conventions have altered radically in the last thirty years. I am not politically active because, while political action may change the course of people's lives, so does art. . . . In some ways being an artist is a much more powerful position to be in. I am, in fact, dealing with real world problems. I'm dealing with morality in those dances" (p. 224).

Nancy Spanier explores sexuality and gender while capturing the range and complexity of human feelings through her melding of movement, music, vocalizations, and humor. Luger (1982) describes *Maiden Forms*, a quartet for women, as a journey through the evolution of woman's consciousness. Spanier puts up to scrutiny the stereotypes of the woman as temptress: the coy, the vamp, the innocent. In another section the dancers "frolic with each other like little girls, or a pack of puppies. On all fours, they nuzzle up to one another, butt, push, and roll over each other. Slowly their play becomes more aggressive. Their bodies . . . become rigid, alert, threatening. They stare at the audience and begin to yowl. They transform from puppies to a pack of menacing she-wolves, advancing downstage." The dance concludes with imagery of the nurturing aspect of womanhood. One by one the dancers slowly wind themselves up in a billowing expanse of white fabric that stretches from one wing of the stage to the other. When all of the dancers are enveloped, a child emerges from beneath the soft, trembling fabric."

Spanier choreographed *Peep Show* as the male counterpart to *Maiden Forms*. First she got twelve men together to deal with their images of women. Then, yelling out concepts upon which the men improvised, Spanier structured, shaped, and edited the movement. The group performed sequences of movements usually performed by or associated with women: chorus lines, stripper bumping and grinding, and sultry and seductive movements. The men "strike body-builder poses, and in a changing series of positions from the Kamasutra, each describes his 'perfect woman.' Throughout the dance they are manipulated by an androgynous figure in a black tuxedo and whiteface. The master/mistress of ceremonies teases and excites them, and at the end of the dance, barebreasted and stripped down to bikini briefs—exposed as a woman—joins their line." The men are clad only in jockey shorts (Luger 1982).

Summary

New danced images combine the virgin and bacchante; indeed, one finds complex women expressing many different facets. Both men and women choreographers now portray women in roles of stature, in the reality and illusion of exerting physical strength, and even in lesbian relationships. Males and females appear to share and to relate to each other in a real world—echoing the 1970s-inspired need for human exchange rather than use of another person as object. Reflecting the liberation movements of the 1960s, both sexes dance with the same physicality.

However, audiences also get pessimistic and angry messages about an unyielding status quo. Women choreographers often cannot shed the ideology of a traditional upbringing, which creates conflicts that they attempt to resolve through dance. We see images of women who suffer for their unorthodoxy. Classical tragedies about male heroes are retold with female heroines or stalwart women, and dances are choreographed with women performing in innovatively defiant and bold ways. Both sexes bring to the stage themes that appear in the news: women as victims of love, fate, bodily violation, and other dominance by males.

Who am I, and with whom and how many I share intimacy are questions the dance illusions raise. Females dance male roles or create dances that attempt to neutralize gender. Moreover, women move in ways formerly considered the province of men. Women could be featured as antagonists beginning in the 1930s, but we rarely saw them touching and supporting each other and men to the extent that they do today.

10

New Moves for Men

This chapter and the last emphasize dances about subcultures that present alternative gender images generally in conflict with the accepted views of the dominant culture. Previous chapters (6, 8, and 9) have shown that in Western theatrical dance, some women heralded a revolution against traditional classical ballet concepts and actions; some men have also participated in these innovations and have offered their own, including male-specific exchanges.

Some early twentieth-century innovations in male ballet roles were made: Michel Fokine eliminated fussiness and ornamentation, Sergei Diaghilev promoted superb male dancers, and Vaslav Nijinsky choreographed ballets about sexuality, gays, androgyny. Since the 1960s, changes have accelerated, partly because Rudolf Nureyev and Edward Villella earn six-digit incomes and have emphasized weight, Mikhail Baryshnikov inspires through exemplary technique, and Jacques d'Amboise has educated children and adults nationwide in public institutions and performances, some of which have been televised.

At the same time that masculinity through athletics in dance was being promoted (by female choreographers too), dance makers were recognizing other male qualities. Traditionally men danced together mostly in competition, battle, or work. Now they might relate as lovers. Another dimension of male liberation has meant breaking the stereotypes of masculinity of strength, directness, and weight. The French showed that men could stretch; blacks showed that men could ripple their torsos and rotate and shift their ribcages. More followed.

Stimuli for innovation in male dancing have included aesthetic impulses as well as male resentment against the nineteenth-century onstage woman-centered ballet and the twentieth-century feminist thrust against male domination through modern dance. These stimuli have encouraged several developments. For example, some male choreographers put men instead of women in the limelight. Second, a few men usurp traditionally female roles and movement. Third, men sometimes obliterate women through unisex movement and role reversal, which from another point of view make women equal to men. Exaggerated assertion of machismo is a fourth response, which goes hand in glove with the appearance of such books as *Real Men Don't Eat Quiche, A Guidebook to All That Is Truly Masculine, The Manly Handbook,* and *Be a Man.* A fifth reaction is derogation of women. Moreover, men now explore onstage gay relations and other "deviations" from the traditional norm. At times gay love is dressed up as something else, such as brotherly affection serving as a metaphor for passionate love. More recent dances are explicit or even actualizations.

Men Reassert Themselves

Serge Lifar, premier danseur of Diaghilev's Ballets Russes, and later of the Paris Opéra Ballet, said, "The masculine history of dancing is Nijinsky, Lifar, Nureyev, Baryshnikov" (in Newman 1982, 25). When Nureyev left the Kirov Ballet and found a home and partner in England's Royal Ballet and Margot Fonteyn, he brought with him a new image of male dancing. It disturbed and eventually benefited the young dancers with whom he came in contact (Clarke and Crisp 1981). Indeed, as indicated in chapters 1 and 6, Nureyev has boosted dance in the United States, especially for men.

The Russian prodigy Nureyev encroached on what had come to be the ballerina's traditional territory. He extended male roles or took over female roles by performing filigree steps, adagio, and unison dance (Hunt 1986, 54). "In *Le Spectre de la Rose,* Nureyev dances a part that Nijinsky himself came to loathe as 'too pretty.' Apart from its exotic aspect, *Spectre* is a *danseur-noble* role carried to an extreme of virtuosity and endurance—virtually a nonstop allegro solo, offset but hardly interrupted by passages of doublework. The Specter guides and shadows the ballerina. . . . Nureyev's insularity reached its peak when, while Denise Jackson waltzed around the stage, he held a high *relevé* in fifth [balancing on the balls of his feet, one in front of the other] with his gaze fixed on her empty chair" (Croce 1982, 165–66).

As mentioned in chapter 8, Béjart changed a female character into a male in his ballet *Salome*. It featured the Paris Opéra star and guest Patrick Dupond, who did "some ballerina imitations that wouldn't be out of place in the Ballets Trokadero [see below]. Then dressers enfold him in a mammoth gown, place his feet in platform shoes and hand him a plastic bust of a head (looking more like Dupond himself than John the Baptist). He kisses it on the mouth. Curtain" (Taub 1986, 32).

Michael Smuin's staging of *Romeo and Juliet* for the San Francisco Ballet, claims Croce, has "lots of appeal for homosexuals—not only in the youth-passion-frustration theme but in the many large roles for male dancers. Until the last act, the ballet belongs mainly to Romeo and his friends (and enemies). Juliet flits palely through, usually wearing a nightgown, while the boys are in tights and codpieces. . . . Audiences applaud the young men who carry the show—applaud them sentimentally for being dancers and outcasts from normal society. . . . *Romeo and Juliet* may be the only ballet in standard repertory that homosexuals can identify with emotionally without distortion." Smuin "doesn't minimize the fact that there are more boy-boy scenes" (1977, 179, 134).

Other examples of men moving into the preserve of women include Kenneth MacMillan's substitution of a squad of Russian naval officers for the traditional corps de ballet in *Anastasia*. For the 1972 Stravinsky Festival put on by the New York City Ballet, Jerome Robbins choreographed *Scherzo Fantastique* in which a pas de deux is backed by an ensemble of three men instead of women.

Gerald Arpino's *Trinity*, *Sacred Grove on Mount Tamalpais*, and *Olympics* are male-featured ballets. Ben Stevenson's *L* for the Houston Ballet is an all-male percussion jazz piece. Besides evincing strength and prowess as they hurtle themselves in all manner of leaps and turns, men hold each other's arms, and they flip each other as they might flip women.

In modern dance, the matriarchs spawned male reactions, as described in chapter 6. Ted Shawn organized an all-male company whose specialty was macho movements. José Limón wanted to restore and redeem the male dancer to his former grandeur. He saw women as evil and bitchy or madonnas, whereas men held power and accomplished things. His men's dances include *The Traitor* (1954) and *The Unsung* (1970). Limón also showed men and women working together. Communal circles characterize *There Is a Time* and *Missa Brevis*.

Bill T. Jones's *Fever Swamp* features six male performers, and though Jones says that "he 'never sets out to make a dance about relationships,' *Fever Swamp*—insofar as it explores the way six men negotiate their way through the fast-paced lifting, supporting, touching sequences—depicts men working together at tasks that evoke trust and cooperation, rather than the traditionally masculine competition. 'I told them to think about occasions when men help each other, like when their fathers taught them how to ride the bicycle,' the choreographer explains. Why did he choose an all-male cast? 'I don't often get the chance to work with so many good male dancers and I wanted to do a cool dance. I felt that if I used men and women together, both performers and audiences would read traditional romantic relationships into the lifting and touching sequences. I want to stay away from that!' " (Pally 1983).

Derogation of Women

Has feminism changed men? One woman said feminism has "made things difficult for some of us who like chivalry and a lot of romance is lost." Another woman came down hard: "Sure, men have changed. They've become sneakier, craftier, angrier, more insecure and more misogynist. They're afraid they're going to be castrated. Speaking generally, men either want to *own* a woman or *be* one."[1]

"Siegfried's revenge," the classical ballet *Swan Lake* in which the lead male's traditional role is to lift the ballerina and look noble, was restaged by Erik Bruhn with a new interpretation. In the old version Siegfried, the hero, is a vascillating playboy who cannot find the right girl. To his mother's dismay, he swears eternal commitment to an enchanted Swan with whom he falls in love. When he returns to his palace, he is tricked into betraying her by a magician's daughter. In despair and suffering, he rejoins his beloved briefly before losing her forever.

Bruhn, a great *danseur noble*, refused to dance *Swan Lake* and proceeded to choreograph a "corrective" version, with the Prince as the central character. In this rendition performed by the National Ballet of Canada, Siegfried resents his bullying mother and meets his downfall by choosing spiritual over sexual love. The villain has become a woman, called the Black Queen, alter ego of Siegfried's domineering mother. This Siegfried isn't any more independent than the nineteenth-century original—he's still the victim of women. But he rebels against their power and bids for the audience's sympathy (Siegel 1977, 104–6).

John Butler's *According to Eve*, choreographed for the Alvin Ailey company, portrayed the biblical brothers Cain and Abel as pawns of their mother. Sex has a lot to do with this murder story, and the mother is blamed for what transpires. Favoring Abel and spurning Cain, she watches the spectacular struggle between the men.

In *Nijinsky, Clown of God*, Béjart reinterprets the life of the great dancer "to show him as an innocent whose art, sanity, and finally his life are destroyed by a predatory woman. A childlike Nijinsky flourishes happily under the thumb of the impresario Diaghilev, his mastermind, father, and lover, until the advent of the classic temptress he eventually marries. The marriage costs Nijinsky his friends, work, and Big Daddy. His sexy wife thereupon turns into a symbol of spiritual love" (Siegel 1977, 107).

Siegel calls Balanchine's *Variations pour une Porte et un Soupir* "a blatant send-up of all those duets between predatory females and impotent males, some of which are found even in the New York City Ballet repertory." In this ballet, stars twitch and throw hostile stares at each other (p. 73).

"A whole series of ballets could be grouped under the title 'The Making of a Homosexual,'" asserts Siegel. "Antony Tudor's *Undertow* (1945) established the genre, with its disaster-prone plot and mandatory meanies: parents who show their rejection of their son by having violent sexual relations, the young girl who's too naive to give him real love, the pack of boys who initiate him into sado-masochistic manhood, the woman of the world who awakens castration fears" (p. 107).

Antiwoman messages astonish in Jerome Robbins's *The Cage* (performed to Igor Stravinsky's Concerto in D, premiered in 1951 by the New York City Ballet, and still performed), a story of a covy of female spiders who gruesomely kill their lovers after using them for impregnation. "It is an angry, sparse, unsparing piece, decadent in its concern with misogyny and its contempt for procreation. It dodges no issues, but cuts to the heart of the matter in hand with sharp and steely thrusts. Its characters are insects, it is without heart or conscience. . . . But in spite of its negations, it is a tremendous little work [less than 15 minutes], with the mark of genius upon it," Martin (1951) wrote. Onstage with a simple web structure of ropes, "the Queen ushers the Novice, the pups, into being. A male is drawn prematurely into this nest of vicious females, only to have his neck broken between the legs of the Novice. A second male is lured into mating, and is tossed aside to destruction once he has served his purpose. What remains is a completely unemotional sense of biological function fulfilled, ritual accomplished, nature ruthlessly observed."

The program notes say that the ballet is based on the phenomenon that "occurs in certain forms of insect and animal life and even in our own mythology" in which "the female of the species considers the male as prey." Some people viewed the cruelties of *The Cage* as metaphors for sex drive and instinct or the stereotypic castrating female. A feminist interpretation *might* be the strength and independence of women. Kirstein viewed *The Cage* as a "ferocious update of the second act of *Giselle* . . . a manifesto for Women's Lib" (1973, 128).

Yet, Siegel, as do others, finds *The Cage* to be daring, provocative, and "ugly." Not only does the male choreographer portray a society of predatory females, but "he disfigures them physically, psychologically, every other way. Melissa Hayden looks like a wrestler in the vivacious central role" (1977, 66). Anderson (1983a) writes: "As for Mr. Robbin's *The Cage*, that's black magic, a ballet about man-devouring female insects that combines a fantastic plot with a pinch of Freudianism. . . . with Heather Watts in its leading role, it was electrifying. Almost totally compulsive in her behavior, Miss Watts made every step something a force beyond her control had driven her to do, except for a few moments when she paused, bewildered, as if trying to take stock of her actions. But compulsion always overwhelmed her and she went her murderous way." In reviewing the 1985 performance of *The Cage*, Anderson (1985) refers to "insects on the march," "belligerent bugs," "a dance-drama about a species resembling the mantis. . . . What makes the ballet disquieting is the fact that the female of this species considers the male as prey and Mr. Robbins may be implying that relationships between human beings can be similar power struggles." *"The Cage* raises the troublesome question of whether character is the result of nature or nurture" (Anderson 1982a).

"Once seen," Dunning (1986) proclaims, *"The Cage* tends not to be forgotten." Kisselgoff (1985) asks, "Why is *The Cage* theatrically alive, even entertaining rather than repulsive? The secret lies in Mr. Robbins's restraint. No matter how extreme his imagery, it never crosses certain lines of implausibility. The emotions he depicts are built into the choreography. Thus, when the female insects begin to nibble away at their victim and when the heroine kills her lover by pulling at his entrails, Mr. Robbins has already set up a frame of reference that keeps such passages from being ludicrous." The Novice appears vulnerable at first, supple and cringing, until the erotic and tough queen bids her attack her male lover. Abruptly transformed, she turns "coldly cruel, rubbing her hands as if she were licking her chops."

A year after *The Cage*'s premiere, The Hague's burgomaster, in 1952, insisted that the New York City Ballet remove the ballet from its programs while in that city. His objection did not center on the ballet's negative view of women but on the costume and movement. Indeed, when two critics saw *The Cage* performed in Florence, they deemed it "pornographic" and "shameless." As government officials led a crusade to get the ballet removed from the programs, the public clamored for tickets, which tripled in price (Schorr 1952). Ironically, two decades later the Dutch national ballet companies flaunted frontal male nudity as thrilling aesthetic innovation. Balanchine opted to approximate the body, unimpeded by redundant adornment, clothing his dancers in music, gesture, locomotion, and body leotards.

In Louis Falco's *Huescape*, two men are interested in a woman and in each other. "The woman represents a threat to their friendship/romance because she's a possible companion to each of them. The dance is played out on the level of movement tensions and balances—a cat's cradle of arrangements and entanglements and undoings—but the dancers as people are rootless, motiveless." In Béjart's *Symphonie pour un Homme Seul*, "The hero, He, and ten pals are working hard at representing Mankind, when the heroine, She, comes around bothering them. Why are they disconcerted? Why does He look so tormented by her advances. Not for any reason we can see, except that She is female" (Siegel 1977, 110).

William Forsythe's *Love Songs*, premiered in the United States in 1983 by the Robert Joffrey Ballet, presents an ugly view of man-woman relationships suffused with women deserving of violence against them. In this way the ballet differs in its portrayal of aggression in human affairs from those dances discussed in the sections "Against Their Will" and "Identity as Victim." *Love Songs* is about hate, "a deliberate mix of shabbiness and elegance, a collage of emotional violence and technical virtuosity." Kisselgoff (1983a) reports that the ballet shocked when the Joffrey presented it in 1982 to celebrate its move to the Los Angeles Music Center: "At least one movie star and other members in the audience found *Love Songs* too ungenteel for a ballet gala." Burt Supree (1985) writes, "To recordings by Dionne Warwick and Aretha Franklin, with its pent-up soloists spotlit in the nowhere of a dark stage, *Love Songs* is irrevocably rude and sleazy. In solos and duets, the dancers fling their bodies in disgust and rage, break and collapse, throw themselves around, work themselves into fits and let their movement dribble away."

Critic Suzanne Levy (1984) calls the work "patently offensive in its portrayal of woman as harpy, temptress, shrew, betrayer and slut, and particularly obscene in its depiction of women as the deserving victims of the sexual and physical assaults of men. . . . A willful misrepresentation of songs . . . this work goes beyond the other contemporary revivals of 'Apache' dance in the manner of its indignities and the extent of its violence."

Unisexuality and Role Reversal

Androgyny and asexuality in dance, reactions not only to the male-derived ballet tradition but also to the female challenge, are two-sided. On the one hand, they equalize the sexes; on the other hand, they eliminate the specific character of a sexual being. Mention has been made of men choreographing for persons irregardless of gender or of blending gender roles in response to the trends of the day and as a way of breaking with mentors.

Béjart's premier danseur, Jorge Donn, champions the choreographer's style and aesthetic philosophy: "For Béjart, ballet is man" (quoted in Philp 1983, 62). Yet it is his vision of man. In writer Richard Philp's assessment, "One of Donn's most fascinating performance qualities is occasionally described as androgynous. In Donn, this is not a confusion of sexual roles, nor is it nonsexual. Rather, it is an expression of sexuality on a plane above individual differences, something like a universal sexuality, which casts a potent spell on both the men and the women in the audience" (p. 62).

Manuel Alum who studied Kabuki in Japan thinks that "a true artist knows and trains for both 'male' and 'female' qualities." Society is becoming more receptive to alternative gender roles and demonstrative emotion by men onstage. Dancer Tim Buckley admits, however, that "you can't get away from society. If a movement vocabulary comes out of a man's body it will reflect his physical and social identity." Crustily but wisely, modern dancer Daniel Nagrin warns, "If you need clear answers, you can't afford to see dance" (quoted in Laine 1981). Ambiguity is often the excitement in art.

Bill T. Jones, with Arnie Zane, in their choreography *How to Walk an Elephant*, makes statements about changing attitudes toward gender and androgyny. Premiered in August 1985, this postmodern dance for the Alvin Ailey Dance Theater, had only unisex costumes (lacework tops, a cross between shirts and shifts, worn over tights and jazz shoes). Males not only lifted and caught each other but they parodied ballet, doing movements females commonly do. For example, men performed the Swan Queen's variation of *fouettées*.

To the unique player-piano compositions with rhythmic, harmonic, and formal complexity of experimentalist Conlon Nancarrow, *Elephant*, Alan M. Kriegsman (1985b) tells us, makes "frequent allusions to George Balanchine's 1934 ballet *Serenade*, in his first choreography in America. Eventually, most of the key images . . . are set forth by Jones and Zane in a kind of in-joke parody, often reversing the original gender, for instance, so that the two women and a man of Balanchine's finale become two men and a woman." In lieu of a woman in arabesque revolving in place while a man on the floor below turns the leg on which she stands, Jones and Zane substitute a tall slim male in arabesque. The team is "cannily perceptive about the racist and sexist undertones of the dance past. A possible scenario: The elephant stands for the huge, lumbering classical ballet establishment (recall that Balanchine once literally choreographed circus elephants for Barnum and Bailey), with its virginal ballerinas and slavishly supportive males. Sure, we all love the ballet, but it's really not of our time, so we've got to teach it to walk, that is, to accustom it to the pedestrian movement and contemporary sensibilities that are the stock in trade of postmodernism."

Critic Sali Ann Kriegsman (1985) sees the piece as an extension of Balanchine's break away from hierarchic ballet roles and his greater use of the ensemble. "*Elephant* is even more egalitarian sexually and racially. Balanchine disposed his dancers in new ways on the stage; Jones/Zane wipe the stage with a phalanx of walking dancers, cleaning the slate. They conceal a soloist behind the ensemble and democratize activity."

A brief digression to a non-high-art role reversal performance is apt here. The various forms of performance do, after all, influence each other. First established during the mid 1970s, the male strip show for women appears on the surface as a role reversal of the scenario of woman as passive sexual object and man as consumer and sexual dominant. (Sally Rand epitomizes the fan burlesque performer.) Geared to the woman consumer, male strip shows in bars and nightclubs are found not only in large metropolitan centers but also in small towns in the Midwest and South. The establishments restrict their clientele to women to avoid attracting gays or other men who might inhibit the women.

At Haskell's Club the female announcer encourages sexual behaviors usually associated with the aggressive societal stereotypes of men (Peterson and Dressel 1982). The announcer's statements, such as "it's equal rights night, ladies; we're gonna let the guys work for us for a change" and "we're going to toast the men who are sitting home waiting for you ladies," set the frame for the interaction between male dancer and female customer. Here, the women stomp their feet, yell cheers and lewd remarks, act rowdy, whistle, and verbally and physically abuse the male stripper. The dancers attempt to explore the fantasies of women. For some women, the performance may offer anticipatory socialization; here encounters with the opposite sex have a minimal risk of rejection. The woman can claim her overture or proposal to the dancer was a joke.

Ginnie's is a discoteque that features a male strip show one night a week and permits men in the club immediately after the two-hour show "to come dance and romance with the ladies who have experienced the ultimate 'Male Review'" (Arnold and Margolis 1985; see *Time* 1979; Lewin 1984). As in all disco performances, the disc jockey "works" the audience. While "equal time for women" is a salient theme, the male show, deeply embedded in the gender hierarchy, reenacts and upholds male dominance. Four of the five "Feelgood Dancers" create the traditional aura of romance and chivalry mixed with overt sexuality and male aggressiveness. The dancers appear as sheriff with six-shooter, lion tamer, escaped convict, sailor returning after years at sea, well-muscled men who enhance their size by dancing on tables and balconies. The disc jockey continually and patronizingly tells the female audience how to behave. He urges, "The more you scream, the more you see," screaming being a stereotypic female act. He urges the women to tip and cajoles them to "dive bomb" (a woman puts a dollar bill in her mouth, gets down on the floor on her knees and sticks the bill into the front of the dancer's G-string), an act symbolic of fellatio and female subservience, availability and vulnerability. The gender role reversal or transcendence is somewhat illusory.

Gay Men

Clive Barnes pointed out in 1974 that many of the greatest male dancers and choreographers, especially in the twentieth century, have been homosexual or bisexual. He asked, "Why then, is the dance world so coy and mealy-mouthed about dealing with the subject on stage?" About a decade later Bill T. Jones rued, "Even among the intelligentsia there's a repressive tendency, a polite agreement not to talk about it. They don't want to know about your sexuality—or your politics" (quoted in Laine 1985). Critic Graham Jackson bemoaned in 1978, "We still don't have a dance that meets the demands of both art and a liberated gay consciousness. Will we ever get one? With all the gay involvement in the dance world, we can certainly say we deserve something better" (p. 103).

In his study of the New York City Ballet, Joseph Mazo (1974) calculated the number of gay male dancers compared to the number of straight: six of the eight principal male dancers and about half of the male soloists were practicing heterosexuals; the corps was "overwhelmingly gay."

The answer to the slow uncloseting of homosexuality is that dance is part of social history. Chapter 6 noted the discrimination against male homosexuals. World War II mobilized American society, disrupted traditional social patterns, and catalyzed single-sex emotional ties formed by the war (D'Emilio 1983). Strictures against repression of the body and feeling loosened in the 1960s. The Beatles helped create a counterculture of millions of people who began to regard themselves as separate from mainstream society by virtue of their youthful sensibility, openness, and distrust of those over thirty. During the pivotal 1960s, the black civil rights, antiwar, and women's movements provided models for a new gay militancy. Ballets with homosexual themes and love duets began to emerge following the Nijinsky forerunners, but with great tact and usually still disguised as something else. "Even the male/female sexual duet," says Barnes (1974), "has to be executed and conceived with a certain kind of taste that establishes it as erotic art and not pornography."

Graham Jackson points out that gay men can be macho dancers as well as dainty ones. And there is room for the androgyne. Jackson asks why a woman can make herself as glamorous and appealing as possible, but a man flaunting his sexuality is considered improper.

The year 1982 marked the appearance of four major Hollywood films with gay themes and gay characters—*Making Love, Victor/Victoria, Personal Best,* and *Partners* showed throughout the United States. Germany's *Taxi zum Klo* played in art theaters. Gay subjects were finally being shown on the popular entertainment screen, after Hollywood through the fifties had shunned gay themes except in offering an oblique picture of gays as either sissies or villains. Thus the film industry helped reinforce messages of gender that had been danced out.

For the most part, the conservative nature of ballet had led gay male ballet choreographers to continue making the "pretty dances for girls in filmy dresses" rather than dealing with a nonfantasy world. Jackson thinks that many gay men were initially attracted to ballet "because of its ambivalence, its latent homoerotic potential, and yes, its reputation for being a sanctuary of 'faggots.' Once 'in,' however, they become very self-protective, very conservative. They are careful not to jeopardize their position with critics, public, or management by being too blatant: an old-boy network is established to ensure the status quo" (1978, 43).

In a *Stagebill* article, Barry Laine describes himself as "a writer, an occasional critic, an enthusiastic audience, an amateur dancer, and in my fantasies—a choreographer. And gay: something I might not have to emphasize if it didn't seem so at odds with so much of what I see and hear around me." He worries about the "homophobia that inhabits one of our most benighted classes; the dance critic." He believes they either ignore gayness in dance or lambaste it. "Even the polite code which claims that the personal lives of artists should not be relevant to their creative work is often really the guarded notion that a revelation of the homosexuality of a choreographer or dancer will cancel out the esteem and worth of his art" (n.d.). Laine speaks of the understanding that gayness and "modernism" in all areas of artistic endeavor have been intimately entwined. What is the "natural stamp of one's life upon one's art?" Diaghilev offered less subsidy than experience and inspiration, which sparked to light the creative fires of his chosen loves in the well-established European and Russian tradition of aristocratic patronage (artistic and sexual) (1980b).

Onstage, gay men have been portrayed in various ways. Choreographic motifs run the gamut: unhappy to joyous, masked to unmasked, lustful to loving, and problematic to admirable woman.

UNHAPPY HOMOSEXUAL

Monument for a Dead Boy, choreographed by Rudi van Dantzig and first performed in Amsterdam on June 19, 1965, by the Dutch National Ballet, was one of the first ballets to portray the making, life, and death of a homosexual. Parents, friends, sexual encounters, and psychic trauma are displayed in fragmentary narrative. "On a stage, empty but for some impressionistic, Noguchi-like set pieces, a young man, the title character, stabs the air with his arms in what seems like a future attempt to break free of his past, and then doubles up in a foetal position while a flock of black-draped furies hover near. The boy, it seems, has been traumatized by a brutal display of parental coitus. He can't make it with a snaky seductress in blue; he feels dirty just thinking about it. He wants to go back to the days when he kissed a little girl among the hollyhocks, but this innocence is irretrievable and he turns to a young man for comfort. For this, the boy is taunted and gang-raped by a pack of school chums. With insult heaped upon injury, the boy kills himself." The choreographer's use of symbolic gesture is sufficiently ambiguous so that alternative interpretations were possible. However, Graham Jackson reports, "The serious young men who had sat through countless *Giselles* and *Swan Lakes*, more interested in the boys in white tights than the prima's pirouettes, took to championing *Monument* as the beginning of a new era in dance" (1978, 38). More ballets with homosexual themes followed, usually with the similar motif of the unhappy homosexual.

When *Monument* was performed in 1973 by the American Ballet Theatre, the "first-night audience occasionally giggled at its moments of high passion or high camp" (Barnes 1973). Anderson sums up his perception of the poor reception: "What has caused *Monument* to crumble is a shift in social attitudes. In 1967, its presentation of homosexuality startled us. Since then, thanks to the sexual liberationists, we have become slightly less self-conscious in our discussion of sexual matters. *Monument* . . . survives from a period in which, possibly to mollify the prudes, an artistic representation of homosexuality had to have a slightly whining tone and an obligatory unhappy ending (quoted in Jackson 1978, 39).

Kenneth MacMillan's 1982 premier of *The Wild Boy*, featuring Mikhail Baryshnikov, created a sensation with its raw power. Natalia Makarova danced the Woman, Kevin McKenzie, her Husband. The sexy ballet portrays what natural man uncovers about socialized humans. His association with a herd of animals symbolizes the boy's initial uncorrupted state. Sharing the Woman with other men symbolizes the crudeness and violence of civilization. Kisselgoff (1982b) found the key passions involved, however, "not with the ballet-coupling of the boy and woman to represent his sexual awakening, but when the boy brings the men together in a kiss." The animals reject the contaminated boy.

DIFFERENT WAYS OF LOVE

During the seventies a number of ballets included pas de deux (or trois) for men that showed the acceptance and beauty of homosexuality. For example, in *The Goldberg Variations* (1971) by Jerome Robbins, the two boys dance together as two girls watch. Critics noticed, "Robbins hints at the differing ways of love with artful nuance" (Emory Lewis quoted in Jackson 1978, 44) and "one of the most beautifully subtle inventive treatments of a male-male duet" (Tobias 1975). *Weewis* (1971), by Margo Sappington for the City Center Joffrey Ballet, had a sexually suggestive male pas de deux that *Time* magazine called "homoerotic." The choreographer said that the sequence was about her husband's relationship with his best friend. *Mutations* (1971), by Glen Tetley for the Netherlands Dance Theater, included one of three "love movements" for three nude men. In another sequence "duos of nude men slapped red paint on one another's bodies; they then smeared it over themselves by rubbing together" (Jackson 1978, 44). Hans van Manen's *The Rite of Spring* (1974), for the Dutch National Ballet, has a tender sequence for two boys in "The Dance of the Adolescents." Whereas the men are attractively clothed in brief briefs, the women appear in "ugly body stockings draped in what look like plant tendrils" (p. 45).

Some ballets are essentially homoerotic but pretend to be something else. *Renard*, Siegel believes, is a "homosexual hors d'oeuvre that Béjart tries to dignify with a philosophical program note about the eternal treachery of Woman. The setting is 1920s-French-silent-movie-playground, all slicked-back hair and becoming tank-top bathing suits.

"The Fox . . . furiously bats her eyelashes and wiggles her hips at the Cock, who is horrified but too weak to resist. He is saved from her clutches by his two friends, the Cat and the Goat, who beat her up cheerfully. But she's not dead; at the end they all go off chummily in a real antique car. . . . Béjart's soft, sensuous movement and heavy-handed kitsch may be the new turn-on, but they mask a virulent antifeminism and a rerouted sexuality that seem to be his real message" (1972, 132).

About Béjart's *Gaîté Parisienne* (1983), George Jackson (1986) writes, "How naughty of him to . . . call a gay *pas de deux* a father-son reconciliation."

In Kenneth MacMillan's *Triad*, premiered in 1972, "we are supposed to be seeing a girl flirting with two brothers [causing them to become romantic rivals] . . . but what we actually see . . . is a girl intervening between two male lovers." One can see them warmly embrace, clasp, cling, entwine, and otherwise touch. The man who loses his male lover cries. About the 1984 rendition, Anderson (1984) remarks, "Unfortunately, because they still must battle against vestiges of the puritanical notion that dance is 'depraved,' choreographers remain squeamish about treating certain sexual themes in a forthright manner. Therefore *Triad*'s men remain shadowy figures."

When Vicente Nebrada staged a male duet in *Gemini* for the Harkness Ballet in 1973, the two young men writhing around on stage were presented as twins. An unabashedly homoerotic pas de deux required them to twine and curve around and lift each other. Siegel, upset with the 1974 Harkness season, dismissed the repertoire as gay liberation propaganda and antifeminism. While the male dancers were the sexual focus, the women were the sirens, vamps, or witches (reported in Jackson 1978, 46).

The Relativity of Icarus (1974) by Gerald Arpino of the City Center Joffrey Ballet is implicitly homosexual, although Arpino denied the homosexual inference. Two male leads represent the mythic airborne figures of Daedalus and Icarus. Nearly naked, they touch each other erotically in a cantilevered duet. "If they're supposed to be, in fact, father and son, there is no discrepancy discernible in age to make this believable" (Jackson 1978, 47).

Although one woman represents the Sun, "the men have the bulk of the choreography, which includes many gymnastic feats, strenuous lifts and reciprocal clinches. They are costumed in something just this side of a G-string and are reflected and multiplied by an admiring accompaniment of stage mirrors. When the ballet premiered in fall 1974 it occasioned outrage in all quarters, and like any true *succès de scandale*, packed them in.

"Deborah Jowitt characterized it as 'not so much sensual as pornographic,' Arlene Croce as 'an endless vision of the young and gay in one another's crotches,' and Clive Barnes as a 'pseudo-mythological half-baked apology for sex'" (Laine n.d.) Barnes (1974) exclaimed, "Arpino can call them Icarus and Daedalus until he is blue in the face, but unless you read the program, what you will see is a male love duet. . . . It is also naughtily daring, with deliberate, slow motion grasps, gropes, and gestures, all signifying things that do not look at all myth to me." Laine (1985) questions what Arpino was doing: "Was he championing a broader, uncategorical sexuality for men, a less restrictive gender identity? Or deftly sidestepping what could have been an awkward admission?"

In an April 17, 1987, interview on National Public Radio, Arpino admitted to being in love with the human anatomy and sexuality: "The relationship is divine." The interviewer noted that critics have commented on Arpino's themes of "male love and orgasms" at the same that he is a "choir boy at heart."

Concerto in F, originally choreographed by Billy Wilson in 1981, effuses ambiguity. Two men appear sleeping adjacent to one another. They awaken, stretch, touch, engage in an arm wrestling gesture. Then a woman enters. Flirting with her reaps fruitless results. She leaves them, and they return to each other, lie down once again, one placing his head on the other's stomach.

Not only may some ballets be about intimate male love under the pretense of something else, but choreographer/dancer intention may be different than audience perception. Lar Lubovitch explains that his *Concerto Six Twenty-Two,* premiered in France in 1985 and the following year in the United States, was motivated by AIDS, "because so many dancers have been stricken with AIDS, something the dancing world doesn't own up to. . . . I felt that I wanted to show a version of male love on a platonic and high-minded level, to show the dignity of men who love each other as friends, that all men do have another man in their lives that they love so dearly, not in a homosexual relationship, but just all men, homosexual or heterosexual, have men that they love in their lives. But it's such a delicate subject, and such an embarrassing subject for so many men, that it's very hard for them to deal with it, [and therefore] it's so rarely dealt with" (quoted in Parks 1986, 56). By 1987, Lubovitch had catalyzed thirteen New York–based dance companies to perform in a benefit, called Dancing for Life, to raise money for organizations involved in research, public relations, and patient care.

The following ballets are illustrative of those presenting more explicit homosexual/erotic relationships. *The Wedding Present* (1962), by Peter Darrell for Western Ballet Theatre, portrays a new marriage and its disintegration when the bride discovers her husband's former homosexual relationship and is driven to nymphomania. *The Scarlet Pastorale* (1975), performed by the Scottish Ballet Theatre, focuses on a jaded nobleman and his hedonistic courtiers in search of new pleasures.

Sir Frederick Ashton's *Death in Venice* (1973), based on the Thomas Mann story, portrays an aging writer obsessed by the beauty of a young boy vacationing with his family in plague-ridden Venice. The Sydney Dance Company from Australia presented a full-length ballet *After Venice* in New York City. The ballet is not a sequel but a retelling of the Mann tale in which choreographer Graeme Murphy embodies the general themes through allegorical figures. Tadzio, the young Polish boy the aging creative artist Aschenbach loves from a distance, is a "little punk intent on self-gratification—sleeping with his mother or cavorting with the boys on the beach, who might be Australian surfers, or leading an all-male steam bath ensemble." Male nudity and the approach to the conflicts attract attention. On the one hand, the artist is enamored of the idea of beauty symbolized by Tadzio and the conflict between decline and youth. On the other hand, Murphy spells out the artist's physical attraction to the boy through allegory. "Lust is personified by . . . a lewd fellow with blue lips who thrusts his pelvis out while wearing suggestively cut jeans. His opposite number is Love . . . in lacy dress with flowers in her hair. . . . Life and Death are conveyed by . . . Aschenbach and the contrasting image of Tadzio" (Kisselgoff 1985).

When Alvin Ailey's company performed Rodney Griffin's *Sonnets*, Anderson (1983b) called it "a cool dance about what some people might consider a hot topic, because it shows how a Dark Lady (April Berry) comes between two male lovers, a Poet (Michihiko Oka) and his Friend (Masazumi Chaya). Nothing is shocking here, and although the male duets are romantically tender, they could offend only a Puritan's eyes." What makes the work acceptable appears to be subtle metaphor rather than concretization or more explicit imagery. George Jackson (1983a) witnessed a sex triangle in which "movement turns into abrupt gesture. There is too much smoothness, however, and too little incisiveness to create impact. Soon, one cares little that Dudley Williams's poet is abandoned by both his boy love, Ronald Brown, and Donna Wood as his lady."

Graham Jackson thinks Hans van Manen's works have none of the vulgarity or pseudomysticism of Béjart's or Arpino's. He describes van Manen's *Metaphors*, first performed by the Dutch National Ballet in 1976. The men utilize familiar steps: "lifts, supported turns and arabesques—the classical syllabus for ballerina and *danseur noble*. In a completely natural, uninhibited manner, it emphasizes tenderness and mutual support. For the women's pas de deux, a striving for harmony, symmetry, and crystalline clarity is most apparent. . . . When the men step in to partner them in 'normal' ballet style, the women remain holding hands, even through lifts and supported turns, as if to emphasize the strength of their communion. Both pas de deux are . . . loving—in an almost political way. . . . [van Manen gives a] positive, deeply-felt statement about the rightness of same-sex relationships" (1978, 54).

Béjart, whose grand spectacles audiences either intensely like or dislike, offers paens to what, to him, is part of a continuum of human nature more than an aberrant anomaly: sexuality, heterosexuality, homosexuality, and pansexuality. Croce charges him with sheer gall in making excess the norm in purveying sensation. "The company these days is more openly a drag show than it used to be. . . . But what Béjart's sense of theatre comes down to is an addiction to greasepaint, flashy costumes, masks, boys cast as girls, dual and triple identities, and silences broken by hideous bursts of laughter" (1982, 160).

Fascinated with the male form and explicitly willing to deal with male homosexual themes, Béjart, Laine believes, is a true innovator in ballet. His men have direct physical contact as they partner and support each other; he may use a cadre of men in place of the traditional female corps. *Our Faust* has the protagonist dance with twelve adolescent males; Lucifer and Mephistopheles join in a duet; Satan, Lucifer, and Beelzebub, in a male trio. Béjart's *Bolero* (1971) had a solo dance performed by a woman and a male corps. Essentially about lust, it was "refreshing because it shoots down several stereotypes of both male and female personality." Another rendition presents a man as sex object dancing on a table for a crowd of women. This can be seen as breaking barriers for women or taunting them with a man they cannot have. A still later version uses a male solo with male corps: "forty men pant and pace, circle nervously and generally cream over a beautiful bare-chested man undulating above" (pers. com.).

Representing lovemaking in dance is part of the Greek heritage. Xenophon described a dance of Ariadne and Dionysus in the act (Davies 1984, 23). Following this tradition in his unique way, Béjart created *Dionysos Suite* (1983) to celebrate the orgiastic world of the god of wine and the enduring passionate impulse in human nature. The homoerotic cult of male beauty is actualized as seminaked muscular young men in a semicircle show off lustily for each other in a frenzied sexual competition. Responding to this bacchanalian sensuosity, critic Sasha Anawalt (1987b) said, "There are so many blooming men onstage gyrating with their shirts off . . . and they dance so well that one would have to be blindfolded and hormone-free not to participate in that vision of heat."

A choreographer of the 1980s, Mark Morris, writes Tobi Tobias, "identifies himself as a gay artist and his sexual orientation and attitudes are evident in his work. In the tender *New Love Song Waltzes*, partnering is as often single-sex as it is boy-and-girl, and loving embraces are similarly treated. The Socrates piece allows its all-male cast to move softly, with sensuous and dignified vulnerability." Formerly with the Eliot Feld Ballet, Morris intoned, "I got tired of pretending to be a straight guy in love with a ballerina" (1984b, HC30; also see Jowitt 1986).

Men Together, a festival of gay male performance organized by Tim Miller in 1981, pointed toward two tendencies in recent gay art, reported Sally Banes (1981): "One is the acknowledgment that the body is both subject and purveyor of a social message. The other is a parodic thrust, from the vantage . . . of a subculture outside the mainstream, aimed not only at sexual mores but at the world at large."

Bill T. Jones and Arnie Zane choreographed and danced in the high-energy gymnastic duet *Rotary Action*, a "loose, limber, swiveling romp, spiked with lifts that were barely credible" (Gurewitsch 1982). They present onstage their shared life commitment offstage. "The couple has been insistent about establishing a parallel legitimacy. . . . They have refused to be coy about being gay (Laine 1985, 23). The men chase each other, wrestle, and perform an old usually heterosexual jitterbug move in which partners hold hands and swing under their arms. The viewer encounters the elfin white Zane hefting the mighty black Jones. In size and looks, each is the antithesis of the other. The performers have often said that they want to make art that puts people on the spot, entertaining but provocative about racism, sexism, and sexuality.

The French-Canadian Le Group Novelle Aire's dances reflect both gay and political influences. Daniel Léveillé said he and his colleagues feel strongly about representing the male point of view as well as stressing the impact of the political crises in Quebec since the 1960s. Paul-André Fortier elaborated: "The dance explosion is a logical form of expression following the cultural explosion in literature and film. The public needs to identify itself. An artist has no choice. It's like being pregnant. You can have an abortion or give birth. Our gestation period is over and our self expression is coming out" (quoted in Citron 1982, 41). Viewing dance as political and universal, Edouard Louk said that "modern dance has often been linked with subversiveness. Culture has to find a way of coping with society, especially when society is in a state of change." Fortier's *Violence*, wrote Paula Citron, appears "to be a feminist nightmare. Three girls provocatively parade around in skimpy outfits and red high heels, causing such agitation on the part of the watching men that one of them uses a garden hose like an extended penis and ejaculates water into a bucket. The three relationships which ensue all have sadomasochistic overtones." The choreographer claims the piece is based "on domination and mutual destruction. I'm pointing out sexual brutality. The audience should be asking, 'Am I that dependent, that macho? Where am I in relation to my partner?'" (p. 39).

Léveillé admits that his predominant interest is sex. "We've had women's liberation for 10 years but the problems for men are intense as well. Men have to change. They can meet to talk about cars and sports because they can't talk about the essentials of life." In *Fleurs de Peau* (*Flowers of Skin*), a dance for four male dancers, there is touching and fantasy, and also violence because it is part of men's lives (Citron 1982, 41).

PARODIES AND PASSING DRAG

I have mentioned that men, seriously or in parody, have sometimes assumed female gender movements and roles in dance. Further discussion of the Western historical and psychological context is warranted to help understand some new moves for men that evolve from everyday exchanges, social, folk, and ritual dances, and individual impulses.

Theatrical female impersonators in Western culture arose from the Judeo-Christian exclusion of women from an active role in religious ritual (Brierley 1979). Religious drama either excluded females as characters or boys played the female roles. This trend carried over into the tradition of secular theater and strolling players, and there was broad social rejection of female actresses as well. The medieval theater was a bawdy, unsanitary place. Even in the seventeenth century women were greeted with hostility and derision. In the Elizabethan theater, males played female parts, but Restoration theater made female actresses acceptable. The first portrayal by a female actress was probably Desdemona in 1660.

During ballet's Romantic era, the ascendancy of the female and the discovery of the charm of danseuse *en travesti* created a revulsion against male dancers. Women danced female and male roles. Men reacted against the female-centered ballet in various ways, one of which was to participate in male transvestite dancing.

Dame parts and drag acts today differ from the female impersonation of Elizabethan theater. Transvestite dancing, long a component of the gay demimonde, surfaced from the semisecret underground of clubs largely frequented by homosexuals to the stages of major theaters of the world capitals, where drag ballet has played to standing-room-only crowds, as well as to the mainstream of Broadway and Hollywood. Contemporary performances depend upon the success with which the audience is kept aware that the female onstage is male. Through innuendo, the dancer provides clues that render the performer's real identity. An Elizabethan female impersonator, by contrast, had no need to exploit the audience's knowledge of his true sex.

Michele Wandor points out that "transvestite theatre has flourished at times of changing attitudes to women in theatre and to sexuality in society—the Restoration, the Industrial Revolution, the suffrage agitation and now, in the second half of the twentieth century. At such times clearly there is a tension between the surface appearance of how men and women are supposed to 'be' and the changing reality. The function of transvestite theatre thus becomes twofold; on the one hand, it is an effort to contain rebellion by ridiculing any departure from the 'norm,' and on the other, it becomes an expression of a rebellion against the status quo. . . . The theatrical traditions of 'camp' and 'drag' thus have their roots in the changing relationship of women to theatre, but because the theatre has been male-dominated, these traditions have, despite a legacy of male impersonation by women, been expressions of male explorations of sexual representation"(1981, 19). [2]

Erika Munk (1985) agrees with these "two plausible takes on drag from the point of view of sexual politics." "Theatrical drag . . . [is] liberating because it reveals the artificiality of sexual roles, the arbitrary quality of those gestures, attitudes, costumes, forms of language, and psychological stances which we usually place as either male or female. If gender can be put on and taken off . . . , the relationship between society and biology is unmasked. . . . For the performer, drag casts off one set of shackles while only contingently imposing another; for the spectators, it is a distancing device which lets them imagine other possibilities, other ways to play our roles or to smash them. In this perspective, drag is part of the topsy-turvy utopian tradition of carnival.

"The opposite reading is that drag reinforces rather than breaks down the status quo . . . and the roles usually done are hostile or patronizing caricatures through which the performer seems to establish not that he is female, and not that femaleness is an irrelevant category, but that he can take on certain attributes of femaleness while remaining safely and smugly, male. Seen this way, drag is not only hostile to every attempt women are making to free themselves, but also inimical to gay men's liberation because it reproduces a sexual structure which weighs down on male homosexuality."

Janice Raymond points out that "all transsexuals rape women's bodies by reducing the real female form to an artifact, appropriating this body for themselves" (1979, 104).

Psychologists' views of transvestism in general might help clarify its onstage dance manifestation (Brierley 1979). The pressure for a man to perform aggressively in a male role may be cause for cross-dressing and related behavior. Travesty recognizes the feminine element in every man's nature, which some women appreciate, and acknowledges that the difference between men and women is not so great. Transvestism may reduce stress, create excitement, and relieve gender demands. Sometimes a caricature of the image of the opposite sex is an attempt to demonstrate the right not to adopt an essentially heterosexual way of life; the parody calls attention to the cultural blueprint and the frequency with which it is disregarded. By being a lie, the duplicity of travesty is also a mockery of preestablished sex roles.

Humor helps people experience the unusual and uncomfortable. Discomfiture is likely for some viewers unless they can assume that the travesty performance is in jest. Laughter at the abnormal may police the marginally committed through self-shame and embarrassment into the accepted mold. Alternatively, travesty may create a self-fulfilling prophecy as inner character becomes congruent with outward appearance. Sexual masquerade may express one's sexual orientation and evoke response as such.

In her study of female impersonators in the United States, Ester Newton discovered that the structure of sex roles is maintained by acquiescence of participants, who accept their fate as natural and legitimate. The fundamental division of the social world into male and female ramifies in the male world of homosexuality. Female impersonators, who tend to be homosexual, are at the lower end of the prestige continuum of theater performers. In the "drag" system of impersonation, the effect is "to wrench the sex roles loose from that which supposedly determines them, that is, genital sex. Gay people know that sex-typed behavior can be achieved, contrary to what is popularly believed" (1972, 103).

Female impersonators may mimic ballerinas, flamenco, or acrobatic dancers. In addition to soloists, there are bare-legged chorus dancers, often simply an excuse for getting good-looking boys on stage. The "exotic dance" is the most common kind of dance act appearing in drag shows. This "strip" dancing must meet the challenge of creating the illusion of femininity with little body covering. Thus these men shave off body hair, avoid heavy labor in order to minimize muscular development, and wear a "gaff" to conceal the genitals by strapping them tightly down and back between the legs. The drag stripper attempts to create the same erotic effects on the audience as a female stripper. For straight audiences, the drag stripper sustains the illusion of "reality" down to the bra and G-string. As a climax he pulls off the bra, revealing a perfectly flat chest. For solely gay audiences, this is unnecessary. "Beating women at the glamour game is a feat valued by all female impersonators and by many homosexuals in general" (Newton 1972, 46). Dance is an auxiliary of glamour.

The slapstick and stand-up comedy acts focus on the glamour mode that presents women at their "best" or most desirable and exciting to men. "Glamour is stylized pornography. . . . The flip side of glamour is prostitution. This relationship is laid bare (literally) in the strip, which begins as a clothing show and ends as a skin show. Both the glamour queen and the prostitute are frankly desirable to men and contrast with the housewife-mother" (Newton 1972, 46).

Dance is one means of manipulating sex role behavior. The drag queen, a visible stigmata of homosexuality, embodies and symbolizes the male who places himself as woman in relation to other men. A drag dancer's performance makes gay men laugh rather than cry. For straights, sexuality, gender, and prestige match, whereas for homosexuals, these are out of joint.

We have seen several examples of men moving into the preserve of women in ballet and modern dance. However, the most dramatic male appropriation of what is female in dance is seen in the travesty performed by several dance companies with the word *Trockadero* in their titles. These companies of men dance female as well as male roles. Viewers have attacked the drag-queen act as pitiful, antiballet, and misogynous. However, Les Ballets Trockadero de Monte Carlo, without subsidy or corporate boards, has been a box office success throughout the United States. Most critics recognize that the company performs entertaining burlesque and physical comedy that lovingly parodies the act of performance, specific ballets, and particular styles through informed in-jokes. In parodying gender and a stylization of it, the Trocks distinguish stylistic differences among ballets and know the ballets they make fun of so perfectly that they portray roles and roles within roles. Spoofingly sturdy men doing dainty steps that ballet tradition has reserved for women emphasizes absurdity. However, the well-trained men excel in the art of ballet (Jackson 1983a).

The company presents dance parodies of *Swan Lake, Go for Barocco,* and *Pas de Quarte,* a spoof of Martha Graham called *Phaedra Monotonous No. 1148,* and bombastic ballets of the Bolshoi with allusions to a crumbling Roman Empire. These attack two styles of choreography with which dance aficionados are familiar. In addition, the company performs fine reproductions of, for example, *Les Sylphides,* the *Harlequinade Pas de Deux,* and *The Dying Swan.* Peter Anastos, artistic director, explained in the *New York Times,* December 12, 1976, that one of the company's purposes was to show that men can do the same things that women can do in ballet. The men render what a ballerina actually does at the same time that they present a critical comment on what she should do. Yet, "the ballerina is a metaphor, who appears before us as a vessel teeming with abstract preliterate suggestions—forever a symbol, never a person" (Croce 1977, 76).

Conclusion

Aesthetic dance traditions evolve from and resonate with the contextual past. The new moves of socially constructed kinetic discourse by and for men discussed in this chapter are in part a reaction to the decline in prestige of male dancers since the time of Louis XIV. Women, banned from public theater at the outset of ballet, ascended in the nineteenth century to the limelight of classical ballet. In the following century, modern dance, birthed by women, gave females even more recognition onstage. Dominant backstage throughout theater history, men have reasserted themselves onstage most forcefully since the 1960s. Choreography has featured men and even men by themselves in complete dances without women; moreover, men have appropriated movements formerly categorized as female. And men once again have performed both men's and women's roles. A range of assertive images play across the stage: macho men, derogated women, and beautiful gay men as men in travesty.

Male homosexual themes at first appear obliquely and then become translucent as the gay liberation movement gives support to uncloseting, and even popular culture explores topics formerly taboo. Dance imagery reflects more preoccupation with sexual conflict than with harmony, genesis of male homosexuality, male communion, casual encounters, self-redemption, and ambiguous options.

11

Coda

Spotlight

This book has focused on a compelling issue of our time: the continuing reconstitution of gender roles and meanings that bear on the perpetual human struggle with questions of self-identity and interpersonal relationships. In an era of challenges to dominance hierarchies and the onset of genetic engineering, an attempt to understand gender construction is of special significance. My intention has been to enrich the discourse on male/female body images and social change by spotlighting and clarifying how gender is socially and culturally constructed and transformed in a critical medium of human communication—the dance.

Notwithstanding its importance, gender in dance as related to society has not been examined in cross-cultural and historical perspective. Every discourse re-creates the world and fashions it according to priorities or unintentional ends. Through their kinetic discourse of moving reality and illusion, dancers, as social beings, create knowledge. We apprehend gender principles from the imaginative emanations encoded in dances we see and hear or read about. The images are among the models that socialize or provoke dance participants, both performers and observers, to act in the social arena. Dance, one of the earliest recorded forms of human behavior, persists in its varied transformations through history and across space, and when repressed or suppressed, dance rises, phoenixlike. In the United States, and many other countries, live theater dance has proliferated, images of dance in frozen pictorial advertisements have increasingly appeared, and dance on film and video has gained the potential to reach nearly every household through television.

That dance is part of life is self-evident. With bare energy finely honed in a dance style, the body, the first form of power, shoots or extends into space and time. The body sustains that power symbolically in the postindustrial society as people have become health conscious and exercise prone. Because the body is ubiquitous and sentient, its appearance in dance taps potent, dramatic, and easy-to-recall sources of images. Sexuality resonates in body and psyche, touches elemental fears and joys, and suffuses dance. Thus, in considering gender, the inherent sexuality in dance must be given its due: sex and gender, and sometimes divinity, conflate.

Dance certainly may be an end in itself—pleasurable to do and needing no excuse or pretext outside itself. However, dance may also be a means to another end. As a form of nonverbal communication that scholars have documented as implicated in interpersonal regulation, dance may convey such messages as what it is to be sexual, what it is to be a man or woman, what it is to come hither, see me, or make love with me. Dance may demonstrate interpersonal liaisons, provide an avenue of social mobility, and offer an option to break out of a mold.

We see dance in its three dimensions of space and in a fourth, time. The fifth dimension is the realm of imagination. Here dance reverberates, mixes past and present, and anticipates the future. Referring to Western culture, Rockwell (1976) pointed out, "If dance has always been a meat market, it's been a dream market, too, and even in its most Romantic or minimalist guise, those dreams can be carnal." The ambiguity or explicitness of human bodies in motion attracts attention. In this way dance may play a role in forming the consciousness and reflexivity of a people. The kinetic images of who performs what, when, where, why, how, with, or to whom, come from and create a climate in which gender roles are defined. Sometimes expressive forms, such as dance, perpetuate the pervading ideology of gender; at other times they impugn and undermine it. Culture, socially transmitted and reproductive, is not static but has transformative potential and operative dialectical processes. Change of ideas is rarely abrupt and absolute; under the veneer of transformation lies a mass of tradition.

Dance, we have seen, is a medium to explore the changing conditions of sexuality, identity, and sex role that occur over the course of the life cycle. The vast array of options, realities and illusions of metamorphosis, tradition and its fissures, and subversion seen on American stages by the 1980s contrasts markedly with the images seen in the nineteenth century, hence the folly of fixed ideas about roles for men and women. With graphic depiction, a dance may have multiple meanings that are recognized or not yet verbally articulated. The visual signs of sexuality and gender portray how the world seems, or how one might desire it to appear. Dance signification often reflects the character or dilemmas of choreographer and performer. Although there are numerous nonverbal signs of gender, most of which are out of most people's awareness, dance observers tend to focus on those manifest in pubescent and adult sexual activity, often a metaphor for other power domains.

Global Occurrence

Worldwide, past and present, one finds differences and similarities among cultures. The commonalities may be affinities, aleatory phenomena, or deep structures of human thought and behavior emanating from the origin of the species and its evolvement in somewhat comparable ecological or socioeconomic contexts. There appear to be recurrent themes in dance production and images irrespective of geographical location or level of economic development ("primitive" or "civilized"): sexuality (love won and lost, reciprocal dependency, and tension between partners), gender scripting, and differentiation through movement and stillness styles that are recognizably male or female, gender role reversals (ridiculing the opposite sex, defining the ideal, warning about excessive gender behavior, appropriating the power/attributes), male dominance and women as objects of male definition, questionable status of the public dancer, dancer as sex object, and tension between surface appearance of how men and women are expected to be and changing realities. I have illustrated how gender images from a global overview of dance bespeak of aphrodisia toward culturally licit procreation; pre- and extramarital entertainment, art, and artifice; love, life, death, and divinity; seduction of forces and shamans; sexual sublimation; sex role scripting; modulating and coping with sex role performance; and transvestite parody and adulation. Sexual orientation and social class are often cross-cutting threads.

For the most part, there is relentless male control over the production and reproduction of knowledge as it appears in the contours and quality of the kinetic discourse of dance. A recurring definition of a female is a body that belongs to somebody. There seems to be more objectifying of women than the obverse. In socially stratified societies, the social stigma attached to dance goes hand in glove with respectability for the talented who become powerful through association with powerful people or acquisition of wealth. When women innovate, men often usurp female creations.

Urban areas are the incubus for much of the change in gender images that echoes worldwide (Hanna 1987d, chap. 8). Cities are generative forces for change for several reasons. Urban areas tend to be relatively heterogeneous and provide a range of social networks and arenas for interaction among different cultures as well as a supportive economic base and critical mass. Urban areas act upon traditions brought to it from rural areas and towns and spawn new forms. Within an urban milieu, there tends to be more opportunity for a creative element to develop because of the minimization of spatial impediments which allows exposure to diversity. The more urban a place, the higher the rate of unconventionality. Not only do urban areas encourage innovation, but it may increase exponentially; existing developments constitute an ever-increasing base upon which future ones can build. Urban residents, because of their exposure to diversity, tend to be relatively more receptive to innovation in dance than are nonurban ones.

The gender meaning of danced designs appears in the array of devices and spheres mentioned in chapter 1. Concretizations, metaphors, and actualizations seem to be most common. Recall that *Song for a Dead Warrior* uses the concretization device to encode meaning and presents violence through brutal rape and fighting scenes. Meaning occurred in actualizations at the Paris Opéra, where dancers advertised their sexual selves and were approached for intimate relationships. The duet in early classical ballet was often a metaphor for social stratification, the cruelty in *The Cage* a metaphor for sexual drives and instincts and woman as cause of problems. Icons appear when dance and religion are intimately entwined as in Africa and Haiti. Metonomy is integral to dance of India.

Dances from Western history and earlier non-Western cultures prefigure what appears in the repertoires of Western theatrical dance. As performing arts observer Richard Schechner (1982) puts it, "If nations jealously defend their boundaries, cultures have always been promiscuous, and happily so." Western theatrical dance owes a spiritual debt to the ritual, social, and other dances of peoples of yesterday and today. Contemporary Western performers use offstage everyday movement, and folk, social, ritual, and popular forms as their raw ingredients and transform them in various degrees for their own purpose. They may validate or attack the status quo. Similarly, quotidian gender realities and stereotypes provide the context for dance viewing and comprehension.

Whether from borrowing or independent invention, there are striking resemblances in gender marking in dance, irrespective of society. At the same time, each culture uniquely confronts the problems of its participants' existence in response to the volatile natural and technological dynamics of a constantly churning world. Yet we all remain members of the human species.

Transformations: The American Scene

The United States has been host to immigrants, slaves, and visitors, who carried with them their dance heritage. For example, Africans in the Americas created dances rooted in their former continent and nurtured in the new one. Their descendants have contributed significantly to America's dance culture. Tap, jazz, and its social dance variants are notable. So, too, are the efforts of Katherine Dunham and Pearl Primus who searched their roots in Africa and the Caribbean, staged dances from these areas in the 1940s, and thereby called to public attention the beauty of African and Caribbean peoples' culture. Choreographer-dancer-designer Geoffrey Holder staged his vision of Haiti's ritual Ghede dance.

Classical ballet and modern dance have drawn upon middle eastern "belly" dancing. Transplanted, it became the rage in the United States in the 1970s. Classes were offered in adult education centers and even department stores. Professional groups invited dancers to their meetings to share their art. At least five paperback books on this dance form appeared in 1975. Feminists picked up the dance that was created by women for women in honor of their ability to create other human beings (Dullea 1974). Moreover, this genre, overcoming its popular image of hootchy-kootchy shows and other synthetic interpretations, made its appearance at New York City's Lincoln Center, apart from the classical ballet and modern dance transformations (Shepard 1978).

An examination of Western theatrical dance forms (primarily ballet, modern, and postmodern seen on American stages, including television) reveals the reciprocity as well as the contest of the sexes. These dynamics are played out in shifting images of the predominance of one or the other gender onstage. Images are associated with genre and the period in which a piece was created. At first, male dancers shine and dominate *onstage*; then females gain a foothold; men protest; females both toe the line and reassert themselves while both sexes transgress dominant society's norms in role reversals, gender blurring, and equal opportunity. Images are safe arenas to deal with anxieties and curiosity. Dances with images that deviate from the accepted societal norm may well help alter the status quo. Thus cultural blueprints fade, are disregarded, or redrawn. Tensions between blueprints and changing reality appear onstage in kinetic images.

Despite some notable exceptions, *backstage*, males tend to be managers of companies and theaters, artistic directors, and choreographers who determine the rules, hierarchical chains of command, a dancer's rank—principal, soloist, or corps member—roles, partners, and general working conditions. Work patterns have shaped notions of masculinity and femininity. Gender participation in the various aspects of the dance occupation illustrates the process by which individuals have been encouraged to do certain jobs and prevented from doing others (Matthaei 1982).

In Western dance there are two dramatic movements toward women's liberation in the male-dictated field of dance. The first occurs within ballet in the nineteenth century when women outshine and outnumber males *onstage*. The second effort toward female assertion takes place through their development of a new form of dance antipodal to ballet at the turn of the twentieth century. Modern dance was in part a demand for freedom from the Victorian era's constraints on women and also a manifestation of the emerging freedom of women in the United States. Dance sometimes is a vehicle through which to indict and attempt to dismantle the "patriarchal" ethos. However, while sexual and sex role liberation are in the air, sexual doubt remains their anchorage. Moreover, the male monopoly over production remains entrenched; when women create something new that wins acclaim, men move into this creative arena and establish their invincibility. Not only have men entered the field of modern dance and its subsequent developments, but male-dominated ballet companies have incorporated the new genres into their ballets; they now hire nonballet choreographers to create dances for their companies. Feminist actions make some men resentful, insecure, and misogynist. Like language, dance is capable of conveying male semantic derogation of women and an insistent stereotypic masculinity as antidote to assaults to their privileged status. At times society and dance hold mirrors up to each other.[1]

About the traditional Western theater, in which we include dance,

Susan Bassnett-McGuire has written: "The status of women has mirrored that of society at large. Women have, at various times, been forbidden to act at all, been forced to wear clothing that distinguished them as actors/whores, been excluded from the processes of planning and devising theatre and frequently have been allowed little more than occasional opportunities to appear in subsidiary roles" (1985, 185).

Classical ballet has more adherents than modern dance, although, as mentioned earlier, many ballet companies have incorporated modern dance movements and themes into their new dances. The appeal of classical forms with their traditional romantic themes and stylization, both in ballet and dances of India, may be the momentary partaking of a nostalgic idealized past. Ballet is associated with the authority and prestige of old Imperial Europe, a royalty Americans never had, as well as with contemporary exemplary body images. Athletic prowess, metered movement, and pointedness in an era of economic unease also attract people to ballet. For men and women, contemporary woman's independence carries with it difficulties, constraints, and fears of the unknown, as does traditional woman's submissiveness. The femininity of the classical is, says Susan Brownmiller (1985) in essence, a romantic sentiment, "a nostalgic tradition of imposed limitations." Romantic sexist dances may also be accepted because of the beauty and skill of a performance.

The label "dancer" tends to categorize a person in a particular social status and to carry the weight of yet another evaluation on a scale of disreputable to reputable. Public dance performance has brought opprobrium throughout the course of Western history. Associated with illicit sexuality, low social class or dispossession of social standing, and female self-assertion in addition to means of economic independence, dance, nonetheless, provided some performers with a vehicle to gain glory and the envy of respectable society for their artistry and association with powerful men. Women past their prime dancing age who did not have good fortune in finding a male benefactor often ended their lives as teachers at best and as street beggars at worse.

What is acceptable in one culture and historical period may be repugnant or outrageous in another. As the social situation of women improved and more economic options became available in the twentieth century, dance as a respectable profession also became recognized. With respectable middle-class women in the public workplace, the stage has become just another career opportunity.

Moreover, attitudes toward the dance career and dance images parallel changes in attitudes toward the body. Society's prudish and puritanical attitudes toward the body, sex, and, consequently, dance (the sexual body attracting public attention), have become more liberated. Mid-Victorians believed that "control of the physical movements of a person in his course of life meant control of the confines of his spiritual attitudes" (Bledstein 1976, 55). "Most Christian theologians have harbored a persistent distrust of the body" (Cox 1969, 52). Erich Fromm (1947) notes that societies that impose shame about the body keep people submissive to societal authority by weakening their sense of individual autonomy. Woman's fertile body is the quintessential incarnation of awe about the mysterious and thus the felt need of men to control it and discount carnal truth. The problems of the fluctuating disreputable/reputable status of the dancer in the Middle East, Orient, Europe, and Latin America were mentioned previously.

The 1960s assault on established mores ushered in an era of sensuosity, a celebration of the natural body, and, not surprisingly, a proliferation of dance activity. Consideration of the body as a biological organism with its proper functioning and failures shifted attention to the body as a locus of pleasure. Coupled with hedonism was painless childbirth, voluntary termination of pregnancy, and a diminution of the need for female and male physiques to be different in spite of *Playboy* and *Penthouse* magazines with their photographs of nude females, the body as object was decried (Jodelet 1984). In the 1980s, however, the liberation of the body appears to have abated with the spread of genital herpes and, more seriously, AIDS; in response to the disease (found mostly within the gay community but spreading beyond it) there has been a new wave of homophobia, fueled also by the resurgence of religious fundamentalism and political conservatism. By 1982, after years of steady increase, there was a decrease in the number of teenagers engaging in premarital intercourse.

In the Western tradition, male dancers, since the demise of the Renaissance court fetes, have felt opprobrium for their career choice. Professional male dancing became associated with homosexuality and low income. Gender streams of reputability/disreputability differ for male and female: social class tends to be associated with female dancers, whereas sexual orientation is linked to male dancers.

As the history of attitudes toward the body and the dance career changes, so does the range of acceptable themes, movements, and costumes, or the lack thereof, onstage. Romantic fairy tales about beautiful ladies and gallant gentlemen upon whom they are dependent exist alongside visions of independent females and males with male lovers.

Dance is sometimes like myth—an idealized disguise to hide unorthodox practice or an ideal achieved by no one. For a long time the homosexual subculture pretended to heterosexual love in this romanticized and nonexistent form, which often symbolized homosexual relationships. The 1960s gave impetus to the homosexual subculture paying attention to itself as itself. Yet the themes and actions were often disguised as something else, such as fraternal rather than passionate affairs. Eventually explicit homosexual relationships were depicted in dance. Gay men have been prominent, as have women, including lesbians, in breaking male-female stereotypic roles. Having broken the norms of their own gender's sexual orientation and career trajectories, homosexuals have then taken steps onstage to reverse gender roles or create unisex patterns.

A choreographer-dancer's success in the dance world is related to more than talent. Breaks, good luck, cultural arbiters, and gatekeepers affect opportunity. So do public interest in novelty, personal preferences of company directors and theater managers, peer review for grants, and government policy. Television accessibility of a dance or dancer may be affected by the same conceptual fabric as the imagery that surrounds other programs. The power of our representational systems may be such that views of sexuality and gender tend to reflect majority views, especially on the major networks. In 1985, for example, three congressmen charged the National Endowment for the Arts with mismanagement of taxpayers' money and funding work that is "patently offensive to the average person" (Battiata 1985).

The twentieth century may well be the apotheosis of challenge to dominance hierarchies by minorities, women, and deviant groups. Social and political turbulence in the latter part of the century, given impetus by the gains of blacks through their protest, had synergistic effects on other groups. Consequently, the spectrum of dance images available in live performance or on film and video is now unprecedented. Moreover, technology has helped make the dance audience greater than ever before.

In democratic societies, artists, as part of social consciousness and as part of an aesthetic norm of innovation, hold up startling images for our scrutiny. They do not venture too far beyond what is acceptable for a particular period because the audience may not understand or become consumed by moral outrage and attempt to prohibit the art. In professional dance there is always an economic factor operative; dancers need a place to perform and a ticket-paying audience to perform for.

Although Western litigious society prevents people from publicly saying many things with words, in the union of action and idea, dance images, with the exception of the display of certain genitally connected behavior, may say these things publicly with impunity. Many "hidden" lessons go unnoticed by authorities because they do not consider dance to be more than entertainment. Of course, as the philosopher/critic Jacques Derrida argues, texts, and we would add dances, are what the reader makes of them.

Many choreographers explicitly recognize the importance of the messages their images purvey, especially when society is in a state of flux. Many performers are aware that what has been historically constructed can be politically reconstructed. The arts alert people. Now the arts have before them the effects of women's progress toward equality by efforts to focus on the supremacy of the traditional patriarchal family and the fetus's right to live. The gay movement has had a frightening turn in fortune. After a steady climb from criminality to illness, to tolerated deviance, to a life-style celebrated in popular film and theater as well as theater art dance, the image of male homosexuality is reverting to public menace, symbol of death, and corruption of the soul.

New Directions

This book essays a matter hinted at but not usually made explicit: dance images of and for sexual and sex role thought and action. More broadly the discussion has been about communication, patterns of dominance, and social and cultural change—a saga that continues as long as the human species does. I have observed the exhibition of gender images in dance as forms of communication resembling cultural texts, tapped perceptions of key audience members (the critics who are shamans of dance and whose writing is historical data), dancers, choreographers, artistic directors, and other members of the dance world about the meaning of widely seen or written about dances, and drawn upon the reports of ethnographers and historians. The data I used synthetically to broaden our understanding of dance, sex, and gender in the arts and society could be otherwise interpreted.

One fact, however, is clear. More attention should be given to how images of dance and its production affirm and challenge basic social arrangements and doctrines about them. The dance performance in the theater (proscenium stage or other space) is a frame, a small-scale spatial metaphor. Dance provides us with glimpses of condensed variants of life as it is or might be. I have tried to show that images in a form of expressive culture that is rarely examined for its insights into everyday life are worthy of being taken seriously and asking questions about. We can grasp a culture's shifts in sexual mores and gender roles through its images.

I hope the material in this volume will stimulate further exploration. In the 1970s a significant body of feminist scholarship related to gender equity and cultural expressions of male and female roles emerged. This development enables us to probe multifarious feminist views, which philosopher Alison M. Jaggar (1983) has classified in four categories. Each approach has its different presuppositions and implications.

The liberal feminist view appears most germaine to dance and to Bandura's theory of modeling which undergirds this book. In simplistic terms, *liberal feminists* believe that nonfeminist women are victims of their socialization or sex-role conditioning; these feminists seek educational reform to eliminate discrimination and to achieve liberty and equality. The structuralist arguments that sexual inequality in the economic sphere requires a refashioning of the environment is surely applicable to male dominance in dance production.[2]

To further understand the dynamics of sexuality and gender, samples of choreographers and dancers of different sexes and sexual orientations, and from different dance genres and geographic locations, could be systematically interviewed. They could be asked what differences they have experienced between male and female in dance recruitment, training, career positions, choreography, and production and in performance images (what males and females do). Their views of the relationship between dance and sexuality could be solicited. Theater audiences could be surveyed regarding these questions. They could be asked if what they have seen onstage made them see gender in a new way? How? Which dances and dancers?

Another potentially fruitful line of inquiry would be to systematically describe the images of televised dances that have the potential to reach the entire nation. Illustrative descriptors could include gender identification for who is passive and assertive; who uses relatively larger or smaller movement in space; who is the subject and object of pushing, propelling, lifting, dipping, grasping another's body parts; who throws the body, clings, or leans and supports; who cries or frowns; who moves a limb as a unit or in parts, takes a wide or narrow postural stance, and uses strong or weak effort. Intensity, duration, and longevity of these variables that impinge on role socialization issues could be taken into account through scaling techniques and analyses across genres of dance that correspond to historical periods.

The appendix to this book contains a code that guided my recent qualitative viewing of dance. Although codes exist to describe nonverbal gender patterns in everyday face-to-face interaction, none has been available for dance, theater, or other ritual activity that draws upon and transforms everyday movement. Nor were the dance analysis methods (e.g., Laban's notation or effort/shape) designed to discriminate gender. Observers trained in movement analysis could operationalize and test the code to insure reliability and validity of the visualization terminology and coding.

Following the coding of a sample of dances, computer data processing and analysis could indicate the frequency distributions of gender dominance patterns and their variance with dance genre to answer such questions as, does classical ballet convey more gender stereotypes than modern dance (which is likely to show women with male characteristics) and postmodern dance (which is likely to show more androgynous or role reversal patterns)? and how does it convey them? Is television a medium whose control of the processes of signification appropriates dancing bodies into the reproduction of established notions of gender even when they appear to change?

As a result of explorations of gender in verbal language during the contemporary ferment in thinking about sex roles in society, we now have guidelines to eliminate sexism in everyday writing and speaking. Studies of gender in several occupations have led to affirmative action to alter discrimination. Awareness of gender patterns in dance production and dance images could have similar results in expunging the tyranny of sexism from the nonverbal in everyday life and the dance world occupations. I do not intend to argue for constraints on the creation of dances and determination of dance programs. Rather my point is to call attention to what dance has the potential to do. Framing values, beliefs, and behavior for scrutiny, dance, as do the other arts, sometimes affirms, introduces, and challenges, even parodying and exaggerating behavior so that people are repelled by it. Dance creates signs and designs about sexuality and gender, particular relationships, and dynamics in the wider world.

Appendix: Coding Variables for Gender Patterns in Dance

Code for each dance or act of full-length ballet:

Name of TV program, series, dance company if not included in title
Date of production release
Choreographer
Choreographer's sex
Date of work's premiere
Soloist dancers and sex
Coder
Date of coding
Genre (classifications determined by NYC critics' usage)
    classical ballet
    contemporary ballet (classical and other twentieth-century dance genre)
    modern dance
    postmodern (after Cunningham)
    ethnic (non-Western classical and folk)
    square and country
    jazz/Broadway/rock/pop/break

Code for the occurrence in a dance of the actions described below (scale for quantity: much, some, little, none):

    Individual
        0 male
        1 female
        2 male and female

Interactive

0 male action to male
2 male action to female
3 male action to male and female
4 female action to male
5 female action to female
6 female action to male and female
7 male and female action to same sex
8 male and female action to opposite sex
9 all permutations

Space: posture, locomotion, gesture, touch

Individual action

wide postural stance predominates (A)
narrow postural stance predominates (P)
relatively larger movement (in verticality, horizontality, distance covered
    excluding effect of body size) (A)
relatively smaller movement (including turning in place, e.g., a spin or
    piroutte) (P)
throws own body (gymnastic moves such as tumbling and handstand,
    falling to knees, rolling) (A)
limb moved as unit (A)
successive, differentiated, or articulated movement within limbs (e.g.,
    break at wrist) (P)
makes fist, flexes bicept (A)
cries (P)
smiles (caring)

Interaction

pushes, propels, lifts, dips, fights other dancer (A)
pushed, propelled, lifted, lowered, defends self (P)
grasps, squeezes, or manipulates other's body parts (e.g., opens legs) (A)
grasped, squeezed, or manipulated (P)
supports a dancer (A)
clings to or leans against other dancer (P)
touches, pats, strokes, brushes other (caring)
stares/glares (A)
stared/glared at (P)

Effort

Strong, tense (A)
Gentle, relaxed (P)

Coding for the following:

　0 yes
　1 no
　2 combination

Costume and/or prop

　Male-female differentiated
　Unisex

Music

　Reinforces gender (e.g., strong/heavy/fast music accompanies male
　　dancing alone, the opposite for female dancing)

Spheres of gender meaning

　Parody
　Whole performance (drama is about gender-related theme)
　Specific movement and/or style identify male and female
　Movement intermeshes with costume or music to indicate gender

Devices of gender meaning

　Concretization (e.g., miming hunting, fighting, child care, praying)
　Metaphor (e.g., white soldier's rape of Indian woman refers to domi-
　　nance patterns of gender and ethnicity)

　A = assertive
　P = passive

Notes

Chapter 1

1. Margaret Wyszomirski, pers. com. 1984. I appreciate her comments on an early draft of this chapter.

2. Thomas Hobbes distinguished between two forms of personation. Mimicry is sustaining a feigned person, whereas self-manipulation is emphatically maintaining one's own person to the extent of crossing the border into exhibitionism (Oakeshott 1946, 105).

3. Smith 1984. Even lawyers now find words alone are insufficient to make a good case. Increasingly they are supplementing their verbal renditions with visual aids, from multicolored charts to computer-generated video animation (Murphy 1986).

4. Bankers Trust Company advertised its philosophy as "Excellence is achieved only through consistency and innovation. And Subtlety." Adjacent to this declaration was a picture from *Swan Lake*, a classical ballet that has been staged and restaged through the years. Five women in tutus in a line on the left, three on the right, frame a man supporting a ballerina on pointe in an arabesque (her weight is on one leg, the other extending backward to form a right angle) (*New York Times*, Aug. 16, 1983, p. D3).

Inside the front cover of the October 1984 *Performing Arts: California's Theatre and Music Magazine* is a picture of a pair of toe shoes. Beneath is Imperial Savings Association's text: "To all Those who Strive for Excellence. When the artist is also the art form, it is dance./Mind and body giving meaning to movement./Stretching the limits of time and space./Defying even gravity, it would seem, to celebrate the human spirit./To do so and to do it well is an art which Imperial Savings is proud to support. It is, after all, an inspiration to value our customer's dreams and goals most highly./By providing all the crucial steps and choreography for financial well-being." Beneath a picture of the Dance Theatre of Harlem, Chase's ad includes, "Just as a working partnership is the basis of doing business within Chase and with our customers, it is also the basis of our relationship with the community" (*Village Voice*, Aug. 7, 1984, p. 8). Another bank, Riggs, associates itself with a picture of a ballerina on pointe in arabesque above this quote: "It is art that makes life and I know of no substitute whatever for the force and beauty of its process—Henry James" (*Stagebill* 13[1984]:43, 1984).

The National Corporate Fund's full-page advertisement proclaims, "Dance has a new partner," written over the skirt of the tutu-attired ballerina standing on pointe, one foot crossed in front of the other. A man in a business suit holds her, and their hands interwine in front of her waist. Beneath the image we read: "Business. 200 corporations know that dance is important to the people important to them. That's why they are investing in seven of America's greatest dance companies . . . Don't let your corporation sit this one out" (*Newsweek*, Aug. 26, 1981, p. 89).

The 3M company analogized its light tape product with the airy quality of a female dancer. The image shows two legs below the knee. A toe shoe fits one foot; the other is adorned with a wing made of tape (*Smithsonian Magazine*, Sept. 1983, p. 109). In the *Harvard Business Review* (84[4]:11, 1984), QVT Terminals advertised its products with a ballerina leaping into her partner's arms. The caption reads, "When you need a dependable partner, we'll be there." Polaroid sells its product this way: a picture of a ballet student tying her shoe has the caption, "To bring out the artist in you" (*Newsweek*, Nov. 12, 1984, p. 105a).

Calibre condominiums appealed to young professionals with an image of a ballet dancer's leg seen below the knee, with ballet-slippered foot and pointed toes. The accompanying text says, "In my ballet troupe we push each other hard. It's not competitive though. We all have high pressure jobs, so a hard work-out clears out minds plus keeps us in shape and looking good. Usually when we finish, everyone comes over to my new Calibre home to relax over a cup of cappuccino. It's great" (*Washington Magazine*, Jan. 1984, p. 63). Encore of McLean, Virginia, announces its luxury high-rise condominium with the phrase "Grand Premiere," adjacent to the image of a ballerina on pointe, her left leg lifted chest high and bent at the knee (*Washington Post*, June 6, 1985, p. 4).

For inside the home, Levolor likens its Riveria Blind to "a true classic." A toe-shoed, ballerina in tutu, on one knee, the other leg extended forward as the pointed toe touches the ground, is shown about to lift the blind (*New York Times*, Apr. 15, 1984, p. 13). JVC company proclaims its superior Network TV with a large picture of a male dancer in a leap across the stage, an image replicated in four TV screens. The text read, "I saw the dancer leap across the stage. He seemed to remain suspended, defying gravity. When he landed, I remembered to start breathing again, and I realized I was in my own house, watching TV" (*New York Times Magazine*, Aug. 7, 1983, p. 9).

Lord and Taylor tried to sell Mystere de Rochas with the image of a classical pas de deux, the dancers perched on the perfume bottle top (*Washington Post*, Dec. 12, 1982, p. A11). Bloomingdale's advertised its repertoire of sport clothing separates by featuring "Breakin' in the New Breed," "action afoot," with the all-male Furious Rockers dancers in thirteen different break poses (*New York Times*, Apr. 13, 1984, p. A17). Loafers are seen on a girl's knee-socked legs. To the left is a full view of a girl in ballet attire bending over an extended pointed toe touching the floor. A caption read: "Get a better feeling for the Classics: Sperry Top-Siders" (*New York Times Magazine*, Aug. 26, 1984, p. 117).

Sellers of leisure items associate them with dance. The statement "I could go for something Gordon" and "the possibilities are endless" appeared to the left of a bottle and glass of gin. Both quotes are beneath a dance studio scene of a black ballerina and male piano accompanist seated next to each other on the piano bench. Note that ballet, as well as ads, are no longer the province of whites only. Resting on the bench edge, the woman's legs are extended outward as her ballet-slippered feet point to the alcohol. She touches the accompanist's shoulder; he returns her flirtatious glance" (*Newsweek*, Dec. 5, 1983, p. 97). Vantage cigarettes heralds "The Taste of Success" with the image of a female ballet dancer in the studio taking a break. Seated at the barre, shoes off, she holds a cigarette (*New York Times*, Jan. 5, 1984, p. A22).

Phillip Morris Incorporated (makers of cigarettes, beer, and soft drinks) took out two full dance-illustrated pages to announce its sponsorship of the Joffrey Ballet. A warrior and a ballerina in a split leap were the top separate images. Below were a pas de deux in which a man bent forward, with one arm thrust backward to hold a leotard-clad woman standing on one toe, her back greatly arched over his; a row of black men above a row of white men in jazz shoes, jumping with arms stretched upright; and a ballerina on pointe in an attitude (standing on one leg, her other is lifted behind her and bent at the knee). After two paragraphs singing the company's praises, the third includes the statement, "In our business as in yours, we need to be reminded that there is always fresh life in old forms and that the only way we can discover it is through individual imagination, individual innovativeness, individual creativity" (*Newsweek*, May 17, 1982, pp. 4–5).

American Express charge card features a man in trousers and a woman in stockings, both in top hats and performing high kicks, with a caption, "Pick Your Favorite Number." "There's that moment when the perfect song and dance come together on stage. It's yours when you use the American Express Card," reads the smaller print (*Stagebill*, November 1983). Elsewhere a man holds a ballerina wearing a tutu; her back is arched, with one leg extended high above his head. One hand clasps the back of her waist, the other grasps her ankle. The caption: "Give Yourself a Lift." The smaller print: "Give yourself that moment when something perfect happens on stage" (*Washington Magazine*, Sept. 1983, p. 84). Another advertisement shows Cynthia Gregory in a rehearsal and the caption, "When you're a prima ballerina only the best is for you" (*TV*, Aug. 2, 1984). Not to be outdone, the Visa credit charge company spotlights a female dancer on pointe in arabesque. Above the image are Robert Louis Stevenson's words: "To be what we are, and to become what we are capable of becoming, is the only end of life" (*Smithsonian Magazine*, Mar. 1984, p. 95).

A New York Telephone Company advertisement featured four females doing ballet exercises in a studio. One is at the same time speaking on the telephone. A caption says, "New York Telephone's low rates help New Yorkers exercise their freedom of speech" (*New York Times*, Mar. 18, 1985, p. B5). The statements, "Because a dancer's leap should know no bounds," "New York Telephone is proud to stand behind Dance Theatre of Harlem," and "Giving New York a cultural ring" accompany the picture of a dancer in a split in the air in another advertisement (*New York Times*, Jan. 25, 1985, p. 63).

Sunoco touts its energy development, responsibility to the American people, and contribution to the American arts with eight small photographs of its various activities; in the foreground is a female ballet dancer about six times the size of the other pictures. She appears from the thigh up, dressed in a leotard, facing front, with arms rounded in front of her hips (*Newsweek*, Apr. 4, 1983, p. 26). Phillips 66 associated itself with Ballet West. Beside a painting of a ballerina in arabesque wearing a vividly colored tutu is the caption, "They lift the spirits of us all" (*Smithsonian Magazine*, May 1983, p. 15). Exxon proclaimed its support of the Dance in America series with images of two men performing low leaps from Paul Taylor's *Arden Court* (*Newsweek*, Sept. 28, 1981, p. 83).

Cities and states, too, rely on dance images to promote themselves. Los Angeles, Montreal, and the state of Florida tried to magnetize visitors with the picture of a ballerina in *New York Times* advertisements.

The concept of excellence in a nondance arena was usually shown with the traditional dance pose of a man holding the woman (2 advertisements), a ballerina alone (3), a male dancer alone (1), a nonhuman symbol of dance (1), and a human symbol (1). The idea of recreation is illustrated by images of a man holding a woman (2), a female dancer alone (4), and a male group of dancers (1). Cooperation and dependability are conceptualized by dance images of a man holding a woman (1), a female alone (1), a male group (1), and a nonhuman symbol (1). The importance of dance is associated with pictures of a male holding a woman (1) and a female alone (1). The value of the arts is depicted by an image of a woman alone (4), a man alone (1), and two men (1).

Chapter 2. Odyssey toward Understanding

1. Some of Mead's work, in the tradition of significant scholarship, has been subjected to scrutiny. Derek Freeman, especially, created a hulabaloo with the charges in his 1983 book, *Margaret Mead and Samoa* (Harvard University Press). Mead detractors and defenders made the national news. Some scholars did not appreciate a man's attempt to demolish a pioneering woman's

authority after she died and could not defend herself. Part of the conflict centered on the debate between evolutionary biologists and cultural anthropologists, a manifestation of the nature/nurture controversy.

2. I draw upon several traditions in anthropology: the study of (1) the transmission of culture (Mead 1942, 1964, 1970; Wolcott 1982; Spindler and Spindler 1982, 1983), (2) maleness and femaleness (Mead 1935, 1949), and (3) nonverbal communication and the meaning of expressive culture. The Bateson and Mead 1942 work on Balinese dance is a landmark. Geertz (1973) and Peacock (1968) are among those whose ethnographies show how expressive culture intertwines with continuity and change. Birdwhistell documented gender differences in gesture and posture (1970); M. Douglas called attention to the body as a symbol of the powers and dangers in society (1966, 1970).

3. Henley 1977, 1984. See also Davis and Skupien 1982; Pearson 1985; Rosenfeld, Kartus, and Ray 1976; Welch et al. 1979.

4. New York has long had pride of place for disciples of terpsichore. In the realm of social dance, the *New York Times*, October 22, 1899, p. 23, reported, "New York people dance very well, much better than most of the foreigners who come here. . . . New York is the headquarters to which out-of-town teachers come, not only from small, but often from large places to learn new cotillion features."

Chapter 3. Sexuality

1. This chapter is not comparative in the technical sense of considering rigorously equivalent units and ultimately asking why A in B and not C. Such a quest is beyond the scope of this book. The overview of cases of sex, gender, and dance herein illustrate the variety and affinities of human experience in addition to the pool of resources that the theatrical arts use for their own creations. Although other scholars have attempted world histories or surveys of selected aspects of the dance, I disavow their theories and methods. Ideally I would present all the examples in a substantial way. However, the data are limited and my purpose is to show the range of human behavior.

2. Quoted in Mason 1975, 649; Abdullah Yusuf Ali's translation, Lois Ibsen al Faruqi (pers. com. 1985) believes, is preferable. She says that "to stand" means to stand up for another in a protective and benevolent way.

3. Thus a woman had some say in birth control measures such as coitus interruptus and could use intravaginal suppositories and tampons. Masturbation was permitted to men and also to a woman alone without a husband to satisfy her needs. Under Shia law, there was also a "temporary marriage" or *mut'a*, "marriage of pleasure," which involved a legal contract of sexual relationship for a specified financial recompense and set time ranging from a day to seven years. This partnership could be one of the most binding forms of marriage available in Islam (Musallam 1983).

4. Lois Ibsen al Faruqi (pers. com. 1985) says that Koran chanters and poetry reciters do this all throughout the Muslim world.

5. Sabbah (1984, 37) points out that "the idea that the cause of prostitution is the great sexual appetite of women and not the economic structure is a strongly rooted and still enduring belief."

6. Sita, heroine of the Ramayana epic (ca. 200 B.C.–A.D. 200), takes pride of place in mythology conveying the ideal wife image. The legend centers on her abduction and subsequent trials of doubt as to her chastity, a requirement of feminity. Mamata Niyogi-Nakra, a dancer, asked, "Would a male god's masculinity be questioned with similar trials of doubt? (pers. com. 1985). Savitri is a princess who accompanies her husband unto death. Draupadi, in the Mahabharata epic (ca. 300 B.C.–A.D. 300), is a tale of selfless devotion to five husbands. She fails to reach the highest honor in heaven because of partiality to one. Lakshmi, goddess of the Diwali festival of lights, is the god Vishnu's wife, who epitomizes the joyous and auspicious side of woman's nature.

Contradictory or plural images surround woman as mother just as they surround woman as courtesan. The Krttika, wives of the sages of the Pleiades, appear as loving mothers with milk flowing from their breasts and also as hideous creatures who try to kill children. Goddess Durga possesses characteristics of beauty, strength, cunning, and ability to kill in battle. Black Kali is her fiercely ugly and angry transformation.

7. Kern 1981, 100; Andrews 1940, 144–45. This religious group dance provided inspiration for modern dancer Doris Humphrey's well-known *The Shakers*, choreographed in 1930 as an interpretation rather than a re-creation of a ritual. An elder woman leads the service while five men and five women move to a stamping wood rhythm, circling, bending, and jumping in prayer. The men and women never touch. A couple yearns longingly after each other, making more overt the seething sexuality that must be denied. The men leap high with split legs.

Chapter 4. Sex Role Scripting

1. Bateson and Mead 1942, 18. They note that on day 210, an infant is taught hand gestures. As an adult the individual will identify not with the characters in a play but with the gestures and body movements.

2. Leacock (1981) suggests that there may be more egalitarian societies than current literature would lead us to believe and that researchers in the field have neglected to ask many questions that should have been asked. She speaks of observers with male-dominated biases who project sex role imagery from class society onto the egalitarian bands. Egalitarian relations have existed until recently in many foraging and horticultural societies, which have been contaminated through contacts with social systems in which males are dominant.

Chapter 5. India's Dance Kaleidoscope

1. See Meyer 1971; Gaston 1982; Jeanes Antze 1982; Sarabhai 1965; Henriques 1962; Penzer 1952; Thurston 1909.

2. In the northwest Karnataka area of India, the *mangalarati jogati* is a nondancing *devadasi* attached to the temple of Renuka; she is bought by temple

priests and is their prostitute, although she may also grant favors to others. She continues to serve until she dies (Patil 1977, 31).

3. Temple dancers had to retire from the temple as they approached menopause and the Brahmans no longer found them sexually desirable. The retirees returned their *tali* necklace which symbolized the *devadasi* marriage to the deity.

Chapter 6. Patterns of Dominance

1. This discussion focuses primarily on ballet and modern/postmodern dance. However, the situation of male dominance succeeded by female challenge is similar in jazz and tap dance. Tap began as a black male street form that was then transformed into theater dance and later became supplanted by innovative Broadway story genres. Because blacks sought new forms and associated tap with the era of black subservience, tap nearly died out. It has been picked up and revitalized by white females who perform by themselves and also with black male old-timers.

Note that women now perform (sometimes in theaters) traditional Irish dances formerly passed down from father to son for generations (Goldman 1985). The mimes' explanation for the absence of women is that it is difficult for women to capture a virile kind of feminity and a nonsexual but poetic and strong masculinity. "Women are also thought not to have sufficient endurance and strength to sustain the tension and weight of mime movements" (Royce 1984, 74–76).

Homosexuality refers to exhibiting sexual desire toward a member of one's own sex. Many homosexual men prefer the term *gay* because of the history of pathology and persecution associated with the label *homosexuality*. Behavior is not confined to two categories, but exists on a homosexual-heterosexual continuum and includes a range of experience.

2. Elsom 1974; Guest 1966, 1970, 1972, 1980; Migel 1972. In the mid-eighteenth century, the relation between sexual ideology and social structure ensnared the world of dance. The Industrial Revolution attracted populations to the city and uprooted the old morality. Victorian England's social underclass was degraded and powerless, yet potentially threatening as a conduit of venereal disease to respectable society. The prostitute was a highly visible symbol of social dislocation attendant upon the new industrial era (Walkowitz 1980).

3. Kriegsman 1982. Nijinska worshipped her brother. She was the model upon whom he tried out new ways for dancers to move. In 1921, three years after his mental breakdown, she began to choreograph for the Ballets Russes. Diaghilev allowed Nijinska to choreograph chiefly because there did not seem to be any men available. She stayed with his company for three years until he hired Balanchine. See Shapiro 1982, on the Eliot Feld production of *Les Noces* staged by Nijinska's daughter Irina.

4. Carol Martin pointed out that Isadora Duncan's interpretation of freeing

the body was also in the image of Greek antiquity. This choice aligned her with a branch of Romanticism and provided her with a pedestal on which she could justify her art of dance. Ruth St. Denis and others often presented divine or exotic characters in their own images, which sometimes contradicted the reality of the sources.

5. Hanna 1987a. The concept of the "Orient" is a resonant metaphor for passion beyond Western civilization.

6. Caroline Sheldon's remarks in *Gays and Film* quoted in Wandor 1981, 19; see Laine 1980b.

7. In Thailand, Scandinavia, Guatemala, the Philippines, Brazil, the United States, and the USSR, certain behavioral elements, including interest in dance, appear to be associated with a homosexual orientation (Whitman and Mathy 1986).

8. Bullough 1976; 565. After 1810 the French were more tolerant than the British. The law leaves unpunished any sexual behavior in private between consulting individuals. Belgium, Italy, Spain, Portugal, Rumania, Russia, and several Latin American countries adopted similar laws. In the United States homosexual sodomy was outlawed in the late 1700s and was a crime in every state until 1962. Twenty-four states and the District of Columbia provide criminal penalties. The AIDS epidemic has engendered the current outbreak of homophobia. Note the Supreme Court decision *Bowers v. Hardwick* 478 U.S. (1986) which holds that homosexuals have no constitutionally protected right to engage in sodomy.

Chapter 7. Sexuality and Gender in Dance Images

1. Davis and Weitz 1981; Eakins 1978; Fortier 1979; Henley 1977; Mayo and Henley 1981; Pearson 1985: See chaps. 1 and 2 in this volume.

2. Gombrich 1982; Leach 1972, 327, 335–37; Mauss 1938.

3. Davis and Weitz 1981; Henley 1977; Mayo and Henley 1981; Pearson 1985; Wolfgang 1984; Stier and Hall 1984.

Chapter 10. New Moves for Men

1. Marian Briffa and Jessica Jackson in Bolotin 1982.

2. Kunzle 1982, in *Fashion and Fetishism*, noted that transvestite fashion is often regarded as an indicator of social anxiety and a press for a redefinition of social roles.

Chapter 11. Coda

1. For example, in the 1980s University of Pennsylvania fraternity men had sex with a coed nearly comatose from a combination of drugs. At Big Dan's bar in Fall River, Massachusetts, men raped a woman as other men held her or looked on. In both these cases there was nothing sensual or erotic. Rather the animating force was hostility toward and fear of women. The male ethic was the sport of showing one's manliness by abuse of women. The defense was, "She asked for it."

2. *Marxist feminists* think that capitalism oppresses workers, that sex oppression is a by-product of the economic system, that marriage resembles feudal vassalage with the husband providing economic support in return for the wife's services and devotion, that prostitution is the paradigm of women's oppression, and that the solution is socialist revolution. *Radical feminists* of the 1960s stress the lack of options for women trapped or deluded by patriarchy, the oppression of women as the root of all other systems of repression, and male control of women's sexual and procreative capacities. In attempting to end male dominance, radical feminists accept a women's culture—with the exception of those values that keep women subservient (such as passivity and self-sacrifice)—women's own institutions, and lesbianism. *Socialist feminists* consider capitalism, racism, imperialism, and male dominance as inseparable and want economic changes to provide economic security for women, sexual choice, and procreative freedom (release from compulsory motherhood and male involvement in child care).

References

Acocella, Joan Ross. 1985. Real Men Don't Point Their Feet. *Village Voice,* April 23, p. 78.

Adshead, Janet, and June Layson. 1983. *Dance History: A Methodology for Study.* London: Dance Books.

Alland, Alexander, Jr. 1976. The Roots of Art. In Richard Schechner and Mady Schuman, eds., *Ritual, Play, and Performance,* pp. 5–17. New York: Seabury Press.

Allen, Catherine. 1984. Adean Women: United We Stand. *Anthro Notes* 6(1):1–2, 14–15.

Alliotts, John. 1982. News around New York. *Dance Magazine* 56(9):6–8.

Ames, David. 1982. Context of Dance in Zazzau and the Impact of Islamic Reform. In Simon Ottenberg, ed., *African Religious Groups and Beliefs,* pp. 110–47. Folklore Institute. Meerut, India: Archana Press.

Anawalt, Sasha. 1987a. Ballet of the 20th Century Sizzles with Sensuality. *Los Angeles Herald Examiner,* February 9, pp. B1, 5.

———. 1987b. Maurice Béjart: The Mystic of Ballet. *Los Angeles Herald Examiner,* February 6, p. 35.

Anderson, Jack. 1970. Merce Cunningham and the Heroic Gesture. *Ballet Review* 3(3):55–58.

———. 1982a. *The Cage. New York Times,* February 5, p. C25.

———. 1982b. Dance: Alvin Ailey with Something Old, Something New. *New York Times,* December 11, p. 17.

———. 1983a. City Ballet: Robbins's *Mother Goose. New York Times,* January 6, p. C13.

———. 1983b. Dance: Trisler Troupe. *New York Times,* December 16, p. C36.

————. 1984. Plotless Dance-Drama That Deals with Emotion. *New York Times*, August 26, p. H16.

———— 1985. Dance: Robbins's *Cage* at City Ballet. *New York Times*, June 25, p. C17.

Andrews, Edward Deming. 1940. *The Gift to Be Simple: Songs, Dances and Rituals of the American Shakers*. New York: Dover.

Angioli, Michael D. 1982. Body Image Perception and Locus of Control in Semi-Nude and Nude Female Dancers. Ph.D. diss., psychology, United States International University.

Arbeau, Thoinot. 1968. *Orchésographie*. Cyril Beaumont, trans. New York: Dance Horizons (orig. Langres, 1588).

Arnheim, Rudolf. 1954. *Art and Visual Perception*. Berkeley: University of California Press.

————. 1969. *Visual Thinking*. Berkeley: University of California Press.

Arnold, Marigene, and Maxine L. Margolis. 1985. Turning the Tables? Male Strippers and the Gender Hierarchy. Paper presented at the American Anthropological Association Meeting.

Bandem, I. Made. 1983. The Evolution of Legong from Sacred to Secular Dance of Bali. In Betty True Jones, ed., *Dance as Cultural Heritage, I: Dance Research Annual XIV* (New York: Committee on Research in Dance), pp. 113–19.

Bandura, Albert. 1972. Modeling Theory: Some Traditions, Trends, and Disputes. In Ross D. Park, ed., *Recent Trends in Social Learning Theory*, pp. 35–61. New York: Academic.

Banerji, Projesh. 1983. *Erotica in Indian Dance*. Atlantic Highlands, N.J.: Humanities.

Banes, Sally. 1980. *Terpsichore in Sneakers: Post-Modern Dance*. Boston: Houghton Mifflin.

————. 1981. Men Together. *Dance Magazine*. 50(3):31–39.

Barnes, Clive. 1967. Dance and Poetry Collide. *New York Times*, April 16, p. D20.

————. 1972. Dance: Adventurous Visitors from Netherlands. *New York Times*, March 29, p. 35.

————. 1973. Dance: Van Dantzig's Monument for a Dead Boy. *New York Times*, January 3, p. 16.

————. 1974. Homosexuality in Dance. *New York Times*, November 3, p. D8.

————. 1978. Dance Criticism. *Stagebill* 8(3):33–34, 43–44, 46.

————. 1983. The Emergence of the Male Dancer. *Ballet News* 4(11):54.

Barrett, John Townsend. 1968. A Descriptive Study of Selected Uses of Dance on Television, 1948–1958. Ph.D. diss., mass communications, University of Michigan.

Bartos, Rena. 1982. *The Moving Target*. New York: Free Press.

Bassnett-McGuire, Susan E. 1985. Towards a Theory of Women's Theatre. In

Herta Schmid and Aloysius Van Kesteren, eds., *Semiotics of Drama and Theatre*, pp. 445–66. Philadelphia: John Benjamins.

Bateson, Gregory. 1977. Play and Paradigm. In Michael A. Salter, ed., *Play and Anthropological Perspectives*, pp. 7–16. West Point: Leisure.

Bateson, Gregory, and Margaret Mead. 1942. *Balinese Characters: A Photographic Analysis*. New York: Special Publications of the New York Academy of Sciences.

Batson, Glenna. 1975. Middle Eastern Dance. *Theaters* 5 (March/April):1–2, 8.

Battiata, Mary. 1985. NEA's Porn Ruckus: Three Lawmakers Attack Funding of Poems. *Washington Post*, September 12, p. C1.

Beckwith, Carol. 1983. Niger's Wodaabe: "People of the Taboo." *National Geographic* 164(4):483–509.

Belo, Jane. 1949. *Rangda and Barong*. Monographs of the American Ethnological Society, no. 16. New York: J. J. Augustin.

Bem, Sandra L. 1974. The Measurement of Psychological Androgyny. *Journal of Consulting and Clinical Psychology* 42:155–62.

Bennetts, Leslie. 1983. City in Performing Arts: No. 1, with a Difference. *New York Times*, March 5, p. 25.

Bentley, Toni. 1982. *Winter Season: A Dancer's Journal*. New York: Random House.

Berger, Peter L., and Thomas Luckmann. 1966. *The Social Construction of Reality*. New York: Doubleday.

Berlyne, D. E. 1971. *Aesthetics and Psychobiology*. New York: Appleton-Century Crofts.

Bharata Muni (see Ghosh).

Birdwhistell, Ray L. 1970. *Kinesics and Context: Essays on Body Motion Communication*. Philadelphia: University of Pennsylvania Press.

p'Bitek, Okot. 1966. *Song of Lawino*. Nairobi: East African Publishing House.

Bland, Alexander, and John Percival. 1984. *Men Dancing*. New York: Macmillan.

Bledstein, Burton J. 1976. *The Culture of Professionalism: The Middle Class and the Development of Higher Education in America*. New York: W. W. Norton.

Block, Katherine. 1976. Letter. *Dance Magazine* 50(9):106.

Bolotin, Susan. 1982. Voices from the Post-Feminist Generation. *New York Times Magazine*, October 17, pp. 28–31, 103, 106–7, 114, 116–17.

Bowers, Faubion. 1953. *The Dance in India*. New York: Columbia University Press.

———. 1956. *Theatre in the East: A Survey of Asian Dance and Drama*. New York: Nelson.

Brierley, Harry. 1979. *Transvestism*. New York: Pergamon.

Brink, James T. 1982. Time Consciousness and Growing up in Bamana Folk Drama. *Journal of American Folklore* 95(378):415–34.

Brownmiller, Susan. 1985. *Femininity*. New York: Fawcett Columbine.

Bullough, Vern L. 1976. *Sexual Variance in Society and History*. Chicago: University of Chicago Press.

Bumiller, Elisabeth. 1986. Bhopal's Days of the Dancing Eunuchs. *Washington Post*, April 17, pp. C1–2.

Buonaventura, Wendy. 1983. *Belly Dancing: The Serpent and the Spinx*. London: Virago.

Busby, Linda J. 1975. Sex-Role Research on the Mass Media. *Journal of Communication* 25(4):107–31.

Carlson, Marvin. 1984. *Theories of the Theatre: A Historical and Critical Survey from the Greeks to the Present*. Ithaca: Cornell University Press.

Chaki-Sircar, Manjusri. 1972. Community of Dancers in Calcutta. In Surajit Sinha, ed., *Cultural Profile of Calcutta*, pp. 190–98. Calcutta: Indian Anthropological Society.

Chaki-Sircar, Manjusri, and Parbati K. Sircar. 1982. Indian Dance: Classical Unity and Regional Variation. In Allen G. Noble and Ashok K. Dutt, eds., *India: Cultural Patterns and Processes*, pp. 147–64. Boulder, Colo.: Westview.

Chee, Maria Wai-ling. 1983. References to Dance in the Shih Ching and Other Early Chinese Texts. In Betty True Jones, ed., *Dance as Cultural Heritage, I: Dance Research Annual XIV* (New York: Committee on Research in Dance), pp. 126–38.

Citron, Paula. 1982. The Well-Choreographed Montreal Dance Explosion. *Performing Arts in Canada* 19(2):38–42.

Claiborne, William. 1984. Dowry Killings Show Social Stress in India. *Washington Post*, September 22, p. 1.

Clarke, Mary, and Clement Crisp. 1981. *The History of Dance*. New York: Crown.

Coe, Robert. 1985. *Dance in America*. New York: Dutton.

Cohen, Selma Jeanne, ed. and commentator. 1974. *Dance as a Theatre Art*. New York: Dodd, Mead.

Coomaraswamy, Ananda. 1971. *The Dance of Shiva*. New York: Noonday (orig. 1957).

Copeland, Roger. 1982. Why Women Dominate Modern Dance. *New York Times*, April 16, pp. D1, 22.

Cox, Harvey. 1969. *Feast of Fools: A Theological Essay on Festivity and Fantasy*. Cambridge: Harvard University Press.

Crapanzano, Vincent, and Jane Kramer. 1969. A World of Saints and She Demons. *New York Times Magazine*, June 22, pp. 14–15, 18, 22, 24–25, 28, 30, 33, 36, 38.

Croce, Arlene. 1977. *Afterimages*. New York: Alfred A. Knopf.

———. 1982. *Going to the Dance*. New York: Alfred A Knopf.

Crouch, Stanley. 1982. Gay Pride, Gay Prejudice. *Village Voice*, April 27, pp. 1, 13–19.

Cunningham, Jean. 1987. East Indian Dance: Tradition and Adaptation in Greater Vancouver. Ph.D. diss. in progress, anthropology of dance, William Lyon University, San Diego.

Dalby, Liza Crihfield. 1983. *Geisha*. Berkeley: University of California Press.

Darwin, Charles. 1965. *The Expression of the Emotions in Man and Animals*. Chicago: University of Chicago Press (orig. 1872).

Davies, J. G. 1984. *Liturgical Dance: An Historical, Theological and Practical Handbook*. London: SCM.

Davis, Martha, and Janet Skupien. 1982. *Body Movement and Nonverbal Communication*. Bloomington: Indiana University Press.

Davis, Martha, and Shirley Weitz. 1981. Sex Differences in Body Movements and Positions. In Clara Mayo and Nancy M. Henley, eds., *Gender and Nonverbal Behavior*, pp. 81–92. New York: Springer-Verlag.

Deaver, Sherri. 1978. Concealment vs. Display: The Modern Saudi Woman. *Dance Research Journal* 10(2):14–18.

Degler, Carl N. 1980. *At Odds: Women and the Family in America from the Revolution to the Present*. New York: Oxford University Press.

———. 1982. The Legitimacy of Scholarship by and about Women. *Chronicle of Higher Education*, September 15, p. 56.

D'Emilio, John. 1983. *Sexual Politics, Sexual Communities: The Making of a Homosexual Minority in the United States, 1940–1970*. Chicago: University of Chicago Press.

Denby, Edwin. 1936. *Looking at the Dance*. New York: Pellegrini and Cudahy. New York Popular Library 1968 reprint with an introduction by B. H. Haggin.

———. 1967. Dance Criticism. In Anatole Chujoy and P. W. Manchester, comps. and eds., *The Dance Encyclopedia*, rev. and enlarged, pp. 231–38. New York: Simon and Schuster (orig. 1949).

———. 1986. *Dance Writings*. Eds. Robert Cornfield and William Mackay. New York: Alfred A. Knopf.

Deren, Maya. 1970. *Divine Horsemen: The Voodoo Gods of Haiti*. New York: Delta.

DiMaggio, Paul, Michael Useem, and Paula Brown. 1978. *Audience Studies of the Performing Arts and Museums: A Critical Review*. Washington, D.C.: National Endowment for the Arts, Research Division Report No. 9.

Dimock, Edward C., Jr. 1966. Doctrine and Practice among the Vaisnavas of Bengal. In Milton Singer, ed., *Krishna: Myths, Rites, and Attitudes*, pp. 41–63. Honolulu: East-West Center Press.

Donnerstein, Edward, and Daniel Linz. 1984. Sexual Violence in the Media: A Warning. *Psychology Today* 18(1):14–15.

Douglas, Ann. 1977. *The Feminization of American Culture*. New York: Alfred A. Knopf.

Douglas, Mary. 1966. *Purity and Danger*. London: Penguin.

———. 1970. *Natural Symbols*. New York: Vintage.

Draegin, Lois. 1984. Twyla Tharp Does It Her Way. *Newsweek*, February 13, p. 87.

Dressel, Paula L., and David M. Peterson. 1982. Gender Roles, Sexuality, and the Male Strip Show: The Structuring of Sexual Opportunity. *Sociological Focus* 15(2):151–62.

Drewal, Henry John, and Margaret Thomspon Drewal. 1983. *Gelede: Art and Female Power among the Yoruba*. Bloomington: Indiana University Press.

Dullea, Georgia. 1974. Belly Dancer's View: It's Women for Women. *New York Times*, March 16, p. 18.

Duncan, Isadora. 1938. *The Art of Dance*. New York: Theatre Arts.

Dunning, Jennifer. 1982a. Ballet: Satoru Shimazaki. *New York Times*, January 9, p. 13.

———. 1982b. A Pennsylvania Night of Dances by Women. *New York Times*, April 9, p. C4.

———. 1982c. Should Dance Sell Itself Any Way That Works. *New York Times*, May 6, p. C20.

——— 1983. Harlem Dancers and Diaghilev Days. *New York Times*, January 28, p. C3.

———. 1984a. Toasting That Magical Toe Shoe. *New York Times*, August 26, pp. H1, 12.

———. 1984b. Women Depicted in Dance Come in Many Guises Today. *New York Times*, September 9, p. H8.

———. 1985. Alwin Nikolais: A Dance Patriarch. *New York Times*, June 13, p. C33.

———. 1986. The Dance: City Ballet in *Cage* by Robbins. *New York Times*, January 9, p. C15.

Durkheim, Emile. 1964. The Dualism of Human Nature and Its Social Conditions. In K. H. Wolf, ed., *A Collection of Essays*, pp. 325–40. New York: Harper Torchbooks.

Dworan, Elizabeth. 1983. WAP vs Willis: Body Politics. *Village Voice*, January 4, p. 10.

Eakins, Barbara Westbrook, and R. Gene Eakins. 1978. *Sex Differences in Human Communication*. Boston: Houghton Mifflin.

Eck, Diana L. 1981. *Darsan: Seeing the Divine Image in India*. Chambersburg, Pa.: Anima Books.

Elsbree, Langdon. 1968. D. H. Lawrence, Homo Ludens, and the Dance. *D. H. Lawrence Review* 1:1–30.

Elsom, John. 1974. *Erotic Theatre*. New York: Taplinger.

Engel, Lehman. 1976. *The Critic*. New York: Macmillan.

English, John W. 1979. *Criticizing the Critics*. New York: Hastings House.

Erdman, Joan L. 1983. Who Should Speak for the Performing Arts? The Case of the Delhi Dancers. *Pacific Affairs* 56(20):247–69.

———. 1987. Performance as Translation: Uday Shankar in the West. *The Drama Review* T113, 31(1):64–88.

Erenberg, Lewis A., 1981. *Steppin' Out: New York Nightlife and the Transformation of American Culture, 1890–1930.* Westport, Conn.: Greenwood.

Fallon, Dennis J., and Mary Jane Wolbers, eds. 1982. *Focus on Dance X: Religion and Dance.* Reston, Va.: American Alliance for Health, Physical Education, Recreation and Dance.

Foley, Kathy. 1985. Dancer and the Danced: Trance and Theatrical Dance in West Java. *Asian Theatre Journal* 2(1):28–49.

Fortier, C. E. 1979. Male-Female Differences in Movement. In C. Schmais and F. Orleans, eds., *Dance Therapy Research: Seven Pilot Studies.* New York: Hunter College.

Foster, Mary LeCron. 1979. Synthesis and Antithesis in Balinese Ritual. In A. L. Becker and Aram A. Yengoyan, eds., *The Imagination of Reality: Essays in Southeast Asian Coherence Systems,* pp. 175–96. Norwood, N.J.: Ablex Corporation.

Foucault, Michel. 1978. *The History of Sexuality 1: An Introduction.* Robert Hurley, trans. New York: Pantheon.

Freeman, James M. 1980. The Ladies of Lord Krishna: Rituals of Middle-Aged Women in Eastern India. In Nancy A. Falk and Rita M. Gross, eds., *Unspoken Worlds: Women's Religious Lives in Nonwestern Cultures,* pp. 110–26. San Francisco: Harper and Row.

Friedman, Lise. 1986. Michael Clark. *Vogue,* September, pp. 637–38, 697.

Fromm, Erich. 1947. *Man for Himself: An Inquiry into the Psychology of Ethics.* New York: Holt, Rinehart and Winston.

Gagnon, John H. 1979. The Interaction of Gender Roles and Sexual Conduct. In Herant A. Katchadourian, ed., *Human Sexuality: A Comparative and Developmental Perspective,* pp. 225–45. Berkeley: University of California Press.

Garafola, Lynn. 1985–86. The Travesty Dancer in Nineteenth-Century Ballet. *Dance Research Journal* 17(2) and 18(1):35–40.

Gardella, Kay. 1979. A Smash: Villella plus Bolshoi. *Daily News,* April 6, p. 83.

Gardella, Peter. 1985. *Innocent Ecstasy.* New York. Oxford University Press.

Gardner, Howard. 1983. *Frames of Mind: A Theory of Multiple Intelligences.* New York: Basic.

Gaston, Ann-Marie. 1982. *Siva in Dance, Myth and Iconography.* Oxford: Oxford University Press.

———. 1983. The Effect of Changing Social Structures in Indian Classical Dance. In *Contributions to the Sociology of the Arts: Reports from the Tenth World Congress of Sociology, Mexico City, 1982,* pp. 197–308. Sophia, Bulgaria: Research Institute for Culture.

Gautier, Theophile. 1983. Fanny Elssler in *La Tempete.* In Roger Copeland and Marshall Cohen, eds., *What Is Dance: Readings in Theory and Criticism,* pp. 431–37. Oxford: Oxford University Press.

Gazzaniga, Michael. 1985. The Social Brain. *Psychology Today* 19(1):29–30, 32–34, 36–37.

Geertz, Clifford. 1973. *The Interpretation of Culture*. New York: Basic.

Gelb, Barbara. 1981. The Pied Piper of Dance. *New York Times Magazine*, April 12, pp. 50–53, 56, 58, 62–64, 66.

Gell, Alfred. 1975. *Metamorphosis of the Cassowaries: Umeda Society, Language, and Ritual*. London School of Economics Monographs on Social Anthropology, no. 51. London: Athlone.

Ghosh, Manomohan G., trans. 1950. *Natyasastra*. Calcutta: Royal Asiatic Society of Bengal.

Gluckman, Max. 1954. *Rituals of Rebellion in South-East Africa*. Manchester: Manchester University Press.

Goffman, Erving. 1979. *Gender Advertisements*. Cambridge: Harvard University Press.

Goldman, Ari. 1985. Women Fiddle While Irish Dance Jigs and Reels. *New York Times*, January 4, p. C3.

Gombrich, E. H. 1982. *The Image and the Eye: Further Studies in the Psychology of Pictorial Representation*. Ithaca: Cornell University Press.

Goodman, Cary. 1979. *Choosing Sides: Playground and Street Life on the Lower East Side*. New York: Schocken.

Gopal, Ram. 1956. Pavlova and the Indian Dance. In A. H. Franks, ed., *Pavlova: A Biography*, pp. 98–110. London: Burke.

Gordon, Suzanne. 1983. *Off Balance: The Real World of Ballet*. New York: Pantheon.

Goswami, Shrivatsa. 1984. Women's Experience of God: A Caitanyite Affirmation. Paper presented at the Conference on God, Seoul, Korea.

Graham, Martha. 1985. Martha Graham Reflects on Her Art and a Life in Dance. *New York Times*, March 31, pp. H1, 8.

Greenberg, Bradley S. 1982. Television and Role Socialization: An Overview. In D. Pearl, L. Bouthilet, and J. Lazar, eds., *Television and Behavior: Ten Years of Scientific Progress and Implications for the 80's*, vol. 2: *Technical Reviews*, pp. 179–90. Rockville, Md.: National Institutes of Mental Health.

Griaule, Marcel. 1965. *Conversations with Ogotemmeli*. London: Oxford University Press.

Gruen, John. 1980. Dancevision. *Dance Magazine* 54(12):112–13.

Guest, Ivor. 1966. *The Romantic Ballet in Paris*. Middletown, Conn.: Wesleyan University Press.

———. 1970. *Fanny Elssler*. Middleton, Conn.: Wesleyan University Press.

———. 1972. *The Ramantic Ballet in England*. Middletown, Conn.: Wesleyan University Press.

———. 1980. *Victorian Ballet-Girl: The Tragic Story of Clara Webster*. London: Adam and Charles Black.

Gurewitsch, Matthew. 1982. Bill T. Jones and Co. *St. Louis Globe-Memorial*, October 18, p. 4B.

Hall, Judith A. 1979. Gender, Gender Roles, and Nonverbal Communication Skills. In Robert Rosenthal, ed., *Skill in Nonverbal Communication:*

Individual Differences, pp. 327–67. Cambridge, Mass.: Oelgeschlager, Gunn and Hain.

Halpern, Rona Hidy. 1981. Female Occupational Exhibitionism: An Exploratory Study of Topless and Bottomless Dancers. Ph.D. diss., psychology, United States International University.

Hanna, Judith Lynne. 1976. The Anthropology of Dance Ritual: Nigeria's Ubakala Nkwa di Iche Iche. Ph.D. diss., anthropology, Columbia University.

———. 1979a. Movements toward Understanding Humans through the Anthropological Study of Dance. *Current Anthropology* 20(2):313–39.

———. 1979b. Toward Semantic Analysis of Movement Behavior: Concepts and Problems. *Semiotica* 25(1–2):77–110.

———. 1983a. The Mentality and Matter of Dance. *Art Education* (Art and the Mind, special issue) 36(2):42–46.

———. 1983b. *The Performer-Audience Connection: Emotion to Metaphor in Dance and Society*. Austin: University of Texas Press.

———. 1981. The Representation and Reality of Divinity in Dance. Paper presented at the Conference on God, Section on Religious Art—Images of the Divine. Seoul, Korea. Published in 1988 in *Journal of the American Academy of Religion* 56(2): 281–306.

———. 1985a. Feminist Perspectives on Classical Indian Dance. Paper prepared for Dance of India Conference, University of Toronto. To be published in David Waterhouse, ed., *Dance of India*.

———. 1985b. The Impact of the Critic: Comments from the Critic and the Criticized. In John Robinson, ed., *Social Science and the Arts, 1984*, pp. 141–62. Lanham, Md.: University Press of America.

———. 1987a. The Anthropology of Dance. In James Humphrey and Lynnette Overby, eds., *Dance: Current Selected Research*. New York: AMS.

———. 1987b. Gender "Language" Onstage: Moves, New Moves, and Countermoves. *Journal of the Washington Academy of Sciences* 77(1):18–26.

———. 1987c. Patterns of Dominance: Male, Female, and Homosexuality in Dance. *The Drama Review* T113, 31(1):24–47.

———. 1987d. *To Dance Is Human: A Theory of Nonverbal Communication*. Chicago: University of Chicago Press (orig. 1979).

———. 1988. *Dance and Stress: Resistance, Reduction, and Euphoria*. New York: AMS.

Havens, Thomas R. H. 1983. Rebellion and Expression in Contemporary Japanese Dance. In Betty True Jones, ed., *Dance as Cultural Heritage, I: Dance Research Journal XIV* (New York: Committee on Research in Dance), pp. 159–65.

Hazarika, Sanjoy. 1981. Past Threatens Future of Indian Women. *New York Times*, January 6, p. 24E.

———. 1984. Age-Old Hindu Barrier Falls: Women are Priests. *New York Times*, July 3, p. A2.

Henke, James T. 1979. *Courtesans and Cuckolds: A Glossary of Renaissance Dramatic Bawdy (Exclusive of Shakespeare)*. New York: Garland.

Henley, Nancy M. 1977. *Body Politics: Power, Sex, and Nonverbal Communication*. Englewood Cliffs, N.J.: Prentice-Hall.

Henley, Nancy M. and Marianne LaFrance. 1984. Gender as Culture: Difference and Dominance in Nonverbal Behavior. In Aaron Wolfgang, ed., *Nonverbal Behavior*, pp. 351–73. New York: C. J. Hogrefe.

Henriques, Fernando. 1962. *Prostitution and Society: A Survey*. New York: Citadel.

Heyman, Alan C. 1966. *Dances of the Three-Thousand League Land*. Seoul: Dang A.

Hoch-Smith, Judith, and Anita Spring, eds. 1978. *Women in Ritual and Symbolic Roles*. New York: Plenum.

Hoffman, Jan. 1984. Sex and the Children's Wear Designer. *Village Voice*, April 17, p. 73.

Holmes, Olive, ed. 1982. *Motion Arrested: Dance Reviews of H. T. Parker*. Middletown, Conn.: Wesleyan University Press.

Hunt, Marilyn. 1986. Paris Opera Ballet at the Met: Compagnie de Cristal. *Dance Magazine* 60(1):50–55.

———. 1987. Antony Tudor: Master Provocateur. *Dance Magazine* 61(5): 36–41.

Hyatt, Ester. 1982. Dance? Don't Ask Me. *Washington Post*, April 14, p. B7.

Indra. 1979. *The Status of Women in Ancient India*. Banares: Motilal Prakashan.

Ingber, Judith Brin, ed. 1985–86. Dancing into Marriage: Collected Papers on Jewish Wedding Dances. *Dance Research Journal* 17(2) and 18(1):51–86.

Inoue, Shun. 1980. Interactions and Interpretations in Everyday Life. *Studies in Symbolic Interaction* 3:1–24.

Jackson, George. 1983a. The Many Disguises of Les Ballets Trockadero. *Washington Post*, October 13, p. D4.

———. 1983b. Speaking up for Béjart. *Ballet News* 5(3):18–19.

———. 1986. Energetic But Stuttering Stuttgart. *Washington Post*, June 4, p. C13.

Jackson, Graham. 1978. *Dance as Dance: Selected Reviews and Essays*. Ontario, Canada: Catalyst.

Jaggar, Alison M. 1983. *Feminist Politics and Human Nature*. Totowa, N.J.: Rowman and Allanheld.

Jeanes Antze, Rosemary. 1979. The World of Indian Dance. *Dance in Canada*, August, pp. 5–9.

———. 1982. Tradition and Learning in Odissi Dance of India: Guru-Sisya-Parampara. M.F.A. thesis, Dance History and Criticism, York University.

———. 1985. Approaching the Life and Role of a Mysore Concert Dancer. Paper prepared for Dance of India Conference, University of Toronto. To be published in David Waterhouse, ed., *Dance of India*.

Jespersen, O. 1922. *Language: Its Nature, Development, and Origin.* London: Allen and Unwin.

Jha, Akhileshwar. 1979. *Sexual Designs in Indian Culture.* New Delhi: Vikas.

Jimenez, Francisco Garcia. 1964. *El Tango Historia de Medio Siglo, 1880–1930.* Buenos Aires: Universitaria de Buenos Aires.

Jodelet, Denise. 1984. The Representation of the Body and Its Transformations. In Robert M. Farr and Serge Moscovici, eds., *Social Representations,* pp. 211–38. Cambridge: Cambridge University Press.

Johnston, Jill. 1971. *Marmelade Me.* New York: Dutton.

Jones, Clifford. 1982. The Effect of Culture Contact on Performance. Paper prepared for the Symposium on Theatre and Ritual, New York, N.Y.

Jowitt, Deborah. 1979. Hothouse Party. *Village Voice,* February 15, p. 79.

———. 1981. A Slack String Won't Resonate: A Tight One Man Snap. *Village Voice,* February 4, p. 75.

———. 1982. Does He Mean You Know What? *Village Voice,* December 21, p. 111.

———. 1983. Crawling into a Womb of Rice. *Village Voice,* February 22, p. 91.

———. 1984a. Please Do It Again, Do It Again, Again, Again . . . *Village Voice,* July 3, p. 93.

———. 1984b. Rites of Spring/King. *Village Voice,* March 13, p. 73.

———. 1984c. Sometimes the Picture Frames the *Frame. Village Voice,* June 12, p. 79.

———. 1986. To Drive the Dark Winter Away. *Village Voice,* January 7, p. 67.

Karlins, Marvin, and Herbert I. Abelson. 1970. *Persuasion: How Opinions and Attitudes Are Changed.* 2d ed. New York: Springer.

Katchadourian, Herant A., ed. 1979. *Human Sexuality: A Comparative and Developmental Perspective.* Berkeley: University of California Press.

Katz, Jonathan. 1976. *Gay American History: Lesbians and Gay Men in the USA.* New York: Crowell.

Katz, Ruth. 1973. The Egalitarian Waltz. *Comparative Studies in Society and History* 15:368–77.

Kealiinohomoku, Joann. 1981. Ethical Considerations for Choreographers, Ethnologists, and White Nights. *Journal of the Association of Graduate Dance Ethnologists,* Spring 5:10–23.

Keil, Charles. 1979. Class and Ethnicity in Polish-America. *Journal of Ethnic Studies* 7(2):37 45.

Keller, Karen. 1980. Freudian Tradition versus Feminism in Science Fiction. In Mary Jo Deegan, ed., *Wimmen in the Mass Media,* pp. 41–52. Centennial Education Program, Lincoln, Nebr.

Kendall, Elizabeth. 1979. *Where She Danced.* New York: Alfred A. Knopf.

Kern, Louis. 1981. *An Ordered Love: Sex Roles and Sexuality in Victorian Utopias: The Shakers, the Mormons and the Oneida Community.* Chapel Hill: University of North Carolina Press.

Kern, Stephen. 1975. *Anatomy and Destiny: A Cultural History of the Human Body*. New York: Bobbs-Merrill.

Kersenboom-Story, Saskia. 1983–84. Devadasis (Temple Dancers) of South India: Their Musical and Dance Traditions. *Progress Reports in Ethnomusicology* 1(4).

Khokar, Mohan. 1984. *Traditions of Classical Indian Dance*. Rev. and enlarged ed. New Delhi: Clarion.

———. N.d. Bharata Natyam and Kuchipudi. Mimeograph.

Kirkland, Gelsey, with Greg Lawrence. 1986. *Dancing on My Grave*. Garden City, N.Y.: Doubleday.

Kirstein, Lincoln. 1967. Blast at Ballet, 1937. In *Three Pamphlets Collected*. Brooklyn: Dance Horison.

———. 1970. *Movement and Metaphor: Four Centuries of Ballet*. New York: Praeger.

———. 1973. *The New York City Ballet*. New York: Alfred A. Knopf.

———. 1984. Beliefs of a Master. *New York Review of Books* 31(4):17–23.

Kisselgoff, Anna. 1980. Maverick of the Dance. *Harvard Magazine* 82(5): 42–46.

———. 1982a. Ballet: Susan Jaffe's Swan. *New York Times*, April 30, p. C24.

———. 1982b. Dance: Ballet Theater Opens with Wild Boy. *New York Times*, April 21, p. C17.

———. 1982c. Dance: Harlem Troupe in Two Holder Premieres. *New York Times*, January 21, p. C16.

———. 1982d. Is Gretzky the Nureyev of Sports? *New York Times*, March 7, p. 12D.

———. 1983a. Ballet: Joffrey in a Forsythe Premiere. *New York Times*, October 21, p. C36.

———. 1983b. Ballet: Nijinska *Biches*, by the Harlem Dancers. *New York Times*, January 29, p. 17.

———. 1984a. Ballet: "Tango," A Martins Premiere. *New York Times*, February 6, p. C15.

———. 1984b. Ballet Theater Makes Room for Formalism and Drama. *New York Times*, May 27, p. 16.

———. 1984c. Ballet Theatre: A Kirkland-McKenzie *Leaves*. *New York Times*, May 3, p. C21.

———. 1984d. City Ballet: *Bugaku*: A Balanchine Revival. *New York Times*, April 29, p. 64.

———. 1984e. Dance: Bausch Troupe Makes New York Debut. *New York Times*, June 14, p. C20.

———. 1984f. Dance: Graham Troupe. *New York Times*, March 4, p. 48.

———. 1984g. Taglioni and Elssler Were 19th Century Superstars. *New York Times*, May 6, p. 9.

———. 1985. Has Modern Dance Lost Its Idealism? *New York Times*, June 4, p. H6.

————. 1986. Early Court Ballet in France Was Varied and Lively. *New York Times*, November 11, pp. 9, 30.

Kleinberg, Seymour. 1980. *Alienated Affections: Being Gay in America*. New York: St. Martin's.

Knauft, Bruce M. 1985a. *Good Company and Violence: Sorcery and Social Action in a Lowland New Guinea Society*. Berkeley: University of California Press.

————. 1985b. Ritual Form and Permutation in New Guinea: Implications of Symbolic Process for Socio-Political Evolution. *American Ethnologist* 12(2): 321–40.

Kohlberg, Lawrence. 1966. A Cognitive-Developmental Analysis of Children's Sex-Role Concepts and Attitudes. In E. Maccoby, ed., *The Development of Sex Differences*, pp. 82–173. Stanford: Stanford University Press.

Kornheiser, Tony. 1984. Your Typical Ballet Fan Rarely Is Worth a Hoot. *Washington Post*, December 27, pp. D1, 6.

Kothari, Sunil. 1968. Gotipua Dancers of Orissa. *Sangeet Natak* 8:31–43.

Kram, M. 1971. Encounter with an Athlete. *Sports Illustrated*, September 27, pp. 93–100.

Kriegsman, Alan M. 1979. Dance on TV: Feld Ballet Sex Appeal. *Washington Post*, May 16, p. B14.

————. 1982. The Wonder of Nijinska's *Noces*. *Washington Post*, May 23, p. E1.

————. 1983. Ballet Choreographer Balanchine Dies at 79. *Washington Post*, May 1, p. A16.

———— 1984a. *Dead Warriors*: Brave Ballet. *Washington Post*, January 16, p. B3.

————. 1984b. From Breaking to Ballet. *Washington Post*, May 27, pp. K1, 5.

————. 1984c. NYCB's Images of Ancient Greece. *Washington Post*, March 8, p. B8.

————. 1985a. Coldblooded Choreography. *Washington Post*, September 16, p. B14.

————. 1985b. Enigmatic *Elephant*. *Washington Post*, August 14, p. C10.

Kriegsman, Sali Ann. 1985. Vienna, Virginia. *Ballet News* 7(6):31.

Kunzle, David. 1982. *Fashion and Fetishism: A Social History of the Corset, Tight-Lacing and Other Forms of Body Sculpture in the West*. Totowa, N.J.: Rowman and Littlefield.

Laine, Barry. 1978. Pilobolus. *Christopher Street*, January, pp. 49–54.

————. 1979. Moving Men. *Village Voice*, May 7, p. 91.

————. 1980a. Christopher Beck. *Advocate*, July 24, pp. 29–30.

————. 1980b. Diaghilev: The Imprint of a Gay Impressario on 20th Century Art. *Advocate*, July 24, pp. 27–28, 31.

————. 1981. Today's Non-Heroic Male Dancer. *New York Times*, April 21, p. 12D.

————. 1982. Down to Earth (Harry). *New York Native*.

————. 1983a. Bejart Believes in Ballet as Theater. *New York Times.* September 18, pp. 1, 30.

————. 1983b. Whose Wave Is It Anyway? The New, the Next, and the Permanent . . . *Dance Magazine* 57(10):59–67.

————. 1984. After Balanchine. *Stagebill* 12(7):7–10.

————. 1985. Trendy Twosome. *Ballet News* 7(2):22–25.

————. N.d. Dancing in the Closet. *Stagebill* ms.

Lambert, Helen H. 1978. Biology and Equality: A Perspective on Sex Differences. *Signs: Journal of Women in Culture and Society* 4(2):97–117.

Langer, Roland. 1984. The Post-War German Expressionism of Pina Bausch and Her Wuppertal Dance Theatre: Compulsion and Restraint, Love and Angst. Trans. Richard Sikes. *Dance Magazine* 58(6):46–48.

L'Armand, Kathleen, and Adrian L'Armand. 1983. One Hundred Years of Music in Madras: A Case Study in Secondary Urbanization. *Ethnomusicology* 27(3):411–38.

Leach, Edmund. 1972. The Influence of Cultural Context on Non-Verbal Communication in Man. In R. A. Hinde, ed., *Non-Verbal Communication,* pp. 315–43. Cambridge: Cambridge University Press.

Leacock, Eleanor Burke. 1981. *Myths of Male Dominance: Collected Articles on Women Cross-Culturally.* New York: Monthly Review Press.

Lee, Byong Won. 1979. Evolution of the Role and Status of Korean Professional Female Entertainers (*Kisaeng*). *World of Music* 21(2):75–81.

Levy, Steven. 1983. Ad Nauseum: How MTV Sells Out Rock and Roll. *Rolling Stone,* December 8, pp. 30–34, 37, 74, 76, 78–79.

Levy, Suzanne. 1984. Multifaceted Joffrey. *Washington Post,* December 10, p. C9.

Lewin, Lauri. 1984. *Naked Is the Best Disguise.* New York: William Morrow.

Life. 1969. Sex, Shock and Sensuality. 66(13):22–34.

Linder, Marc. 1983. Self-Employment as a Cyclical Escape from Unemployment. In Ida Harper Simpson and Richard L. Simpson, eds., *Research in the Sociology of Work,* pp. 261–74. Greenwich, Conn.: JAI Press.

Livingston, Lili Cockerille. 1983. Encounters with Balanchine: Inside Interview with Mr. B. *Dance Magazine* 57(7):46–51.

Lohr, Steve. 1982. The New Face of Kabuki. *New York Times Magazine,* May 30, pp. 13–17.

Loomis, Terrence M. 1981. Twisi-na Mama, Twisi-na Papa: The Performance of Gender in Cook Islands Dancing. Paper presented to the Colloquium on Gender and Fertility, University of Adelaide, November 24–27.

Lowe, Marian. 1983. The Dialectic of Biology and Culture. In Marian Lowe and Ruth Hubbard, eds., *Woman's Nature: Rationalizations of Inequality,* pp. 39–121. New York: Pergammon.

Luger, Eleanor Rachel. 1982. Nancy Spanier's People Dances. *Dance Magazine* 56(7):47–48.

Luger, Eleanor Rachel, and Barry Laine. 1978. When Choreography Becomes Female. *Christopher Street*, November, pp. 65–68.

Maher, Vanessa. 1978. Women and Social Change in Morocco. In Lois Beck and Nikki Keddie, eds., *Women in the Muslim World*, pp. 100–123. Cambridge: Harvard University Press.

Manfredi, John. 1982. *The Social Limits of Art*. Amherst: University of Massachusetts Press.

Manor, Giora. 1978. The Bible as Dance. *Dance Magazine* 52(12):56–86.

Marglin, Frederique. 1980. Wives of the God-King: The Rituals of Temple Courtesans. Ph.D. diss. anthropology, Brandeis University.

Marks, Bruce. 1969. The Male Image. *Dance Perspectives* 40:25–29.

Marshall, Donald S. 1979. Sexual Behavior on Mangaia. In Donald S. Marshall and Robert C. Suggs, eds., *Human Sexual Behavior: Variations in the Ethnographic Spectrum*, pp. 103–62. New York: Basic.

Martin, John. 1933. The Dance: The Far East—The Message of Shan-kar That Art to Further a Cause Must First Be Art. *New York Times*, October 15, p. IX:7.

———. 1936. *America Dancing: The Background and Personalities of the Modern Dance*. New York: Dodge.

———. 1937. The Dance: Its March from Decadence to a Modern Golden Age. *New York Times Magazine*, December 12, pp. 10–11, 30.

———. 1951. Ballet by Robbins in Local Premiere. *New York Times*, June 15, p. 17.

———. 1961. Male Performers and Choreographers Monopolizing the Modern Field. *New York Times*, December 17, p. 14.

Martland, T. R. 1984. Question: When Is Religion Art? Answer: When It Is a Jar. In Diane Apostolos-Cappadona, ed., *Art, Creativity, and the Sacred*, pp. 250–61. New York: Crossroad.

Mason, John P. 1975. Sex and Symbol in the Treatment of Women: The Wedding Rite in a Libyan Oasis Community. *American Ethnologist* 2(4):649–61.

Matthaei, Julie A. 1982. *An Economic History of Women in America: Women's Work, the Sexual Division of Labor and the Development of Capitalism*. New York: Schocken.

Mauss, Marcel. 1938. Les technique du corps. *Anthropologie et Sociologie*. Paris: Presses Universitaires de France.

Maynard, Olga. 1979. Suzanne Farrell. *Dance Magazine* 53(1):45.

Mayo, Clara, and Nancy M. Henley, eds. 1981. *Gender and Nonverbal Behavior*. New York: Springer-Verlag.

Mazo, Joseph H. 1974. *Dance Is a Contact Sport*. New York: Dutton.

Mazrui, Ali A. 1973. Phallic Symbols in Politics and War: An African Perspective. Paper read at an Interdisciplinary Colloquium on African Systems of Form, African Studies Center, University of California at Los Angeles.

Mead, Margaret. 1935. *Sex and Temperament in Three Primitive Societies.* London: William Morrow.

―――. 1942. Educational Effects of Social Environment as Disclosed by Studies of Primitive Societies. In W. W. Burgess et al., eds., *Symposium on Environment and Education*, pp. 48–61. Chicago: University of Chicago Press.

―――. 1949. *Male and Female.* New York: William Morrow.

―――. 1964. *Continuities and Discontinuities in Cultural Evolution.* New Haven: Yale University Press.

―――. 1970. *Culture and Commitment.* Garden City, N.Y.: Doubleday.

Meyer, Johann Jakob. 1971. *Sexual Life in Ancient India: A Study in the Comparative History of Indian Culture.* Delhi: Motilal Banarsidass.

Migel, Parmenia. 1972. *The Ballerinas: From the Court of Louis XIV to Pavlova.* New York: Macmillan.

Miles, Margaret R. 1985. *Image as Insight: Visual Understanding in Western Christianity and Secular Culture.* Boston: Beacon.

Miller, Judith. 1984. American Belly Dancers Undulate in Middle East. *New York Times*, March 9, p. B6.

Mitchell, G. 1981. *Human Sex Differences: A Primatologist's Perspective.* New York: Van Nostrand.

Mitchell, Juliett. 1971. *Women's Estate.* New York: Random House.

Money, John. 1985. *The Destroying Angel.* Buffalo: Prometheus Books.

Money, Keith. 1982. *Anna Pavlova: Her Life and Art.* New York: Alfred A. Knopf.

Montagu, Ashley. 1974. *The Natural Superiority of Women.* Rev. ed. New York: Macmillan (orig. 1952).

―――. 1981. *Growing Young.* New York: McGraw-Hill.

―――. 1986. *Touching: The Human Significance of Skin.* 3d rev. ed. New York: Harper and Row (orig. 1971).

Mork, Ebbe. 1976. Nudity Is Natural for the Royal Danish Ballet. *New York Times*, May 16, sec. 2, p. 1.

Mullins, Edwin. 1985. *The Painted Witch: How Western Artists Have Viewed the Sexuality of Women.* New York: Carroll and Graft.

Munk, Erika. 1985. Drag: 1. Men. *Village Voice*, February 5, pp. 89–91.

Murgiyanto, Sal. 1983. Basic Principles of the Javanese Court Dance. In Betty True Jones, ed., *Dance as Cultural Heritage, I: Dance Research Annual XIV* (New York: Committee on Research in Dance), pp. 179–84.

Murphy, Anne. 1985. Rebel with a Cause. *Ballet News* 6(12):14–19.

Murphy, Caryle. 1986. Lawyers Turning to Show and Tell. *Washington Post*, July 7, pp. D1, 5.

Musallam, Basem F. 1983. *Sex and Society in Islam: Birth Control before the Nineteenth Century.* New York: Cambridge University Press.

Nadel, S. F. 1947. *The Nuba: An Anthropological Study of the Hill Tribes in Kordofan.* London: Oxford University Press.

Namboodiri, M. P. Sankaran. 1983. Bhava as Expressed through the Presentational Techniques of Kathakali. In Betty True Jones, ed., *Dance as Cultural Heritage, I: Dance Research Annual XIV* (New York: Committee on Research in Dance), pp. 194–210.

Nanda, Serena. 1984. The Hijras of India: A Preliminary Report. *Medicine and Law* 3:59–74.

New York Times. 1908a. The Call of Salome: Rumors That Salomania Will Have a Free Hand This Season. August 16, pt. 5, p. 4.

———. 1908b. The "Salome" Dance Gets into Politics: Actress Marie Cahill Writes to Party Heads Urging Suppresson of the Dance. August 24, p. 2.

———. 1908c. Salome Dinner Dance: Tale of London Society Women Dining in Maude Allan Undress. August 23, pt. 3, p. 3.

———. 1912a. Daring Ballet Stirs the Paris Critics: Production by Russian Dancers Condemned but Public Rushes to See It: Rodin Is Its Defender. June 2, p. 3, p. 4.

———. 1912b. Moral Reaction in Paris. June 3, p. 8.

———. 1932. Says Dance Aids Culture. February 10, p. 20.

———. 1937. Tele-Ballet Wins Applause. August 29, p. X10.

Newman, Barbara. 1982. *Striking a Balance: Dancers Talk about Dancing.* Boston: Houghton Mifflin.

Newsweek. 1980. The Legal Mating Dance. December 1, p. 111.

Newton, Ester. 1972. *Mother Camp: Female Impersonators in America.* Englewood Cliffs, N.J.: Prentice-Hall.

Nicholls, Robert W. 1984. Igede Funeral Masquerades. *African Arts* 17(3): 70–76, 92.

Nikolais, Alwin. 1967. Dance, Sexual Dynamics in Contemporary. In Albert Ellis and Albert Ararbanel, eds., *The Encyclopedia of Sexual Behavior,* 1:313–25. New York: Hathorn.

Oakeshott, Michael, ed. 1946. *Levianthan.* Oxford: Oxford University Press.

Oaks, Robert. 1980. "Things Fearful to Name": Sodomy and Buggery in Seventeenth-Century New England. In Elizabeth H. Pleck and Joseph H. Pleck, eds., *The American Man,* pp. 53–76. Englewood Cliffs, N.J.: Prentice-Hall.

O'Flaherty, Wendy Doniger. 1980. *Women, Androgynes, and Other Mythical Beasts.* Chicago: University of Chicago Press.

Oldenburg, Veena Talwar. 1984. *The Making of Colonial Lucknow, 1856–1877.* Princeton: Princeton University Press.

Olsin-Windecker, Hilary. 1983. Characterization in Classical Yogyanese Dance. In Betty True Jones, ed., *Dance as Cultural Heritage, I: Dance Research Annual XIV* (New York: Committee on Research in Dance), pp. 185–93.

284   *References*

Ortner, Sherry B., and Harriet Whitehead, eds. 1981. *Sexual Meanings: The Cultural Construction of Gender and Sexuality*. New York: Cambridge University Press.

Oswald, Genevieve. 1983. Myth and Legend in Martha Graham's *Night Journey*. In Betty True Jones, ed., *Dance as Cultural Heritage, I: Dance Research Annual XIV*, pp. 42–49.

Pace, Eric. 1966. Belly Dance Gets the Go-Go in Cairo. *New York Times*, December 22, p. 19.

Pally, Marcia. 1983. A Guest Artist Brings a Dance to the Ailey. *New York Times*, May 8, p. H19.

Panov, Valery. 1978. *To Dance*. New York: Alfred A. Knopf.

Parks, Gary. 1986. New Lease on Lar. *Dance Magazine* 60(11):54–56.

Patil, B. R. 1977. The Jogatis. *Man in India* 57(1):23–47.

Peacock, James. 1968. *Rites of Modernization: Symbolic and Social Aspects of Indonesian Proletarian Drama*. Chicago: University of Chicago Press.

Pearson, Judy Cornelia. 1985. *Gender and Communication*. Dubuque, Iowa: Wm. C. Brown.

Penney, Phyllis Annette. 1981. Ballet and Modern Dance on Television in the Decade of the 70's. Ed.D. diss., fine arts, University of North Carolina at Greensboro.

Penzer, Norman Mosley. 1936. *The Harem: An Account of the Institution as It Existed in the Palace of the Turkish Sultans, with a History of the Grand Seraglio from Its Foundation to the Present Time*. London: Harrap.

———. 1952. Sacred Prostitution. In Richard Dorson, ed., *Poison Damsels and Other Essays in Folklore and Anthropology*, pp. 131–84. London: Charles J. Sawyer.

Perper, Timothy. 1985. *Sex Signals: The Biology of Love*. Philadelphia: ISI.

Perron, Wendy. 1980. Lesbians in Hystory: Loie Fuller, Innovator of Motion and Light. *Green Mountain Dyke News* 1(5):1, 5, 7.

Perron, Wendy, and Stephanie Woodard. 1976. When a Woman Dances, Nobody Cares. *Village Voice*, March 1, pp. 59, 61–62.

Peterson, David M., and Paula L. Dressel. 1982. Equal Time for Women: Social Notes on the Male Strip Show. *Urban Life* 11(2):185–208.

Philp, Richard. 1983. Donn! *Dance Magazine* 58(1):61–64.

Philp, Richard, and Mary Whitney. 1977. *The Male in Ballet*. New York: McGraw-Hill.

Pleck, Joseph H. 1979. Men's Power with Women, Other Men and Society: A Men's Movement Analysis. In Barry M. Shapiro and Evelyn Shapiro, eds., *The Men Say/The Women Say: Women's Liberation and Men's Consciousness*, pp. 255–61. New York: Dell.

———. 1981. *The Myth of Masculinity*. Cambridge MIT Press.

Plummer, Kenneth. 1975. *Sexual Stigma: An Interactionist Account*. London: Routledge and Kegan Paul.

Pollard, Percival. 1908. "Salome" Craze Raged in Europe Long Before It Came

Here: Some History of Famous Dancers, from Lola Montez to Isadore (*sic*) Duncan. *New York Times*, August 23, pt. 5, p. 7.

Popescu-Judetz, Eugenia. 1982. Kocek and Cengi in Turkish Culture. *Dance Studies* 6:46–58.

Procter-Smith, Marjorie. 1983. Women in Shaker Community and Worship: A Feminist Theological Analysis of the Uses of Religious Symbolism. Ph.D. diss., theology, University of Notre Dame.

Quigley, Colin. 1982. An Analysis of Traditional Dancing in Rural Newfoundland as Nonverbal Communication. *Journal of the Association of Graduate Dance Ethnologists*, Spring, 6:14–21.

Rao, Vissa Appa. 1959. Kuchipudi School of Dancing. *Sangeet Natak Akademi Bulletin*, no. 11–12 (April): 1–8.

Rappaport, Roy A. 1971. Ritual, Sanctity, and Cybernetics. *American Anthropologist* 73(1):29–76.

Raymond, Janice. 1979. *Transsexual Empire*. Boston: Beacon.

Read, Margaret. 1938. The Moral Code of the Ngoni and Their Former Military State. *Africa* 11:1–24.

Research and Programming Services. 1978. *Dance in America: The Effects of a Television Appearance on Professional Dance Companies*. San Francisco, Calif.

Richards, Audrey I. 1956. *Chisungu: A Girls' Initiation Ceremony among the Bemba of Northern Rhodesia*. New York: Grove Press.

Rigby, Peter. 1972. Some Gogo Rituals of "Purification": An Essay on Social and Moral Categories. In William A. Lessa and Evon Z. Vogt, eds., *Reader in Comparative Religion: An Anthropological Approach*, pp. 238–47. New York: Harper and Row.

Rimer, Sara. 1985. D'Amboise Makes PS 29 Feel Like Dancing. *New York Times*, May 6, pp. B1, 4.

Robertson, James Oliver. 1985. *America's Business*. New York: Hill and Wang.

Rockwell, John. 1976. Eros—The Greatest Dance Master. *New York Times*, April 11, pp. 1, 11.

Root, Deane L. 1981. *American Popular Stage Music, 1860–1880*. Ann Arbor: UMI Research Press.

Rosaldo, Michelle Zimbalist, and Louise Lamphere, eds. 1974. *Women, Culture, and Society*. Stanford: Stanford University Press.

Rosenberg, Charles E. 1973. Sexuality, Class and Role in 19th-Century America. *American Quarterly* 35(2):131–53.

Rosenberg, Rosalind. 1982. *Beyond Separate Spheres: Intellectual Roots of Modern Feminism*. New Haven: Yale University Press.

Rosenfeld, Lawrence B., Sallie Kartus, and Chett Ray. 1976. Body Accessibility Revisited. *Journal of Communication* 26(3):27–30.

Rosenwald, Peter J. 1982. Dance: Margot Fonteyn's Sparkling Hour of Dance. *Wall Street Journal*, November 5, p. 33.

Ross, Stephen Davis. 1982. A *Theory of Art: Inexhaustibility by Contrast.* Albany: State University of New York.

Rothfield, Otto. 1920. *Women of India.* Bombay: Taraporevata.

Rowe, Karen. 1979. Feminism and Fairy Tales. *Women's Studies* 6:237–57.

Roy, Manisha. 1972. *Bengali Women.* Chicago: University of Chicago Press.

Royce, Anya Peterson. 1984. *Movement and Meaning: Creativity and Interpretation in Ballet and Mime.* Bloomington: Indiana University Press.

Saal, Hubert. 1983. Farewell to Ballet's Mr. B. *Newsweek,* May 9, pp. 89–90.

Sabbah, Fatna A. 1984. *Women in the Muslim Unconscious.* Trans. Mary Jo Lakeland. New York: Pergamon.

Sanday, Peggy Reeves. 1981. *Female Power and Male Dominance: On the Origins of Sexual Inequality.* Cambridge: Cambridge University Press.

Sarabhai, Mrinalini. 1965. *The Eight Nanikas: Heroines of the Classical Dance of India. Dance Perspectives,* no. 24.

———. 1976. *Longing for the Beloved: Songs to Siva-Nataraja in Bharata Natyam.* Gujarat: Durpana.

Sargent, Alice G, ed. 1977. *Beyond Sex Roles.* New York: West.

Sartre, Jean-Paul. 1956. *Being and Nothingness.* Trans. H. Barnes. New York: Philosophical Library (orig. 1943).

Schechner, Richard. 1982. Introduction to Intercultural Performance. *The Drama Review* T94, 26(20):3.

Scheflen, Albert E., with Alice Scheflen. 1972. *Body Language and the Social Order: Communication as Behavioral Control.* Englewood Cliffs, N.J.: Prentice-Hall.

Schmidt, Jochen. 1983. The Granddaughters Dance Themselves Free: From Fanny Elssler to Pina Bausch or from Female Other-Directedness to Self-Determination in Ballet. *Ballet International Koln* 5(1):12–19.

Schneider, Harold K. 1979. Romantic Love among the Turu. In Donald S. Marshall and Robert C. Suggs, eds., *Human Sexual Behavior: Variations in the Ethnographic Spectrum,* pp. 59–70. New York: Basic.

Schorr, Daniel. 1952. Disputed Ballet Wins an Ovation. *New York Times,* July 4, p. 9.

Sebeok, Thomas, ed. 1987. *Encyclopedic Dictionary of Semiotics.* Berlin: Mouton-de Gruyter.

Shapiro, Laura. 1982. Nijinska Stages a Comeback. *Newsweek,* October 28, p. 82.

———. 1986. Dance: BAM: Sex and Decibels. *Newsweek,* November 10, p. 85.

Shelton, Suzanne. 1981. Reviews VII. *Dance Magazine* 50(50):156–59.

Shepard, Richard F. 1978. A New Spin on Belly Dancing. *New York Times,* January 13, p. C24.

Sherman, Jane, and Barton Mumaw. 1986. *Barton Mumaw, Dancer: From Denishawn to Jacob's Pillow and Beyond.* New York: Dance Horizons.

Shorter, Edward. 1982. *A History of Women's Bodies*. New York: Basic.

Siegel, Elaine V. 1984. *Movement Therapy: The Mirror of Ourselves*: A *Psychoanalytic Approach*. New York: Human Science.

Siegel, Marcia. 1972. *At the Vanishing Point: A Critic Looks at Dance*. New York: Saturday Review.

———. 1977. *Watching the Dance Go By*. Boston: Houghton Mifflin.

———. 1979. *The Shapes of Change: Images of American Dance*. Boston: Houghton Mifflin.

Simpson, Ida Harper, and Richard L. Simpson, eds. 1983. Research in the Sociology of Work: Peripheral Workers. *Research Annual 2*. Greenwich, Conn.: JAI.

Singer, Milton. 1972. *When a Great Tradition Modernizes*. New York: Praeger.

Sinha, A. P. 1967. Procreation among the Eunuchs. *Eastern Anthropologist* 20(20):168–76.

Smith, Sally Bedell. 1984. Average Family Viewing Passes 7 Hours a Day. *New York Times*, January 18, p. 47.

Solway, Diane. 1983. Follow the Leader. *Ballet News* 4(11):18–20, 53.

Sommer, Sally R. 1985. What's Old? *Village Voice*, July 2, p. 90.

Spalding, Murray. 1983. A Mission in Dance. *Washington Post*, October 24, p. C7.

Spindler, George, and Louise Spindler. 1982. Do Anthropologists Need Learning Theory? *Anthropology and Education* 13(2):109–24.

———. 1983. Anthropologists View American Culture. *Annual Review of Anthropology* 12:49–78.

Srinivasan, Amrit. 1976. *Ascetic Passion: The Devadasi and her Dance in a Comparative Context*. Delhi, n.d.

Stayt, Hugh. 1931. *The Bavenda*. London: Oxford University Press.

Steinberg, Cobbet, ed. 1980. *The Dance Anthology*. New York: New American Library.

Steinbrink, Mark. 1983. Perpetual Motion. *Stagebill* 11(9):9–10, 48.

Steir, Deborah S., and Judith A. Hall. 1984. Gender Differences in Touch: An Empirical and Theoretical Review. *Journal of Personality and Social Psychology* 47(2):440–59.

Stodelle, Ernestine. 1984. *Deep Song: The Dance Story of Martha Graham*. New York: Schirmer.

Stoop, Norma McLain. 1984. The Canadian Cosmopolitan Montreal's Brian Macdonald. *Dance Magazine* 58(4):62–65.

Subramaniam, V. 1985. Class and Caste Affiliations of Artists and Connoisseurs in South India, 18th–20th Centuries. Paper presented at the Conference on Dance of India.

Suleiman, Susan Rubin, ed. 1985. The Female Body in Western Culture: Semiotic Perspectives. *Poetics Today* 6(1–2).

Supree, Burt. 1985. New Guy on the Block. *Village Voice*, April 2, p. 86.

Taper, Bernard. 1984. *Balanchine: A Biography*. New York: Times Books.

Taub, Eric. 1986. New York. *Ballet News* 7(9):32.

Taylor, Julie. 1976. Tango: Theme of Class and Nation. *Ethnomusicology* 20(20):273–92.

Taylor, Margaret Fisk. 1967. *A Time to Dance: Symbolic Movement in Worship.* Philadephia: United Church Press.

Taylor, Shelley, Susan Fiske, Nancy L. Etcoff, and Audrey J. Ruderman. 1978. Categorical and Contextual Bases of Person Memory and Stereotyping. *Journal of Personality and Social Psychology* 36:778–93.

Ten Raa, Eric. 1969. The Moon as a Symbol of Life and Fertility in Sandawe Thought. *Africa* 39(1):24–53.

Terry, Walter. 1976. *Ted Shawn: Father of American Dance.* New York: Dial.

————. 1978. *Great Male Dancers of the Ballet.* New York: Anchor.

————. 1982. *How to Look at Dance.* New York: William Morrow.

Thernstrom, Stephan, ed. 1980. *Harvard Encyclopedia of American Ethnic Groups.* Cambridge: Harvard University Press.

Thorne, Barrie, and Nancy Henley, eds. 1975. *Language and Sex: Difference and Dominance.* Rowley, Mass.: Newbury House.

Thurston, Edgar. 1909. *Castes and Tribes of Southern India.* Madras: Government Press.

Time. 1979. And Now, Bring on the Boys. March 6, p. 69.

Tobias, Tobi. 1975, Ballet Partners—Matches Not Made in Heaven. *New York Times,* August 17, pp. 1, 6.

1984a. A Conversation with Martha Graham. *Dance Magazine* 58(3):62–64.

————. 1984b. Manchild in the Promised Land: Mark Morris. *Dance Magazine* 58(12):HC28–30.

Tomalonis, Alexandra. 1984. North Carolina Dance Theatre. *Washington Post,* April 30, p. C11.

Tuchman, Gaye, and Nina E. Fortin. 1984. Fame and Misfortune: Edging Women Out of the Great Literary Tradition. *American Journal of Sociology* 90(1):72–96.

Turnbull, Colin M. 1981. Mbiti Womanhood. In Frances Dahlberg, ed., *Woman the Gatherer,* pp. 205–19. New Haven: Yale University Press.

Turner, Victor. 1957. *Schism and Continuity in an African Society: A Study of Ndembu Village Life.* Manchester, England: Manchester University Press.

————. 1969. *The Ritual Process: Structure and Anti-Structure.* Chicago: Aldine.

————. 1974. *Dramas, Fields, and Metaphors: Symbolic Action in Human Society.* Ithaca: Cornell University Press.

Umiker-Sebeok, Jean. 1981. The Seven Ages of Woman: A View from American Magazine Advertisements. In Clara Mayo and Nancy M. Henley, eds., *Gender and Nonverbal Behavior,* pp. 209–52. New York: Springer-Verlag.

Update Dance USA. 1983. National Endowment for the Arts Holds Two-Day Dance Seminar. 2(5):1–7.

Vance, Carol, ed. 1984. *Pleasure and Danger*. Boston: Routledge and Kegan Paul.

Van der Leeuw, Gerardus. 1963. *Sacred and Profane Beauty: The Holy in Art*. London: Weidenfeld and Nicolson.

Van Gulik, Robert. 1961. *Sexual Life in Ancient China: A Preliminary Survey of Chinese Sex and Society from ca. 1500 B.C. till 1644 A.D.* Leiden: E. J. Brill.

Van Kesteren, Aloysius. 1985. Theatre and Drama Research: An Analytical Proposition. In Herta Schmid and Aloysius Van Kesteren, eds., *Semiotics of Drama and Theatre*, pp. 19–66. Philadelphia: John Benjamins.

Vatsyayan, Kapila. 1968. *Classical Indian Dance in Literature and the Arts*. New Delhi: Sangeet Natak Akademi.

Vaughan, David. 1982. Reviews. *Dance Magazine* 56(11):46–47, 96.

―――. 1983. Those Bright Young Things. *Ballet News* 4(7):15–17.

Villella, Edward. 1969. The Male Image. *Dance Perspectives* 40:39–48.

Waghorne, Joanne Punzo, and Norman Cutler, in association with Vasudha Narayanan, ed. 1985. *Gods of Flesh, Gods of Stone: The Embodiment of Divinity in India*. Chambersburg, Pa.: Anima Press.

Walkowitz, Judith R. 1980. *Prostitution and Victorian Society*. Cambridge: Cambridge University Press.

Wandor, Michelene. 1981. *Understudies: Theatre and Sexual Politics*. London: Methuen.

Warner, Marina. 1985. *Monuments and Maidens: The Allegory of the Female Form*. New York: Atheneum.

Webbink, Patricia. 1981. Nonverbal Behavior and Lesbian/Gay Orientation. In Clara Mayo and Nancy M. Henley, eds., *Gender and Nonverbal Behavior*, pp. 253–59. New York: Springer-Verlag.

Weeks, Jeffrey. 1985. *Sexuality and Its Discontents*. London: Routlege and Kegan Paul.

Weigert, Andrew J., J. Smith Teitge, and Dennis W. Teitge. 1986. *Society and Identity: Toward a Sociological Pyschology*. Rose Mongraph Series. New York: Cambridge University Press.

Welch, Renate L., Aletha Huston-Stein, John C. Wright, and Robert Plehal. 1979. Subtle Sex-Role Cues in Children's Commercials. *Journal of Communication* 29(3):202–9.

Wheeler, Mark Frederick. 1984. Surface to Essence: Appropriation of the Orient by Modern Dance. Ph.D. diss., history, Ohio State University.

Whitam, Frederick L., and Robin M. Mathy. 1986. *Male Homosexuality in Four Societies: Brazil, Guatemala, the Philippines and the United States*. New York: Praeger.

Wild, Stephen A. 1977–78. Men as Women: Female Dance Symbolism in Walbiri Men's Rituals. *Dance Research Journal* 10(1):14–22.

Williams, Drid. 1968. The Dance of the Bedu Moon. *African Arts* 2(1):18–21.

Williams, John E., and Deborah L. Best. 1982. *Measuring Sex Stereotypes: A Thirty Nation Study.* Beverly Hills, Calif.: Sage.

Wilshire, Bruce. 1982. *Role Playing and Identity: The Limits of Theatre as Metaphor.* Bloomington: Indiana University Press.

Wolcott, Harry F., ed. 1982. Special Issue: Anthropology of Learning. *Anthropology and Education Quarterly* 13(2).

Wolff, Deborah Goleman. 1979. *The Lesbian Community.* Berkeley: University of California Press.

Wolfgang, Aaron, ed. 1984. *Nonverbal Behavior.* New York: C. J. Hogrefe.

Wood, Leona, and Anthony Shay. 1976. *Danse du Ventre*: A Fresh Appraisal. *Dance Research Journal* 8(2):18–30.

Wynne, Shirley. 1970. Complaisance, An Eighteenth Century Cool. *Dance Scope* 5(1):22–35.

Wyszomirski, Margaret Jane, and Judith H. Balfe. 1985. Coalition Theory and American Ballet. In Judith H. Balfe and Margaret Jane Wyszomirski, eds., *Art, Ideology, and Politics*, pp. 210–36. New York: Praeger.

Yati, Nitya Chaitanya. 1979. *Love and Devotion.* Varkala, India: East-West University of Brahmavidya.

Yinger, J. Milton. 1982. *Countercultures: The Promise and the Peril of a World Turned Upside Down.* New York: Free Press.

Youskevitch, Igor. 1969. The Male Image. *Dance Perspectives* 40:13–23.

Zimmer, Hendrich. 1946. *Myths and Symbols in Indian Art and Civilization.* Ed. Joseph Campbell. New York: Pantheon.

Index

DATE DUE
